Ethnicity, Identity, and Conceptualizing Community
in Indian Ocean East Africa

Indian Ocean Studies Series

Richard B. Allen, series editor

Richard B. Allen, *European Slave Trading in the Indian Ocean, 1500–1850*

Erin E. Stiles and Katrina Daly Thompson, eds., *Gendered Lives in the Western Indian Ocean: Islam, Marriage, and Sexuality on the Swahili Coast*

Jane Hooper, *Feeding Globalization: Madagascar and the Provisioning Trade, 1600–1800*

Krish Seetah, ed., *Connecting Continents: Archaeology and History in the Indian Ocean World*

Pedro Machado, Steve Mullins, and Joseph Christensen, eds., *Pearls, People, and Power: Pearling and Indian Ocean Worlds*

Burkhard Schnepel and Julia Verne, eds., *Cargoes in Motion: Materiality and Connectivity across the Indian Ocean*

Jane Hooper, *Yankees in the Indian Ocean: American Commerce and Whaling, 1786–1860*

Daren E. Ray, *Ethnicity, Identity, and Conceptualizing Community in Indian Ocean East Africa*

ADVISORY BOARD

Edward A. Alpers
  University of California, Los Angeles (emeritus)

Clare Anderson
  University of Leicester

Fahad Ahmad Bishara
  University of Virginia

Erik Gilbert
  Arkansas State University

Devleena Ghosh
  University of Technology Sydney

Hans Hägerdal
  Linnaeus University

Pedro Machado
  Indiana University

Rila Mukherjee
  University of Hyderabad

Burkhard Schnepel
  Martin-Luther-University, Halle-Wittenberg (emeritus)

Alicia Schrikker
  Leiden University

Julia Verne
  Johannes Gutenberg University

Kerry Ward
  Rice University

Ethnicity, Identity, and Conceptualizing Community in Indian Ocean East Africa

Daren E. Ray

OHIO UNIVERSITY PRESS
ATHENS, OHIO

Ohio University Press, Athens, Ohio 45701
ohioswallow.com
© 2024 by Ohio University Press
All rights reserved

To obtain permission to quote, reprint, or otherwise reproduce or distribute material from Ohio University Press publications, please contact our rights and permissions department at (740) 593-1154 or (740) 593-4536 (fax).

Printed in the United States of America
Ohio University Press books are printed on acid-free paper ∞ ™

Library of Congress Cataloging-in-Publication Data
Names: Ray, Daren E., 1982– author.
Title: Ethnicity, identity, and conceptualizing community in Indian Ocean East Africa / Daren E. Ray.
Other titles: Indian Ocean studies series.
Description: Athens, Ohio : Ohio University Press, [2024] | Series: Indian Ocean studies series | Includes bibliographical references and index.
Identifiers: LCCN 2023013525 (print) | LCCN 2023013526 (ebook) | ISBN 9780821426135 (paperback) | ISBN 9780821426128 (hardcover) | ISBN 9780821426142 (pdf)
Subjects: LCSH: Ethnicity—Africa, East—History. | Communalism—Africa, East. | Africa, East—Ethnic relations.
Classification: LCC DT429 .R29 2024 (print) | LCC DT429 (ebook) | DDC 305.8009676—dc23/eng/20230321
LC record available at https://lccn.loc.gov/2023013525
LC ebook record available at https://lccn.loc.gov/2023013526

kwa wanangu

Rhys, Iris, Niall

Contents

List of Illustrations ix

Acknowledgments xi

Note on Language xiii

Introduction Disentangling Ethnicity from Its Ancestors in Littoral Kenya   1

PART I: ANCESTORS OF ETHNICITY

Chapter 1 Ancestors in the Doorway
Claiming Kith and Kin in East Africa before 500 CE   29

Chapter 2 Making a Peaceful Home
Organizing Clans through Knowledge along Sabaki Frontiers, ca. 150 BCE–1250 CE   52

Chapter 3 Dancing with Swords
Domesticating Commerce through Clan Confederations in the Western Indian Ocean ca. 1000–1700 CE   80

PART II: INNOVATING ETHNICITY

Chapter 4 Polarizing Politics
Imperial Ventures in Dar al-Islam, 1498–1813   111

Chapter 5 Practicing Muslims, Marginalized Pagans
          *Accommodating Arab Orthodoxies in the
          Zanzibar Sultanate, 1813–1895*   137

Chapter 6 Gazetting Identity
          *Assembling Tribes and Demarcating Districts in
          the British East Africa Protectorate, 1895–1920*   166

Chapter 7 Historicizing Tribalism
          *A Kaleidoscope of Communities in the Colony
          and Protectorate of Kenya, 1921–1953*   191

          PART III: TRANSCENDING ETHNICITY?

Chapter 8 Transcending Ethnicity?
          *Nationalist Sentiments and the Appeal of Autonomy
          during Kenyan Decolonization, 1953–1962*   217

Epilogue   Reconciling Ethnicity and Nationalism   238

           Notes   247
           Bibliography   295
           Index   319

Illustrations

MAPS

	Reference Map: Western Indian Ocean	xvi
1.1.	East African languages, ca. 1000–500 BCE	41
2.1.	Modern languages and historic pottery wares	57
3.1.	Conurbations in littoral Kenya	87
3.2.	Segeju Corridor	99
4.1.	Mombasa and neighboring communities	129

FIGURES

I.1.	Rabai's rural landscape	16
1.1.	Palm-wine ceremony	30
1.2.	Proto–Mashariki Bantu and Proto–Sabaki Bantu tree diagram	33
2.1.	Proto–Sabaki Bantu divergence	64
3.1.	*Goma* dance, Lamu	81
5.1.	*Zefe* procession, Mombasa	138
6.1.	Paziani borderland	183
8.1.	Mwambao	231
8.2.	"Digo Coast and Hinterland"	235

Acknowledgments

How do you calculate over a decade of support? Though I take responsibility for any deficiencies in this book, I am grateful for the many friends and colleagues who shaped my writing. Adria LaViolette, Cynthia Hoehler-Fatton, John Mason, Roquinaldo Ferreira, Lydia Wilson, and Noel Stringham offered advice and support during my time at the University of Virginia and many times since. Chris Basgier, Tracy O'Brien, and Joni Lakin read drafts of nearly every chapter in our weekly writing group at Auburn University. Many thanks to Leo Garofalo and Joyce Bennett (Connecticut College); Kate Craig, Elijah Gaddis, Xaq Frolich, Heidi Hausse, and Matt Malczycki (Auburn University); Matthew Mason, Christopher Jones, Stewart Anderson, Brian Cannon, Leslie Hadfield, and Shawn Miller (Brigham Young University [BYU]); and Myles Osborne and David Bresnahan for comments on various chapters. I also thank the organizers and participants of the Southeast Regional Seminar in African Studies (SERSAS) and the Rocky Mountain Workshop on African History for their insightful feedback.

Monetary support for research in Kenya and Zanzibar came from a 2008 Dissertation Proposal Development Grant (Social Science Research Council), a 2009 Fulbright-Hays Dissertation Research Abroad Grant (US Department of Education), and a 2017 New Faculty Research Grant (Auburn University). Bruce Lawrence and Charles Kurzman taught me the nuts and bolts of field research, research proposals, and publishing through the Social Science Research Council workshops on "Muslim Modernities" in 2008 and 2013.

The Research Institute of Swahili Studies in East Africa (National Museums of Kenya) sponsored my research permit. Director

Kassim Omar also provided office space, access to museum facilities and events, and introductions to my research assistants. My research would have been impossible without Amira Mselem in Mombasa, William Tsaka in Rabai, and Mohamed Hassan in Lamu. My consultants are too numerous to list here, but I deposited digital files for most interviews in the Ray Research Deposit at Mombasa's Fort Jesus Audio-Visual Department.

My research depended on the generous staff and faculty at the Kenya National Archives (in Nairobi and Mombasa), the Wakf Commission in Mombasa, the Kenya Land Office, and the University of Nairobi. Henry Mutoro personally escorted me around the University of Nairobi, and Professors Milcah Amolo Achola and Mary Mwiandi provided access to the University of Nairobi History Department's research project archive. Stambuli Nassir and Ahmed Sheikh Nabahany shared with me copies of their personal collections in Mombasa.

Many people contributed to the production of the book. Richard Allen, Rick Huard, and several anonymous reviewers at Ohio University Press helped me better communicate the book's contributions to African and Indian Ocean history, and Beth Pratt, Tyler Balli, and Laura André helped usher the book through production and marketing. Eli Allen and Abner Hardy from the ThinkSpatial Lab at BYU's Geography Department crafted excellent maps, and SIL International granted permission to use map shapes from *Ethnologue* for map 2.1. Kevin Blankinship confirmed an Arabic translation from al-Idrisi's report on East Africa. Thomas Hinnebusch, Derek Nurse, Ellen Contini-Morava, and David Schoenbrun graciously provided linguistic data.

Reynolds Richter shared his home and many meals throughout our time together in Kenya. Jared Staller, who outpaced me in graduate school, deserves special thanks for his stellar friendship. To my late adviser Joseph Miller I express appreciation for years of incisive critiques and unflagging support. We all miss you very much. My parents and siblings have always expressed curiosity and support on this long journey to publication. To my wife Patience and our three children: thank you for bearing with me in my (early) years as an academic nomad.

Note on Language

I apply the convention of distinguishing Kiswahili (a language) from Swahili (a people) to each member of the Sabaki language family: Chimijikenda, Kipokomo, Kielwana, and Shicomorian are languages spoken by Mijikenda, Pokomo, Elwana, and Comorian peoples. I also mark words from reconstructed Bantu protolanguages with an asterisk. This convention of historical linguistics indicates that the word is not attested in written or spoken language but is a reasonable approximation of how the speakers of past languages pronounced it.

The historical classification and grouping of Bantu languages is ongoing. I use the classification adopted by the authors of the sources from which I gathered linguistic data, instead of adapting all data to a consistent classification. If tone markings were unavailable in the source material, I consulted the *Bantu Lexical Reconstructions 3 (BLR3)* database maintained by linguists at the Royal Museum for Central Africa in Tervuren, Belgium. Readers may consult cited sources for distribution data. All non-English words in the text are glossed in parentheses when mentioned for the first time in each chapter. I also italicize all non-English words, aside from a handful of frequently used words. I retain the prefixes with which Bantu nouns denote number and class but write verbs in unconjugated forms.

I use Standard Kiswahili spellings found in Frederick Johnson's *A Standard English-Swahili Dictionary* for Arabic and Portuguese loanwords into Sabaki languages. When spelling Arabic words without Kiswahili equivalents (e.g., names of people or texts), I follow the transliteration system of the Library of Congress. Arabic words that are common in English (e.g., Qur'an, qadi, and imam) are neither italicized nor transliterated.

Ethnicity, Identity, and Conceptualizing Community
in Indian Ocean East Africa

REFERENCE MAP: Western Indian Ocean. Map created by ThinkSpatial.

INTRODUCTION

Disentangling Ethnicity from Its Ancestors in Littoral Kenya

> Swahili-speaking people [are] a community within the communities in Kenya, or perhaps more specifically at the Kenyan Coast.
> —Prof. Abdullah Said Naji

IN APRIL 2010 National Museums of Kenya invited dance troupes throughout littoral Kenya to represent their ethnic groups in a friendly competition at Malindi, a tourist town on the Indian Ocean. Malindi's marine attractions draw many European visitors, but the organizers marketed the festival to local Kenyans—and they turned out in droves. The organizers separated spectators and performers in the sandy field between the Malindi Museum and the ocean dunes by assigning each troupe a roped-off square to practice.

As intended, this arrangement formed a living exhibit in which spectators observed the competitors' "intangible cultures." On one end of the field, Waata performers built two small grass sheds and demonstrated their skill at jumping vertically into the air. Opposite them, Kamba dancers formed two parallel lines and danced to the deep beat of a double-sided barrel drum. In the center of the field, a Mijikenda troupe wove arches out of palm fronds to frame the entrance of their square and placed a mortar wrapped in blue cloth as a shrine at the center. The women danced in traditional skirts (*hando*) as the men played drums, gourd shakers, and a trumpet shaped from an antelope horn. The Pokomo troupe was a crowd favorite; they wore reed headdresses and pantomimed spats between men and women. But a young Swahili troupe stole the show with its gender-bending performance of the salacious *chakacha* dance. Though structured as a competition, the organizers presented the festival as a celebration of Kenya's diverse cultures.

A few hundred yards away, retired chemistry professor Abdullah Said Naji led a public forum in a rooftop veranda. The meeting focused on how Kenyans could use the Kiswahili language to repair the national cohesion that had been shattered by Kenya's postelection violence in 2008.[1] Identifying himself as Swahili, Professor Naji began by noting that the "Swahili-speaking people [are] a community within the communities in Kenya, or perhaps more specifically at the Kenyan Coast." Then he paused. Before discussing the pride he took in his Swahili heritage, he wanted to clarify: "Some of you may be surprised to hear me say that—that I support ethnicity, but I want to qualify it with positive ethnicity. I am totally against negative ethnicity because that will not take us anywhere."[2] Professor Naji's remarks revealed two fundamental tensions at the festival. First, the clarification that his own ethnic group belonged to Kenya—but specifically to Kenya's coastal region—alluded to the marginalization of littoral communities in national politics. Second, by emphasizing the differences of each ethnic group—by roping them off from one another and inviting them to compete—this celebration of Kenya's cultural diversity validated the ethnic loyalties that Kenyans blamed for their recent political crisis.

Substitute "ethnic group" for tribe, caste, race, or religion, and the dilemma faced by Kenya's littoral communities resembles situations throughout the Indian Ocean. Postcolonial projects of nation building in Sri Lanka, India, Mauritius, the Philippines, East Africa, and elsewhere have struggled to accommodate "communalist" fragments.[3] Scholars and laypeople alike consider these "subnational" communities vestiges of a distant precolonial past.[4] For instance, many Kenyans regard ethnic identities as an ancient, immutable trait that people inherit at birth and pass down through descent.[5] They regard their ethnic groups both as kin and the legitimate custodians of their ancestral heritages.[6]

This book distinguishes ethnicity from other kinds of collective identity in order to reimagine how littoral communities in the Indian Ocean formed and then adapted to ever-shifting political constraints over several centuries. Historians like Pier Larson and Leif Manger have shown that Indian Ocean communities inspired new forms of identity as they extended their diasporas into the sea.[7] These identities include categories based on religion, nationality, status, occupation, and race, but scholars of the Indian Ocean (and elsewhere) often use *ethnicity* as a catch-all category for any culturally defined group, regardless of historical era.[8] This approach differs from research on collective identities by many historians of Africa who view ethnicity as a particular kind of identity that Africans first embraced in the colonial period.[9] In Kenya alone scholars have identified colonial origins for Kikuyu, Gusii, Luo, Maasai, Taita, Kalenjin, Kamba, Luhya, Swahili, Mijikenda, and other ethnic identities.[10] Their research on ethnicity seeks to dispel the myth of African tribalism—that the continent is and has always been populated by tribes—by tracing how Africans created novel identities.

Yet, other historians have argued that Africans also formed ethnic groups in precolonial eras. For example, Allen and Barbara Isaacman have argued that there "is no compelling theoretical or empirical reason to presume that all ethnic identities were simply a product of the complex and contested colonial encounter."[11] This introduction will counter this assertion in the next section by explaining why scholars should reserve ethnicity as a model for understanding only modern identities. However, instead of emphasizing a sharp break between precolonial and colonial identities, this book also traces continuities in the elements with which earlier communities and modern ethnic groups distinguished themselves. The collective identities for which earlier Africans created these enduring elements are the ancestors of ethnicity.

Elizabeth Tonkin once lamented that "African apprehensions of collective identity before colonialism have rarely been preserved."[12] Indeed, most precolonial identities can never be recovered if historians continue to rely mostly on oral traditions and written documentation or limit their focus to the origins of modern identities. This book overcomes these limitations in three ways.

First, instead of focusing on the history of a single ethnic group, it examines the formation of multiple ethnic groups that share a common linguistic heritage: the Sabaki language family. This group of Bantu languages emerged around 500 CE and now includes the languages spoken by members of the Swahili, Mijikenda, Pokomo, Comorian, and Elwana ethnic groups. Historians of Africa have sometimes extended their investigation of ethnic identities into precolonial times.[13] However, most of them have organized their research around single ethnic groups in colonial states.[14] Adopting a linguistic framework that encompasses multiple ethnic groups permits a broader analysis of collective identities in colonial and precolonial eras.

Second, this book centers on coastal Kenya, where speakers of most Sabaki languages reside. The geographical characteristics of this littoral zone highlight that these speakers were never isolated from one another or surrounding regions. Rather, communities from both Africa and other regions of the Indian Ocean influenced Sabaki speakers' collective identities in different eras. Focusing on the Kenyan coast also reveals how communities in one part of East Africa formed a littoral society in the first millennium CE before adapting to the Indian Ocean's shifting political topography in the following centuries. The first Bantu settlers to join other indigenous communities on the shore around the first century CE could not have anticipated their descendants' participation in the Islamic *umma;* the Portuguese, Omani, and British empires; or the African nation of Kenya. Each of these reconfigurations of littoral Kenya's position within the Indian Ocean motivated residents to reimagine their inherited identities and innovate new ones. Early research on the Indian Ocean often excluded East Africa as too different and isolated to be relevant.[15] More recent scholarship has incorporated African perspectives and contributions to the wider ocean, but most of these studies have remained focused on modern times.[16] Tracing a succession of the identities that residents of littoral Kenya developed over the past fifteen hundred years will enable scholars to evaluate how the peoples of East Africa compared to and contributed to other littoral societies in the Indian Ocean.

Third, this book draws on a wide array of evidence generated by archaeologists, linguists, and anthropologists, as well as historians. Communities have preserved some of the elements (i.e., the words, symbols, places, objects, and ideas) with which their forebears formed earlier communities as the intangible heritage of their ethnic groups. This book traces these elements from their innovation in distinct precolonial eras through their entanglement with ethnicity in the colonial era, thus correlating and sequencing archaeological, linguistic, ethnographic, and documentary evidence to reconstruct the identities that I describe as the ancestors of ethnicity. By disentangling how people historically incorporated elements from these earlier identities into their ethnic identities, I stress that the invention of ethnicity was not merely a disruption imposed by colonial governments. Innovating ethnicity was also an incremental elaboration of ancestral strategies that littoral East Africans had long used to move with the shifting tides of the Indian Ocean.

THE NOVELTY OF ETHNICITY

The novelty of ethnicity seemed obvious to scholars of Africa in the 1960s.[17] They joined with Africa's nationalist politicians in castigating tribes as European inventions that distracted Africans from uniting against their common colonial enemy. In contrast, the proponents of ethnic identities in the same era argued the opposite: that they represented the interests of communities that had existed since time immemorial.[18] When historians began tracing the origins of specific ethnic identities in Africa to the colonial era, they learned that Africans contributed much to inventing ethnicity. Colonial officials imposed constraints on what kinds of collective identities they would recognize in policy and law, but Africans often supplied the names, territorial claims, histories, traditions, and rituals that distinguished their respective ethnic groups.[19]

First, a word on terminology. Laypeople and scholars unfamiliar with scholarship on Africa commonly refer to African communities as "tribes," whether they are small groups living in remote areas or large populations spanning urban and rural locales.[20] In contrast, since the 1960s Africanist scholars have routinely replaced the term *tribe* with *ethnic group* in the hope that they could extinguish the connotations of barbarism, violence, and primordialism that Europeans and Americans associated with African tribes.[21] However, replacing the word *tribe* with *ethnic group* did not change politicians' rhetoric or government policies that presumed each person ideally belonged to just one community. In addition, most Africanist scholars have retained a common definition of *tribe* when discussing ethnic groups: a group of people who claim common ancestry, territory, and culture.

Though Africanist scholars largely failed to convince others to adopt their preferred euphemism, associating so-called tribes with ethnicity brought Africans' histories into wider conversations about other modern identities like race and nation.[22] The diversity of African ethnic groups also propelled debates about the definition, origins, and persistence of ethnicity on a continental scale.[23] Compared to Africanists, scholars of the Indian Ocean have engaged in less debate over the definition and application of ethnicity to different eras. They found ethnicity most useful for managing the dizzying array of collective identities they encountered in their research. For example, in Mauritius, scholars have used ethnicity as a framework for analyzing relationships among Hindu and Sino-Mauritian communities, even though membership in the former is determined by religion and in the latter by geographic origin.[24] Ananya Chakravarti has suggested that historians of the Indian Ocean rely too often on "unexamined modes of ethnic identification" to ascribe motivation to the subjects of their narratives.[25] Although scholars of these two overlapping regions have applied ethnicity in different ways, they all rely on principles that anthropologist Richard Jenkins describes as the "basic social anthropological model of ethnicity."[26]

A Modern Model for Ethnicity

The basic social anthropological model of ethnicity is most often associated with the work of sociologist Fredrik Barth, who in 1969 challenged prevailing anthropological approaches that divided humanity into relatively fixed cultural systems.[27] The model he articulated, and which later scholars expanded on, emphasizes that ethnic groups dynamically modify their criteria for inclusion and exclusion to fit changing situations rather than preserving static cultural traits inherited from primordial times. It also recognizes that individuals can shift among various ethnic identities because of recognized boundaries among ethnic groups, not in spite of them. Since people create ethnic boundaries to distinguish "us" from "them," this model also asserts that ethnic groups cannot form in isolation. As Thomas Eriksen notes, ethnicity requires a "common field" in which people can distinguish their respective ethnic groups.[28] This principle of complementarity also means that ethnic groups are mutually exclusive. They cannot overlap, even though individuals move among them situationally. In practice, this model is inextricable from the contexts of modern states, which uniquely developed efficient bureaucratic systems like censuses that require people to identify as members of mutually exclusive categories recognized (though not always created) by governments.[29]

Barth's model built on previous work by sociologists who suggested that new urban spaces motivated Africans to form the first ethnic groups.[30] Migrants who moved to cities engaged with strangers much more frequently than in their homelands. The pressures of securing housing and other scarce resources led them to seek out people hailing from similar "tribes" and form ethnic groups to compete with other ethnic groups emerging in the same times and places. David Horowitz and other scholars extended this logic to show how the common fields created by colonial states promoted the emergence of ethnic groups on large scales throughout the modern world.[31]

These general statements on the origin of ethnicity appealed to scholars focused on contemporary periods, but they did not satisfy scholars interested in the collective identities of precolonial communities. The basic social anthropological model of ethnicity presumes that each ethnic group is a historical construction with identifiable origins. However, the model does not account for the transition from earlier kinds of collective identities to ethnicity. This elaboration may have seemed unnecessary because the universal application of ethnicity to human groups in any time or place is one of the model's supposed strengths.[32] Yet over four decades of research by Africanist historians suggest that the utility of seeing ethnicity everywhere (and in every era) fades as scholars trace the origins of collective identities into the precolonial past.

The Limits of Ethnicity in Africa

Most historians of Africa neglected the history of specific ethnic groups until 1983, when Benedict Anderson, Ernest Gellner, Eric

Hobsbawm, and Terence Ranger introduced methods for analyzing nationalities in Europe and Asia as "imagined communities" held together by "invented traditions."[33] Leroy Vail extended this conversation to ethnicity in Africa by convening a conference to discuss the "creation of tribalism" in southern Africa. Vail argued that tribalism, or ethnicity, was the mutual construction of colonial officials, missionary linguists, and the few African intellectuals whom missionaries educated.[34] Since then historians have applied this "constructivist" analysis of ethnicity to trace the formation of dozens of African ethnic groups to the colonial era.[35] Historians have pursued similar research in other areas of the world, particularly Asia, where they have documented a profusion of ethnic groups in the wake of modern imperialism.[36]

Historians of Kenya have been especially prolific in their writing about ethnicity. John Lonsdale's foundational writings on Kikuyu ethnicity distinguished *moral ethnicity* (which examines how people stake their claims as members of a shared community) from strategies of *political tribalism* (which defends a community's interests against people categorized as outsiders).[37] Gabrielle Lynch's study of the Kalenjin emphasized the exclusionary logic of ethnicity that discourages people from belonging to more than one ethnic community at once.[38] Julie MacArthur's research on Luhya communities demonstrated how ethnic groups can construct their collective identity around shared territory without also asserting common ancestry.[39] Though scholars have sometimes pondered the relationship between modern ethnic groups and earlier communities in Kenya, they have focused on colonial contexts.[40]

Other historians have supported Allen Isaacman and Barbara Isaacman's claim (quoted above) that Africans formed ethnic groups before colonialism. This position has proven theoretically inconsistent. Specifically, historians have found it necessary to abandon or modify aspects of the basic social anthropological model of ethnicity to make it fit precolonial contexts.[41] As one example, Pier Larson's study of precolonial communities in Madagascar emphasized how their collective identities often overlapped. Although he recognized that these identities violated the principle that ethnic identities are mutually exclusive, he persisted in describing them as ethnic anyway. He justified these modifications with the common refrain that ethnicity existed in precolonial Africa, but "it took on a very different form."[42] The theoretical elasticity in this line of thinking is also apparent in Paul Nugent's definition of ethnicity as "any form of 'we-they' distinction."[43] Scholars should reject this approach because ignoring or adjusting the basic social anthropological model of ethnicity diminishes their ability to compare ethnicity and ethnic groups in different times and places. It also hampers cross-disciplinary communication. Historians' failure to consistently apply this basic social anthropological model of ethnicity to precolonial contexts suggests that ethnicity is not so universal after all.

Debates over the history of Kenya's Swahili and Mijikenda ethnic groups further clarify the challenge of articulating the precise relationship between the concept of ethnicity and its ancestors. Between 1970 and 1985, Thomas Spear wrote two monographs and numerous articles that traced the precolonial histories of these two peoples separately.[44] His method presumed that these communities shared an ancient linguistic heritage but had separated from one another centuries ago and developed as isolated tribes. His narrative thus treated their relationship after coming back into contact in the sixteenth century as interactions between two distinct societies.

However, when Justin Willis wrote a history of Mombasa in 1993, he showed that both the Swahili and Mijikenda ethnic groups were colonial-era inventions that developed in tandem with each other.[45] Engagement, rather than isolation, set the contours of their ethnic boundaries. He also suggested that ethnic groups differed categorically from networks organized around Big Men in precolonial times. Since these communities did not identify themselves as Swahili or Mijikenda prior to the twentieth century, he suggested that it was inappropriate for scholars to do so.

Spear then responded in an influential article about the limits of "invention" that the Mijikenda ethnic group was indeed formed in the colonial era, but it was a "super tribe" that had consolidated smaller, precolonial groups that shared an underlying cultural unity. He summarized the position of those who insist on the antiquity of ethnicity by asserting that "ethnic concepts, processes and politics predated the imposition of colonial rule" and "extended through the colonial and post-colonial periods as well."[46]

Spear's intervention corrected the faulty presumption of a decisive rupture between the precolonial and colonial past—as implied by the word *invention*. Yet, the examples he surveyed came from very different contexts. Migration, resistance to the slave trade, commercialization, urbanization, and the formation of states and diasporas certainly led Africans to reimagine their collective identities in precolonial times. However, Spear did not explain why the communities that precolonial Africans formed should be characterized as ethnic groups besides the fact that they involved historical processes of inclusion and exclusion—a definition so expansive that it applies equally well to the formation of any group. His survey did not clarify how or why Africans formed groups during colonial rule that consistently fit the basic social anthropological model of ethnicity, but collective identities they formed in precolonial eras did not fit that model. In addition, retreating to the terms *tribe* and *super tribe* demonstrated that historians recognize a difference between ethnic groups and their nonethnic ancestors but struggle to characterize the relationships and continuities between them.

Differentiating Ethnicity

This book resolves this theoretical conundrum by expanding on anthropologist Ronald Cohen's approach to ethnicity. For Cohen each ethnic identity is a nonrandom, historically derived "series of nesting dichotomies of inclusiveness and exclusiveness."[47] While nationalists gain followers through strategies of assimilation that efface other identities, proponents of ethnic identities incorporate a diverse set of elements from earlier collective identities. However, they arrange them into a hierarchy of identities that range from local kin groups to extensive societies.

Cohen illustrated this process with historical documentation from the nineteenth and twentieth centuries about Ndendeuli communities in Tanzania.[48] He outlined the chronological sequence in which Ndendeuli people nested first political, then religious, and finally occupational elements into their ethnic identity over the course of a century. Cohen used this example to illustrate the layered or nested logic that distinguishes ethnic groups from nationalism. When applied to a wider array of collective identities, his approach can also answer the broader question of how modern peoples came to form groups that fit the basic social anthropological model of ethnicity.

In addition to the generic definition that ethnic groups are communities that claim to share ancestry, territory, and culture, the basic social anthropological model clarifies that ethnic groups are mutually exclusive communities, which modify their cultural elements as they engage with one another. Cohen's approach shows how the interior dimensions of ethnic identities can be differentiated to discern elements adopted from earlier collective identities. This book expands on Cohen's method by situating the Swahili, Mijikenda, and other ethnic groups from the same language family within a longer chronological sequence of collective identities in littoral Kenya. It neither attempts to shoehorn every collective identity into the theoretical constraints of the basic social anthropological model of ethnicity nor discards that model, which so usefully conveys the relationship between ethnic groups and modern states.

A FLEXIBLE AFRICAN LITTORAL: REORIENTING MOMBASA AND ITS INLAND HILLS

The notion of "littoral societies" in Indian Ocean studies can resolve distortions that historians introduced into the history of coastal Kenya when they organized their research around ethnic groups. As Abdul Sheriff and Engseng Ho summarized, "oceanic movements and connections" and the "creation of new societies" are two major themes of Indian Ocean studies.[49] The first historians of the region focused on identifying natural and political structures that enabled oceanic commerce.[50] Later historians have traced the expansion of diasporic communities hailing from Gujerat, Malabar, Sind, Madagascar, Oman, Portugal, and elsewhere that sustained these commercial connections.[51] The narratives of travel that dominate this research most often attribute historical change to movement: expanding diasporas brought new products and ideas to relatively stationary communities (often characterized as states, chiefdoms, ethnic groups, or tribes). This focus on mobility in Indian Ocean history often diminishes the contributions of shore-bound communities whose histories before contact with oceangoing migrants are relegated to historians focused on continental interiors or remain unexamined. One remedy for this oversight is to examine the histories of littoral societies, which necessarily include both people who traveled the seas and those who remained on shore.

A littoral society is a collection of interdependent communities that occupy the transitional zone between a sea and its mainland. Members of these communities often pursue occupations related to the sea, such as fishing or maritime trade. So the initial contours of littoral societies are determined by ecological features like the availability of certain plants and animals and meteorological features like winds, rains, and tides. However, as littoral societies extend their influence inland, they integrate people who do not derive their livelihood from the sea.

Historian Michael Pearson introduced the notion of "littoral society" to Indian Ocean studies in order to emphasize the integrity of that ocean as a historical space that people lived in rather than traveled through. By treating littoral societies as units comparable to states or cities, he suggested that scholars could determine if "shorefolk have more in common with other shorefolk thousands of kilometers away . . . than they do with those in their immediate hinterland."[52] He offered fish-rich diets, salt production, coral building materials, and a common Arabic-derived lexicon as the shared features of littoral societies in the Indian Ocean. Other historians have offered case studies that confirmed Pearson's initial impressions that littoral societies are similar throughout the Indian Ocean.[53] They also emphasized the commercial and cosmopolitan qualities of littoral societies.[54] However, there has been a dearth of research on how littoral societies first emerged in different parts of the Indian Ocean or how they came to be so similar to one another. In recent years, archaeologists have collaborated with linguists, botanists, and geneticists on the multidisciplinary SEALINKS project to investigate the beginning of long-distance seafaring and connectivity in the ancient Indian Ocean, but historians have so far stayed on the margins of this conversation.[55]

This book will draw greater attention to how littoral societies formed by exploring how communities on the East African rim of the Indian Ocean developed cosmopolitan qualities, which—besides proximity to water— are the hallmarks of littoral societies. As with empires, states, and religious movements, the extent of a specific littoral society waxes and wanes according to its political and economic fortunes. However, littoral societies have populated the entire Indian Ocean almost as long as people have lived near the sea. As such, they are more suitable units than states or port towns for tracing centuries-long developments of collective identities.

Treating the residents of coastal Kenya as members of a single littoral society can also transcend the boundaries of the ethnic groups and colonial states that have distorted research in African history. Although direct comparisons between the Atlantic and Indian Ocean worlds are often ill advised, the research agenda proposed by Pearson can be complemented by what David Armitage has labeled cis-Atlantic history. Pearson suggested that the history of littoral societies need not be "restricted to the sea," because some influence "can come from far inland."[56] Armitage similarly offered that the ocean "provides the link but is not itself the object of analysis" in cis-oceanic histories.[57] Instead of tracing perambulations of people, products, and ideas around the sea, a cis-oceanic history examines the consequences of their movements into a specific coastal region. Sebastian Prange's *Monsoon Islam,* for example, could be described as cis-oceanic because it focused primarily on the transformations of the Malabar coast; in contrast, the transoceanic work of Pedro Machado's *Ocean of Trade* examined how a Hindu merchant community developed effective trading networks on two sides of the ocean (western India and Mozambique).[58] Both works acknowledge, but only partially detail, how the experiences of inland partners shaped those of shore folk. This book will deploy the term *cis-oceanic* in the following chapters to highlight the contributions of inland African communities to Kenya's littoral society.

More importantly, as Armitage suggested a cis-oceanic framework may "overcome artificial, but nonetheless enduring, divisions between histories usually distinguished from each other as internal and external, domestic and foreign, or national and imperial . . . by studying the local effects of oceanic movements."[59] A cis-oceanic approach helps transcend the ethnic divisions of littoral Kenya that are sustained both by oral traditions and scholarly narratives. The following overview of settlement patterns in littoral Kenya demonstrates how a cis-oceanic perspective disrupts over sixty years of research that artificially consigned Swahili, Mijikenda, and other ethnic groups in littoral Kenya to separate histories.

For a long time visitors to the East African coast have assumed that the urban architecture and seafaring occupations associated with its port towns were contributions from Persians or Arabs.[60] This perception is incomplete. Seafaring immigrants settled on the shores of East Africa since at least the first century CE, but they usually joined established communities rather than founding new settlements.[61] East African port towns welcomed immigrants and traders; but residents balanced debts to these creditors from the sea with commitments to inland suppliers. Although intimate ties of marriage, commercial partnership, and military alliances promoted these exchanges all along the East African coast, it is only in Kenya that shore folk share over a millennium of linguistic heritage with their inland neighbors.[62]

The first Bantu speakers to reach the shore of the Indian Ocean probably spoke dialects of Proto–Northeast Coast Bantu. Around 500 CE those who lived near the Kenyan coast articulated a new language that linguists call Proto-Sabaki. The speakers of Proto-Sabaki then began extending their reach along the coast to southern Somalia and the Comoros Islands. As they drifted apart, they formed new speech communities that articulated the Sabaki languages of Kiswahili and Chimijikenda—as well as Kielwana, Kipokomo, and Shicomorian. (The prefixes differentiate languages from the ethnic groups that speak them; e.g., Comorians speak Shicomorian, but speakers of Shicomorian have not always claimed a Comorian identity.) Kiswahili speakers began to distinguish their language as they settled the areas around Mombasa Island as early as 600 CE.[63] Around the same time, the forebears of Chimijikenda speakers simultaneously extended their settlements along the inland hills that form an escarpment from Mount Mwangea in the north to the Shimba Hills in the south, a distance of nearly 120 miles.[64] The material remains of abandoned settlements near Rabai, fifteen miles west of Mombasa, show that cultivators have also occupied that site intermittently since the tenth century CE.[65]

Most modern-day residents of the coast and the escarpment claim descent from these pioneering speakers of Sabaki languages. However, they also began making claims to these contrasting landscapes as mutually exclusive ethnic groups in the twentieth century. Swahili communities often imagine their histories through the urban ruins that line the coast.[66] Wealthy residents commissioned buildings of worship, and later their homes, to be built with mined coral beginning around 1000 CE. They erected the first of these "stone towns" in the Lamu Archipelago; but builders soon brought their skills southward, and their architectural techniques became widespread by the fifteenth century CE.[67] Portuguese soldiers razed Mombasa's grandest buildings in the sixteenth century, and Omani soldiers followed suit in the nineteenth century. Ironically, Portugal also built Mombasa's most enduring monument: Fort Jesus. The massive walls of the fort have towered over the entrance to Mombasa's northern harbor since its completion in 1596. A few mosques have also endured for several centuries, but Muslim immigrants from other parts of the Indian Ocean built most of Mombasa's mosques in the twentieth century.[68] Modern Swahili communities value these ties to the wider Islamic world, but they claim the old stone towns as their distinctive ethnic heritage.

The acres of visible ruins along the coast contrast sharply with the seemingly ephemeral settlements around which Mijikenda communities imagine their collective history. From the crest of Benyegundo Hill near Rabai, Mombasa appears as a white blur against the eastern horizon. Yet settlements along the escarpment were not merely the hinterland suppliers of Mombasa. Settlers established their communities at Rabai as part of the "*kaya* complex" that drew people into the hills.[69] The Chimijikenda word *kaya* (pl. *makaya*) means "town" but also refers to dozens of ritual sites in hilltop clearings. So Benyegundo Hill provides a view not only to Mombasa at the sea but also to the expansive network of makaya on neighboring hills, whose residents welcomed political exiles, trading partners, and relatives from Mombasa for centuries.[70]

Although no one has taken up residence atop Benyegundo Hill for generations, the people of Rabai maintain the forest that encloses its abandoned settlement through dutiful neglect. They let the forest grow. The climb to the top of the hill is strenuous, and most residents of Rabai have never personally set foot in it or any other kaya. The elders who maintain the kaya forbid anyone from collecting firewood from the hilltop, but they occasionally call upon their

FIGURE I.1. Rabai's rural landscape. Photograph by author.

clans to maintain paths and clearings in the forest. Those few people who visit must observe special rules when they reach the clearings, such as removing footwear. Just as the Swahili claim the stone towns of the coast, the Mijikenda regard the makaya as their distinguishing ethnic heritage.[71]

The oral traditions of Kenya's littoral ethnic groups (and the scholarly narratives that reference them) have used these coastal and hilly landscapes to project the contemporary divisions of Swahili and Mijikenda ethnicity onto times long past. Swahili narratives assert that their ancestors descend from Persian and Arab immigrants who intermarried with African residents of the coast centuries before the Mijikenda migrated from the interior.[72] Mijikenda narratives acknowledge this migration, and the timing, but dispute how deep Swahili territory runs inland. From an archaeological perspective, both the urban ruins and forested ritual centers testify to a much longer occupation by large communities of farmers (most likely Bantu speakers) on both the shore and the escarpment.[73] This longer history of contact between the coast and the escarpment is supported by a subset of oral traditions that acknowledge a shared past in Shungwaya, a mythical homeland thought to be north of the

Somali-Kenya border. Yet even these traditions reinforce ethnic divisions by treating the Swahili as distinct from the Mijikenda, Segeju, and Pokomo communities, who separated as they fled Oromo raids in Shungwaya.[74]

The debate between Spear and Willis described above derives from their different analyses of these migration traditions. Spear treated the itineraries recounted in them as mostly accurate descriptions of an overland migration event in the sixteenth century.[75] Hence he wrote two books—one on the Mijikenda, another on the Swahili—that treated these groups as distinct societies in early and modern times.[76] Willis questioned the events narrated in the traditions and argued that they merely reflected the territorial aspirations of emerging ethnic groups in colonial Kenya.[77] Neither scholar questioned the basic assumption of the oral traditions—that the forebears of the Swahili and Mijikenda ethnic groups were also distinct peoples. This book affirms Willis's argument that speakers of Sabaki languages did not innovate Swahili or Mijikenda ethnic identities until the twentieth century. Yet it also extends the narrative back to their Proto-Sabaki-speaking forebears in the sixth century to show that these speakers established a single, shared littoral society centuries before Spear's migration narrative even began. Instead of welcoming and incorporating Mijikenda migrants into a Swahili coast, the forebears of both these ethnic groups worked from the beginning to establish Kenya's littoral society.

The proximity of Rabai to Mombasa alone should cast serious doubt on the assertion from Swahili and Mijikenda oral traditions that their respective communities formed in isolation. At high tide Mombasa's creek laps at the foot of Benyegundo Hill in Rabai. Following the ebb and flow of tidal creeks that join the escarpment to the coast, some residents "face both ways," claiming to be either Swahili or Mijikenda as their situations demand.[78] Others emulate the practices of the other ethnic group even as they describe these practices as foreign.[79] Rather than trespasses of ethnic boundaries, some of these seeming appropriations are a testament to a shared heritage that binds the stone towns and makaya to one another, other African communities, and the Indian Ocean. Reorienting Kiswahili speakers as participants in the kaya complex of the escarpment and Chimijikenda speakers as participants in Kenya's stone towns disrupts the presumed antiquity of the ethnic boundaries around which scholars have organized their research.[80] However, replacing Swahili and Mijikenda ethnic labels with geographical labels—"coastal" and "escarpment"—should only be an intermediary step in disrupting a division that projects these modern identities onto past times: these labels potentially validate violent political claims that treat ethnic boundaries as if they were as natural and immutable as the physical features of the landscape.[81] So rather than approach Kenya's coast and escarpment as fixed ecologies for two equally exclusive ethnic groups, this book traces their mutual contributions to a shared littoral society.

East Africa in the Indian Ocean

A cis-oceanic history that transcends ethnic boundaries also challenges how scholars have incorporated East Africa into the Indian Ocean. Though most scholars regard Kiswahili speakers as active participants in the Indian Ocean world, they usually exclude Mijikenda and other inland communities. On the one hand, they consider loanwords from Arabic, Persian, Hindi, and Portuguese in Kiswahili as emblematic of the ocean's cosmopolitan connections. For instance, Sheriff classified the Swahili alongside Arabs and Mappilas as a "dhow culture."[82] Scholars have also treated Arab and African heritages as distinct fonts of culture from which the Swahili uniquely drew. On the other hand, they suggest that hinterland peoples like the Mijikenda, Kamba, and Pokomo drew solely on an undifferentiated and ahistorical African or Bantu heritage disconnected from oceanic history.

Yet the emphasis on mobility and the formation of transoceanic diasporas that has distinguished Indian Ocean studies hardly applies to the Swahili either. There is little evidence that merchants from littoral Kenya went beyond the relatively close Arabian coasts to trade in early times.[83] Nor did they establish diasporic communities in Oman until the mid-twentieth century.[84] Aside from a few Kiswahili loanwords, most of the African "survivals" that scholars have positively identified in South Asia originated in Ethiopia, Madagascar, or Mozambique rather than areas populated by Kiswahili speakers.[85] Instead of vague references to syncretism and cosmopolitanism, a cis-oceanic history requires attention to the history of each element that people used to form their littoral societies, whether they emerged from deep in the continental interior, far across the sea, or right along the shore.

Flexibly extending the Kenyan littoral to include not only Kiswahili speakers but also speakers of other languages remedies the exclusion of many indigenous African communities from Indian Ocean studies. K. N. Chaudhuri, a founder of the field, claimed that "indigenous African communities appear to have been structured by a historical logic separate from the rest of the Indian Ocean."[86] Later, more expansive visions of the Indian Ocean have countered this dismissal.[87] Nevertheless, scholars' focus on early modern and modern diasporic communities overlooks the experiences of the shore-bound communities who accommodated seafaring migrants. A cis-oceanic history that explores how indigenous Africans incorporated elements circulating throughout the Indian Ocean is just as essential to understanding the formation of littoral societies as the transoceanic histories of migrants and diasporas who joined them. By detailing the "historical logic" of Kenya's littoral society, from its initial formation to decolonization, this book aims to improve the circulation of detailed knowledge about the region so that scholars can better compare it to the formation and transformation of other littoral societies in the Indian Ocean and beyond.

TRACING VERNACULAR EXPRESSIONS OF ETHNICITY THROUGH SCHEMAS

Historians of ethnicity in Africa have relied primarily on ethnographic descriptions, oral traditions, and documentary evidence, which provide only limited perspectives on Africa prior to 1800 CE. Jonathon Glassman's work on Zanzibari nationalism, for example, illustrated how closely examining the discourses of racial thinking can distinguish Africans' intellectual innovations from those of Europeans.[88] However, he could only assert, rather than confirm, that Zanzibaris' racialized thinking had deeper precolonial roots because his documentary sources were limited to modern times. In contrast, historians who have investigated earlier identities usually limited their studies to precolonial times, preventing them from detailing how modern communities entangled their inherited identities with ethnic identities in the colonial era.[89]

This book bridges this temporal divide through a multidisciplinary approach that considers archaeological and linguistic evidence alongside conventional evidence from documents, oral traditions, and ethnographies. Though these methods cannot always be correlated precisely, together they illuminate the original contexts of elements that people later repurposed to imagine other identities, including ethnic ones.[90] Instead of tracing the permutations of a single culture, complex, or identity over time, this book reconstructs the sequence in which speakers of Sabaki languages and their neighbors who spoke other languages in Kenya's littoral society distinguished their respective communities from one another in a vernacular schema.

Schemas are the protean products of categorization—the cognitive process that people use to sort elements in the world around them into categories.[91] Though individuals create idiosyncratic schemas, people also develop shared schemas so they can understand one another.[92] As shared mental maps, schemas are similar to cultures, except they are not bound to ethnic, national, or linguistic groups in popular or academic discourse. While cultures are conceptually circumscribed by the boundaries of collective identities, schemas cut across and transcend political allegiances, language barriers, religious affiliations, and cultural boundaries. Writing about schemas clarifies how people from different communities share categories in a common field, without resorting to phrases like "cross-cultural interaction" that reinforce political claims. Schemas thus provide a flexible framework for examining how people from multiple groups conceptualized themselves and others across centuries. So while most histories of ethnicity focus on the origins and development of a single ethnic group, this book uses the concept of schemas to examine the formation of multiple communities and ethnic groups in tandem. It would be inappropriate to identify a single "Sabaki schema" since speakers of Sabaki languages borrowed categories and shared a schema with speakers of other Bantu and non-Bantu languages from Africa, Asia, and Europe. However, this book will sometimes refer to "Kenya's littoral schema" to emphasize the unique qualities of the vernacular concepts that Kenya's coastal communities shared.

In addition to reconstructing schemas though evidence from the past, this book examines ritual practices through which Sabaki speakers express and perform various identities in Kenya. In the introduction to each chapter, I narrate brief vignettes of formal rituals or quotidian practices I observed in 2010 that suggest how modern expressions of ethnicity resonate with practices from past eras.[93] These vignettes should not be misunderstood as an argument that people performed all of these practices, unchanged, through all the intervening years. Rather, just as historians plumb oral traditions for nuanced understandings of vernacular epistemologies, drawing connections between these rituals and the past demonstrates how everyday life illuminates history in littoral Kenya and vice versa.[94]

The precise provenance and development of ritual symbols and practices in precolonial Africa have proven almost impossible to discern through archaeological, anthropological, or documentary evidence in isolation. However, some ritual elements can be traced to earlier periods of time if they are encoded in speech. When participants speak about rituals, they make ritual elements amenable to historical linguistic analysis. Linguistic historians interpret linguistic evidence to perceive distinct horizons in the past that make the cognitive world of earlier speech communities accessible.[95] So instead of simply outlining the formation of the Swahili and Mijikenda ethnic groups, I use linguistic methods to trace the origins and development of the precise elements that Sabaki speech communities nested into their expressions of ethnicity.

When this book mentions Proto-Sabaki speakers, it refers to a speech community in a specific era (around 500 CE) prior to the division of the Sabaki language family, whose speakers I will collectively refer to in later eras as either Sabaki speakers or speakers of Sabaki languages. As with schemas, readers should not mistake speech communities for ethnic groups or any other kind of self-conscious community. *Speech community* is merely the term linguists use for people who speak the same language. These kinds of communities are not congruent with ethnic or national boundaries, in part because many people, including most East Africans, are multilingual and participate in several speech communities. While ethnic groups self-consciously maintain subjective boundaries through cultural criteria, linguists identify speech communities with objective linguistic characteristics, such as how speakers pronounce a particular sound or organize a sentence. When linguists refer to speech communities, they are explicitly referring to shared patterns of language—not the social groups that people use languages to imagine.

Of course classifying communities according to objective linguistic data is itself a subjective process that rarely conforms with the identities people claim for themselves.[96] So while this book refers often to specific speech communities as acting in concert, or at least pursuing similar strategies, readers should regard these actions as common behavior that was prevalent enough in a particular era to leave traces in the modern languages from which linguists take their data.

The methods that linguists use to reconstruct past languages and speech communities will be outlined briefly in chapter 1, which reviews linguistic evidence to explore how the forebears of Proto-Sabaki speakers conceptualized kinship. At this juncture, I will use the linguistic history of a single word, *muji* (pl. *miji*), to illustrate how littoral Kenyans reimagined their collective identities to accommodate new political constraints in the Indian Ocean.

The etymology of *muji* stretches back to the earliest Bantu times (ca. 3000 BCE) when it was pronounced **mu-gì* and meant "village." This basic meaning held for centuries and across thousands of miles as Bantu speakers extended into new environments and encountered new peoples. However, when the Proto-Sabaki speakers of littoral Kenya started organizing towns around the middle of the first millennium CE, they shifted the meaning of *muji* to refer to this new kind of town community and coined the word *kijiji* (pl. *vijiji*) to denote a village. They divided early towns into neighborhoods, each occupied by a clan that specialized in exploiting different kinds of natural and esoteric resources. Bringing these different lifeways into a single community introduced a cosmopolitan ethic of complementarity that Sabaki speakers continued to elaborate as new communities entered their littoral society.

Miji continues to mean "towns" in the twenty-first century. However, speakers of Sabaki languages added a new meaning to the word by the middle of the second millennium CE (if not earlier) when they began using town names as metonyms for the networks of towns, villages, and homesteads that collaborated as members of the same clan confederation. That is, *miji* could mean either "towns" or "clan confederation," depending on context. For example, the two clan confederations that occupied Mombasa Island in the nineteenth century referred to each other as Miji Tatu (Three Towns) and Miji

Tisa (Nine Towns). The indigenous patrician clans of Mombasa later adopted the alternatives of *taifa* (e.g., Thenashara Taifa) from Arabic and *tribe* (e.g., Twelve Tribes) from English in the nineteenth and twentieth centuries to translate their evolving notion of what the word *miji* could mean for Omani and British imperialists.

Sabaki speakers in the mid-twentieth century returned to the word *miji* as the best representation of the communities they wanted to imagine into existence: *miji wa pwani* denoted the Kiswahili-speaking communities of the coast in the influential writings of Sheikh al-Amin bin Ali al-Mazrui, while Chimijikenda-speaking labor activists partnered with rural elders to organize the Mijikenda Union. Kenya's politicians deprecated the Mijikenda Union and other tribal associations after Kenya's independence to promote nationalism. However, when the government lifted a ban on them in the 1980s, Kiswahili speakers, who claimed Old Town Mombasa as their ancestral home, once again repurposed *miji* by naming their cultural revival organization the Wamiji Association. Finally, though Swahili and Mijikenda have appeared as ethnic categories in Kenya's national census since the country's independence in 1964, many Sabaki speakers wrote the names of their ancestral *miji* confederations on 2009 census questionnaires when asked to identify their tribe.[97]

As this brief sketch suggests, *miji* was not simply passed down among Kiswahili and Chimijikenda speakers from a primordial Bantu past. Rather, as their forebears scaled up *miji* in size and complexity, they changed its meaning while adopting new elements, including collective identities that cut across clans and confederations. The crosscutting categories that Sabaki Bantu speakers helped to innovate include age-sets and councils adapted from Central Kenya Bantu speakers who settled along the coast in the sixteenth century; political and religious identities that became more salient in the competition between the Portuguese and Omani empires of the seventeenth and eighteenth century; racial and sectarian identities they negotiated with the Omani Sultanate in the nineteenth century; and finally, ethnic identities they articulated in the twentieth century to engage with the British Empire. Throughout these centuries, speakers of Sabaki languages forged economic and military alliances that routinely crossed these boundaries as they competed with one another to establish a regional "coastal" polity.

Ethnic identities can never be completely disentangled from the ancestors that Sabaki speakers incorporated into their expressions of ethnicity; but some of these linguistic elements, like the word *miji,* can be sequenced into distinct historical contexts in which earlier speech communities created and transformed them. Instead of merely asserting that a particular element is from a primordial African or Arab past, historians can combine the insights and data of historical linguistics with other evidence to identify when and where an element first emerged and trace its transformations through succeeding eras, just as Indian Ocean scholars have done in regions with more extensive documentary sources. Historians seeking to understand how people formed littoral societies throughout the Indian Ocean must consider a wider array of identities than those which are salient in modern times.

ORGANIZATION

The chapters in this book, divided into three parts, outline the chronological sequence in which Sabaki speakers and their neighbors formed novel collective identities in the precolonial past and adapted these ancestors of ethnicity to a succession of imperial governments since the sixteenth century. The title of each chapter highlights (1) a new innovation in how they imagined their communities and (2) the novel cis-oceanic contexts to which their innovations responded in each era.

"Part 1: Ancestors of Ethnicity" synthesizes evidence published by archaeologists, linguists, and ethnographers to demonstrate that the interdependence of Sabaki speakers continued uninterrupted since their divergence around 500 CE rather than in the sixteenth century (as suggested by the oral traditions collected by Thomas Spear).[98] This synthesis also illustrates how to investigate the complexities of identity in littoral societies throughout Indian Ocean history in times and places where states had little influence. Specifically, it reconstructs the sequence in which Kenya's littoral society developed the lineages, marriage alliances (chapter 1), clans (chapter 2), clan confederations, age-sets, and title societies (chapter 3) that later speakers of Sabaki languages would nest into their various ethnic identities.

"Part 2: Innovating Ethnicity" shifts focus to documentary evidence to explore how Sabaki speakers drew on the heritages of earlier speech communities to develop new collective identities, including ethnicity, once they became subjects of imperial states and citizens of nation-states. As they accommodated the disruptions of foreign rule by Portugal, Oman, and Great Britain, speakers of Sabaki languages experimented with more extensive communities based on military alliance (chapter 4), religious devotion (chapter 5), tribal solidarity (chapter 6), and political ideology (chapter 7). Sabaki speakers strove to maintain their autonomy by adapting the categories that imperialists tried to impose onto their schemas in ways that made sense to them. Successive extensions of oceanic empires motivated most residents of littoral Kenya to reimagine the ancestors of ethnicity as the interior components of ethnic groups.

"Part 3: Transcending Ethnicity?" examines efforts by littoral Kenyans to transcend (but not discard) ethnic affiliations. This part of the book outlines the role of Swahili and Mijikenda communities in the decolonization movements that mobilized for Kenyan independence between 1953 and 1962 as well as their efforts in 2010 to heal Kenya as a nation following the 2007–2008 postelection violence. After outlining the incompatibility of African and Arab nationalism in Kenya, chapter 8 documents how Sabaki speakers continued to modify the categories of the colonial schema they shared with British imperialists and how these communities articulated who belonged to their "coastal" society.

The book's concluding epilogue offers two final vignettes from 2010: the celebration of Swahili New Year on Mombasa Island and an installation ceremony of a new Mijikenda elder on the Malindi seashore. Though Swahili and Mijikenda participants framed these events as ethnic celebrations, they also used media to offer their ethnic and religious rituals as a national heritage that all Kenyans should celebrate. Regardless of how Sabaki speakers choose to reimagine their communities, the Indian Ocean remains a constant horizon for them in littoral Kenya. Even as they claimed membership in the Kenyan nation, both ethnic groups chose to celebrate their ceremonies within sight of the sea.

PART I

Ancestors of Ethnicity

ONE

Ancestors in the Doorway

Claiming Kith and Kin in East Africa before 500 CE

> We are all descended from Mbodze and Mutsedzi,
> the co-wives of Muyeye.
>
> —Bukardi Ndzovu

Hunayo!—"We have it!"—the women shouted as their brother passed their niece's bridewealth to their sister. Their cheers signaled a successful marriage engagement to those waiting outside a concrete home in Rabai, fifteen miles west of Mombasa. Moments later the prospective bride entered to greet each of her future in-laws with a handshake. She honored her mother's ancestors by pouring a few drops of palm wine from a wooden cup inside the doorway of the home. Then her father—absent during the negotiations—entered to drain the cup in a single gulp with all the dregs. He drank a second serving with a homemade straw that filtered fibers from the locally distilled alcohol. Finally, the eldest brother of the bride's mother, who led the proceedings, invited each member of the groom's delegation to introduce themselves by name.

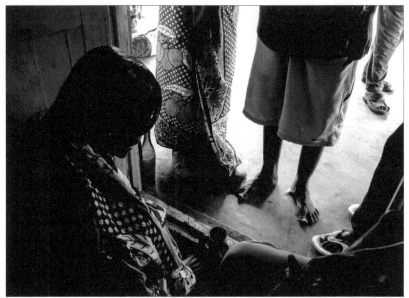

FIGURE 1.1. Palm-wine ceremony honoring maternal ancestors. Photograph by author.

When the groom's delegation first arrived in the morning, the bride's family had regarded them as strangers. The families arranged themselves in two lines to shake hands in greeting, but the hosts then sent their guests to an isolated corner of the homestead to wait. After more than an hour, the bride's maternal uncle formally received them with a gift of a live goat for the groom's father and grandfather.[1] Only then could the visitors enter the house in which negotiations would take place. Since the families spoke different dialects of Chimijikenda, the groom's family hired a Rabai man to conduct engagement negotiations on their behalf.

Modern exchanges of bridewealth for brides illustrate three dimensions of kinship that extend deep into the history of East Africa. First, kinship is more than an accounting of biological genealogy; it is membership in a corporate descent group with shared assets.[2] Researchers may trace biological descent through DNA, but these measurements do not account for how people obligate one another to act as kin. The shouts of "We have it!" claimed the bridewealth for all the bride's kin, not just her mother. Conversely, a groom can afford to pay bridewealth only if his kin share their collective resources. Second, guarding the site of negotiation expresses the underlying tensions between a family who gives a daughter and the family who receives her as a daughter-in-law. Even families who speak similar Chimijikenda dialects and follow nearly identical customs hire brokers to handle these sensitive matters. Finally, the difference in reckoning kinship between these Mijikenda families—one organized around maternal relatives, the other around paternal relatives—is a testament to the historical contingencies of kinship. Scholars often note a "family resemblance" between ethnicity and kinship because proponents of both kinds of identity rely on metaphors of descent to argue that their communities are natural.[3] Yet when making this analogy scholars rarely emphasize that kinship is also constructed. By attending to the historical intricacies of these metaphors—not generic notions of descent—this chapter shows what makes ethnic affiliations seem as authentic, intuitive, and essential as kinship claims.

Few topics have been subjected to more academic theorization than kinship in Africa. Instead of retreading these theories of kinship, this chapter uses the elaboration of Bantu kinship categories to illustrate how people create shared schemas over time. The forebears of Sabaki speakers maintained an array of kinship roles and descent groups over centuries through everyday conversations and practices as well as choreographed rituals. However, they also adapted these elements to new contexts and added new categories to facilitate their collaborations with speakers of other languages. Coordinating evidence from ethnography, linguistics, and oral and written literature clarifies how schemas accommodate changes while maintaining the values and strategies of past communities.

This chapter also focuses on some of the elements that the forebears of Mijikenda families include in their bridewealth negotiation rituals. When the bride offered a palm-wine libation to her maternal ancestors in the doorway, she reinforced the conceptual links among doors, houses, settlements, and descent groups that Bantu speakers have compiled over generations. The kinship schema that earlier Bantu speakers formed is foundational to the ways that Sabaki speakers in Kenya express relationships among their modern ethnic groups. By embedding the rituals and ideologies that create kinship into ceremonies and ideologies of ethnic belonging, speakers of Sabaki languages often affiliate with ethnic groups as collective networks of kin rather than as individuals.

Though some scholars have lamented that it would be futile to identify the origins of specific African patterns of kinship, linguistic historians have been doing precisely this work for several decades, albeit as part of wider-ranging reconstructions of vocabulary related to environments, political strategies, and technologies.[4] The historical narrative in this chapter draws on their reconstructions to explore how speakers of Sabaki languages and their forebears incrementally organized their kinship categories into a gradient of intimacy rather than a single division between an in-group and an out-group. It then describes how Mijikenda and Swahili ethnic groups drew on the kinship schema traced below as they formed in the twentieth century. Specifically, they used stereotypical interactions among the children of co-wives as a model for explaining the agonistic and mutually dependent relationships among their ethnic groups in modern times.

By synthesizing even a narrow slice of the work that linguistic historians have done to reconstruct the East African past, this chapter emphasizes that scholars should no longer refer to an undifferentiated African or Bantu heritage to describe the heritage of specific communities. In order to reimagine the littoral societies of the Indian Ocean, they must account for movements of peoples and ideas from continental interiors as well as from the ocean. So instead of beginning this history of littoral Kenya with the settlement of generic Bantu speakers at the coast, this chapter first considers how communities who spoke dialects of Proto–Mashariki Bantu reimagined their families as they settled around the Great Lakes of East Africa.

A PRIMER IN LINGUISTIC HISTORY

Tracing the development of past ideas and practices that speakers of modern languages retained requires two types of language history. First, linguists establish a framework for how languages within a given region developed over time. They compare the features of modern languages, including their sounds (*phonology*), word forms (*morphology*), vocabulary (*lexis*), and grammar (*syntax*). Second, they examine the histories of individual features to trace how speakers of each dialect innovated and borrowed them. Combining these two types of analysis, linguists can determine (1) the sequence in which speech communities adopted or innovated specific features, (2) whether speakers borrowed those features from neighboring speech communities, and (3) when speakers shifted the meaning or form of those features—all relative in time to other features and other speech communities.[5]

Linguists cannot reconstruct the entire language of a past speech community, but they can reconstruct sets of features (including full words) that objectively distinguish past speech communities from one another. They call these sets *protolanguages*. They also visualize relationships between successive protolanguages and modern languages as a timeline in the form of a tree. Each node in the tree represents a protolanguage, and the lines between each node indicate how *daughter* languages derived from *mother* languages. Linguists refer to languages derived from the same protolanguage as *sisters*. They place modern languages (without a *proto*-prefix) at terminal branches. In some cases sister languages may continue or resume interactions after diverging, or they may adopt similar innovations from the same unrelated languages. Linguists describe these groupings as *areal* groups. Figure 1.2 shows that Proto-Sabaki is the sister of Proto-Pare and a daughter of Proto–Northeast Coast (NEC) Bantu, which is itself derived from an areal grouping of Proto–Mashariki Bantu dialects that Christopher Ehret classifies as Kaskazi.[6] It also shows the major daughter languages of Proto-Sabaki, which constitute the Sabaki language group.

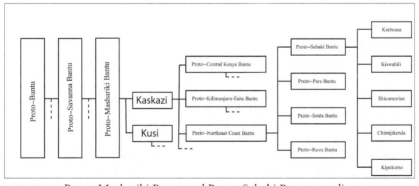

FIGURE 1.2. Proto–Mashariki Bantu and Proto–Sabaki Bantu tree diagram.

Ancestors in the Doorway   33

Tree diagrams are representations of linguists' hypotheses about how languages diverged over time, and scholars often propose competing trees. They refine their hypotheses with the *comparative method*—a technique for systematically reconstructing and sequencing innovations of sounds, forms, and grammar among related languages. The comparative method can also help determine when and where protolanguages were spoken through a rule of parsimony called the *least moves principle*. On the scale of centuries it is less likely that many related speech communities independently converged in the same location after moving several times and more likely that just a few related speech communities departed a single location. So the area with the greatest linguistic diversity within a language family is the most likely place from which daughter languages diverged from their mother protolanguage.

Beyond the relative chronologies and geographies that linguists reconstruct through the comparative method, scholars can estimate calendar dates for the divergence of protolanguages and their daughters by calibrating probabilistic models with archaeological evidence.[7] Regardless of the dating method, firm archaeological data that correspond clearly with "linguistic events" are required to calibrate these measurements with a high degree of certainty.[8] These estimates of calendar dates are never absolute, and their efficacy is highly debated; but they are statistically significant enough to date the formative contexts for many Bantu words.

MAKING KIN: A GENEALOGY OF DESCENT IN EAST AFRICA

When linguists reconstruct ancient kinship categories, they often associate them with one of six formal kinship systems described by anthropologists, such as Crow or Iroquois kinship.[9] They thus present the constellation of words that denote kinship roles and categories in modern languages as retentions of widespread strategies for reckoning unilineal or cognatic descent among past speech communities. In unilineal descent either the father or the mother claims their children as members of their respective patrilineage or matrilineage; conversely, cognatic descent groups consider children to be linked to kin through both their fathers and mothers. In the marriage negotiation described above, the maternal uncle represented the bride's matrilineage, and the paternal grandfather represented the groom's patrilineage.

These formal classifications sometimes convey the impression that kinship is a stable structure that people pass down unchanged for generations. Anthropologist Wyatt MacGaffey has clarified that kinship systems are not "a true description of what exists in real life now or at any time in the past"; instead, each kinship system is an "agreed formula for making political claims."[10] They are schemas for categorizing relationships among people and their resources. Centuries-old words suggest strategies that people consistently found useful and relevant, but they do not determine the precise forms that families took from generation to generation.

At the center of all these negotiations is the notion that people are kin if they share blood from a common ancestor. Classificatory siblings, adopted dependents, blood brothers, and other kinds of fictive kin can embody roles reserved for people born to a member of a descent group; but they do so through ritual and rhetorical transformations that render them equivalent to people related by blood. In this book I use the term "kin" for people who are both related to one another through blood and "unrelated" people who have been formally claimed as kin. For example, in a patrilineal system, children are related by blood to their mother and father but only claimed as kin by their father's family, thus separating his children from their mother's descent group. I use the more expansive term "kith" for dependents, friends, and affines (people related by marriage). This usage may not be suitable for complex analyses of kinship, but it usefully distinguishes the core concept of blood descent from its metaphorical uses, such as when people in clans and ethnic groups assert common descent from a distant ancestor but cannot identify precise genealogical links. It also aligns with the way that Sabaki speakers and their forebears have distinguished gradients of family intimacy.

Contingencies of Claiming Kin

Some of the ceremonies practiced among Mijikenda and Swahili communities illustrate how speakers of Sabaki languages have claimed people as kin in relatively recent times. For example, ethnographer Arthur M. Champion recorded a naming ceremony from the Giriama Mijikenda that dates back at least to the early 1900s.[11] When Giriama Mijikenda children were about one year old, their paternal grandfathers would give them their *dzina la nyumbani* (name of the house) by laying them on their back across the *mriango* (doorway) of their home.[12] He would then pour a few drops of water on their lips, hold their ears, and enjoin them to hear and guard the names of their fathers. Next, he would give the children their personal names and the "name of the house" of their fathers.[13] In another ceremony documented from twentieth-century Lamu, mothers rooted their infants in the household by taking them to each room and explaining its purpose.[14] Some Mijikenda and Swahili families marked the arrival of a new baby through the practice of "bringing out the child." A few days after the birth of a child, the mother or her midwife would bring the newborn outside for the first time to introduce the baby to neighbors.[15] When a grandfather tells a newborn to honor the name of his or her father or a mother bears a child in her arms through her neighborhood, these adults claim stewardship and rights over children as kin.

Yet, both Mijikenda and Swahili communities have adjusted their family schemas as local contexts changed, demonstrating the flexibility of kinship. For example, Champion's early twentieth-century informants explained that children previously received their mother's name as their "name of the house," suggesting that the mother's lineage previously claimed her children.[16] The substitution of the father's lineage in this naming ceremony declared novel, patrilineal claims. One motivation for this change may have been the increase in marriages to formerly enslaved women who escaped coastal plantations in the nineteenth century but had no maternal kin available to claim their children.[17]

The wide variety of methods for organizing kin among contemporary Mijikenda or Swahili communities is the result of choices that speakers of different Sabaki languages made after separating. Among the Mijikenda, Giriama families tend to follow principles of patrilineal descent, Duruma prefer matrilineal descent, and Rabai practice double descent, in which unilineal descent is reckoned through both the father's and mother's line for different purposes. Historically, wealthy Swahili communities followed patrilineal descent to preserve property, but those of humbler circumstances preferred the flexibility of cognatic descent.[18] The Swahili system is so varied that anthropologist A. H. J. Prins regarded Swahili kinship as "somewhat intricate and confused. . . . Seemingly inconsistent information applies to separate usages in different sections of the population."[19] It is reasonable to question whether their common linguistic forebears would have been any less varied in following patrilineal, matrilineal, or cognatic descent.

Scholars who examine the terms for kinship categories shared throughout the Bantu-speaking world often argue whether these terms indicate a patrilineal or matrilineal system.[20] Yet, recognizing the additive process of constructing kinship emphasizes that Bantu speakers used both patrilineal and matrilineal principles of descent as complementary strategies that shifted as circumstances merited. Instead of identifying a fixed-kinship system handed down unchanged from Proto-Bantu times, this book examines kinship terminology to reveal the iterative elaboration of a widely shared schema that made different kinds of descent groups available for later generations to adapt as their contexts changed.[21] As Bantu speakers encountered peoples speaking other languages along their expanding settlement frontier, they gradually developed more elaborate and precise terminology for deciding who counted as kin, kith, or strangers.

BANTU ANCESTORS, KIN, AND KITH, CA. 3000 BCE–1 CE

Linguists have firmly established the historical framework of Bantu languages in East Africa, at least compared to other regions. Taking the chronology in reverse order, Proto-Sabaki speakers began articulating distinct languages around 500 CE as they entered southeastern Kenya and diverged from Seuta, Ruvu, and Pare—the other daughters of Proto–NEC Bantu. The first speakers of Proto–NEC Bantu settled in the hills adjacent to the Tanzanian coast after venturing toward the Indian Ocean in the last few centuries BCE.[22] They drew on the heritage of their forebears in the Southern Nyanza and Kaskazi areal groups of Proto–Mashariki Bantu, whose speakers settled near the Great Lakes around 500 BCE.[23] In turn these speakers inherited elements of their kinship schema from earlier Proto–Mashariki Bantu speakers, who entered the savannas of East Africa around 1000 BCE, and Proto-Bantu speakers, who entered the rain forests of western Central Africa at least five thousand years ago.[24] This section traces how speakers of these earlier protolanguages developed the kinship roles and descent groups that speakers of Sabaki languages would later adapt in littoral Kenya.

Proto-Bantu speakers organized their kin into three categories that emphasized their relationships to ancestors and descendants. They included a single term for descendants (*jánà), two gendered terms for parents (*màà [mother] and *tàátá [father]), and one term for ancestor (*dímù).[25] Linguists disagree about whether Proto-Bantu speakers also organized their families into unilineal descent groups, but they derived a general term for kinship (*dòngò) from a verb that meant to "arrange" or "heap up." Proto-Bantu speakers also used *dòngò to indicate "a line or row." This word could have been an early metaphor for lineage because lineage members succeed one another, generation by generation, in order through time.[26] However, Kathryn de Luna noted that the distribution of meanings for *dòngò across Bantu-speaking regions include divergent notions, such as *kiongozi* (leader) in Kiswahili and *mulongo* (bond friendship) in Ila (a Bantu language in Zambia).[27] So these meanings may have referred to the act of assembling cognatic kin (or the wealth they shared), but they do not indicate the notion of blood descent on their own. The lack of distinct kinship roles that later Bantu speech communities created suggests that the earliest Proto-Bantu speakers had not yet developed lineal strategies of descent and inheritance.

It was the speakers of the Kaskazi cluster of Proto–Mashariki Bantu dialects who first associated unilineal descent groups with doorways in the bridewealth ceremony that opened this chapter. By the time Proto–Mashariki Bantu speakers extended into the eastern reaches of the equatorial rainforest around 1000 BCE, they had elaborated two sets of kinship roles.

The first set formalized enduring relationships among lineages whose members exchanged marriage partners in successive generations. For example, Jeff Marck and Koen Bostoen have reconstructed words that speakers of Bantu languages in eastern Africa used to classify the opposite- gender siblings of their parents as matchmakers: *cé-n-kádí (paternal aunt [lit. female father]) and *máá- dúmè (maternal uncle [lit. male mother]). Cultivating relationships with these relatives helped arrange marriages between *biádá* (cross-cousins), a preference indicated by a pair of words with dual meanings: **cébiádá* (father of cross-cousin) also meant "father-in-law" while **màamá-biádá* (mother of cross-cousin) also meant "mother-in-law."[28] These roles sustained lineages by reproducing the relationships they shared with other lineages in succeeding generations.

The second set of words expressed novel attention to the relationship between grandparents and grandchildren: **tàatá-kúdú* (grandfather), **máá-kúdú* (grandmother), **kúdú* (elder brother/sibling), and **jíjùkùdù* (grandchild).[29] Appending the root **kúd* (to grow up) or **kúdú* (adult) to words for father and mother signified grandparents rather than ambiguous "ancestors." As grandparents began to identify their grandchildren with themselves through naming ceremonies, they created a system of alternating generations: instead of a lineage that extended in a line through time, it became a cycle in which every other generation reproduced the relationships among kin and kith through their grandchildren.[30]

Another new role, **jípòà* (child of a man's sister), acted as a bridge between lineages.[31] Schoenbrun noted that the word specifically denotes nieces or nephews that have been "lost" to an in-law's lineage through their sister's marriage.[32] The emphasis on the loss of a sister's children indicates that patrilineal descent had become normalized. Categorizing **jípòà* as a kind of kith rather than kin opened opportunities for novel kinds of collaboration with those who were lost to another lineage. For example, excluding **jípòà* from one's patrilineage made the children and grandchildren of the **jípòà* eligible for marriage without violating taboos of incest. They could also assist in ritually dangerous activities like washing the bodies of their mother's kin before burial.[33]

These new words suggest that Proto–Mashariki Bantu speakers were more concerned than their forebears with defining roles that relatives performed in their **dòngò* (unilineal descent groups), which they also began to pronounce as **lòngò*. Consolidating three alternating generations in a single household through cross-cousin marriage preferences increased the honor and status of grandparents. Conversely, defining kin more precisely increased Proto–Mashariki Bantu speakers' ability to exclude others from shared assets while continuing to collaborate with kith in other ways.

These innovations also suggest that Proto–Mashariki Bantu speakers were more involved than their forebears in exclusionary, competitive activities. Marck and Bostoen suggest that men left for long periods of time for hunting or "missions of aggression and defense with respect to aborigines" as they extended the Bantu frontier eastward.[34] Alternatively, Proto–Mashariki Bantu speakers could have created more exclusionary kinship criteria because they were moving into new ecologies in which familiar forested environments seemed rare enough that families wanted to assert privileged access. The wider distribution of people across the landscape would have accentuated the problem of securing marriage partners and organizing labor, particularly as they learned new agricultural techniques that fit a more varied ecology.

Some Proto–Mashariki Bantu speakers added grain cultivation to their ancestors' horticulture and foraging strategies between 1000 and 500 BCE as they entered the Great Lakes region of East Africa.[35] As linguist Christopher Ehret shows, they learned these techniques from two different sets of speech communities from the Nilo-Saharan language family. In the wooded highlands of western Uganda and Tanzania, they met Central Sudanian speakers who grew sorghum. Then, farther east, they encountered Eastern Sahelian speakers who farmed pearl millet.[36] Both of these Nilo-Saharan speech communities supplemented their grain harvests by herding cattle, hunting wild game, and foraging.

Ehret has used loanword evidence to show how Proto–Mashariki Bantu speakers relied on these indigenous peoples.[37] For example, several loanwords refer to different kinds of porridge or gruel (e.g., *papa, *ùgì, and *nya from Central Sudanian; *kímà and *gàlì from Eastern Sahelian). These meals, offered in hospitality, would have been these Bantu speakers' first introduction to domesticated grains. Other words indicate that established pastoralists helped the newcomers learn to raise cattle.[38] The immigrants also adopted iron-working skills, which they passed westward to speakers of other Bantu languages.[39]

Before mastering each of these new technologies, Proto–Mashariki Bantu speakers needed to learn about the diverse ecologies of the Great Lakes from strangers who conceptualized kinship in unfamiliar ways. Schoenbrun has suggested that the reconstructed word

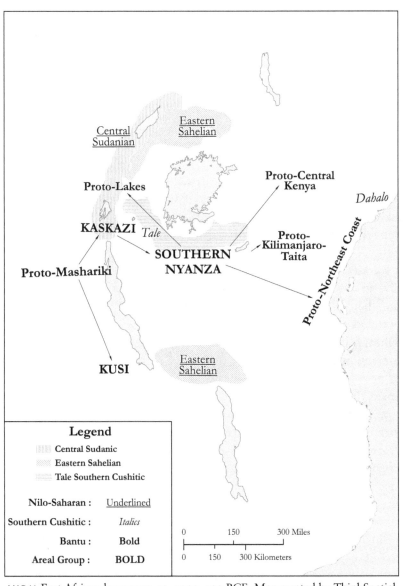

MAP 1.1. East African languages, ca. 1000–500 BCE. Map created by ThinkSpatial.

ihanga (foreigner) is an artifact of these multilingual encounters around the Great Lakes.[40] However, since variants of this word are limited to Proto–Lakes Bantu languages, it is unlikely to have been current among their Proto–Mashariki Bantu forebears. Nor did these early settlers apply the inherited Proto-Bantu word **ba-tûa* (forager, forest specialist) to speakers of Nilo-Saharan languages. Rather than create a single, abstract word for strangers, they coined words for descent groups more exclusionary than **lòngò* (lineage).

The areal groupings that Proto–Mashariki Bantu speakers formed as they drifted apart make it possible for linguists to reconstruct the novel descent groups they created as speakers of different Proto–Mashariki Bantu dialects established communities around the Great Lakes. Proto–Mashariki Bantu speakers divided into at least eleven speech communities, each with its own protolanguage. Sabaki Bantu languages derive from Proto–Northeast Coast (NEC) Bantu—one of eight speech communities that Ehret grouped into a Kaskazi (north) areal group.[41] Since speakers of Kaskazi dialects diverged from the Proto–Mashariki Bantu speech community sometime before 500 BCE, they inherited the Mashariki kinship schema outlined above. However, as they associated with speakers of Nilo-Saharan languages more frequently, they developed specific words for unilineal descent groups. Instead of enforcing a binary division of people into the categories of kin and nonkin, these groups enabled them to create gradients of intimacy between kin, kith, and strangers. They also materialized this gradient in the complex organization of their domestic spaces.[42] Daily interactions reinforced the degree to which people were related because the physical boundaries of gates and doorways managed which people could enter a settlement or household.

According to Ehret and Schoenbrun, Kaskazi speech communities coined **lìàngò* and **nyùmbá* to denote two kinds of unilineal descent groups.[43] The first of these drew inspiration from the layout of novel **ka* (homesteads).[44] In the villages organized by Proto-Bantu speakers in equatorial rain forests, residents lived in structures centered around a single lane. This settlement pattern persisted as they left the rainforest. However, some Proto–Mashariki Bantu speakers adopted their new neighbors' practice of establishing isolated homesteads. If speakers of Kaskazi dialects tended to use *liàngò* to reckon descent through paternal kin, this tendency could have eased marriage exchanges with speakers of Nilo-Saharan dialects, who also organized patrilineal families.[45]

The consolidation of an entire descent group within a homestead fence, rather than a house, made the gate that excluded outsiders from the domestic spaces of the lineage a physical symbol of their kinship.[46] Their perception of this link is evident because they merged the meaning of **lòngò* (lineage) with **liàngò* (doorway).[47] Doorways became both a metaphor of descent and the location for ceremonies that renewed ties with ancestors. The rituals associated with bridewealth negotiations and child naming, both described at the beginning of this chapter, would not have been practiced precisely in the same way since then; but the metaphors that lend these ceremonies symbolic weight likely date from this early era.

Kaskazi speech communities also created **nyùmbá* as an intimate space from which they excluded even some members of their **ñàngò*. This word denotes a round house with a thatched roof that some Kaskazi speakers began using as a replacement for the rectangular, gabled **júbò* houses of earlier generations.[48] They also used **nyùmbá* to refer to a descent group comprised of their maternal kin.[49] Though children might reside in different homesteads upon marriage, those who shared membership in the same **nyùmbá* could expect their siblings, their mother, and their mother's relatives to support one another. By associating motherhood with individual structures, speakers of Kaskazi languages could retain ties with maternal relatives that cut across the patrilineal descent groups that organized villages and homesteads.[50] They nested several **nyùmbá* (maternal homes) behind the **liàngò* (gate, doorway) of every **ka* (homestead).[51] The networks of maternal kin that these spaces sustained would have been particularly valued by women who left their families to bear and raise children in communities speaking a different language.

The innovation of **liàngò, *nyùmbá,* and related terms does not mean all Kaskazi speech communities practiced this particular combination of unilineal descent strategies. For example, Janice Irvine's ethnography suggested that Pokomo communities eventually reversed the hierarchy of these terms as practiced earlier in the Great Lakes.[52] For Pokomo *nyumba* (house) designates clans or incipient lineal descent groups, with *tumbo* (stomach) denoting a clan segment and *midyango* (doors, derived from **liàngò*) denoting siblings who share both parents. Still, the distribution of these terms among Kaskazi languages that are now located across East Africa affirms that they formed part of a widely shared schema for claiming kin.

Kaskazi communities may have been motivated to form these new descent groups to manage networks of kin dispersed among isolated homesteads.[53] Articulating who belonged to which descent group enabled them to claim kin; but as they committed more fully to the agricultural cycles of grain cultivation, they occasionally needed to recruit a larger number of people for labor-intensive tasks like clearing and harvesting. Instead of relying solely on kin for these projects, they could have reached out to affines with whom they had arranged marriages.

A later, slightly smaller areal group of Kaskazi protolanguages that Ehret labeled Southern Nyanza Bantu invented the word *lukólò* to designate this wider kind of network near the end of the first millennium BCE. Whether this new category coalesced networks of maternal **nyùmbá* or patrilineal **liàngò* is unclear. However, this new word may have reflected an increase in crosslinguistic collaboration with speakers of Central Sudanian languages and a group of Southern Cushitic languages called Tale (ta-lay). The root word **kòlò* meant "taproot" or "lower trunk" in Proto-Bantu; but Ehret noted that it also sounded like a word from a modern Central Sudanian language (*ólá* from Lugbara) that means "root" and was used as a metaphor for the "descendants of a particular ancestor."[54] Extending the logic of marriage exchange beyond two lineages created sets of multiple intermarrying lineages for whom the offspring of all would be considered the common children of the **lukólò*.

Linguists usually gloss *lukólò* as "clan," but the different lineages that composed a *lukólò* would have regarded one another as kith rather than kin. The logic of unilineal descent divided the lineages in these marriage alliances into unambiguously distinct families—else cross-cousins could not marry one another. Maintaining distinct lineages within the wider *lukólò* also would have enabled families speaking different languages to benefit from marriage alliances without abandoning their respective heritages. Over several generations, the descendants of Bantu speakers who married their daughters to speakers of Nilo-Saharan and Tale Southern Cushitic languages gained the latter's distinctive knowledge about the Great Lakes environment, cattle husbandry, and grain cultivation.[55] Drawing together metaphors from the Bantu and Nilo-Saharan language families, the coiners of *lukólò* obscured their deliberate exclusion of affines from the status of kin (e.g., **liàngò* or **nyùmbá*) by ascribing their commonality to a "taproot"—an imaginary ancestor whose genealogical connections were untraceable because they did not exist. However they did share descendants—both the children who would carry on their respective lineages and their nephews and nieces (**jìpúí*) who could perform rituals or other activities that were taboo for kin. Members of the same clan secured their alliance through mutual investments in the future but imagined their relationships through a fictive, ancestral past.

The speech communities that made up the Southern Nyanza areal group moved away from one another near the end of the first millennium BCE. Several remained around Lake Victoria or moved to the southern highlands of Tanzania. Proto–Upland Bantu speakers nestled into the foothills of Mount Kenya and the Taita Hills, while Proto–NEC Bantu speakers moved, quite rapidly it seems, across the savannas to the wooded hills of eastern Tanzania.[56]

As Proto–NEC Bantu speakers left the good, green lands of the Great Lakes for more arid regions to the east, they settled in communities with lower population densities. As part of the Southern Nyanza areal group, Proto–NEC Bantu speakers would have been familiar with cattle pastoralism. Yet most of them founded villages with shade and water (where their gardens could flourish) instead of isolated homesteads. As less populous communities, they also abandoned more extensive groupings led by chiefs, diviner-doctors, and rainmakers that Proto–Lakes Bantu societies retained; but they kept the title **muéné* (steward, trustee), which signified a person with stewardship over the direct and lateral descendants in their lineage. They also retained the term **liàngò* to signify paternal relations and the term **nyùmbá* to reference maternal ones, while *lukólò* included the lineages of in-laws and prospective spouses.

Sometime after settling near the Indian Ocean, Proto–Sabaki Bantu speech communities diverged from Proto–NEC Bantu. They also shifted the meaning of the word **ilumbu* from "opposite-gender sibling" to "full sibling" to emphasize even more intimate relationships.⁵⁷ While *nyùmbá* networks connected children to their mother's relatives living elsewhere, the term **ılumbu* refers to siblings who were raised in the same home or who were children of the same mother in contrast to half siblings, who shared only one parent. A similar development is indicated by the shift in meaning of **lìàngò* (patrilineage) to *midyango* (children who share both parents) in Kipokomo. The more intensely exclusionary meaning of this Kipokomo word hints at domestic instability or, rather, women's social mobility. This word may have emerged as women more often exercised their prerogative to leave their marriages and seek new husbands. The intimate association of sharing a mother could have transcended, or at least cut across, the obligations of her children to their respective fathers' lineages.

Alternatively, coining a word for full sibling may suggest that some men formed polygynous households where each cowife guarded the interests of her children and taught them to rely more closely on one another than their half siblings. In Kiswahili and Chimijikenda, the word for cowife is *mke mwenza*. *Mke* is a generic word for "woman" that also means "wife," while *mwenza* is derived from the verb *enza*, which the missionary-linguist John Ludwig Krapf translated as "to look at or visit one, to inquire how one fares" in nineteenth-century Kimvita, the Kiswahili dialect spoken in Mombasa.⁵⁸ Another common derivation of the verb is *mwenzi* (friend). The compound word *mke mwenza* thus captures an idealized situation in which co-wives would support one another.

Some Swahili proverbs, on the other hand, characterize relationships among co-wives in decidedly negative terms. To a prospective cowife, a woman might say: *Naona ni shoga yangu; kumbe ni mke mwenzangu* (I saw you as my friend, alas! You are my cowife), suggesting that friendship is at best improbable among co-wives.⁵⁹ To a husband considering an additional marriage, a wife might reply: *Mke Mwenza! Haa! Mezea* (Cowife? Ha! [Just try and] swallow it!), indicating disdain for the prospect of sharing her husband.⁶⁰ Although the word *mke mwenza* is shared by several Sabaki languages, it could have been loaned from Kiswahili speakers whose polygynous unions were sanctioned by Islam, rather than having been inherited from an earlier time. Yet the word **ılumbu* (full sibling) suggests this marriage pattern was also possible among Proto-Sabaki Bantu speakers unfamiliar with Islam. Even if very few men were able to assemble the resources and alliances necessary to form polygynous households, the tensions among co-wives were salient enough to find expression in proverbs and oral traditions.

To review this genealogy of descent among Bantu speakers in East Africa, *dòngò (kinship) was a strategy of shared descent innovated in Proto-Bantu times (ca. 3000 BCE). The Proto-Mashariki Bantu settlers of the Central African plains changed the term's pronunciation and meaning to *lòngò (lineage) around 1000 BCE. In the meantime their forebears also coined words for cross-cousins, grandparents, and nephews/nieces. These roles helped them reproduce their families as unilineal descent groups when they began living in dispersed homesteads and associating with speakers of Nilo-Saharan languages. Around 500 BCE, the eight Bantu protolanguages that constituted the Kaskazi areal group articulated *lìàngò as patrilineal settlements and *nyùmbá as maternal households—complementary strategies that enabled siblings to maintain relationships with each other and dispersed maternal relatives. After separating from Proto-Lakes Bantu communities, the speech communities of the Southern Nyanza areal group formalized the term for marriage alliances as *lukólò* before separating to settle the eastern frontiers of East Africa. The Proto-Sabaki branch of Proto-NEC Bantu speakers then embedded their distinctive concerns for maintaining relationships with their cosiblings in the word *ilumbu (full sibling). The Bantu linguistic heritage that speakers of Sabaki languages employ to claim kin was not simply inherited from Proto-Bantu times. Rather, their ancestors developed these roles over thousands of years as they elaborated the notion of kinship to draw one another and the peoples they encountered into a nested set of descent groups while simultaneously excluding others as kith or strangers.

Proto-Sabaki speakers' retention of kinship roles and descent groups over more than a thousand years since diverging from Proto-NEC Bantu is a testament to the intuitive and persuasive power of the schema they inherited. Few speech communities draw on all these ancestral categories, and different Bantu speech communities use them inconsistently. But these variations are contingent on historical experiences rather than being random. Whenever speech communities draw on this heritage—by referring to their maternal relatives as *nyumba,* naming a child after their grandparent, barring entrance into an interior space, or offering palm wine in a doorway—they renew and embody the kinship schema of their ancestors. These practices thus pass on cognitive connections beyond the conscious range of any individual's memory.

EXPRESSING ETHNICITY AS KINSHIP

Examining how speakers of modern Sabaki Bantu languages use kinship terms created by their ancestors in everyday conversation and performances cannot reveal precisely how their ancestors used them; but their modern expression in proverbs, rituals, and other performances emphasize that these words were coined to obligate kin and kith to act in prescribed ways. The words for kinship roles and descent groups helped channel complex social dynamics into predictable, agreed-upon formulas for ordering society. Therefore, it is not surprising that speakers of modern Sabaki languages use these kinship metaphors to explain relationships among their ethnic groups.

When telling the origin of the Mijikenda ethnic group to Thomas Spear in the 1970s, for instance, many Mijikenda men asserted that all the ethnic groups that speak Sabaki languages were descended from a single man and his two wives. Joseph Denge explained: "Muyeye had two wives. Mbodze and Matsezi. They were not sisters; they were co-wives. Mbodze is our mother. . . . Matsezi is the mother of the Bajun [northern Swahili] and the Arabs." Bukardi Ndzovu, another of Spear's informants, explained: "We are all descended from Mbodze and Mutsedzi, the co-wives of Muyeye. . . . Mbodze was the first wife and she gave birth to the Digo and the Ribe. . . . Matsezi, the second wife, gave birth to the Pokomo, the Giriama, the Taita, and the Gunya [northern Swahili]."[61] Spear's two consultants disagreed on which particular groups were descended from which mother, but they both drew extemporaneously on the metaphor of a polygynous family to indicate the degrees of intimacy they perceived among contemporary ethnic groups and clan confederations.

By mixing patrilineal and matrilineal descent metaphors, Spear's informants made seemingly contradictory claims. Claiming unilineal descent back to a single male used the logic of patrilineage (*liàngò) to emphasize similarities among neighboring ethnic groups with related languages. However they also drew on maternal households (*nyùmbá) and relationships between co-wives to emphasize their differences from one another. Considering the work that Sabaki language-speaking intellectuals did to distinguish Swahili and Mijikenda ethnicity in the decades preceding Spear's research, these differences could not be lightly dismissed in the 1970s. Yet the relationships between patrilineal and matrilineal descent groups in their shared kinship schema allowed Spear's informants to entangle these distinct ethnic groups as members of an extended family— perhaps closer to kith than kin but certainly not strangers. As a clear expression of this perspective, the Mijikenda word for the Swahili ethnic group is *adzomba* (uncles). The kinship metaphors that speakers of Sabaki languages use to describe their ethnic identities thus contradict conventional models that describe ethnic boundaries as exclusionary binaries by depicting them instead as complex gradients of intimacy.

While Mijikenda oral traditions show the complementarity of patrilineal and matrilineal claims, Kiswahili literature shows how they can also be set in opposition to one another. Swahili communities rarely claim shared descent with the Mijikenda, but they rely on similar lineage metaphors to express ethnic affiliation.[62] However, Swahili metaphors are complicated by a patrilineal system supported by Islamic ideologies introduced by immigrants from Arabia and Persia. These immigrants' integration into coastal society is a major theme in Kiswahili historical chronicles transcribed from oral sources between the sixteenth and nineteenth centuries.

The writers of these chronicles present patrilineal and matrilineal descent as opposing principles that require reconciliation. In the *Kilwa Chronicle,* for example, tensions between an immigrant Persian prince and his local father-in-law are only resolved with the birth of a grandchild who can claim authority over Kilwa through both his mother, whose kin settled the island, and his father, who purchased it.[63] This chronicle and similar traditions affirm the precedence of patrilineal descent as prescribed in Islamic law, while noting that matrilineal inheritance can be accommodated in exceptional circumstances.

In contrast, stories, poems, and songs about the folk hero Fumo Liyongo told among Swahili and Pokomo communities in northeast Kenya present patrilineal and matrilineal claims as irreconcilable. Liyongo was a folk hero famed for his prowess with the bow, his near invincibility, and his skill as a bard. However, he struggled with his maternal uncle's son Fumo Mringwari over who should lead the community. The dispute rested on whether matrilineal or patrilineal principles of descent should be given precedence, with Liyongo claiming to be the successor of his mother's brother and Mringwari claiming the title as his father's son.[64] Unlike the *Kilwa Chronicle*, the dispute was resolved not by the hope of a new generation but by the fatal betrayal of Liyongo by his own son.

The oral and written literature of Sabaki speakers thus emphasize that the kinship schema inherited from various epochs of the Bantu past provides a reservoir of concepts, ideas, and resources, but this schema does not determine which political claims they use these elements to make. As speakers of Sabaki languages drew on kinship metaphors to express ethnic affiliations in the twentieth century, they manipulated the elements in their shared schema in many ways. Kinship metaphors may sometimes shape how people collaborate as members of an ethnic group, but they are mostly important because proponents of ethnic identities can use their knowledge of the intricacies of kinship to lend authenticity to newly imagined communities.

As I recorded a prospective bride kneeling in the doorway of her mother's home to offer a libation of palm wine to her ancestors, my research assistant William Tsaka whispered to me, "This is symbolic." He wanted to make sure I did not miss the climax of the day's events; but his statement also emphasized that the action was a deliberately choreographed moment. The bride wore special clothing and was coached word by word to seek the blessing of her ancestors. The family chose a traditional liquor, which they placed in a hand-carved wooden cup; and they sipped it with a homemade straw and filter. These deliberately archaic touches made the ceremony appear as ancient as the ancestors. Later, the bride's maternal uncle explained that she had poured palm wine in the doorway because the ancestors were in the doorway.[65]

Despite the relationship between ancestors and doorways in the ceremony, Chimijikenda speakers rarely use their word for doorway (*muryango,* derived from **liàngò*) to mean "lineage" (as do some Kiswahili speakers) or "children who share both parents" (as do some Kipokomo speakers). Instead, they use the word *mbari* (lineage, clan), which they borrowed from Central Kenya Bantu speakers. So Chimijikenda speakers have preserved the tight cognitive link between domestic spaces and kinship in a ritual practice instead of a word. Only by examining the Mijikenda rituals within the wider context of Sabaki language heritage does the millennia-old provenance for the symbolic connection between doorways and descent groups become apparent.

A cis-oceanic approach that transcends geographical and historiographical boundaries also helps reveal overlooked connections. The littoral society that speakers of Sabaki languages helped form along Kenya's coast did not extend to the Great Lakes. Yet the intricacies of a kinship schema first elaborated hundreds of miles from the sea are as crucial to understanding the formation of a littoral society in coastal Kenya as the ideas that flowed from distant shores around the Indian Ocean.

TWO

Making a Peaceful Home

Organizing Clans through Knowledge along Sabaki Frontiers, ca. 150 BCE–1250 CE

> When one is asked who he is, it is not enough to be Giriama.
> One is asked what sort of Giriama; what mbari [clan]?
>
> —Bukardi Ndzovu

GONA DZOKA COMPLAINED of a mild headache when we visited him near Rabai. So before turning his attention to our questions, he gathered a handful of twigs and spoke to them in a quiet voice. His daughter then took the twigs to make into a tea. He told us this blessing was *uganga*—medicine or spiritual healing. Dzoka did not present himself as a *mganga*—a person who treats the sick with herbal treatments, incantations, prayers, and dances. However, he did claim he could fashion protective wards to prevent the theft of crops and amulets to protect against lions. He regarded these uganga as commonplace, but he also spoke of a rare technique that could make the forest around Rabai appear as the ocean. Enemies who approached their settlements would drown because the vision was so convincing.[1]

Mijikenda elder Thomas Govi offered a different perspective on uganga in an interview with Thomas Spear decades earlier. He described uganga not as common knowledge but as the assets of clans. "Each *mbari* [clan] had its own *uganga*. . . . There was *uganga* to evade an epidemic, *uganga* to stop an epidemic from spreading further, *uganga* for starting war, *uganga* to win a war, *uganga* to evade a war, and *uganga* to stop a war. You cannot divide all these by a few *mbari*; people of the same *mbari* were given two or three different types of *uganga*." Govi affirmed that clans must assist one another because all these different uganga were necessary to "make a peaceful home."[2]

Cognates for the Kiswahili word *uganga* (medicine) stretch throughout the Bantu-speaking world.[3] However, as Dzoka and Govi's descriptions suggest, the conventional gloss of "medicine" does not capture the full range of meanings that speakers of Sabaki languages associate with uganga. As a category, uganga includes the healing arts but also techniques of ironworking, rain making, carving grave markers, and communicating with ancestors. So uganga is better defined in littoral Kenya as esoteric knowledge—techniques that draw power from the unseen world of ancestors, spirits, and gods. Though some kinds of uganga have become common knowledge, speakers of Sabaki languages consider many of these techniques to be the exclusive property of different clans.

This chapter draws on the link between uganga and clanship articulated by Thomas Govi to reimagine the settlement history of littoral East Africa.[4] The word *uganga* has not changed for thousands of years, and its derivations are limited to words for medicine man and a generic word for roots. Conversely, the linguistic history of "clan" in Proto–Sabaki Bantu languages is difficult to reconstruct because words for the same concept vary across Sabaki languages. Proto-Sabaki speakers initially added the meaning of "clan" to **lukólò* (marriage alliances). However, the speakers of each daughter language articulated new words for this novel social category as they adapted them to incorporate strangers into their communities.[5]

So instead of tracing changes in the linguistic history of uganga and clan, this chapter uses these words as presented in Mijikenda oral traditions as a source of vernacular theory.[6] These traditions are neither eye-witness accounts nor unaltered narratives passed down from the first millennium CE. Rather, they reflect relationships among different kinds of people that matter in the present because they also mattered in the past. Weaving oral traditions around linguistic, archaeological, and documentary evidence brings the historical knowledge that African communities have curated about their past into dialogue with academic narratives. These academic narratives have often used intermarriage, trade, and religious conversion to explain how residents first mastered the ecologies of Kenya's littoral zone and then increased their commercial entanglements in the Indian Ocean.[7] Focusing instead on how speakers of Sabaki languages transformed their settlements through clanship suggests that local rivalries over knowledge increased these speakers' capacity to integrate new practices into their inherited schemas, from techniques of grain farming to Islamic devotional practices.

RETHINKING CLANS

Anthropologists conventionally define clans as unilineal descent groups whose members claim a common ancestor but cannot precisely trace their genealogy to a founder. However, the notion of clans among speakers of Sabaki languages more closely resembles Neil Kodesh's description of Ganda clans near the Great Lakes.[8] Kodesh emphasized that scholars should not be distracted by claims that members of the same clan are literal kin. Rather, clan members use descent as a metaphor to assemble people who are unrelated by blood, just as members of ethnic groups and nations do.

Kodesh's analysis of Ganda oral traditions demonstrated that they formed clans by drawing people from noncontiguous areas into shared networks of healing. This practice enabled them to acquire many kinds of knowledge. Even in the twenty-first century, "clanship serves as a way to organize and deploy . . . various skills for the collective good of clan members," from college-educated professionals to traditional healers, Christian bishops, and Muslim imams.[9] For Kodesh, treating clans as groups with stewardship over knowledge instead of descent groups challenged the emphasis on centralized authority in conventional narratives of the Buganda Kingdom's founding in the eighteenth century.

In the settlement history of littoral East Africa, linking uganga to clanship explains why crosslinguistic collaborations were limited as Proto–Northeast Coast (NEC) Bantu speakers settled into the region between 150 BCE and 600 CE but more common as their successors who spoke Proto-Sabaki languages stretched out between 500 and 1250 CE. Since they regarded communities as the owners of knowledge, they could not settle the varied ecologies of littoral Kenya until they developed a strategy for bringing people who spoke unrelated languages and practiced different subsistence strategies into the same settlements.

So a major difference between the two overlapping phases of settlement in littoral Kenya rests on a shift in settlers' strategies for collaborating as distinct communities. As detailed in the previous chapter, Proto–NEC Bantu speakers regarded *lukólò as marriage alliances that reproduced relationships between kith and kin over succeeding generations. However, as Proto- Sabaki speakers diverged from this speech community around 500 CE, they added the meaning of "endogamous clan" to "*lukólò" to distinguish their relationships with affines (their kith) from people who belonged to other *lukólò. Sustaining marriage alliances was an internally directed strategy for binding lineages dispersed among several settlements; reconceptualizing "*lukólò" as "clan" made it the operative unit for collaborations with nonkin, nonkith people who lived in the same settlement. Negotiations among clans over space and influence in their shared towns created a new dimension of public familiarity without discarding the marriage alliances that reproduced relationships among kith and kin in domestic life. Mijikenda oral traditions indicate uganga would have been a critical feature for distinguishing who belonged to which clan. As speakers of Sabaki languages diverged, they also materialized the physical boundaries of their clans by marking off distinct spaces for each clan that shared a town. Entrusting the stewardship of knowledge and space to clans was the key innovation that enabled them to stretch out their settlements from Mozambique to Somalia, as well as the Comoros Islands, the inland estuary of the Tana River, and Kenya's escarpment. The other speech communities that branched off from Proto–NEC Bantu (Ruvu, Seuta, and Pare) remained stationary in comparison.[10]

Archaeologists use material culture to distinguish three populations who lived in littoral East Africa. Pots are not people, as archaeologists often caution.[11] Still, examining pottery wares alongside other material remains can reveal techniques of food production and artisanship that scholars can associate with distinct lifeways. For instance, archaeologists have interpreted animal remains, pottery, and other artifacts to show that agropastoralists made temporary camps along the plains to graze their herds in East Africa before 700 CE; but they lived for much of the year in more permanent settlements near rivers or highland locations where they foraged, hunted, and grew crops.[12] Archaeologists have also identified strategies that distinguish foragers and early ironworking farmers in the first millennium CE of littoral East Africa.[13]

When researchers can trace words for practices identified by archaeologists back to the same period of time, as in littoral East Africa, the correlation between past speech communities and specific lifeways described by archaeologists is relatively strong. The remains of stone tools likely indicate regular encampments of autochthonous foragers, Pastoral Neolithic pottery identifies the settlements of Southern Cushitic speakers starting around 2500 BCE, and Kwale pottery indicates the locations settled by Proto–NEC Bantu speakers starting around 150 BCE. The work of classifying pottery wares and reconstructing protolanguages inherently privileges descriptions of past peoples as isolated, bounded populations; but loanwords, shared aesthetics, and technology transfers hint at more complex relationships among these populations.[14]

Settling In, ca. 150 BCE–600 CE

The settlement of Proto–NEC Bantu speakers in coastal East Africa between 150 BCE and 600 CE is attested primarily by archaeological evidence, with a small number of linguistic innovations and loanwords that indicate limited engagements with agropastoralists who spoke Southern Cushitic languages. There are also a few tantalizing passages from the *Periplus of the Erythraean Sea* that offer the earliest written testimony of East Africa's littoral society. Though the evidence suggests some interactions among early foragers, Proto–NEC Bantu speakers, and Southern Cushitic agropastoralists prior to 600 CE, these three populations often confined their activities to the

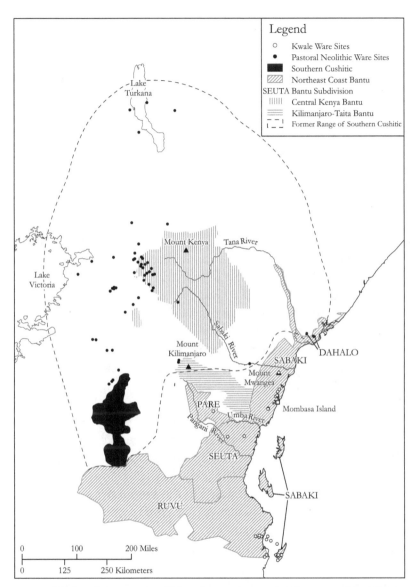

MAP 2.1. Modern languages and historic pottery wares. Map created by Think-Spatial. Language zones based on "Country Map of Kenya" and "Country Map of Tanzania" in David M. Eberhard, Gary F. Simons, and Charles D. Fennig, eds., *Ethnologue: Languages of the World* (Dallas: SIL International, 2022). Used with permission. Further redistribution prohibited without permission.

ecological niches in which their respective lifeways could flourish; they also avoided each other where those environments overlapped.

The *Periplus* was a first-century guidebook for Indian Ocean traders, written by an anonymous Greek-speaking Egyptian merchant. He noted that fishermen in a coastal region of East Africa that he called Azania were "very big-bodied men" who caught turtles and other sea animals in wicker traps. They also fished from dugout canoes and sewn-plank boats. The writer reported that the sultan of Musa (in southern Arabia) attempted to collect tariffs through representatives at a coastal trading center called Rhapta, but the residents asserted their autonomy "each in their own place, just like chiefs." These local communities offered ivory, rhinoceros horn, tortoise shell, and palm oil to Arabs and other visiting merchants, who provided wine and grain to foster goodwill but also married into local families. Indian Ocean merchants found that their trading partners in East Africa most valued glass and iron tools—lances, hatchets, daggers, awls, and so on. The author also wrote that the people of Azania spoke a single language.[15]

Although some of the people who traded at the coast may have been indigenous foragers or Southern Cushitic agropastoralists, several lines of evidence suggest that the residents of Azania who most often traded with seagoing merchants spoke dialects of Proto–NEC Bantu. First, foragers and agropastoralists in the region used stone tools even after immigrating smiths made iron tools accessible.[16] As late as the tenth century, Chinese chronicler Tuan Ch'eng-shih recorded that pastoralists in coastal East Africa fought "with elephant's tusks, ribs, and wild cattle's horns as spears."[17] Apparently they were uninterested in the forged metals offered by merchants at the coast, whereas producers and consumers of local iron would have recognized their value. Second, archaeologists have found the remains of shellfish, fish, and turtles at many settlements associated with ironworkers, confirming their connection to the sea. Third, archaeologists date Kwale ware—the pottery found most often in the settlements of ironworking farmers—from as early as 150 BCE to around 600 CE, inclusive of the time when the *Periplus* was written.[18] Fourth, the spatial distribution of Kwale ware corresponds to the territories of modern NEC Bantu speech communities (see map 2.1).[19]

Archaeologists have recovered enough samples of Kwale ware to indicate that early Bantu speakers on the coast extended their settlement frontier northward from near the Tanzanian coast toward Kenya. Although littoral Kenya has a large cluster of Kwale ware sites dating from the second century CE, the earliest finds are from around 150 BCE in Limbo, Tanzania. Even before these potsherds were found, linguist Thomas Hinnebusch postulated a similar trajectory because the northernmost NEC Bantu language families (Sabaki and Pare) share linguistic features with the Saghala Bantu language in the Taita Hills.[20] These areal innovations suggest they had already separated from the other NEC Bantu language families (Ruvu and Seuta)—still located in northeast Tanzania—before extending northward.

As Proto-NEC speakers worked their way north over multiple generations, they relied on foragers' knowledge of the landscape to extend their reach. These relationships could have resembled the interactions between farmers and foragers described by Bukardi Ndzovu to Thomas Spear. He said, "The Laa [a forager group] told them [where to settle]. The Giriama [a Mijikenda clan confederation] originally were not men of the forest, but they had made friends with the Langulo [foragers]. A Langulo would come, ask for a ram, and then he would show you a nice area in the forest where he hunted."[21] Richard Helm's survey of ironworking sites in Kenya's escarpment indirectly confirms the impression given by this oral tradition. He found that iron workers settled in places where foragers had previously camped; for example, he recovered stone tools at Mgombani below strata in which he found sherds of Kwale ware.[22] Yet surveys of forager and farmer sites, which were contemporaneous in the early first millennium, show no signs that they traded items or otherwise shared a common material culture, even when located within walking distance of one another. Archaeologists have thus concluded that foragers and ironworking farmers did not interact frequently in the "pioneer phase" of Bantu settlement.[23]

Proto–NEC Bantu settlers similarly limited their association with neighbors who spoke Southern Cushitic languages prior to 500 CE. Most speakers of modern Southern Cushitic languages reside along the Rift Valley of central Tanzania. However, the distribution of Pastoral Neolithic ware indicates that Southern Cushitic speakers also occupied much of eastern and central Kenya before 700 CE, including the plains along the upper Tana and Sabaki Rivers that formed a wide arc north and west of Kwale ware users (see map 2.1). The distribution of these settlements reflected their inhabitants' respective ecological preferences.

Despite this physical separation, Proto–NEC Bantu speakers in Tanzania and Kenya adopted Southern Cushitic words related to local wildlife, such as the word for "gazelle" (*nswala* from **tsawad*) as well as the word for "sorghum" (*mutama* from **tyaam*), which agropastoralists cultivated.[24] Proto–NEC Bantu speakers who settled in littoral Kenya (but not those in Tanzania) also drew on their neighbors' aesthetic sensibilities as they decorated their pottery.[25] Since pottery decorations can vary infinitely, archaeologists often interpret shared aesthetics as evidence that potters deliberately sought to affirm their relationships, in this case across linguistic boundaries. The shared designs suggest that occasional exchanges of marriage partners may have facilitated an exchange of knowledge between the two populations. However, the forms, shapes, and production methods of Kwale and Pastoral Neolithic ware remained distinct because of the physical distance. Still, the borrowed designs bear witness to collaborations that made it possible for Proto-Sabaki speakers to live in more varied environments after 500 CE.

Stretching Out, 500–1250 CE

As the Proto–NEC Bantu speakers who lived in Kenya expanded their territory between 500 and 1250 CE, they articulated the Proto-Sabaki language and six daughter languages.[26] These speech communities pursued more varied subsistence strategies that could support larger settlements. In addition to continuing the old strategy of gaining knowledge through exchanging marriage partners, Proto-Sabaki speakers innovated a cosmopolitan ethic that promoted cooperation (and competition) among people with different kinds of knowledge. To encourage these collaborations, they formed towns.

The earliest Proto-Sabaki speech communities lived south of the Sabaki River along Kenya's coastal escarpment around 500 CE.[27] The location of the Sabaki homeland has been the subject of much debate. Nurse and Hinnebusch suggest it was north of the Tana River because oral traditions about these speech communities' Shungwaya homeland

and the archaeological research that was available several decades ago indicate extensive settlements in northern Kenya and Somalia but not elsewhere in Kenya. However, linguistic evidence suggests they extended northward from the region between the Umba and the Sabaki rivers—in other words, Kenya's coastal escarpment—rather than southward. In addition, the mainland near Mombasa is the only place along the East African coast with speech communities from both Northern and Southern Kiswahili, as well as from Northern and Southern Mijikenda. More recent archaeological surveys also support a Sabaki homeland in the vicinity of the escarpment west of Mombasa. A single sherd of Kwale ware that Helm found on Mount Mwangea is the most northern evidence of Bantu settlements inland from Kenya's coast before 600 CE.[28] In addition, his site surveys indicate a radiation of settlements from similar environments in Kenya's coastal escarpment to more diverse environments throughout the region.

As Proto-Sabaki speakers expanded into environments with less permanent water supplies, they would have depended more on rainfed crops. Some of the Proto-Sabaki words that Nurse and Hinnebusch have reconstructed indicate that these settlers developed techniques for growing and processing grain before dispersing from their homeland. For instance, Proto-Sabaki speakers elaborated an ancient Bantu word for "sifting" to describe the process of clearing fields and winnowing. From *ced (sifting) they coined the word *wucelo (cleared ground for planting grain) as well as *lucelo (winnowing tray). A third word, *mucele (grain), suggests they had started cultivating grains other than sorghum (for which they used the word *mutama) that also required sifting and winnowing, such as pearl millet and finger millet.[29] Archaeologists have found traces of these other grains in ironworking settlements as early as 600 CE.[30]

Proto-Sabaki speakers likely learned how to grow all these crops from Southern Cushitic agropastoralists. Their word *soola (pounding grain) came from a Proto-Southern Cushitic word (*shool [pulverize]). However, this word is shared only by the northernmost Sabaki speech communities.[31] So it may have been borrowed in later centuries after the daughter languages of Proto-Sabaki had already separated. Regardless of the source of this innovation, the ability to grow food away from a consistent water supply made many more places suitable for settlement.

Ethnographic descriptions of agricultural practices in modern Sabaki-speaking communities suggest that Proto-Sabaki speakers would have regarded this novel rain-fed agriculture as a new kind of uganga whose practices were protected and passed on through rituals overseen by "guardians of the soil." These specialists were responsible for divining the best time for planting, selecting areas for cultivation, and keeping track of the solar calendar.[32] Even mundane, technical knowledge was mediated through the unseen world.

As speakers of new Sabaki languages expanded their settlements, they displaced foragers; but Mijikenda traditions describe their ancestors' relationships with foragers in positive terms because of the valuable uganga that foragers contributed. For example, Toya wa Kiti considered the foraging communities active in his own time (1971) to be the successors of the foragers mentioned in his community's oral traditions. He told Spear, "The Laa were like the Langulo or the Boni. I can't explain exactly who they were, but they were *waganga* [medicine men]."[33] Others that Spear interviewed emphasized that Laa foragers taught them rituals, war strategies, and ways to hunt (and fight) with bows and arrows.[34] Their reasoning lends support to archaeologists' interpretation of material remains that they usually associate with ironworking farmers but appear in foraging sites in the later first millennium CE. These finds include pottery made by East African farmers and oceanic imports. Instead of focusing on foragers' displacement or their status as trading partners, Mijikenda traditions emphasize that Bantu-speaking communities integrated foragers into their communities to benefit from their uganga.

Archaeologists have correlated the increased interactions between foragers and farmers with the growing variability and scale of farmers' settlements in the second half of the first millennium CE.[35] These changes in settlement sizes also correspond to the replacement of Kwale ware with Early Tana Tradition (ETT) ware. ETT ware resembled Kwale ware but had more prominent incised triangle designs and distinctive forms.[36] Those who used Kwale ware invariably built villages less than 3.2 hectares (eight acres) in size. In contrast, those who used ETT ware established settlements that varied in size from tiny hamlets of just a few houses to a large site at Mtsengo that measured eight hectares (twenty acres). In addition, escarpment residents doubled their settlements between 500 and 1000 CE, an increase that is comparable to the growth of settlements closer to the coast. Users of ETT ware established these larger, more numerous, and more varied settlements by stretching into the more arid western edge of the coastal escarpment, the hilltops around Kaloleni, the northern Shimba Hills, the uplands near Kwale, and the coastal plain.[37]

In contrast to ETT ware found elsewhere in the East Africa littoral, the Sabaki speakers' variant in Kenya is distinguished by features it shares with Pastoral Neolithic ware.[38] These similarities are even more pronounced than those found on the earlier Kwale ware, suggesting that Sabaki speakers had strengthened their associations with Southern Cushitic speakers as they moved into new territories and coined new Sabaki languages. As members of these different speech communities exchanged food, raised children together, and married one another, it is not surprising that they also influenced one another's sense of style. The disappearance of Pastoral Neolithic ware from the archaeological record after 700 CE suggests that the two populations had started to coalesce around shared settlements.

LINGUISTIC MIGRATIONS

The settlement history of littoral East Africa that archaeologists reconstruct from material culture cannot effectively distinguish among languages and lifeways once ETT ware became ubiquitous after 600 CE. However, the linguistic research of Derek Nurse, Thomas Hinnebusch, and their collaborators clarifies several intermediary stages in the extension of Sabaki speakers' settlements. Scholars often cite this research as confirmation that Kiswahili is a Bantu African language and the Swahili are an African people. Their contributions are much more extensive. The linguistic sequences they have reconstructed provide a baseline chronology for investigating historical relationships among the speech communities of Sabaki and other language groups. They also corroborate archaeological evidence that supports an increase of collaboration across linguistic boundaries in the latter half of the first millennium CE.

Nurse and Hinnebusch traced the divergence of six speech communities from the Proto-Sabaki speech community in the following order: Pre-Kielwana, Proto-Kiswahili, Pre–Upper Kipokomo,

Proto-Shicomorian, Pre–Lower Kipokomo, and Proto-Chimijikenda. Figure 2.1 illustrates in schematic form this division of Sabaki languages over several hundred years. In the second two stages, the speech communities on the top of the chart expanded in a northerly direction past the Tana River, while the speech communities on the bottom of the chart expanded eastward and along the coast of the Indian Ocean. The final stage indicates a division between Lower Kipokomo to the north and Chimijikenda to the south. As with all tree diagrams, these divisions do not represent abrupt shifts or migrations of people but their gradual separation from one another.

Nurse and Hinnebusch referred to the core speech community as Proto-Sabaki throughout their description of this sequence; I have added the labels Middle Proto-Sabaki and Late Proto-Sabaki to clarify for nonlinguists that Proto-Sabaki speakers, who remained in contact with one another, continued to innovate after other Sabaki speech communities moved away. Indeed, the groups that moved away from this core group were often more conservative than those they left behind. I have also added a Northern Sabaki areal group of languages that came back into contact with one another (or a similar intermediary speech community) after they had separated.

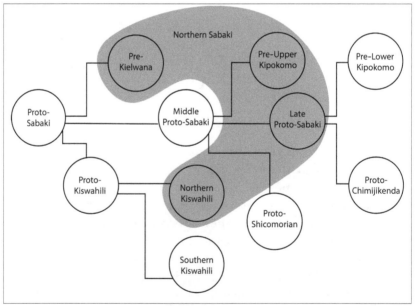

FIGURE 2.1. Proto–Sabaki Bantu divergence.

64   ANCESTORS OF ETHNICITY

Around 500 CE, Proto-Sabaki speakers divided into three speech communities. Pre-Kielwana and Proto-Kiswahili speech communities extended into new environments while the remaining population remained in place as they articulated linguistic innovations that distinguish Middle Proto-Sabaki.³⁹ An arid scrub-brush desert to the west of Kenya's coastal escarpment discouraged expansion in that direction; Proto-Sabaki speakers who moved south likely assimilated with other Proto–NEC Bantu communities. Those who moved north and settled along the plains near the upper reaches of the Tana River became Pre-Kielwana speakers; around the same time, Proto-Kiswahili speakers moved eastward to settle closer to the coast. Pre-Kielwana speakers were conservative because of their relative isolation. For instance, they alone retained seven vowels in their language (*a, e, i, ɪ, o, u, ʊ*), while other Sabaki dialects merged two pairs of vowels (*i* and *ɪ* became *i*; *u* and *ʊ* became *u*). Proto-Kiswahili speakers similarly retained Proto-Sabaki features that others discarded while innovating new grammatical tenses. These changes indicate their relative isolation from Middle Proto-Sabaki speech communities.⁴⁰

After Proto-Kiswahili speakers had established themselves at the coast and learned to travel along the seashore, they expanded to the north and south and developed many more dialects than speakers of any other Sabaki language.⁴¹ Those who expanded northward created dialects of Northern Kiswahili, which closely resemble one another; the more varied dialects of the Southern Kiswahili constitute an areal group that reflects their wider dispersion and contacts with communities speaking Bantu languages other than Sabaki.

Around 700 CE Pre–Upper Kipokomo and Proto-Shicomorian diverged from the core Middle Proto-Sabaki group. Those who remained articulated a few more sound shifts that distinguish Late Proto-Sabaki.⁴² Following in the footsteps of Pre-Kielwana speakers, Pre–Upper Kipokomo speakers settled along the Upper Tana River, but directly on the riverbanks. They began fishing and farming the riverine environment, leaving Pre-Kielwana speakers to cultivate and forage the lands around it.

Meanwhile, Proto-Shicomorian speakers transitioned to life at the coast. As they learned to build boats and harvest the sea, they adopted features otherwise unique to Kiswahili.⁴³ Like Northern Kiswahili dialects, Shicomorian speakers substitute the sounds *s* and *z* in words that speakers of other Sabaki languages pronounce with the sounds *f* and *v*. They also share complicated phonological and grammatical features unique to Southern Kiswahili dialects. So although they first settled alongside speakers of Northern Kiswahili, they must have also spent some time in proximity to communities speaking Southern Kiswahili dialects.[44] Although many of them likely assimilated to Kiswahili speech communities, others retained Middle Proto-Sabaki features in their dialects as they moved farther south along the coast. They established the first towns on the distant Comoros Islands between 840 and 1070 CE.[45]

Sometime in the ninth century CE, Late Proto-Sabaki speakers also extended their reach to the Tana River. There they joined a Northern Sabaki areal group that included the dialects of Kielwana, Upper Kipokomo, and Northern Kiswahili.[46] Although they maintained their respective dialects and may not have been in direct contact with one another, they all borrowed sounds from speakers of Southern Cushitic languages. Specifically, they learned to produce and distinguish dental sounds made with their teeth from sounds made with the alveolar ridge (between the teeth and the hard palate). This sound change is subtle enough that linguists assume it came from Southern Cushitic–speaking parents who raised children with Sabaki speakers. Nurse and Hinnebusch tentatively date the timing of these collaborations between 800 and 1000 CE, but the Northern Sabaki group may also correspond to the fading of Pastoral Neolithic ware from the archaeological record of eastern Kenya around 700 CE. As Southern Cushitic pastoralists settled into towns, they mostly adopted the dialects and material culture of Sabaki speakers but also passed along some of their own pronunciations.

By 1000 CE, Late Proto-Sabaki speakers diverged to form Pre–Lower Kipokomo and Proto–Chimijikenda speech communities. Pre–Lower Kipokomo speakers occupied a string of settlements along the lower Tana River toward the coast. Nurse and Hinnebusch argue that they relexicalized their language: they borrowed from Pre–Upper Kipokomo speakers a large proportion of their vocabulary related to the riverine ecology. However, they retained the linguistic features that distinguished Late Proto-Sabaki speakers. As these two populations of river dwellers formed a new Kipokomo synthesis, Proto-Chimijikenda speakers extended their settlements to the immediate south. They entered previously unoccupied territory in the escarpment and coastal plain, but they probably integrated with communities who spoke other dialects of Proto–NEC Bantu as well.[47] The vestiges of this synthesis, rather than a later divergence, may explain some of the distinctions between Northern and Southern Chimijikenda, as well as a nearly universal acknowledgment in Mijikenda oral traditions that the Digo confederations (in the south) were the first people to settle in the region.

The pottery wares that archaeologists use to distinguish stages in the settlement history of coastal East Africa is not as granular as the linguistic sequence just narrated. However, triangulating both narratives suggests that the isolation of farmers, agropastoralists, and foragers in different territories prior to 500 CE dissolved as they moved into transitional environments that required all their respective uganga to flourish. These crosslinguistic collaborations suggest that language barriers were not very important for their communal identities, nor was shared culture a necessary precondition for collaboration. Instead, the speech communities that participated in the Northern Sabaki areal group integrated Southern Cushitic speakers into a shared littoral society that began to extend its settlements throughout littoral Kenya and beyond.

PLANNING TOWNS, MATERIALIZING CLANS

Proto-Sabaki speakers set the stage for collaborating across linguistic and cultural boundaries with their most important and distinguishing innovation: towns. They did not simply build towns as larger villages; they organized spaces that encouraged people who followed different lifeways to live alongside one another. Archaeologists distinguish towns from villages in the region by their larger size and organization into multiple components (i.e., neighborhoods).[48] This arrangement reflected innovations in how Proto-Sabaki speakers reimagined schemas for people and spaces. They still claimed their children as members of *liàngò (lineages) and *nyùmbá (maternal relatives), and they assembled these lineages in *lukólò (marriage alliances). However, when marriage alliances began clustering in the same settlement, they also needed to manage relationships with co-residents who were neither kith nor kin, but who were not quite strangers either. As members of different marriage alliances settled together, they recharacterized those who participated in the same marriage alliances as members of the same clan; endogamy excluded residents of the same town from intimate family affairs.

As previewed at the beginning of this chapter, scholars should distinguish Sabaki speakers' understanding of clanship from kinship because they limited proprietary knowledge, or uganga, to members of their respective clans. Though marriage alliances enabled lineages to pass the expertise of a spouse to their shared children, clustering members from different clans into the same town made the knowledge of entire communities—or rather, the products of their knowledge—available to all co-residents. A town of clans could shape and harvest the surrounding lands, rivers, forests, and ocean more effectively than a village with a single lineage or marriage alliance. In addition, if crops faltered, fishing failed, or livestock succumbed to disease, people could seek help from clans who gathered or produced other resources, without physically relocating. These collaborations enabled them to settle in transitional ecologies—like the littoral zones near the coast.

The ecological mosaic of littoral East Africa that motivated collaborations across linguistic boundaries presented similar environmental pressures as did the Inland Niger Delta of Mali. Archaeologists Susan Keech McIntosh and Roderick McIntosh suggested that heterarchical collaborations were the key to developing and sustaining urbanization at Jenne-jeno in Mali.[49] Instead of supporting specialized craft and knowledge production by making an abundance of a few grains controlled by centralized governments (as in Egypt and Mesopotamia), the communities of Jenne-jeno created large urban clusters and organized exchanges among castes that produced different kinds of food. Thomas Govi's insightful connection between clans and knowledge points to clans as the most likely corollary in East Africa to the castes of West Africa.

In order to accommodate communities with different uganga, Proto-Sabaki speakers reorganized their settlements so that clans could claim spaces of their own. Four Proto-Sabaki words reconstructed by Nurse and Hinnebusch illustrate how these speakers elaborated this spatial schema before diverging.[50] First, they shifted the meaning of *muji from "village" to "town." Second, they coined a diminutive form of **muji*—**kijiji*—to distinguish the villages that they continued to organize in more marginal or newly settled areas. Third, they extended the meaning of **mutala* (an alternative word for "village") to designate a neighborhood or cluster of homes. The meaning of a fourth word, **luwanja*, has a range of meanings in modern Sabaki languages—"workshop," "yard," "clan space," and so forth—that indicate Proto-Sabaki speakers reserved open spaces for various communal activities.[51] They materialized each of these features—the distinction between towns and villages, neighborhood clusters, and open spaces—in the settlements they built after 500 CE.

Shanga Town

The most complete reconstruction of a transition from village to town life among Sabaki speech communities comes from Shanga in the Lamu Archipelago. Archaeologist Mark Horton's excavation there revealed a sequence in which a small village became a cluster of neighborhoods around a town square and then a large coral-built "stone town" over the course of six centuries. Shanga's centuries-long development illustrates how the spaces of the town accommodated diverse subsistence strategies and motivated residents to develop new craft specialties, trading activities, and spiritual practices. The relationship between the town's mosques and other communal structures also suggests that Shanga's residents conceived of Islam as just one of several uganga until the eleventh century CE, when they began to prioritize mosques at the expense of other religious structures. In addition to demonstrating the foundations of urbanization in littoral East Africa, Horton's excavations at Shanga detail how its residents incrementally centered all their clans around Islam to form a shared Muslim identity.[52]

The evident care with which the founders of Shanga organized their initial settlement suggests they followed a well-established schema. This schema provided open spaces and closed structures for people to congregate as lineages and clans but also as a town community. Around 760 CE settlers established Shanga around 500 feet (150 meters) from the seashore near a clump of trees by digging a well—a relatively new technology that enabled them to settle closer to the sea. They burned the vegetation around the site and dusted the ground with white sand from the surrounding dunes. Then they marked the boundaries of the village with a light wooden fence to create a rectangular enclosure of 2 acres (0.8 hectares), centered on the well. They erected houses with wooden posts, keeping them clear of the area around the central well and trees. They also buried a hoard of cowrie shells under the eastern entrance to the enclosure, perhaps to serve as a protective ward. For food they ate chicken, shellfish, and sea turtles—but few fish or domesticated livestock. They also baked bread in ceramic ovens. From the beginning of the settlement, they worked iron, ground shells into small disk-shaped beads, and acquired small amounts of glass and pottery that sailors imported from the Persian Gulf.

Between 780 and 850 CE, the next few generations of residents expanded their village into a town by removing their homes from the enclosure and building new ones outside. Within the enclosure, they built at least one hall and two mosques in succession—the hall aligned along cardinal directions, while the mosques oriented toward Mecca. A series of gates through which people passed to access the hall suggests they wished to limit casual access to its interior. They surrounded the 36 m^2 (387 ft^2) square building with a 100 m^2 (1,076 ft^2) fence to create a large yard with an access gate on the north side. Copper knives found near the hall would have been poor instruments for daily use, but their intrinsic value (and natural antimicrobial properties) would have made them suitable for circumcision, drawing blood for oaths, and other ceremonies. By analogy to the *makaya* (fortified towns) of Chimijikenda speakers in the nineteenth century, Horton suggested the hall could have been either a "clan house" or a structure similar to a *moro* (council house), in which leaders kept war trophies and other talismans.[53] In any case, the hall materialized a spiritual association among at least a portion of the town's residents.

The two mosques' locations suggest that residents increased their appreciation for Islam over just a few generations. They located the first, smaller mosque near the western gate, at the very edge of the enclosure. They built the second, larger mosque just a few meters east of the well at the center of town. The small mosque would have held fewer than a dozen worshippers and was eventually abandoned; but even the larger mosque in the center of the town held only a minority of the community—maybe twenty-five people.

However, the residents gave the second mosque a prominent place in the town by felling and burning a prominent tree by the well. This action suggests that many residents in Shanga had begun to value Islam, whether they attended daily prayers or not. In the two burials that Horton encountered from this period, the surviving kin arranged the bodies of the deceased to face Mecca.[54] These burials were the first evidence that some of Shanga's residents, rather than visitors, practiced Islam.

Scholars often suggest that Africans adopted Islamic practices to engender trust with traveling Muslim merchants. However, residents at Shanga may have also sought instruction in Islamic techniques for healing maladies, praying for rain, and guarding against malevolent spirits. Just as clans relied on one another to provide a wide variety of food and resources from the surrounding land—and seascapes—they valued multiple forms of spiritual power, including Islamic ones.

Together, the hall and the large mosque materialized the social foundations of the town community: there were at least two (possibly overlapping) groups who shared the town but accessed spiritual power in different ways. From the perspective of those who spoke Proto-Kiswahili and other Sabaki languages, these structures were not only houses of worship but also dedicated spaces for teaching and practicing different kinds of uganga. Unlike the subsistence strategies that belonged exclusively to individual clans, these spaces could have promoted unity among all the town's clans. Just as marriage alliances integrated lineages as members of a single clan, these sacred spaces could have incorporated all the town's constituent clans into a co-residential community.

Like the speakers of Sabaki languages who elaborated Southern Cushitic grain-processing techniques with inherited Bantu vocabulary, Proto-Kiswahili speakers like those at Shanga would have articulated their understanding of Islamic practices through familiar concepts. The testimony of Muslim writers who visited the coast in the late first millennium CE shows that it may have been relatively simple for Sabaki speakers to extend their notions of uganga to include Islam. Bantu speakers had long ago developed the notion of a Creator God.[55] In addition, Muslim writers described many of the activities they observed in East Africa as religious. In the tenth century Abū Zayd al-Sīrāfī reported that men "who devote themselves to a life of piety [preach] to them, calling on them to keep God in their minds . . . and describing to them the fate of their people who have died."[56] Abū al-Ḥasan al-Masʿudi (896–956) wrote around the same time that East African communities "have an elegant language and men who preach [obedience to God] in it."[57] Abu Abdullah al-Idrisi (1100–1165) reported that non-Muslim East Africans called these people *maganga* as late as the twelfth century.[58] This last word means a big or important *mganga* (healer), emphasizing that in the minds of Muslim observers, uganga was a religious practice comparable to Islam. The Proto-Kiswahili speakers at Shanga may have made the obverse conclusion that Islam was a kind of uganga, or perhaps many kinds of uganga.

This view of Islam as a collection of spiritual techniques rather than a single abstract religion is precisely how Buzurg ibn Shahriyar described a tale about the conversion of an East African community to Islam in the tenth century. Allegedly told in the voice of an East African ruler whom Arab traders enslaved, the tale characterizes conversion to Islam as a gradual unfolding of ritual knowledge. After Arab merchants kidnapped the ruler in East Africa, they sold him to a slaveholder in Oman, who took him to Basrah. There the ruler learned to pray and fast as well as read parts of the Qur'an. After being sold to a man in Baghdad, he "completed [his] knowledge of the Qur'an and prayed with the men in the mosque." Later the enslaved ruler absconded with a caravan headed for Mecca, and the pilgrims taught him how to perform the ceremonies of hajj (pilgrimage). After completing his pilgrimage, the ruler followed the banks of the Nile to return home, resumed his place as king, and taught his people the "precepts of Islam," which he summarized as "true faith, prayers, fasting, the pilgrimage, and what is permitted and what is forbidden."[59]

Though this apocryphal tale does not represent the authentic voice of any specific ruler in East Africa, it demonstrates that the tenth-century Arabs who told the story regarded Islam as a repertoire of spiritual techniques, just as Mijikenda orators describe uganga in their oral traditions. Scholars sometimes attempt to identify when various sects of Islam arrived in different parts of Africa; examining Islam from the perspective of uganga emphasizes instead the specific

Islamic practices that Africans integrated into their schemas. As particular clans in Shanga learned these techniques—to pray, to recite the Qur'an, to perform pilgrimage—they also gained better access than other East Africans to the trade goods that Muslim merchants circulated around the Indian Ocean. Closer relationships with traders may have encouraged more people to seek proprietary Islamic knowledge for their clans, though no clan could possibly monopolize all Islamic knowledge.[60]

Shanga's residents did not need to worship in a mosque to benefit from Muslim traders. From 850 to 920 CE, they dedicated more space in the central enclosure for kiosks in which they made or displayed crafts for trade.[61] They stopped grinding shells into beads, but they intensified their working of iron. Arab geographers even began describing iron implements as a major export from the region.[62] Residents also reminted coins from imported silver to facilitate exchanges.

The growing prosperity of the town attracted people with more varied lifeways. All Shanga residents in the late ninth century raised more small livestock and ate more fish, but residents in one of the town's neighborhoods also began eating beef. Southern Cushitic speakers, or perhaps Bantu speakers who had learned from them to raise cattle, had joined the town.

Residents celebrated their prosperity by investing in improvements to the structures in the central enclosure. They rebuilt both the large mosque and the hall with large wooden timbers. They kept the large mosque about the same size, but they added a long gallery to its northeast side. They enlarged the hall to around 100 m² (1,000 ft²), divided it into seven rooms, and placed a cut-coral basin by its western door— one of the first examples of coral carving in East Africa. Carvers cut out sections of living *porites* coral underwater in nearby reefs, transported them to shore, and then shaped them before they could harden. This new technique subsequently became common in religious architecture along the coast, again indicating the spiritual character of the hall. Increased trade and a more diverse subsistence base around the turn of the tenth century supported experiments in such time-consuming, labor-demanding, and ingenious crafts.

The cutters and shapers of coral must have honed their craft within a few generations, because from 920 to 1000 CE they rebuilt the entire town center with the material. They replaced the wooden fence of the enclosure with a coral wall, rebuilt the hall and central mosque in coral, and added three more coral halls. They used floor plans similar to the first hall and placed the new halls at the center of each enclosure wall near a gate. In the west of the enclosure, they added a small two-room structure with benches outside. Horton called this structure the "priest's house" because of its proximity to the original hall.[63] Residents also added walls within the enclosure to restrict access and separate the halls from the kiosks.[64] To cleanse the town (physically and perhaps spiritually), they spread white beach sand inside the enclosure and its buildings. Shanga's residents also erected seven clusters of coral tombs in a cemetery to the northeast of town. Horton correlated these clusters with seven neighborhoods in the town, taking a cue from modern Swahili communities who associate cemeteries with the clans of particular *mitaa* (neighborhoods).[65]

Before 1000 CE, Shanga's residents seemed to place Islam on an equal footing with other esoteric uganga by providing dedicated spaces to each of them within the town center—but their attitudes changed in the eleventh century. As more clans gained access to Islamic techniques, they invested less effort in organizations dedicated to other kinds of uganga. In the first half of the century they rebuilt the mosque in coral but stopped maintaining the four halls and the "priest's house." Debris gathered in and around the halls, and they stopped spreading fresh sand to surface the courtyards and paths. The roof of the priest's house collapsed, but no one repaired it. By the middle of the century residents began systematically dismantling the halls, and they used the reclaimed coral to rebuild their own timber homes in coral. They also burned the coral debris to make lime for a binding agent and for whitewash. After the thatch roof of the mosque caught fire, residents repaired and enlarged the structure to accommodate over a hundred worshippers. By the end of the century, residents had dismantled the wall around the enclosure. The mosque, rather than the enclosure, became the new center of the town.

However, Shanga's increasing commitment to Islam did not diminish their hospitality toward new, presumably non-Muslim, communities who joined their town. Newcomers in the eleventh century included camel pastoralists who left behind camel bones and used a "wavy-line pottery" similar to what pastoralists in southern Sudan made at the time.

From 1100 to 1250 CE, Shanga also attracted new residents through its focus on craft production and fishing. In addition to expanding the town outward, residents crowded close around the mosque, building workshops for tanning leather and weaving textiles, at least one large corral for cattle, and private homes. They also acquired more imports than in the past and varied their diet by eating more varieties of fish, including shark and barracuda caught in deeper, offshore waters. For the first time Shanga's residents built a mihrab—a semicircular alcove that marked the direction toward Mecca and amplified the voice of the prayer leader to those standing behind him. Horton suggested this feature signaled a transition to the Sunni-Shafii sect from the Kharaji-Ibadi sect of Islam.[66] Though there is no evidence of the political contexts attending this sectarian transition, the physical construction of the mihrab may have been the culmination of a movement that had led residents to neglect and then dismantle the non-Muslim halls in the preceding century. The Muslim reformers who brought a new Sunni-Shafii orthodoxy may have been less tolerant of maganga and their "halls" than the earliest Muslims, who would have depended on the good will of these ritual specialists to build their first mosques and attract followers. If Shanga's residents had previously regarded Islam as one of several uganga connected to part of the community, it now took precedence as the singular focus of the entire town.

After 1250, Shanga's residents stopped making iron or weaving textiles themselves, but they began to acquire more imports from the Indian Ocean, including from China. As more ships passed Shanga on their way to gold supplies at Kilwa in southern Tanzania, the residents focused less on craft production and more on brokering exchanges between Indian Ocean merchants and inland allies who could provide ivory, gum resins, and other salable local resources, including enslaved people.[67]

While residents in the north of the town continued productive activities such as pastoralism and fishing, many of those in the southern neighborhoods close to the shore redesigned their homes to accommodate traveling merchants and engage in trade. They added reception rooms at the front of their homes, off which they placed single bedrooms and lavatories. This arrangement provided a place for their guests to stay and preserved the intimacy and security of their homes' interior spaces, in which they built specialized storage compartments, wall pegs, and nooks to store and display material wealth.

Though not as extravagant as the multistory homes in later "stone towns," these single-story homes could be expansive, housing multiple generations of a single lineage in adjoining houses. The family who lived in Shanga's Structure 60, in the northeast part of town, started with a simple two-room house with a walled yard. Over several generations, they roofed the yard, added three rooms (two to the front, another to the rear), two lavatories (front and back), and a storage area in the heart of the home. The home shared a wall, but no evident doors, with Structure 58 to the north. They must have had a closer relationship with the residents in Structures 61 and 62, with whom they shared an open courtyard.[68]

Similar house complexes demonstrate that Shanga's residents not only divided their town into neighborhoods, or *mitala (sg. *mutala), for clans but also divided each *mutala into spaces for lineages. They used doorways (*liàngò) that granted access to intimate family spaces to materialize their lineage (also called *liàngò). In addition, bread ovens located at different parts of a single structure indicated separate cooking areas within the larger household, possibly for groupings of either maternal kin (*nyùmbá) who shared meals with one another or siblings (*ılumbu) who gathered with their respective mothers in polygynous households. The shared courtyards and additions to these homes materialized family histories of lineages that grew with each new generation. Instead of founding a new village, they just built a few new walls. While the transformation of Shanga's religious buildings shows a deeper identification with Islam over time, the architecture of domestic spaces illustrates both the materialization of the kinship schema residents inherited from their ancestors as well as the novel clans they innovated to form more complex "town" communities.

Sabaki Legacies

As scholars worked to overturn earlier presumptions that Persian or Arab foreigners built the cities and complex trade networks of coastal East Africa, they often focused on the shared experiences of

Kiswahili-speaking communities. For example, since Shanga's excavation in 1994, scholars have considered the town as representative of early Swahili society. Urban, Islamic, and mercantile, the eighth-century village turned tenth-century town and thirteenth-century trading center demonstrates that Swahili society was an indigenous African achievement rather than a colonial transplant from Arabia.

Yet Shanga was not only a Swahili town but also a Sabaki one. Widening the scope from Kiswahili communities to a cis-oceanic perspective that includes speakers of all Sabaki languages shows they acquired new forms of knowledge through a shared schema that associated clan identities with specific uganga. Though not definitive on this point, archaeological surveys indicate that Sabaki speakers began to associate uganga with clanship around the same time they started organizing towns: towns started to appear only after speakers of Sabaki languages began to live in more varied environments. In addition, the variation of foods in each neighborhood suggests residents followed distinct diets.

Speakers of every Sabaki language except Elwana founded towns everywhere they went—along the Tana River, the coastal escarpment, and the distant Comoros Islands. The closest corollaries to Shanga's physical layout are not the quintessential Swahili towns of the coast but the Mijikenda makaya (fortified towns), whose residents marked off clan spaces and central enclosures that resemble the organization of Shanga's earliest phases. The makaya seem to have uniquely retained spatial strategies inherited from early Proto-Sabaki speakers.

Unfortunately, only Kiswahili and Shicomorian speakers built in coral. Since the speakers of most Sabaki languages built their settlements with perishable materials, it may be impossible to reconstruct their development over time or to even determine the extent to which their layouts resembled Shanga's. However, archaeologist Richard Helm's survey of Kenya's coastal escarpment has at least confirmed that the range in settlement sizes and the expansion of settlements into more varied ecologies kept pace with trends at the coast.[69]

In these towns, speakers of Sabaki languages exchanged people, commodities, products, and services; produced tools and instruments; deliberated in public and private; and celebrated and worshipped together. These shared spaces helped speakers of Sabaki

Bantu and Southern Cushitic languages create the innovative fusion of speech, lifeways, pottery, and collective knowledge that supported the Sabaki expansion and the formation of Kenya's littoral society. They needed a lot of uganga to make a peaceful home.

As the population of littoral Africa increased, speakers of Sabaki languages and their collaborators did not just build larger villages; they reorganized their settlements as towns that could accommodate multiple marriage alliances. Nor did they assemble all the town's lineages into one large marriage alliance. Instead, they reconceptualized marriage alliances as components of a larger society—as knowledge-bearing clans.

This incremental cognitive shift illustrates that they constructed the interior dimensions of their collective identities by creating a series of boundaries nested within each other. The boundaries of endogamy that defined the outer limits of a marriage alliance became internal boundaries of towns that separated clans from one another. Speakers of Sabaki languages still use metaphors of blood descent to describe the bond shared by clan members because clans continue to be a collection of lineages, but they also define them according to the spaces they claim and the knowledge they guard.

The evident population growth and social organization that motivated the expansion of Proto-Sabaki speakers and their descendants throughout littoral East Africa reflects the success of organizing knowledge through clans. Reinterpreting the settlement history of littoral Kenya as a quest by clans for knowledge clarifies precisely how they relied on the foragers and agropastoralists who preceded them, why they extended their territorial reach more than other NEC Bantu speakers, and how they integrated new religious practices, including Islam, into their communities. Although the wider range of food production techniques probably helped Proto-Sabaki speakers increase their population through natural reproduction, they also expanded their speech communities by encouraging speakers of other languages to contribute to a shared, newly littoral, society.

Although residents in East Africa traded with visitors to their shore since the first century CE, they did not establish their first towns in places conducive to trade, as is often assumed. Rather, they located the first coastal settlements in areas suitable for producing food and other resources.[70] In order to live in these transitional ecologies, they first worked out ways to collaborate among (at least) three distinct populations, which followed different lifeways. They also developed their cosmopolitan ethic— a distinguishing characteristic of littoral societies—before they increased their engagement with Indian Ocean traders. Examining these various African populations from a cis-oceanic perspective suggests that it was local rivalries that motivated them to forge a littoral society that linked land and sea, at least as much as their efforts to engage in commerce with seaborne foreigners.

THREE

Dancing with Swords

Domesticating Commerce through Clan Confederations in the Western Indian Ocean, ca. 1000–1700 CE

> A *kaya* is ... the capital town of all the clans.
> —Johnstone Muramba

THE BRIGHT CLANG of swords rang through the square beside Lamu's Riyadha Mosque. Dressed in white ankle-length *kanzu* (tunics), *kofia* (embroidered caps), and rubber sandals, two men wielded heirloom swords in a mock duel. The younger of the two bounded across the square toward the elder, timing his strides to the beat of the drums; but they paused before striking blades to hold spectators in suspense. The younger man then retreated to the edge of the roped-off square for another round. About a dozen men and boys wearing the same attire faced them, witnessing the fight as they stood shoulder to shoulder in a line. They sang and swayed long *fimbo* (walking sticks) to the directions of their chorus leader in the dignified *goma* dance.[1] Two other troupes performed the dance in their own roped-off areas as they competed for attention from tourists and pilgrims at the annual Maulidi ya Nabi festival that celebrates the birth of the Prophet Muhammad.

Dancing with metal swords is uncommon in littoral East Africa, but swordplay with sticks has long been a pastime among Kiswahili speakers.[2] John Ludwig Krapf, the first Christian missionary to reside in Kenya's coastal escarpment, observed a similar practice among Chimijikenda speakers at Rabai in the nineteenth century. He recorded that the young men "displayed their *heshima* [respect, honor] by shouting, dancing, brandishing their swords and bows, and all the show of joy, which they manifest on extraordinary occasions."[3] Krapf associated these displays of mock violence with trade. Whenever inland communities welcomed a stranger, they performed "a great *heshima*, i.e. with show and shouting, with giving him a present and receiving another in return. . . . All the great merchants of Mombas[a] always resigned themselves to this custom."[4]

Coastal communities also practiced this custom on the southern end of littoral East Africa in 1497, when the sultan of Mozambique Island tried in vain to convince Vasco da Gama that it was a harmless war dance rather than a challenge to battle.[5] Their bravado demonstrated their ability, and their right, to deal lethally with

FIGURE 3.1. Goma Dance, Lamu. Photograph by author.

Dancing with Swords   81

whoever might approach their territory, but withholding actual violence signaled their willingness to trade with those who accepted their autonomy.

The sword dances that Swahili communities inherited from their ancestors evoke conflicts that accompanied commercial exchange even before the close of the fifteenth century, when Europeans rounded the Cape of Good Hope. For at least as long, men who aspired to elite standing in the Islamic, commercial, and urban communities of littoral Kenya donned long tunics similar to *kanzu*. Wearing fine cloth exhibited a portion of a person's wealth, making elite status materially visible. Wielding swords protected that wealth from rivals.

This chapter considers the consequences of commerce and violence on the schemas of littoral Kenya between the tenth century CE, when speakers of Sabaki languages intensified their participation in overseas trade, and the early seventeenth century CE, when the shocking raids of Oromo-speaking pastoralists inspired new narratives for organizing Kenya's littoral communities. Scholars have celebrated these centuries as the height of Swahili civilization because of the many "stone towns" built during the period.[6] Yet, the remains of these towns also reveal the tensions of wealth inequality. Elaborate mosques and multistoried coral houses decorated with imported pottery sharply contrast with the earthen homes in which most people lived; and the amount of imports excavated from inland settlements pales in comparison to the tremendous wealth of those at the coast. The ruins of defensive walls hint at the violence that these visible inequities inspired. Though oral traditions recount this violence in vivid detail, the oral traditions of Mijikenda communities also explain how speakers of Sabaki languages formed heterarchical organizations like clan confederations, title societies, and age-sets to seek political consensus; that is, they formed organizations that diffused power across many people rather than arranging hierarchical institutions that centralized authority in individual rulers.

Oral traditions collected in the twentieth century cannot compensate for the scarcity of direct observations by writers in the first half of the second millennium CE. However, they suggest possibilities about how these heterarchical organizations may have functioned among speakers of Sabaki languages. They assembled their clans into confederations composed of many settlements to organize defense and support commercial endeavors. They maintained the internal integrity of their clan confederations through title societies, whose members shared their wealth to defuse tensions over visible inequities in status. They also formed age-sets that defined the boundaries of their confederations and military alliances. Together, title societies and age-sets inspired fraternal bonds that cut across clan boundaries and redirected the martial energies of the rising generation toward the defense of their respective clan confederations. These organizations did not prevent violence, but they made it more predictable. Archaeological and linguistic evidence surveyed in this chapter suggests that speakers of Sabaki languages formed the kinds of organizations presented in oral traditions before the arrival of Portuguese visitors, and these data directly confirm the feasting practices now associated with title societies, perhaps as early as 1000 CE.

Speakers of Sabaki languages reimagined some of their clan confederations as tribes in the twentieth century before assembling them into larger tribal conglomerates bounded by language and religion; but they first developed them to manage the inequities and violence that accompanied their participation in Indian Ocean commerce. Since these conflicts pitted clan confederations of relatively equal strength against one another, speakers of Sabaki languages and their neighbors did not coalesce into larger political alliances. However, they began to conceptualize one another as members of a single littoral society after incoming raiders, who spoke non-Bantu Oromo languages, exceeded the bounds of expected violence.

REAPPRAISING THE FLIGHT FROM SHUNGWAYA

Applying the insights of Mijikenda oral traditions to the first half of the second millennium CE requires a reappraisal of the flight from Shungwaya with which these traditions usually begin. The Mijikenda orators who narrated their traditions to Thomas Spear in the 1970s presented a relatively consistent accounting of their shared history: they depicted the flight from Shungwaya as a story of retreat from an unrelenting enemy in their Shungwaya homeland who chased them south into Kenya's escarpment.[7] In this telling, the people separated as they fled, eventually settling in nine different *makaya* (hilltop forts, sg. *kaya*)—one for each of the nine clan confederations that constitute the modern Mijikenda ethnic group. Orators from different clan confederations recited nearly identical lists of named age-sets, with which Spear estimated the date of their southward migration to the late sixteenth century.[8] They also described complicated political strategies for seeking consensus, which Spear called the "kaya complex." The Shungwaya myth gives the impression that the kaya complex (and the Mijikenda ethnic group) came fully formed from Shungwaya.

Several historians have reappraised the Shungwaya tale as a mythic charter, more attuned to the complexities of identity politics in the twentieth century than the contexts of the sixteenth century.[9] Yet archaeologist Richard Helm's research suggests that at least some elements of the myth developed along Kenya's coastal escarpment centuries before the supposed flight from Shungwaya. As detailed in the previous chapter, he demonstrated that Proto-Sabaki speakers and their Chimijikenda-speaking descendants extended their settlements throughout the escarpment nearly a thousand years earlier than the date that Spear had reconstructed through age-set lists. Helm also confirmed that the oral traditions of his informants correctly (and independently) sequenced settlements into pre-kaya, kaya, and post-kaya periods of time.[10] Chimijikenda speakers passed down knowledge about their settlement history in spatial mnemonics and oral traditions for much longer than five hundred years.[11]

Crucially, Helm's survey dated the transition from dense settlement in makaya to more dispersed "rural" living in post-kaya settlements to around 1650. In other words, Chimijikenda speakers abandoned their makaya around the time Spear suggested they were founded. So although the episode of flight can be accurately dated through Portuguese sources, much of the historiological reasoning that Mijikenda orators presented to Spear and others about establishing and living in makaya may refer to earlier periods of time. This reordering of episodes and elements is an expected feature of oral traditions.[12] Instead of focusing on when the story of Shungwaya emerged as a coherent, integrated myth, this chapter considers how, why, and when speakers of Sabaki languages organized the confederations, title societies, and age-sets that populate the myth. In addition to extending the establishment of these heterarchical organizations further back in time, reappraising the Shungwaya myth shows that the strategies Spear associated with the kaya complex were not distinctive to Chimijikenda-speaking communities but shared more widely among speakers of other Sabaki languages in littoral Kenya.

CLAN CONFEDERATIONS:
SABAKI STRATEGIES FOR COMMERCIAL COLLABORATION

By 1250 CE speakers of Sabaki languages had positioned themselves in nearly every ecological niche of littoral Kenya and expanded their efforts to collect commodities that Indian Ocean merchants wanted to buy: ivory, ambergris, mangrove poles, gum copal, iron, rock crystals, cured fish, leather, and so on. In return for these commodities, they received imported products that symbolized prestige: glazed Chinese and Iranian pottery, worked bronze metal, glass beads, and especially cotton textiles from India.[13] They also began grouping their towns and villages into larger, geographically extensive communities bound not only by blood, knowledge, and proximity but also by commercial collaboration and political expediency.

Scholars refer to these larger communities as clan confederations, federations, alliances, or city-states, but Sabaki languages have their own words for them, like *kyeti* (in Kipokomo) and *ntsi* (in Shicomorian). Chimijikenda and Kiswahili speakers expanded the meaning of their respective words for "town" (*kaya* and *muji*) to include all the towns and settlements affiliated with a clan confederation. As Johnston Muramba explained to Thomas Spear, "A *kaya* is a town. People think it means forest, but it is the *capital town of all the clans*. In the kaya were all the leaders who organized people both inside and outside the kaya. All matters of the country were dealt with in the *kaya*."[14] However, since *capital* usually indicates a city that is the formal bureaucratic center of a territorial state, I refer to the principal settlement of each clan confederation as its "anchor town." This term recognizes the role of the principal coastal towns in harboring the ships of Indian Ocean traders, but it also emphasizes that inland speakers of Sabaki languages, as well as those at the coast, regarded their towns as ritual centers that anchored the collaborations of clans, trade partners, and other followers from surrounding communities.

Archaeologically, the clan confederations of the past appear as conurbations—groups of settlements distributed to access various resources within a few days' walk.[15] In the Lamu Archipelago, Horton and Middleton distinguished five conurbations that linked farming areas to the anchor towns of Kau, Lamu, Pate, Faza, and Omwe. Malindi and Mombasa extended their respective conurbations to encompass those of Kilifi and Mtwapa, respectively, before overlapping and inspiring a centuries-long rivalry. Meanwhile Vumba, Vanga, and Wassin contended for primacy within a single conurbation near the Umba River (see map 3.1). Along the escarpment the conurbations of Chimijikenda speakers ranged in number from at least the two documented by Portuguese writers in the sixteenth century to as many as twelve in the nineteenth century.[16] Sabaki speakers formed additional conurbations along Tanzania's Mrima coast between Bagamoyo and Kilwa, the Tana River, the Comoros Islands, the offshore islands of Zanzibar and Mafia, and countless inland areas that await archaeological surveys.[17]

In littoral Kenya these conurbations included three tiers of settlements: villages, country towns, and anchor towns.[18] Villages rarely had any coral structures, though they may have been important sites of craft production.[19] Country towns were larger than villages but too small to anchor an autonomous confederation. They contained only one or two coral houses or a single coral tomb.[20] Although inland anchor towns never reached the same scale as the largest anchor towns at the coast, they coordinated the collection and redistribution of trade goods in similar ways and were visibly larger than other inland settlements. This three-tiered settlement pattern distinguished the communities that spoke Sabaki languages in the early second millennium CE from the more uniform villages of their Proto-Sabaki-speakingancestors.[21]

Jeffrey Fleisher's analysis of settlements on Pemba Island illustrates how the influence of clan confederations varied over time. Brokers in northern Pemba established five country towns and several coral mosques between the twelfth and sixteenth centuries, probably from their profits in selling rice, which Kiswahili speakers began to prefer over millet after the eleventh century.[22] With favorable winds, sailors could bring supplies of rice to buyers at Mombasa in the morning and return to Pemba in the evening.[23] As the volume of trade goods to East Africa increased in the middle of the sixteenth century, the commercial alchemy of transforming food into cloth and porcelain slipped out of the hands of Pemba's local middlemen, and residents started to abandon the country towns. Brokers on Pemba lacked ivory and other goods that attracted overseas merchants directly to their shores, and Mombasa was close enough for rice suppliers to bypass Pemba's brokers. Fleischer suggested that the ostentatious display of twenty-two imported bowls

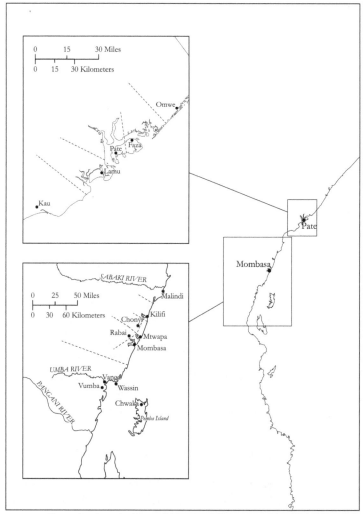

MAP 3.1. Conurbations in littoral Kenya. Map created by ThinkSpatial.

Dancing with Swords

in a mosque at the country town of Chwaka in Pemba was a belated effort by local brokers to cling to their roles as patrons.[24] Like other country towns along the coast, Pemba Island lost its urban zones as people scattered to rural villages by the sixteenth century.[25]

Modern language maps offer a rough proxy for the most successful conurbations in littoral Kenya.[26] Chimijikenda speakers developed as many as eight dialects after 1000 CE, and Kiswahili speakers articulated over a dozen. Rabai has endured as a clan confederation in some form since at least the sixteenth century, when Portuguese visitors first recorded its name as Arabaja; but it first became a conurbation of settlements on and near Benyegundo Hill around 1000 CE. Residents then distinguished their Chirabai dialect as they communicated more frequently with one another than Chimijikenda speakers in other locales.[27]

Some dialects emerged because of the physical distance between their speech communities. Yet the language features that speakers of Sabaki languages share belie colonial-era assumptions that clan confederations were isolated tribes. For example, Southern Chimijikenda speakers replaced their inherited vocabulary with many words from the Kimvita dialect of Kiswahili spoken in Mombasa.[28] In turn, Southern Chimijikenda speakers influenced the pronunciation of certain sounds in the Vumba and Chifundi dialects of Kiswahili south of Mombasa.[29] Speakers of Kimvita who lived on Mombasa Island did not adopt this inland pronunciation. Instead, their direct involvement in oceangoing commerce motivated them to emulate the accents of communities in the Lamu Archipelago.[30] The sustained contact among these speech communities indicate that lineages, clans, and individuals regularly moved among clan confederations to pursue wealth and status. The next three sections draw on the traditional names and rulers of Mombasa Island to illustrate how speakers of Sabaki languages used heterarchical organizations to manage their sometimes-violent commercial competitions.

DOMESTICATING COMMERCE: MERCHANTS AND HOUSE POWER

Mombasa's poets remember the name of the island's earliest town as Kongowea, a name that could allude to several meanings in modern Kiswahili dialects. Frederick Johnson, in his 1939 English-Swahili dictionary, defined *kongowea* as a verb meaning "greet, salute, accost, but with excessive humility or show"—a reference, perhaps, to the *heshima* greeting ceremonies described at the beginning of this chapter.[31] After explaining that *konga* meant "to welcome" in his Kimvita dialect, one educator in Mombasa proposed that *konga* had become part of a folk etymology for Kongowea.[32] If so, poets may have coined the town's name to lend Mombasa this meaning of "welcome/greeting" as well as all the other meanings of the root word *konga:* "grow old," "quench thirst," and "assemble things or people."[33] The weeks of sailing between Mogadishu in the north and the gold of Kilwa to the south made Mombasa's protected harbors a welcome sight to sailors.[34] There, travel-worn traders quenched their thirst and rested in the comfort of homes designed for hosting. In 1331 the famed traveler Ibn Battuta (1304–1369) described refreshing meals of rice, bananas, chicken, fish, mangos, and citrus in Mombasa. Unlike littoral communities elsewhere in the Indian Ocean, those in East Africa rarely built markets.[35] Instead, local brokers domesticated commerce by assembling the people and things that lent them status and authority in their homes.

Hans Meyr's description of Mombasa offers a glimpse of what residents had managed to assemble on the island by 1505: "The houses are . . . three storied and all are plastered with lime. The streets are very narrow, so that two people cannot walk abreast in them. . . . The town has more than 600 houses which are thatched with palm leaves."[36] Meyr observed that Portuguese soldiers pillaged silk, gold-embroidered clothes, rugs, rice, honey, butter, grain, "countless camels," cattle, and two elephants. He estimated the population to be ten thousand, including thirty-seven hundred men.[37]

Brokers competed for the attention of visiting Muslim merchants by demonstrating their superior hospitality.[38] This competition encouraged Kiswahili-speaking communities to make coral architecture more suitable for family homes, in which they could feed and house their guests.[39] Instead of cutting out porites coral underwater and carving it into large blocks for public buildings, they mined coral rag from surface deposits and burned it to make a lime mortar that could bind rubble. Besides lasting longer than earthen homes, coral foundations and walls could better support multiple stories in towns in which clans had claimed all the space within the town walls. Shanga solved the problem by tearing down its wall and building another one farther out from the town center; but as Mombasa and Kilwa adopted coral architecture in the following centuries, they expanded their homes upward. The immense resources and backbreaking labor required for building multistoried coral houses meant they were out of reach for the majority of the towns' residents, who continued residing in earthen homes.[40]

Outward ostentation could threaten brokers' careful balance of obligations with local trading partners. So they concealed movable merchandise in private spaces to make commerce less divisive.[41] The homes at Gedi to the west of Malindi, for example, include outside porches and stepped courtyards at the front for entertaining; but only guests who entered private family spaces would see porcelain pottery displayed in plaster niches, textiles hung on pegs, and storage rooms for other trade items.

As coral houses became the locus of wealth, they also became a foundation for political influence—if located in the right place. The members of wealthy clans in Gedi built walls to separate their coral-built neighborhoods from poorer residents as much as to defend against raiders. Building a coral house required enough material wealth to compensate (or purchase) laborers, but brokers also needed to acquire the right kind of blood, or descent, for their grandchildren if they wanted them to live among the clans who owned the neighborhoods within the town wall. So Kiswahili speakers domesticated trade not only by conducting business in coral houses but also by inviting upstart brokers and foreign traders to join with their daughters in making a home. To the extent that the founding families could control the privileges that came with marriage into their lineages, they could also control who shared elite status in their towns.

While brokers sought traditional honors by marrying into the lineages of *wenyeji* (founders, lit. town owners), they also sought kinship with foreign (usually Arab) Muslims who could extend their commercial relationships in the Indian Ocean. Conversely, this strategy paved the way for foreigners to exert local influence. For example, the Batawi family of Pate arranged a marriage with the Nabahani lineage from Oman in the sixteenth century. At first Nabahani men established local standing by emphasizing their descent from a woman of the Batawi clan. After a few generations, one of them reasserted his patrilineal Nabahani ancestry to claim the title of sultan of Pate, though Pate's *wenyeji* lineages repeatedly contested the claim.[42] The Nabahani ascent in Pate shows how material wealth and the prestige of being a Muslim from Arabia could threaten the primacy afforded to the original founders of a town.[43]

While Kiswahili speakers strengthened their associations with foreign merchants through marriages and their shared commitment to Islam, they conceptualized relationships with inland communities through terms usually reserved to denote kinship. Chimijikenda speakers often married their daughters to Kiswahili-speaking men at the coast, but Kiswahili-speaking Muslims usually refused to marry their daughters to Chimijikenda speakers who had not converted to Islam. It is unclear when they initiated this imbalance, but the social distancing was first documented by Kiswahili speakers' identification of inland people as *kafiri* (unbelievers) to Portuguese visitors in the sixteenth century.[44] Long-standing friendship and these unidirectional marriage alliances, rather than religious communion, served as the foundation and motivation for inland communities to do business with Muslim patricians at the coast.

These strategies helped elite families exclude or assimilate rivals, but they also made distinctions in status and wealth more visible. As lineages and clans assembled material forms of wealth and status, they invited accusations of greed from their neighbors and unwanted attention from other confederations. Around 1450, Pate sacked Shanga and permanently dispersed its residents.[45] As commercial competition heightened, towns built defensive walls, and they founded new settlements in more secure positions on nearby islands as well as hilltop makaya along the escarpment.[46] The inequities and violence that accompanied greater participation in commerce are clear from the ruins of coastal stone towns; but historians must rely on oral traditions and ethnographic analogies to imagine how speakers of Sabaki languages organized title societies and age-sets to manage these problems.

CONTINGENT CONSENSUS: COUNCILS AND TITLE SOCIETIES

Speakers of Kiswahili used Arabic-derived titles like sultan, sheikh, vizier, qadi, and amir, but they rarely centralized power in royal courts or restricted authority through a hierarchical political schema. Even those who held the venerated Kiswahili title of *mfalme* (king) were severely limited: as al-Mas'udi noted in the tenth century, an *mfalme* could be executed and all his descendants forbidden to take the title if he asserted himself too strongly.[47] Also, although Kiswahili speakers prized patrilineal Arab descent, they emphasized matrilineal ties by celebrating named queens as the founding rulers of major anchor towns.[48] The name of Mombasa's mythical foremother Mwana Mkisi may derive from *kisi,* which means "to tack a sailboat," a technique for making forward progress into the wind by switching the orientation of the sails.[49] If so, her name evokes the tension between the communal ethos of reciprocity that held confederations together and an emerging commercial ethos that encouraged accumulation of individual and family property.

Some of the political titles that Kiswahili speakers derived from Sabaki roots suggest that they organized political power in heterarchical organizations, which asserted authority over knowledge required for different activities.[50] At Lamu a *mwinyi mui* (town trustee) represented the interests of all the town's clan confederations to outsiders, but he was selected by the *wenyeji* (town owners). They also selected an *mkuu wa pwani* (grandee of the beach) from a designated lineage, who divined the proper time to set sail on trading voyages. In many places, guardians of the soil (e.g., *jumbe la wakulima, mwizi,* and *mvyale*) were often women who kept track of the solar calendar to determine the proper time for planting crops and performing related rituals.[51] Some of these titles were the prerogative of esteemed lineages or clans. Other titles were claimed by those who organized exclusive title societies that cut across clan boundaries. These title societies protected knowledge regarded as too powerful for any single clan to control.

Although these heterarchical organizations distributed authority instead of centralizing it, they did not prevent social stratification. Confederations often functioned as oligarchies, led by an elite class of titled men. The Pokomo *wakijo,* Mijikenda *avyere,* Comorian *waferembwe,* and Swahili *waungwana* were all patricians—mature, married men and women of means who claimed stewardship over their respective confederations by virtue of their descent, ritual knowledge, and material wealth.[52] The Shicomorian word *waferembwe*—a compound of *wafe* (council members) and *rembwe* (to be decorated)—is a literal description of these patricians, but the Kiswahili word *waungwana* suggests a more nuanced notion of their status. *Waungwana* comported themselves as civilized Muslim freepersons in contrast to *washenzi* (barbarians, sg. *mshenzi*), *kafiri* (pagans, sg. *kafiri*), or *watumwa* (enslaved people, sg. *mtumwa*). Krapf, expounding on this term's root word (*unga* [to join]), explained that "free men hold together, assist each other in word and in everything, but slaves do not and cannot, because they are dependent on their master and cannot join others."[53] Not all patricians who spoke Sabaki languages involved themselves directly in commerce. Yet they held in common a notion of elite status that made their influence contingent upon reciprocal obligations within their clan confederations.

Beyond this ethic of reciprocity, no patrician could purchase absolute authority or resort to violence because their rivals and followers could simply move away to another confederation. Speaking of two Mijikenda confederations, Dahlu wa Mombare explained to Thomas Spear: "The Ribe were always fighting for leadership in the town. The Kambe, being very peaceful people, not only gave them the leadership but gave them the whole town and went to search for a new one. They left them with these words: 'We shall see whether you will be able to run it' and they haven't been able to run it since. In fact, when we left that town the Ribe also had to leave and settle outside it."[54] As this oral tradition suggests, leaders could "run the town" only if they could organize consensus among the resident clans. In practice patricians organized themselves into councils and title societies, rather than royal courts, to redistribute material wealth and resolve disputes among clans within the same confederation.

People claimed and preserved patrician status through their lineages, whose resources they depended on to engage in conspicuous generosity. Initiation fees varied over the centuries, but ethnographic analogies to modern practices suggest that initiation fees required candidates to develop positive social relationships with people in all levels of a clan confederation. For example, a Giriama man seeking patrician status in the early twentieth century needed to provide initiated elders with six bulls, enough maize to purchase seven more bulls, and grain, fruits, and vegetables sufficient to accompany a celebratory meal. In addition, his clan needed to contribute to the feast, an important measure of his ability to inspire confidence and loyalty beyond his lineage.[55] If a patrician desired to acquire esoteric knowledge and regalia that conferred authority beyond their clan, they needed to pay additional fees to join more exclusive title societies.[56] Though title societies were theoretically open to any men, initiation fees and the expense of hosting feasts excluded anyone who could not convince their clan to support their aspirations. Women also formed societies, such as the *lelemama* clubs of Mombasa or Mijikenda *kifudu* societies in the twentieth century. Though women's societies were less exclusive, they did not include all women.[57]

Titled men flaunted their commercial success through their clothing. Just as *waungwana* at the coast donned white *kanzu* and metal swords, Giriama men who joined the *luvoo* title society in the early twentieth century wore clothing that signified their commercial connections: a *luvoo* (ivory armband), a *kitambi* (black skirt) tied at the waist with a red sash, and a white cloth over one shoulder—imported textiles they forbade others from wearing.[58] In the nineteenth century patricians could purchase the right to represent the commercial interests in Mombasa for one of twelve Chimijikenda-speaking clan confederations—the fee of six hundred Maria Theresa dollars (approximately US $10,000 of silver in 2020) suggests this privilege was quite lucrative.[59] These modern historical examples are suggestive of the strategies earlier title holders may have used to assert their elevated status.

Patricians also received fees for resolving disputes, which people paid in the form of cattle or other movable goods. European observers in the nineteenth century had a poor opinion of patricians, but they still managed to describe some of the essential work that titleholders performed. Charles New noted (disapprovingly) that the "chief occupation" of these societies was feasting on dues, fees, and fines.[60] For example, the *vaya* society in nineteenth-century Rabai held diviners and healers accountable by ensuring they did not use their medicine (*uganga*) to harm people with witchcraft (*utsai*).[61] The vaya empowered its members by teaching them the hyena oath (*kirao cha fisi*)— a trial by ordeal of poison to determine guilt for heinous crimes like murder.[62] Not many aspired to make weighty decisions over life and death, but vaya members were honored with exclusive feasts and special funeral rites.[63]

However, some people accused title societies of witchcraft if they could not halt droughts, epizootics, and epidemics, or if they violated expectations of generosity and morality. The relict distribution of cognates for "witch" and "witchcraft" in Bantu languages indicates that speakers of Sabaki languages inherited their notions of witchcraft from a Bantu speech community that predated even their Proto–Mashariki Bantu ancestors (i.e., before 1000 BCE).[64] Mijikenda notions of witchcraft explicitly connect it with the practice of taking and concealing wealth. Mitsanze Mwamure told Spear that the vaya used witchcraft because "they used to hold their meetings in the bush and ate their feasts there."[65] Chibo wa Mundu, of Chonyi, reported to Spear that the vaya were "very evil people who deprived others of their things unlawfully. For example, they would march together singing to warn people that they were approaching. Everyone had to go inside or hide so as not to see them. Anyone who remained outside was seized and his relatives had to give the *vaya* a calabash of palm wine and two *reale* [coins] before they would free him. If no one came to his rescue, the *vaya* would sleep with him whether he was a woman or not."[66] Though title societies ostensibly granted membership to those who demonstrated generosity and self-sacrifice, oral traditions that associate the vaya society with witchcraft, greed, and physical abuse underscore the tension between amassing personal wealth and meeting community obligations.

Bantu speakers throughout Africa organized title societies, suggesting that these organizations extend deep into their shared past.[67] Yet as ephemeral institutions, they left few material or linguistic traces. Linguists cannot precisely sequence specific title societies in time because their names are too localized. However, the similarities of these organizations among modern Sabaki speech communities indicate their continuous relevance over many centuries. Krapf described how some title societies had diminished in authority because people began to doubt the efficacy of the oaths they used. For the *kirao cha fisi* (hyena) oath of the vaya society, he noted: "The transgressor was supposed to howl like a hyena when [they were] going to die. Such a case being very rare, it was thought *the oath was not much dreaded,* and it was therefore *superseded* by the Musafuma

[oath]."[68] Krapf also recorded that the hyena oath had replaced a previous *kirao cha kidudu* (insect oath). This succession of oaths shows that title societies could recruit new members only so long as people respected their authority; conversely, patricians could rejuvenate their authority and privileges by forming new societies and creating new oaths. Krapf's observations suggest that clan confederations formed several societies with overlapping memberships, with each society carving out distinct responsibilities to prove their value to their confederation.[69] Clan confederations with overbearing or stingy leaders would lose members to less demanding, more generous neighbors.

Although it is impossible to identify the specific title societies that speakers of Sabaki languages organized in the early second millennium, archaeologists have found tantalizing evidence of feasting practices that oral traditions and ethnographic reports associate with modern title societies. For instance, they have found large, imported bowls for feasting throughout coastal East Africa that date from the twelfth century. Not only could these vessels hold copious amounts of food but they also revealed intricate interior designs, and thus the identity of its owner, as the meal was consumed.[70] This decoration suggests that the feasts would have been sponsored by patrons who wanted recognition for their generosity. Fleisher argued that this practice may have extended back as far as the tenth century, when local potters emulated the decoration of imported Iranian bowls but used locally produced red pigment instead. Since these distinctive vessels were relatively rare in the region, they may indicate some of the earliest efforts by patricians to signal their status with material goods.[71]

In any case, the general transition from necked jars in Early Tana Tradition ware before 900 CE to the open bowls of the Late Tana Tradition ware along the Kenyan coast in the following centuries indicates that feasting became common throughout the region—just as their engagement with Indian Ocean commerce accelerated. These feasts continued into the fourteenth, fifteenth, and sixteenth centuries in littoral Kenya. An excavation by Stephanie Wynne-Jones at Vumba Kuu positively associated large serving bowls with feasts by identifying the pottery along with copious amounts of fish bones in the site's public spaces between the fourteenth and sixteenth centuries.[72] So while coral houses show how elite Kiswahili speakers assembled and concealed their wealth, changes in pottery suggest that patricians from the twelfth century onward found political advantage in publicly sharing their abundance.

Although patricians could deflect accusations of hoarding with generosity, flaunting their wealth could also attract suspicion. Playing up this inherent contradiction in patrician status enabled competing patrons and succeeding generations to replace the faltering societies of their rivals or elders by charging them with corruption or impotence. Councils and title societies could only maintain authority by achieving consensus, contingent on their ability to prevent catastrophe and sponsor feasts. As Krapf observed, "The established feasts . . . unite them more closely and stronger than anything else."[73]

ROUTINES OF VIOLENCE:
SLAUGHTERING CATTLE AND CUTTING AGE-SETS

If memories of Kongowea and its ruler Mwana Mkisi reflect the delicate maneuvers of domesticating commerce and cultivating consensus in littoral Kenya, those of Shehe Mvita recall the violence of commercial rivalry. Kiswahili oral traditions describe the founder of Mombasa's Mvita town as an immigrant from Shiraz in Persia, but his name derives from a Proto-Sabaki word for "war."[74] When a Portuguese fleet raided Mombasa in 1504, the invaders met stiff resistance from residents accustomed to battle. The ill-fated defenders met Captain Francisco de Almeida's soldiers with swords, spears, and poisoned arrows. They pinned down the invaders in narrow alleys and threw stones down from their multistoried houses. The leading patricians retreated to a grove of trees in the interior of the island while others erected barricades around the town. They also called on allies from inland towns to fortify their defenses. They had prepared these weapons, fortifications, and alliances to protect their town against local rivals long before Europeans arrived. Linguistic evidence suggests that speakers of Sabaki languages adopted some of these tactics and routines of violence from a subset of Central Kenya Bantu communities called Mosseguejos, thus emphasizing the importance of a cis-oceanic framework that also traces inland influences on Kenya's littoral society.

Most Central Kenya Bantu speech communities flourished in Kenya's central highlands, but the Mosseguejos and communities who spoke early dialects of Kamba also established settlements closer to the coast. As far as modern Mijikenda and some Swahili clans are concerned, their ancestors met the Mosseguejos forebears of Segeju communities when they all lived together in the mythical homeland of Shungwaya. Mijikenda versions of the tradition describe the Segeju (i.e., the Mosseguejos) who fled from Shungwaya as one of the first groups to settle along the escarpment; but they disparage the Segeju as lowly servants who tended their ancestors' cattle. In contrast, Portuguese chroniclers described the Mosseguejos as fearsome warriors.

Evidence of linguistic borrowing also confirms the extensive influence of the Mosseguejos on speakers of Sabaki languages. Martin Walsh identified dozens of loanwords in Chimijikenda dialects that appear to come from Central Kenya Bantu languages.[75] He argued that the Mosseguejos created a "Segeju corridor" through the territory of Sabaki speakers (see map 3.2). Their predecessors first encountered Sabaki speakers as early as the twelfth century CE, when they influenced changes in the sounds and vocabulary of Kielwana on the upper reaches of the Tana River.[76] Then Portuguese visitors reported the presence of the Mosseguejos near Malindi in 1589.[77] As Mosseguejos speech communities extended through the escarpment and the arid plains to the west, most of them joined Sabaki-speaking communities. By the nineteenth century, their descendants who lived in Tanzania still spoke a Central Kenya Bantu language called Daisu, but their posterity along the Kenya-Tanzania border had fully adopted a Chimijikenda dialect called Segeju.[78]

Central Kenya Bantu loanwords may have also come from hamlets immediately west of the Mijikenda communities, whose residents spoke Pre-Kamba (i.e., dialects that developed into modern Kamba). These settlements eventually served as waystations for the caravan routes that connected the coast to Ukambani in the nineteenth century—but some Portuguese sources indicate that the Pre-Kamba speakers who founded them had started visiting the coast as early as 1689.[79]

Central Kenya Bantu loanwords in Chimijikenda and Kiswahili suggest that speakers of Sabaki languages added words for techniques

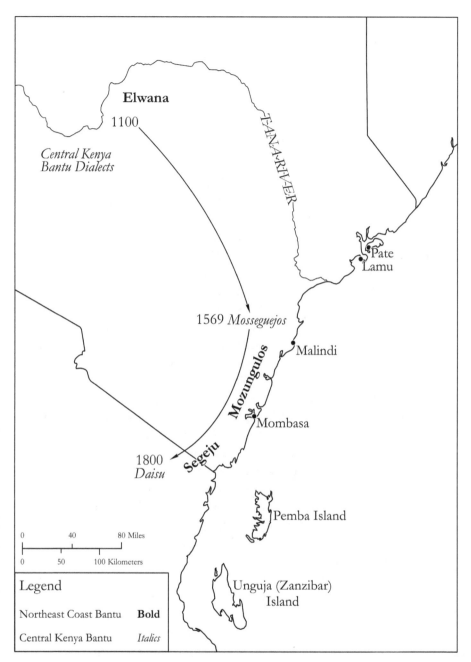

MAP 3.2. Segeju Corridor. Map created by ThinkSpatial.

in cattle husbandry, new regalia, and procedures for title societies, as well as practices for organizing age-sets to Kenya's littoral schema.[80] Loanwords include terms for "male calf" and "castrated animal" and the verbs "to look after" livestock, "to brand" livestock, and "to churn" milk.[81] These loanwords related to cattle husbandry suggest Central Kenya Bantu speakers joined this littoral society a short time before the sixteenth century, since that is when archaeologists have confirmed that people in the region began to eat more beef. In 1505 Hans Meyr reported that nearly every house in Mombasa was connected to a cattle stall. Oxen did not plow fields or carry burdens in the region; they were prized for their meat. Since the island's ecology could not support large herds of cattle, the cattle traded to coastal towns must have been supplied in part from inland locations.

The Mosseguejos may have established some of the small settlements that appeared in the sixteenth century throughout the arid scrub brush west of the coastal escarpment. Chimijikenda and Kiswahili speakers call this area the *nyika* (wilderness).[82] Father Monclaro, a Jesuit priest who visited Malindi in 1569, described the Mosseguejos as pastoralists. Without permanent homes or crops, they "ha[d] large numbers of cattle, and subsist[ed] upon their blood and milk mixed together," indicating that they may have been the initial suppliers of beef to the coast.[83] However, Chimijikenda speakers took over the nyika and the role of supplying cattle to the coast by 1700, when a Portuguese mapmaker equated a century-old epithet for Chimijikenda speakers (Mozungullos) with a new one: Wanyika (people of the bush).[84] Though now regarded as derogatory, the name could have referenced mastery over the arid nyika plains, which supported cattle raising better than the hilly terrain of the escarpment.

As Chimijikenda speakers made cattle more available, their Kiswahili-speaking trade partners replaced fish with beef in the feasts that promoted patrician authority. In one Kiswahili chronicle about the founding of Rabai, a shared feast of three cows formalized an agreement between Rabai's settlers and the people of Jomvu.[85] Cattle thus became not only a sign of wealth but an important resource for diplomacy after the sixteenth century CE.

The Mosseguejos also introduced new rituals associated with title societies. For instance, Monclaro's description of the Mosseguejos reported that they "cover their heads with stinking clay."[86] Centuries later, in the 1860s, Charles New observed a Chimijikenda-speaking candidate for a title society crafting a clay helmet. At least one ceremony performed by Rabai council members in recent times also required the use of such a helmet.[87] Besides this material innovation, Chimijikenda speakers borrowed Central Kenya Bantu words that suggest a strong influence on the work of councils. These include words for resolving disputes like *bako* (gifts for reconciliation), *kirurumo* (fine paid to an elder), and *voya* (to beg, ask for, pray). Others indicate ceremonial places, such as *dhome* (meeting place of the council) and *aro* (house of uncircumcised youth).[88] The loanwords *kambi* (council of initiated elders) and *mutumia* (elder, pl. *watumia*) expressed the need to clearly define the leaders of clan confederations. Although these loanwords are concentrated in Chimijikenda, speakers of Kipokomo and the Mombasa dialects of Kiswahili adopted some of them as well. One of the strongest signs of influence from Central Kenya Bantu speakers is that Chimijikenda and some Kiswahili speakers replaced their inherited words for clan and lineage with the loanword *mbari*.

However, age-sets (*marika*) were likely the most transformational organization that Central Kenya Bantu speakers introduced to speakers of Sabaki languages. Proto-Bantu speakers had formed age-sets that they called *kúlà as early as 3000 BCE.[89] By 2000 BCE, Bantu-speaking men joined age-sets by "entering circumcision and initiation rites" (*alik) from which Proto–Mashariki Bantu speakers derived the noun *liika* (initiated age-set). When Proto–Central Kenya Bantu speakers diverged from other members of the Southern Nyanza Bantu areal group, they preserved the word for age-set as *riika (pl. *mariika). However, Proto–NEC Bantu speakers (the forebears of Sabaki speakers) must have abandoned age-sets—elsewise, the distinctive sound changes in their dialects would have led them to pronounce the word as *zika.[90] By the time Central Kenya Bantu speakers reintroduced age-sets to Sabaki speakers as *marika*, the clan confederations could sustain age-sets better than isolated villages could in earlier eras. In addition, the aggressions of other age-set organizations in East Africa—such as the Oromo *gada* and later the Maasai *murran*—would have consistently reinforced the military value of age-sets.[91] The violence of this era of contact is also indicated by at least ten loanwords in Chimijikenda from Central

Kenya Bantu related to warfare, with meanings such as "plunder," "revenge," and "commit atrocities."[92]

While title societies distributed power horizontally among patrician men, age-sets introduced a hierarchy that systematically excluded younger men from formal authority. Mijikenda oral traditions present a complex, idealized process for organizing age-sets and elevating them through three age grades: the *ahoho* (children), the *nyere* (youth), and the kambi (elders). So for instance, boys between the ages of five and twenty-five became ahoho first. Two or three decades later, their age-set received a formal name (e.g., Amwendo) after entering the nyere grade. They retained this name when they entered the kambi grade after several more decades. Clan confederations entrusted members of the nyere grade to protect the community and engage in commercial pursuits, but only members of the kambi grade were permitted to become *watumia*, or "elders" who could sit on councils and acquire titles.[93] Though all men of the same age-set were elevated to the next grade together, in practice they selected leaders from each clan called *akirimu* (noble, generous people) to represent them in initiation ceremonies.[94]

Mijikenda oral traditions also detail rituals with which age-mates progressed together through each age-grade. The most important of these ceremonies was *mung'aro*, which elevated ahoho to the nyere grade. Since only established kambi could elevate nyere to the next age-grade, the mung'aro ceremonies became pivotal moments of generational tension. Every few years the eldest nyere could join the ranks of the kambi, but none of the ahoho could ascend to the nyere grade until all members of the previous, older age-set had moved from the nyere grade to the kambi grade. By that time some of the ahoho could be nearly fifty years of age. The youngest men in each age-set endured much of their lives subordinated to the nyere and kambi, only to be supplanted by their juniors a few years after achieving prominence.[95] Since the retiring age-set was responsible for initiating the rising age-set, they could delay the necessary ceremonies as they saw fit. However, as more and more kambi succumbed to old age, it was difficult to carry on the work of leading their clan confederations. The eldest ahoho needed to persuade the youngest surviving kambi to initiate them as nyere. Conversely, the prospect of leading the clan confederation helped assure commitment to it and dissuaded "young" men from setting off on their own.

The mung'aro dance routinized this fraught transition of authority between age-sets and directed violence away from internal rivals toward external threats. In order to prepare for the ritual, the ascending age-set would gather in their respective clans near a body of water, such as a river or a pond, at which they would cover their skin with clay or mud.[96] Then they would participate in feats of strength, such as carrying a heavy load on one's head or jumping up to bring down an animal skin from a branch using only one's teeth.[97] Most traditions about mung'aro assert that "before [participants] could dance *mung'aro* and cut a *rika* [i.e., officially ascend to the next age-grade], . . . a person had to be killed."[98] The victims might include rivals or wrongdoers within the confederation, but most oral traditions suggest that the initiates needed to kill a stranger. The rituals demonstrated participants' capability as warriors and their willingness to take up arms for their clan confederation, instead of just their clans.

The mung'aro ritual also established the effective external boundaries of a clan confederation. Selecting an appropriate victim required the initiates to identify who belonged to their confederation. In addition to establishing friendly relations by exchanging cattle, some Mijikenda clan confederations claimed they held joint age-set initiations in recognition of their alliance. For example, some Giriama reported that they timed their *rika* initiations to coincide with those of the Ribe on the same night, no small matter for a ceremony that came only once per generation and involved years of preparation.[99] Allied clan confederations presumably did not target one another for their ritual sacrifices. The alliances that clan confederations established with one another through slaughtering cattle and "cutting *rika*" did not necessarily reduce violent skirmishes in the region, but these rituals provided expectations for managing when violence was acceptable and who could be targeted.

Since age-sets lent credibility to threats of force, the Chimijikenda also used them to secure parity with seaside suppliers. Brokers at the coast hoarded trade goods in expectation of future exchanges rather than redistributing them immediately to clients; so they were a convenient focus of attack. The Portuguese chronicler Bocarro even described the people of Mombasa as "prisoners of the Mozungullos" because "they have to pay them a large tribute in cloth in order to be allowed to live in security."[100] The clan confederations of Mombasa learned that they fared better in collaboration with, rather than competition against, the Giriama, the Rabai, and other inland confederations.

Though it is possible that several Central Kenya Bantu loanwords entered Sabaki vocabularies after 1600, the documented presence of the Mosseguejos by then suggests these age-set practices extended at least to that time. Regardless of when speakers of Sabaki languages adopted these practices, age-sets remained the preferred strategy of Chimijikenda as well as Kiswahili speakers for securing the loyalty of the rising generation to their confederations from the fifteenth to the early twentieth centuries. Instead of regarding the kaya complex, with its title societies and age-sets, as a coherent set of practices carried from Chimijikenda speakers as they made their way south from Shungwaya, Central Kenya Bantu loanwords show the continued influence of the African interior on the schema, which was shared throughout littoral Kenya.

THE GALLA THREAT

Though speakers of Sabaki languages and their neighbors competed with one another, their experiences with Oromo speakers inspired them to see one another as members of a cohesive littoral society. Mijikenda traditions explicitly blame the flight from Shungwaya on Oromo speakers they derided as "Galla." As documented by contemporary Portuguese writers, Oromo-speaking herders extended their territory from Ethiopia and Somalia into northern Kenya in the sixteenth century. Their raids forced many communities to relocate to islands, retreat to hilltop forts, or seek shelter in caves. Oromo-speaking communities eventually reached as far as Malindi, which they occupied from 1623 until Omani planters expelled them in the nineteenth century.

As Sabaki-speaking refugees from these raids streamed south, they spread the disturbing news of an enemy who accosted women on their way to fetch water and stabbed spears through the walls of grass huts while people slept.[101] The Oromo- speaking raiders depopulated villages rather than simply raiding them. The speakers of Kipokomo and Northern Kiswahili dialects eventually appeased Oromo invaders with promises of tribute, while Chimijikenda speakers engaged them in trade, and the Kiswahili speakers of Pate even came to rely on them as allies in warfare.[102]

However, the refugees' tales of a hurried retreat endured as a framework for slotting local settlement and clan histories into a generalized schema of migration from Shungwaya. As people from many confederations repeated these tales, they generated a shared narrative among Kipokomo, Kiswahili, and Chimijikenda speakers that promoted anti-Oromo sentiments. Though local rivals continued to raid one another, the "Galla threat" was salient enough that oral traditions singled them out as the enemies against whom residents needed to unite for protection.[103] In contrast to the detailed accounts of rivalries among clan confederations, Mijikenda traditions describe the Galla as a homogenous, amorphous, and ever-present threat.[104]

Changes in settlement patterns after 1600 suggest that the Galla threat helped retain Chimijikenda speakers' loyalties to their respective clan confederations. Though the Shungwaya tradition associates the founding of makaya (hilltop forts) with Galla raids, archaeological surveys show that the incursions of Oromo speakers in the seventeenth century coincided with the abandonment of makaya. As Oromo speakers razed northern towns, people in the southern part of the escarpment were already abandoning town living. They established a settlement pattern that persisted into the twenty-first century in which each lineage forms a homestead on agricultural land claimed by a clan, resulting in a mosaic of clan lands in each *lalo* (location). However, clans continued to affiliate with confederations by maintaining clan spaces (*lwanda*) within the otherwise abandoned anchor towns to which they returned for rituals and refuge.

Some lineages may have preferred living outside of makaya for the same reasons brokers in coastal towns preferred to live in coral houses: a homestead allowed them to conceal their wealth. Krapf's informants associated the Chimijikenda words *dendana* (to ridicule one another) and *fomorera* (to demolish) with the time when their ancestors lived in towns. For *dendana*, Krapf noted that "this is said to have been much the practice in former times, when they lived more together in their kayas"; concerning *fomorera,* he explained, "This happened especially when one built his hut on the *chansa* [cleared area] of another in the kaya."[105] While "ridicule" indicates enmity that would cause some residents to leave and establish a new settlement, the rivalries conveyed by the word *fomorera* (the destruction of a squatter's home) suggest that Chimijikenda speakers in the nineteenth century preserved an assumption from earlier generations that life in the close quarters of a kaya could be difficult. As Chimijikenda speakers spread out into homesteads, they could maintain their affiliations to a confederation through their clans but achieve independence and privacy comparable to what coral houses afforded coastal brokers—without clustering together. Since most Chimijikenda speakers did not live in towns during the nineteenth century, the grievances they reported about the tensions of town living may have conveyed social memories that predated the Galla threat.

Oromo raids coincided with new commercial opportunities provided by Portuguese visitors. The honor of joining title societies offered enough incentive for wealthy men to affiliate with an anchor town. However, ambitious but less prosperous men needed some persuasion to remain. For patricians trying to dissuade people from leaving, the threatening caricature of fearsome and incomprehensible Galla warriors became a compelling argument for remaining safely within walking distance of a kaya defended by young warriors, as well as within the collective ethos of the clan confederations.

The Galla are also a clear example of a stereotyped "other" whose foreignness helped speakers of Sabaki languages imagine their respective communities as components of the same littoral society. Portuguese writings demonstrate how Sabaki speakers had already begun to craft caricatures of one another. The Wanyika, Mozungullos, and Mosseguejos, all of whom Kiswahili speakers called *kafiri* (unbelievers), occupied the escarpment and the nyika plateau. However, these labels of perceived religious and linguistic difference did not dissuade them from military, trade, or even marriage alliances. Since the Galla threat was common to all the communities of littoral Kenya, it transcended local rivalries and linguistic boundaries to inspire a nascent regional identity. The foreign dialects and frequent hostility of Oromo speakers fostered a wider recognition of the commonalities shared by all speakers of Sabaki languages, just as they were organizing wider political alliances with one another to manage Portuguese intrusions.

This chapter has examined oral traditions about how speakers of Sabaki languages used clan confederations, title societies, and age-sets to mitigate the divisive potential of commerce. The sequence in which they created these institutions remains unclear, but archaeological, linguistic, and documentary evidence indicates that they organized them prior to the mythical flight from Shungwaya in the late sixteenth century and possibly as early as 1000 CE.

As settlers filled the landscapes of littoral Kenya with commercially oriented towns after the tenth century, local brokers exchanged commonplace resources for prized products imported from overseas. Their material wealth granted them a privileged status as patricians that had previously been reserved for the founding lineages of the towns (*wenyeji*). Yet they also channeled this competition for status toward joining title societies responsible for mediation and socially valuable rituals. The coral houses of brokers at the coast and the exclusive feasts in the groves of the vaya society along the escarpment violated expectations of generosity, but they also reinforced an ethic that visible distinctions in wealth should be hidden. By the end of the fifteenth century, brokers had oriented most commercial activities away from marginal country towns to relatively crowded anchor towns. However, just a century later, inland communities partially abandoned their anchor towns, confident they could maintain their confederations through unifying ceremonies. The Galla threat persuaded refugees and immigrants to affiliate with clan confederations that maintained fortified (if often empty) towns for protection.

Reappraising the timing of these heterarchical organizations in the Shungwaya myth makes it possible to reimagine the kaya complex of Chimijikenda speakers as part of Kenya's littoral society rather than a belated intrusion into it. In this cis-oceanic perspective, Chimijikenda speakers did not migrate to the escarpment west of Mombasa in the sixteenth century. Rather, as early as 1000 CE they joined with Kiswahili speakers and speakers of other Sabaki languages in building a commercial society that struggled to preserve the communal ethos of their confederations.

When threatened in the colonial era, Chimijikenda speakers drew again on the heritage they shared with other Sabaki speakers. They recast clans and confederations as internal boundaries within Mijikenda ethnicity, and they reorganized councils and title societies to compete over the stewardship of Mijikenda interests.[106] Though age-sets proved more difficult to sustain in the colonial era, Mijikenda orators used the memory of past age-sets to narrate a shared history and symbolize a comradery that extended beyond the boundaries of any one clan confederation. As Richard Waller observed, "Although age systems maintain social and cognitive order, they do so through accommodating disorder or at least uncertainty and debate."[107] Speakers of Sabaki languages used age-sets to focus debates about leadership without descending into inexplicable violence. They even transformed age-sets into the chronological markers of time in the metanarrative of Shungwaya so that every clan—the lynchpin between intimate lineages and extensive clan confederations—could find a place for their story.

PART II

Innovating Ethnicity

FOUR

Polarizing Politics

Imperial Ventures in Dar al-Islam, 1498–1813

Kongowea [Mombasa] is an unforgiving place, do not enter with pride.
Its affairs bewilder, . . . even the informed do not comprehend.

—Muyaka bin Haji al-Ghassany

THE HOUR OR so before the sun sets in coastal Kenya, men gather to play *bao,* the game of choice in East Africa for those who enjoy matching their wits. Bao is deeply rooted in Bantu intellectual history, as indicated by cavities pecked into stone boulders at Mapungubwe in the eleventh century.[1] Enthusiasts have devised versions of this count-and-capture game throughout Africa and shared it with Indian Ocean communities as far away as the Philippines. The game played along the East African coast—*bao la Kiswahili*—is particularly complex. Two players face each other across a board with thirty-two cavities arranged in four rows. They take turns placing one of twenty-four additional seeds into one of their occupied holes. After each placement, they take the seeds from that hole in hand

and sow them one by one into adjacent holes, expanding the range of options for future turns. If they end in an occupied hole that faces one of their opponent's occupied holes, they seize the seeds from the other side of the board and continue sowing on their own front row.[2] The game ends when all the cavities of a losing player's front row have fewer than two seeds, while their opponent's holes overflow with the seeds they have captured. As John Iliffe noted, bao is a game devised by people dedicated "to building up [their] numbers."[3]

By 1658, when a European traveler recorded the first written description of bao in East Africa, the game was already competing with card games as a pastime.[4] Portuguese sailors introduced these games of chance when they entered the Indian Ocean regions of Dar al-Islam (the realm of Islam) at the turn of the sixteenth century. The gambling that accompanied card games made them exciting. Several people could join each game, and lucky players could double or triple their wagers in a few rounds. They could also lose everything, which incentivized cheating. The elements of luck and deception in card games offered lessons in the high-stakes, no-holds-barred commerce that Portuguese mariners promoted after their 1498 arrival in the Indian Ocean.

As zero-sum, adversarial games that reward calculated risk, both bao and card games exemplify the polarized politics that drew Europeans and speakers of Sabaki languages together in the Indian Ocean.[5] While Portuguese officials and merchants often focused on short-term commercial profits, East Africa's littoral communities played a longer game. As the successive ventures of Portuguese, Ottoman, and Omani imperialists failed over two centuries, coastal communities built their numbers. Kiswahili speakers often suffered the leveling effects of seaborne cannons because of their proximity to the coast. Yet they steadily built alliances that extended inland to include speakers of Chimijikenda and Kipokomo as well as newcomers who spoke Central Kenya Bantu languages like Kisegeju and the Oromo dialects of the Eastern Cushitic language family. The disruptive "Portuguese period" in East Africa was also a time of consolidation.

Though virtually no speakers of modern Sabaki languages claim Portuguese ancestry, many trace the formation of their clan confederations to conflicts and alliances motivated by the Portuguese presence along the coast. They continue to draw on imperial ventures of the seventeenth and eighteenth centuries to narrate the formation of the political communities they reimagined as tribes in the twentieth century. So this political history is as integral to the formation of ethnic identities in littoral Kenya as the intricacies of kinship and clans.

MAKING MOIETIES

Historians often gloss over the details of local rivalries in littoral Kenya as they focus on imperial competitions over commerce in the Indian Ocean.[6] This chapter reexamines familiar episodes in these imperial ventures but focuses on how speakers of Sabaki languages reshaped their political schema as they allied with foreigners to their shores. The outline of ancestral elements presented in part 1, from oral traditions, linguistics, and archaeology, presented an idealized and orderly image of how speakers of Sabaki languages thought their littoral society should function. Part 2 continues to explore novel kinds of communities and identities that they added to Kenya's littoral schema. However, it also takes advantage of more plentiful documentary evidence after 1500 CE to explore how they managed conflicting principles for organizing lineages, clans, age-sets, and clan confederations.

For example, this chapter explores how speakers of Sabaki languages managed tensions among different scales of community by forming moieties—polarized political alliances—in each town. Anthropologists describe moieties as a structural feature of Swahili society through which *wenyeji* (town owners) tried to limit the influence of *wageni* (guests) immigrants.[7] However, Chimijikenda and Shicomorian speakers also organized moieties; and in several Kiswahili-speaking towns, each moiety had a mix of *wenyeji* and *wageni*. Much as age-sets organized the transfer of leadership between elders and youth, moieties structured debate among a clan confederation's patricians by grouping their respective clans and lineages into just two factions. Instead of presenting a unified front, these moieties often cultivated relationships with people in other clan confederations and foreigners. Thus the polarization of domestic town politics often mirrored imperial rivalries. Speakers of Sabaki languages likely organized moieties before Portuguese incursions, but the efforts of imperial officials to impose centralized governance on them raised the stakes of their rivalries. In addition, although the realm of Islam had extended to the coast of East Africa centuries earlier, Portuguese writers offer the first documentary evidence that speakers of Sabaki languages formalized political alliances with Muslim polities to their north. Though Kiswahili speakers sometimes equated political betrayal with apostasy from Islam, their faith did not stop them from seeking foreign assistance from Christians or other unbelievers.

PORTUGAL'S MALIGN NEGLECT

Beginning with Vasco da Gama's first encounters along the coast of East Africa in 1498, Portuguese captains demanded the conversion of their hosts to Christianity and their submission as vassals to the king of Portugal. Ruling distant territories entailed neglect to some degree. However, as Portuguese captains ventured into Dar al-Islam, they added a measure of malice. Captains showed their disregard for Muslim communities by dripping hot oil on captives to gather intelligence, holding public executions, and sacking towns.

Portuguese writers referred to Muslims in East Africa as "Mouros" (Moors). Like Portugal's historical adversaries in Iberia and North Africa, Kiswahili speakers lived in towns built of stone, traveled the seas, worshipped in mosques, and (some) could speak Arabic. Ironically, as historian Jeremy Prestholdt observed, this antagonistic familiarity led the Portuguese to view East Africa from the perspective of Kiswahili speakers. Portuguese writers adopted their habit of referring to non-Muslim Africans as *caffres* (from Arabic *kāfir* [unbelievers]), and the foreigners relied on them as nautical pilots, trading partners, military allies, and lovers. Since prominent lineages along the coast emphasized descent from Arab men, Portuguese visitors and settlers considered East Africa an extension of Arabia and Dar al-Islam rather than Bantu-speaking societies like Kongo, which they had encountered in Equatorial West Africa.[8]

Kiswahili speakers called the Portuguese *wareno* (kingdom-people). They borrowed the term from Portuguese contacts who used the word *reino* to distinguish recent arrivals from Portugal and *castiços* born in India to Portuguese parents.[9] *Reino* also meant "kingdom"—the European style of feudal, patrilineal monarchy that Portuguese captains introduced to East Africa. For communities accustomed to heterarchical organizations that diffused power, the notion of submitting to the authority of a single person was odd. Though Arab travelers such as Ibn Battuta had identified men who led coastal towns as sultans, Kiswahili-speaking sultans also relied on councils, title societies, and age-sets that sought consensus. The gold entrepôt of Kilwa appears to offer a major exception to this observation, but even its sultans faced removal if they could not maintain their famous generosity.[10]

As long as Portuguese captains contented themselves with collecting annual tributes enforced by occasional raids, speakers of Sabaki languages pursued their own interests with minimal interference. However, once the Portuguese established a permanent fort in Mombasa, they instigated conflicts among littoral Kenya's towns and clan confederations as well as within the al-Bauri lineage that claimed authority as the vassal of Portugal's king.

Ruling from a Distance

Portuguese kings' attempts to rule from a distance were not exactly unprecedented along the East Africa coast, but the strategy had never been very successful. The Yemeni trade monopoly in the first century CE described in the *Periplus of the Erythraean Sea* was porous to say the least, and neither states in South Asia nor China ever attempted to directly rule the coast south of the Red Sea. When Zheng He (1371–1433) of the Ming dynasty brought his treasure fleet to Malindi in the fifteenth century, he returned with a giraffe as an auspicious souvenir but did not demand tribute or otherwise assert Chinese dominion in East Africa. The Ottoman Empire limited most of its patronage to the eastern parts of the Indian Ocean. In East Africa they rarely reached past the forts they built along the coast of Eritrea to defend their claims in the Red Sea from Christian Ethiopia.[11] The societies ringing the Indian Ocean generally observed the principle of mare liberum (free seas) until the arrival of Portuguese captains who had the temerity to claim sovereignty over the ocean.[12]

Though not averse to meddling in local politics at key anchor towns like Kilwa and Mombasa, the Portuguese were constrained by their reliance on letters and wind-born ships. They coped by narrowing their ambitions. Instead of controlling expansive territories where farmers produced spices, Portuguese captains patrolled the seas and collected customs at conquered ports. Their most important settlement was Goa, on the western coast of India, where a viceroy coordinated Portuguese interests from Mozambique to Japan. Fortunately for Indian Ocean merchants, Portuguese armadas were hardly up to the task of properly enforcing their claims to the seas, and so "smuggling" was rife.[13]

For much of the sixteenth century, Portuguese captains neglected East Africa. Some Portuguese merchants and clerics settled at Malindi, Zanzibar, and elsewhere on the coast to provision and host the sailors of passing Portuguese ships. Yet most Portuguese crews hunkered down on Mozambique Island and then sped toward India as soon as the winds permitted. From 1505 onward coastal towns suffered occasional Portuguese raids, and after Captain Nuño da Cunha's (1487–1539) punitive sacking of Mombasa in 1528, they paid tribute to the annual Portuguese patrol to avert them. Though spared the imposition of hosting large numbers of Portuguese soldiers and settlers until the late sixteenth century, East Africa's anchor towns suffered as Portuguese armadas impeded traffic to their ports.

An Ottoman Conspiracy

Portuguese priorities shifted in 1585 when an Ottoman corsair named Mir Ali Bey captured three Portuguese ships, sixty prisoners, and 150,000 *crusados* of booty in East Africa. Mir Ali found enthusiastic support for Ottoman protection against Portugal in many coastal towns but not Malindi, whose leaders in the al-Bauri lineage accepted vassalage in 1498 to counter the influence of rivals at Mombasa.[14] When a Portuguese commander pillaged Mombasa and Faza as a punishment for their hospitality to the Ottomans, the towns sent delegates to seek help from Mir Ali's superior, an Ottoman governor in Yemen. However, as historian Giancarlo Casale has deduced, the governor and Mir Ali were part of a conspiracy without the full backing of the empire.[15] Although they wanted to increase the Ottoman Empire's presence in the Indian Ocean, they could only muster a handful of ships for Mir Ali to command. When he responded to Kiswahili speakers' pleas for help in late 1588, he did so with only five ships and what he thought was sufficient artillery to hold Mombasa Island.

He was wrong. The Portuguese viceroy in Goa had mobilized twenty ships to repel the Ottoman fleet as soon as spies confirmed Mir Ali's arrival in East Africa. In addition, when the Portuguese fleet arrived in January 1589 to uproot the Ottoman forces from Mombasa, they were astonished to find the island was already under siege by thousands of "Zimba cannibals."[16] Though commonly associated with the Zimba people of Mozambique, this invading force was most likely made up of Chimijikenda speakers who occupied the adjacent mainland. Mir Ali had prepared for a seaward invasion, so his entrenched artillery proved useless against forces invading from the direction of the mainland. He was also unlucky. His cannons failed to hit a single ship as the Portuguese armada secured a beachhead position. Mir Ali and his local allies took refuge in the middle of the island.

After a few days of fruitless negotiations, the mainland invaders struck a deal to ensure that the seaside invaders would not interfere; then they started their final assault. Rather than risk capture by the supposed cannibals, Mir Ali's forces fled toward the sea, where the Portuguese longboats waited to receive them as prisoners of war. With the corsair in custody, Portugal left Mombasa at the mercy of the mainlanders. (Portuguese reports of a Mombasa raid against Malindi within the next three years suggest the town recovered quickly.)[17] The corsair retired to prison life in Europe, the viziers who financed his adventure abandoned their designs, and the Ottoman Empire withdrew from East Africa.[18]

Though the Ottomans never looked back, the Portuguese court feared the worst. Instead of abandoning the coast, the monarchy decided that a robust presence was necessary to dissuade future Ottoman aggressions. By 1593 the walls of Fort Jesus were going up, and Portuguese cannons commanded the entrance to Mombasa's southern harbor. Portuguese settlers congregated at Mombasa once the government directed ships visiting the coast to pay their customs there.[19] Portuguese garrisons, a Christian mission, and settlers formed the Gavana neighborhood of Mombasa near the fort, only a short walk from the Kiswahili-speaking town of Mvita.

Casale has described Portugal's dispute with the Ottoman corsair as an example of how obscure, historically elusive actors like the supposed "Zimba cannibals" could determine the outcome of imperial confrontations. However, it was also a major turning point in the history of littoral Kenya. Not only did the Ottoman conspiracy motivate a more effective Portuguese occupation but the presence of a foreign military force fundamentally changed the calculus for political confrontation among and within the region's clan confederations. Foreigners offered an alternative, if sometimes unpredictable, source of leverage.

The Portuguese Occupation of Mombasa

At first the new Portuguese settlement on Mombasa had difficulty securing local supplies from the mainland because the people of Mvita had fled. According to oral traditions, at least some refugees settled at Jomvu, west of the island.[20] However, the Portuguese occupation also drew new Kiswahili-speaking communities onto Mombasa Island. Ahmed al-Bauri, the sheikh of Malindi, and his followers relocated to Mvita, where al-Bauri secured recognition from the Portuguese king as ruler of the "kingdom of Malindi and Mombasa." The Portuguese occupiers also urged Kiswahili speakers from the nearby mainland to establish the town of Kilindini on the southwest side of the island.[21] Soon it surpassed the population of Mvita, whose former residents started to return. Both towns swelled as refugees from Oromo raids to the north trickled in during the seventeenth century.

Portugal's occupation of Mombasa thus directly inaugurated the rivalry between Kilindini and Mvita that defined Mombasa's politics until the twentieth century. The clan confederation anchored around Kilindini was called the Miji Tatu (Three Towns) and was divided among three clans: Kilindini, Tangana, and Changamwe. Most members of the latter two clans remained in mainland settlements directly across the creek from the island. In contrast, the number of clans in the Mvita confederation fluctuated over the centuries as immigrating lineages became large enough to form clans named for the anchor towns from which they hailed. By the nineteenth century the Mvita confederation was called the Miji Tisa (Nine Towns) because it included members from nine coastal towns. These included the original Mvita, Jomvu, Mtwapa, and Kilifi clans as well as newcomers from the northern confederations of Pate, Shaka, Faza, Katwa, and Bajun.[22] Since the Malindi immigrants of 1593 lived in Mvita, their lineages formed part of the Miji Tisa, but they usually formed a moiety with the Miji Tatu in disputes between the two confederations. Since the Miji Tisa had settled on the island first, the Miji Tatu often relied on foreign patronage for support.

Once Portuguese officials occupied Mombasa, they used their positions to make personal fortunes. Official collections were usually insufficient to meet the expenses of maintaining the fort. However, safe from prying eyes in their isolated outpost, officials embezzled money from other projects with impunity, extorted bribes from ships without the proper papers, and farmed out the management of the customhouse. Though Portuguese captains could use their position in Mombasa to profit without risking their wealth in trade, few resisted the temptation. Michael Pearson detailed staggeringly high gross profits on the ivory, cloth, and gold trade between India and East Africa, with merchants earning ten times or even six hundred times their initial investment in revenue.[23] Even those plying the standard routes between Mombasa and India could count on doubling their original investment. Like a game of cards, a talent for playing the odds and an inclination for cheating offered great rewards.

Since overseas merchants needed to stop at a Portuguese customhouse before enjoying the hospitality of a local broker, Portugal's customs regime interfered in the flows of commerce through the private homes with which local lineages had previously amassed wealth and status. Some families adjusted by seeking personal connections with the Portuguese monarchy. They soon learned the peril of seeking favors from a neglectful king halfway around the world, whose unscrupulous representatives enjoyed minimal supervision.

The King of Malindi and Mombasa

The wrangling within the al-Bauri lineage over the title "King of Malindi and Mombasa" illustrates the risks of royal patronage as well as the tension between the organizing principles of age-sets and lineages in the schema of littoral Kenya. Some members of the al-Bauri lineage and likeminded Kiswahili speakers tried to follow the Portuguese model of patrilineal succession (which some already followed within their lineages) to political succession. However, they encountered resistance from relatives who continued to favor generational succession, in which young men were ineligible to lead until all the previous age-set had passed away. This disagreement led some members of the al-Bauri family to fracture the solidarity of their lineage in pursuit of political authority. The details of this family tragedy show how speakers of Sabaki languages manipulated Portuguese officials to pursue their own political agendas and the challenges of adopting new principles of succession.

After Ahmed al-Bauri died in 1609, his son Hasan competed with Ahmed's brother Munganaja (perhaps a Portuguese rendering of "Mwinyi Naji") to claim the title king of Mombasa. After a three years' delay, King Philip II (1527–1598) conferred the title on Hasan, but Munganaja continued presenting himself as the true representative of the al-Bauri family.[24] In 1612 Munganaja even persuaded a Portuguese captain to fire the cannons of Fort Jesus toward his nephew's home. He and his allies must have thought it unacceptable to elevate a youth to rule over an elder. Either solidarity with his age-set transcended his loyalty to his lineage or the precedents of generational succession gave him a reasonable justification for personal ambitions.

Hasan eventually smoothed things over with the captain of Fort Jesus; however, a new captain arrived in 1614 with a warrant for his arrest. Hasan fled inland to the Chimijikenda-speaking confederation of Rabai for asylum, but his supposed allies murdered him in return for the two thousand pieces of cloth that the new Portuguese captain offered as a bounty.[25] The people of Rabai preferred the generous patronage of a foreign captain over that of a junior patrician with a tenuous hold on his own town. The new captain proudly returned Hasan's head to the viceroy at Goa as evidence of his success.

King Phillip II was upset by the brutal treatment of his vassal. When the letter detailing the viceroy's plans to arrest Hasan had reached Lisbon in February 1615, the king had belatedly countermanded the order. When he heard of Hasan's death a month later, he ordered an inquiry to determine who was at fault, but his officials in Goa and Mombasa hampered this effort. Ultimately, the king attempted restitution for Hasan's murder by sponsoring the education of his orphaned son Yusuf in Goa. Yusuf soon accepted baptism as a Christian and took the name Don Jeronimo Chingulia.

Yusuf's return as king of Mombasa and Malindi in 1630 at the age of twenty-five proved tragic. He expected to be accorded royal honors. Yet in his own words, "Since my accession I have frequently had cause to complain of the gratuitous insults offered me by the Captain, Marcal de Macedo, in front of my own people. . . . No respect was paid to my person, and my treatment did not accord with my station."[26] After a year enduring these indignities, he gathered three hundred men to massacre the celebrants at a Christian feast on August 15, 1631. His retinue then killed all but five of the remaining Portuguese residents.[27]

Yusuf bin Hasan al-Bauri's experiences show the flexibility of religious commitments in East African politics and the degree to which his family's status in Mombasa relied on vassalage to Portugal. In Mombasa's historical chronicle, Yusuf is remembered as an insufferable boor.[28] He flaunted his Christianity and humiliated his subjects by forcing them to eat pork in violation of Islamic law. However, shortly before his rebellion, he was found praying at the grave of his father, in a manner that his tattlers described as Islamic. When he launched his rebellion, he cast off his Christian name and claimed to act in defense of Islam. Unfortunately, by removing the Portuguese settlers, he had extinguished his legitimacy. Sheltered in Goa since childhood, perhaps he misunderstood the weakness of his position as a member of the al-Bauri lineage—they were immigrants from Malindi with no standing among Mombasa's *wananchi* (sons of the soil). Or perhaps he thought his newfound commitment to Islam could overcome his pedigree as a newcomer. He incorrectly supposed that the people of Mombasa would accept his political legitimacy once he reidentified as a Muslim. Instead, they pressed him to leave. After weathering a Portuguese assault on Fort Jesus in December 1631, he lost local support and departed in 1632.

Yet Yusuf fully committed to his anti-Portuguese revolt. For the next five years he lent his aid to towns rebelling against Portuguese dominance from Pate down to the Comoros Islands, inspiring a succession of epic but fruitless manhunts. Eventually, Yusuf sought reconciliation. In a letter explaining his actions to the viceroy of Goa, Yusuf wrote that he was merely seeking justice for the execution of his parents and bringing the king's attention to how the "Captains treated his royal brother."[29] For Yusuf justice included restitution for murder but also an acknowledgment of the indignities that he, a royal peer of the king, suffered at the hands of a mere captain. Instead, he suffered an ignominious death at the hands of pirates near Jiddah in 1638.[30] After Portuguese soldiers reoccupied Fort Jesus, they continued to coordinate local matters with a sheikh from the al-Bauri lineage, but they never again recognized a king of Mombasa.[31]

Portugal's Eviction

Given the hazards of vassalage, many coastal patricians avoided such entanglements and sought instead to evict the Portuguese occupiers. The alliance with the Ottomans proved futile. However, when discontented residents of Mombasa heard that the imam of Oman, Sultan bin Seif al-Yarubi (r. 1649–1679), ousted Portuguese soldiers from Muscat in 1650, they sent delegations to seek his assistance. The sultan responded by sending a navy in 1652 to raid Portuguese stations in Pate and Zanzibar; and in 1660 his soldiers briefly liberated the residents of Mombasa Island, though they failed to seize Fort Jesus.

After a nearly forty-year hiatus, the imam's son and successor, Seif bin Sultan al-Yarubi (r. 1692–1711), resumed the campaign for naval dominance in East Africa by laying siege to Fort Jesus. In the meantime, Portuguese officials drew support from Kiswahili-speaking allies (the prince of Faza and the queen of Zanzibar) as well as Chimijikenda-speaking allies (e.g., the king of Chonyi).[32] With their assistance the Portuguese soldiers held off the siege from 1696 until 1698. However, when the viceroy at Goa finally managed to send relief ships, they found Omani commanders in possession of the fort. For the next thirty years, malcontents in succession disputes and town rivalries across coastal East Africa ventured south to Mozambique to petition for the return of Portuguese rule, despite the Europeans' Christian convictions.[33] Though Portugal briefly retook Fort Jesus in 1728, their allies had diminished. After failing to extend control to the town outside the walls of the fort, the Portuguese departed Mombasa for the last time in 1730.

Most of the clan confederations along the coast welcomed the Portuguese eviction. For two centuries, Portuguese soldiers had razed the East African coast, tortured captives, and executed whomever they considered rebels. However, the violence of Portuguese occupation often overshadows the fact that the littoral societies of East Africa assimilated Portuguese elements into their schema. They retained the forts and customhouses, began committing oral chronicles to writing, added skills in shipbuilding, and played cards and dice in their free time. Most importantly, Portugal's occupation of Mombasa after the swift expulsion of the Ottomans and the Zimba raid led to the founding of Kilindini, a permanent rival to Mvita on Mombasa Island. The suffering under Portuguese rule also strengthened littoral Kenyans' comity with other Muslims in Dar al-Islam. After the last Portuguese soldiers deserted Fort Jesus, the people of Mombasa locked it up, entrusted the keys to representatives from each clan to prevent disputes, and sent a delegation in 1730 to invite the imam of Oman to occupy the fort once more. Appointing a king from one of the local moieties would have been disastrous; but inviting foreign occupiers that each moiety could hope to manipulate was an acceptable compromise.

FROM TOWNS TO COUNTRY: OMANI MEDIATIONS AND SABAKI RIVALRIES

Mombasa's delegation to Oman in 1730 included representatives from not only its two towns but also several Chimijikenda-speaking confederations.[34] Their inclusion shows that clan confederations throughout littoral Kenya had begun working in concert to safeguard their shared interests. Portuguese soldiers had created walls and forts to guard the mainland approach to Mombasa Island. Yet the clan confederations of Rabai, Ribe, Chonyi, and Giriama, among others, had made alliances with their coastal counterparts in return for annual gifts of cloth. The linguistic and religious boundaries between coastal and escarpment confederations proved to be less important than political rivalries among Kiswahili speakers; some Kiswahili-speaking confederations invited *kafiri* (unbeliever) Chimijikenda speakers to join them in raids against other Muslim Kiswahili speakers.

Speakers of Sabaki languages sought their first formal alliances with Islamic states in the Indian Ocean because of commercial interests and Portuguese settlers' disdain for their Islamic faith. Although the sole Ottoman attempt to expel Portugal from East Africa failed spectacularly in 1589, the imams of Oman enjoyed more success after 1701. However, they also found it difficult to enforce their will from afar. Their representatives generally had to fend for themselves and depended on local support for authority. As these representatives became embroiled in coastal politics, their personal rivalries began to mirror those of the towns they claimed to rule. Within a few generations, Omani appointees declared independence from the imams in Oman and began to contend with each other to unify the confederations between Pate and Pemba into a single, politically unified country.

Omani Administration

Omani Arabs distinguished themselves along the coast by refusing to marry their daughters to local families and by limiting government titles to members of Omani Arab clans.[35] Maintaining strict boundaries for their lineages also held them above the fray of moiety rivalries. However, they shared a closer affinity with Kiswahili-speaking communities than the Portuguese soldiers and settlers had. Most Omani Arabs practiced Ibadi Islam, a movement that had rejected both Sunni and Shi'a leadership in the late seventh century CE. However, they referred to Sunni Muslims, like those in East Africa, as "our people."[36] Kiswahili speakers, for their part, offered men to fight alongside Omani forces, taught them to speak Kiswahili, and married their daughters to the sons of Omani immigrants. They valued Omani officials as mediators in disputes among their moieties.

Kiswahili speakers adopted thousands of Arabic words that show these collaborations with the Omani encompassed far more than commercial exchange or political tribute. Like Portuguese loanwords, they include nautical and administrative terms, but Arabic loanwords into Kiswahili also relate to religion, food, kinship, law, personal ornaments, and measurements. Though merchants from Yemen had dominated commercial exchanges with littoral East Africa for centuries, most Arabic loanwords in Kiswahili date to the formal political alliance that coastal towns made with Oman at the turn of the eighteenth century.[37]

Like the Portuguese kings, the imams of Oman appointed representatives, called *maliwali* (governors, sg. *liwali*). These maliwali established customhouses (*forodha*) at the port towns they occupied in the Indian Ocean and supervised the imams' mercenaries from Baluchistan and Arabia who accompanied them.[38] In Mombasa the imams usually selected members of the Mazrui clan to represent them. At Pate the descendants of its first liwali, Bwana Tamu al-Nabahani, considered his appointment as a recognition of his de facto authority as Pate's sultan.

Members of the Mazrui and Nabahani clans were two of several Omani clans who had lived as merchants along the coast for generations. In addition to participating in raids against Portuguese ships, they exported ivory for India and timber for Arabia. They also transported enslaved Africans to serve as soldiers or laborers on date-palm farms in Oman. However, the eighteenth-century imams of Oman focused most of their commercial activities at Basrah in the Persian Gulf and the ports of western India.[39]

Since the Omani imams' commercial interests lay elsewhere, they left the maliwali in East Africa to fend for themselves. The Mazrui even offered to "find [their] own expenses" to avoid burdening the finances of the imamate.[40] It was a relatively simple matter for the maliwali to redirect customs fees to themselves, because the Portuguese regime had accustomed merchants to paying duties on their trade goods. It is less clear how they managed to acquire shipping privileges, fishing rights, and the option to prepurchase ivory exported through Mombasa. By the middle of the nineteenth century, French traveler Charles Guillain (1808–1875) reported that a liwali had imposed a grain tax called *kikanda*. He required each grain supplier to pay around ninety pounds (forty-two kilograms) of millet for each of their enslaved laborers or around one hundred pounds (forty-five kilograms) for every mile of cultivated land.[41] The *Pate Chronicle* similarly described how their Nabahani rivals in Pate levied "three loads of produce for every gang of slaves," or a kikanda equivalent to "one hundred eighty pounds."[42]

The *Pate Chronicle* and Guillain's reports of Mombasa likely exaggerate the extent of the maliwali's authority in these towns. Their influence initially rested on the military protection that Oman offered the towns of East Africa, but it always relied as well on the assent of the townspeople. After the Omani forces expelled Portuguese occupiers for the first time in 1698, the imam appointed Nasir bin Abdalla al-Mazrui as liwali (r. 1698–1728). Though well liked by the townspeople, Nasir lost the support of his enslaved soldiers in 1728.[43] They placed him in chains and proclaimed their own leader, Sheikh Rumba, as the ruler of Mombasa. To Rumba's dismay, a sheikh from the Malindi clan and three men (one from each clan of the Miji Tatu in Kilindini) rejected his claims and tried to evict him from the fort. They eventually succeeded with the help of Portuguese soldiers, who had been summoned to address a succession dispute in Pate.[44]

Just like Yusuf bin Hassan al-Bauri a century earlier, Sheikh Rumba learned that it was the people of Mombasa who determined which foreigners they allowed to rule. The returning Portuguese occupiers also ignored this lesson. Once the soldiers began requiring patrician men to labor and "violat[ing] their women," the people of Mombasa laid siege until they abandoned the fort.[45]

When Mombasa's clan confederations invited Omanis to return after 1730, the confederations swept the new maliwali up in their local rivalries. They helped convince the next liwali, Muhammad bin Sa'id al-Ma'amiri (r. 1730–1735), to distribute "all the wealth and goods" in Fort Jesus as a show of goodwill to the townspeople.[46] Then the Miji Tisa of Mvita convinced Sa'id al-Ma'amiri's successor, Liwali Salih bin Muhammad al-Hadhramy (r. 1735–1739), to evict the Miji Tatu of Kilindini from Mombasa Island, along with the Malindi clan that lived in Mvita—in other words, the communities who had settled on the island at the invitation of Portuguese occupiers a century earlier.

When Liwali Salih and his soldiers left to resuscitate the essential trade in food with Pemba Island, the sheikh of the Malindi clan, Ahmad bin Shaikh, took his revenge. According to the *Mombasa Chronicle*, "together with the Kilindini, [he] had sent an army of Nyika [Chimijikenda speakers] to make war in the old quarter of Mombasa [Mvita]; and the people in this part of the town were killed and plundered for their support of the governor."[47] The episode shows again that the political alliances of moieties paid little heed to linguistic and religious boundaries.

The imam promptly removed al-Hadhramy in 1735 and appointed Mohammed bin Uthman al-Mazrui (r. 1739–1745) as liwali of Mombasa, thus returning the office to the Mazrui clan. Like al-Ma'amiri, al-Mazrui began his tenure by distributing wealth from the fort and inviting the outcasts to return to Kilindini town. He also cultivated personal relationships with the leaders of Mombasa and the Chimijikenda-speaking confederations of Rabai and Chonyi.[48] The Mazrui intervention earned appreciation from the Miji Tatu of Kilindini, the Malindi clan in Mvita, and a few Chimijikenda-speaking clan confederations along the escarpment—but also the ire of the Miji Tisa.

Mombasa's two moieties also opposed each other when the ripples of Oman's dynastic transition reached its shores. In 1743 Ahmed bin Said al-Busaidi (1694–1783), then serving as the liwali of Sohar in Oman, seized control of the imamate from the al-Yarubi clan. When Liwali Mohammed bin Uthman heard this news in Mombasa, he refused to transfer his loyalty to the new imam because they had previously held equal positions and status. The new Busaidi imam then sent agents who pretended to be defectors seeking protection. After secretly securing support from the Kilifi clan of the Miji Tisa, the infiltrators assassinated Mohammed bin Uthman in his quarters.[49]

While most of the Miji Tisa accepted the liwali appointed by the new Busaidi imam, the Miji Tatu and the Malindi clan refused. With the help of soldiers loyal to the Mazrui, they helped Mohamed bin Uthman's brother Ali bin Uthman escape from Fort Jesus. Then they called on their Chimijikenda-speaking allies to capture and execute the new Busaidi-appointed liwali.[50] The Kilifi clan of the Miji Tisa had plotted to use the succession conflict to eliminate Mazrui influence in Mombasa. Instead, the Miji Tatu frustrated their plans and secured Mazrui autonomy from Oman. The Omani succession dispute exemplifies how speakers of Sabaki languages used imperial competitions to increase their leverage in moiety rivalries.

Sabaki Alliances and Factions

As at Mombasa, the maliwali at Pate and every other port town except Zanzibar refused to pledge loyalty to the new Busaidi imam. Busy consolidating his control in Oman, the new imam abandoned his efforts to secure the ports in East Africa. The rift between Oman and Mombasa meant that the leaders of the Mazrui clan no longer received appointments as maliwali from Oman. Instead, their authority derived solely from the patricians of Mombasa. While the word *liwali* still denoted a "subordinate governor" in Omani Arabic, it became a synonym for "ruler" in Kiswahili.

This new arrangement may have motivated the Mazrui liwali to formally recognize as advisers a council (*kambi*) of sheikhs, which included representatives from each of Mombasa's twelve clans. Their positions as advisers enabled them to insist on some aspects of their preferred political schema. For instance, the French traveler Charles Guillain relayed historical reports that the people of Mombasa "intervened several times to appoint the brother and not the son of the deceased, when this son was not a mature and experienced man."[51] Though they did not force the Omani-descended Mazrui to establish formal age-sets, they preferred generational succession and refused to accept the leadership of immature youths.

As Mombasa and Pate shrugged off the protection of foreign rulers after 1745, they each embarked on imperial ventures of their own to consolidate the coast. Mombasa failed to take Zanzibar (Unguja) Island in a campaign that cost the first independent liwali, Ali bin Uthman (r. 1746–1753) his life. But his successors managed to appoint representatives in Pemba and parts of the Tanzanian coast.[52] Mombasa also extended their alliance to include the Chimijikenda-speaking clan confederations inland from Mombasa. For example, the people of Rabai received a chair, a ring, and a staff that symbolized their friendship with the Mombasa liwali.[53] Pate mirrored Mombasa's efforts by cultivating military alliances with the feared Oromo-speaking communities to their north and south that sometimes helped them intimidate the towns of Faza, Siu, and Lamu into submission. The Sabaki River near the abandoned town of Malindi served as a notional boundary between the two polarized domains of Mombasa and Pate.[54]

Yet internal disputes within Mombasa blurred these political boundaries, as demonstrated by W. E. Taylor's report of an oral tradition about the *rika* of Nguli Kibanda. Sometime in the latter half of the eighteenth century, this age-set of eighty young men from Mombasa absconded to Ribe, a clan confederation of Chimijikenda speakers. Then they refused an order from Mombasa's military commander to return.[55] Although Ribe's patricians rebuffed Mombasa's requests to expel the *rika*, the young men decided to leave for Pate. With Pate's assistance, they then conducted three raids against Mombasa, during which they killed people and carried off several

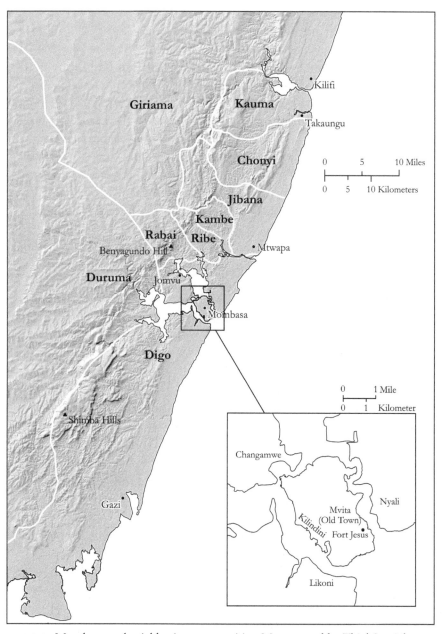

MAP 4.1. Mombasa and neighboring communities. Map created by ThinkSpatial.

women. Shortly afterward, they reconciled with Mombasa's military commander and joined him in a raid on Pate. Another version of the story identifies the Nguli Kibanda as a faction within the ever-troublesome Kilifi clan of Mombasa's Miji Tisa confederation, who had relatives among the "lowest" of the people of Pate.[56]

In any case, the young age-set's temporary alliances with both Ribe (an ally of Mombasa) and Pate (a rival of Mombasa) show the continued relevance of the littoral schema in the coastal towns of Kiswahili speakers. The generational tensions inherent in the creation of age-sets exacerbated conflicts among rival clan confederations. The purported kinship between the Kilifi clan of Mombasa and families in Pate is also a testament to the mobility among clan confederations. Clan confederations operated as large-scale littoral political rivalries, but they also needed to accommodate movements of lineages and clans through defections and asylum seeking that complicated the distinction between *wenyeji* (owners of the town) and *wageni* (guests). Political identities tied to clan confederations were even more contingent than those of their constituent clans.

Proud Pate

In Pate the Nabahani rulers discarded the title of liwali in favor of sultan to assert singular, centralized authority. They also burnished a reputation for ruthlessness.[57] One version of the *Pate Chronicle* described how an early Nabahani sultan summoned the townsmen who opposed him to a feast at which he "butchered them all."[58] The grandiose chronicle of Nabahani conquests not only extended their presence on the coast back to 1200 CE, but it also claimed their sovereignty extended from Somalia to Mozambique. In truth they were relatively recent arrivals on the coast who only occasionally exerted their influence over other towns in the Lamu Archipelago. When the channel to Pate Island filled with silt in the eighteenth century, merchants diverted their trade to Lamu. This led part of the Nabahani lineage to split their time between the two islands, and some even married into Lamu's patrician families.

This relocation motivated new moieties to form in both towns. In Lamu patricians formed the Suudi and Zena factions. The Suudi resented Pate's meddling in the affairs of Lamu's town council, while the Zena welcomed them as a check against the imperial ambitions of Mombasa. Meanwhile, the Nabahani lineage divided as two cousins claimed the title of Pate's sultan. Their respective branches of the family traded turns in exile for decades.

Meanwhile, the competition between Mombasa and Pate came to resemble two large-scale moieties: they divided the stretch of coast between Somalia and Tanzania between them, but they were themselves riven by internal disputes. Just as moieties sometimes worked together to protect their towns, Pate and Mombasa managed to arrange a détente to prevent the Busaidi rulers of Oman from reasserting their claims. After narrowly repelling an Omani force around 1747, the sultan of Pate invited the Mazrui governor of Mombasa to station a garrison of soldiers at his town, but only if Pate could also garrison soldiers on Pemba. This would provide Pate with military support against Oman and guarantee access to Pemba's agricultural exports.

Mombasa's leaders agreed to the terms; but they evicted Pate's garrison from Pemba in 1776 without withdrawing their own from Pate, a barefaced assertion of primacy. After decades of wrangling, the Mazrui of Mombasa intervened decisively in Pate's 1807 succession dispute, ending the impasse between Pate's two moieties. The new sultan, Ahmed bin Sheikh (r. 1809–1813), returned the favor by acknowledging Mombasa's supremacy over Pate and Pemba.[59]

The Portuguese, Ottoman, and Omani rivalry for supremacy over the seas during the sixteenth and seventeenth centuries sometimes led Mvita and Kilindini, as well as Mombasa and Pate, to ally with one another, but they were almost as likely to encourage imperial allies to attack each other's towns. Both Mombasa and Pate aimed to unite the coast as they embarked on their own imperial ventures—deploying troops, collecting tributes, and imposing taxes. Once Pate submitted to Mombasa, they both turned their sights on Lamu.

Defiant Lamu: In Defense of a Moral Economy

With Portugal's and Oman's commercial monopolies in abeyance during the late eighteenth century, new avenues for trade and production were opening up, not just with merchants from India but also with those from England, France, and the United States.[60] Like so many others who faced the disruptions of an emerging capitalist economy in the Indian Ocean, the clan confederations of littoral Kenya sought to prosper without sacrificing the integrity of their communities. After Mombasa resolved its rivalry with Pate, it was on the verge of forming a single regional polity with itself at the center. However, Mombasa's plans faltered and their alliances unraveled after Lamu turned instead to Oman for protection. Though the egalitarian sentiment that the people of Lamu had institutionalized in its town council motivated their resistance, they also expressed reservations about the economic transformations that accompanied Mombasa's imperial ventures.

During the eighteenth century, Lamu's population rose quickly to nearly twenty thousand residents as it received trade diverted from Pate's silty channels.[61] In order to sustain this growth, the town's clans relied on laborers from the adjacent mainland who transformed pastures and swamps into productive farmland. These farming communities included Bajuni fishermen (who spoke a dialect of Kiswahili) and Boni foragers. They also included *watumwa* (enslaved people) from throughout the region.

As it became clear that Pate would no longer protect Lamu from Mombasa, Lamu's Suudi moiety that opposed external meddling rallied the town to defend itself. Trusting in a classic forum for seeking consensus, the leaders of Lamu's moieties organized a *gungu* dance, during which they presented their options in poetic verse.[62] Sheikh Zahidi bin Mngumi of the Suudi faction went first, eloquently arguing that submission to Mombasa would corrupt bonds of fidelity between Lamu's patricians and the mainland clients who had sustained the town's growth in the past century. Zahidi acknowledged their contributions, singing:

> *Tuna kori za aswili tusizoyuwa mipaka*
> We have farming lands of old, we do not know their boundaries.
> *Hulima sote wajoli tukivuniya shirika*
> All of us farm it [as] fellow servants, we share the harvest.
> *Kuna nokowa jamali atashiye kutubuka*
> There is an elegant slave driver, he intends to whip us;
> *Kunyamaa tumetoka, mwatupa shauri gani?*
> We will not be silent, what advice do you give us?
> *Mula shokowa la Pemba na hapa ataka kula*
> He eats the tribute of Pemba, and he wants to eat here.[63]

The archaic word *wajoli* translated here as "fellow servants," is sometimes translated as "enslaved people." The related word *ujoli* (feeling of shared striving) thus encompasses a more patristic notion of clientage and bondage compared to chattel slavery, in which slaveholders value enslaved persons primarily for their productive or exchange value. The image of the "elegant slave driver" who flogs his workers makes the comparison between the two forms of bondage explicit, and the passing mention of Pemba's tribute obligations identifies the target of the poem as Liwali Ahmed bin Muhammad al-Mazrui (r. 1780–1814) of Mombasa.

Historian Randall Pouwels noted that the poem refers to the tax on local production that Mazrui governors had introduced in Mombasa and Pemba.[64] Recall that the kikanda taxes collected by Mombasa's maliwali could be valued either according to land or the number of enslaved people a person claimed to own. Pouwels's translation of the poem makes Zahidi's reference to *'ushr* land taxes clearer by translating the reference to "boundaries" in the first line of the poem as "fencing lines." As a land tax, the *'ushr* required people to demarcate land to demonstrate individual ownership, but this would complicate their traditional principles of collective clan ownership.[65] Zahidi's assertion that Lamu's lands have no borders suggests he saw these investments as contrary to customs of collective trusteeship. Placing fencing lines in Lamu would call disruptive attention to the different levels of wealth in the community, instead of obscuring such distinctions in harvests shared by all. This behavior would be a clear violation of the reciprocal obligations that *waungwana* (patricians) prided themselves on upholding. In addition, the kikanda tax on enslaved laborers would have established a clear hierarchy between slaveholders and those whom they kept enslaved. Instead of including a wide spectrum of relationships that included followers, clients, refugees, and pawned or purchased people, the tax would have forced patrons to determine which of their followers were emancipated and which were enslaved.

While surely containing an idealized view of slavery in Lamu, Zahidi's poem asserts that the harmony between patricians and their clients was threatened by the hard-driving, violent commercialization of agriculture that was just starting to take hold in the Indian Ocean. In the seventeenth century Portuguese settlers relied on enslaved laborers to work their Zanzibar fields, though describing their farms as plantations is probably an exaggeration. Since the seventeenth century, however, Omani imams had derived much of their income from extensive date groves tended by enslaved laborers.[66] In addition, the French colonies of Mauritius and Reunion were importing enslaved captives from Mozambique and Madagascar to grow sugar as early as 1730.[67]

The peak of monocrop agriculture associated with chattel slavery in the Atlantic Ocean was still a few decades off in East Africa. Yet the taxes that Mombasa's independent maliwali wanted to collect suggest that coastal landowners, including recent Omani immigrants, had begun to alienate and demarcate land. Enslaved labor, whether pawned youths from inland communities or imported prisoners from Mozambique, would help recoup their investments. While the taxes that Omani governors and sultans collected on production did not necessarily promote slave-worked plantations, they suggest that reaping profits from enslaved labor was a growing trend supported by Mombasa's leading patricians. The term *shokowa* in the poem, used in the sense of "forced labor" in some Mijikenda oral traditions, suggests the suffering that Mazrui rule entailed for the local communities of Pemba.[68] Zahidi emphasized instead the common interests of all the people of Lamu and their partners on the adjacent mainland who tilled the earth together and shared the fruits of their labor.

Zahidi's second quatrain extended for three more lines, impressing the urgency of Mombasa's pending invasion on his listeners. His despairing language elicited the desired response. According to modern poets, the other leaders of the Suudi faction replied as follows: "We refuse to be pack-asses," "Our guns are cocked and our gunpowder horns and flints are ready," and finally "We have cannons and mortal arrows, with sinewy limbs to fire them! And the Suudi regiment have swords."[69] The Suudi had resolved to fight, but the Zena moiety refused to stand against Pate (whose residents included their kith and kin). Lineage and clan loyalties seemed to hold firm even in the face of their town's imminent subjugation.

The allied forces of Mombasa and Pate, supported by Giriama archers, landed eighty vessels around two miles from Lamu Town at Shela beach around 1813. But a rainstorm ruined their gunpowder and rendered their muskets useless. Undeterred, they pressed on with swords and poisoned arrows until they reached Hedabu Hill, a sandy mound overlooking the town of Lamu. At that time the Zena moiety had a change of heart. They joined the Suudi in common defense of their town and routed the allied forces.

Although Lamu won the battle, it feared another confrontation. Returning to a now familiar formula, Lamu's elders sent a delegation to Seyyid Sa'id al-Busaidi (1791–1856), who had recently secured the leadership of Oman. By asking to resume an Omani alliance of protection, Lamu dashed Mombasa's imperial ventures; but its request ended a half-century period in which littoral Kenya was free of foreign meddling along the coast, ushering in the economic transformations Lamu had judged immoral.

About half a mile from Lamu's shore stands a crooked monument in an abandoned lot that locals refer to as a "Portuguese pillar."[70] Barely remembered and never celebrated, the landmark is a testament to the deprecated legacy of Portuguese imperialism. Even the imposing walls of Fort Jesus is an afterthought to most residents of Mombasa. Once a barracks, then a prison, and now a tourist trap, it is a place where few residents bother to enter except for museum employees and buses of school children who come for field trips. On the other hand, the fort's walls offer much shade. So as older men gather for bao, young men gather in the shadow of the fort to play soccer. Ali Mazrui, a prominent Swahili historian and descendant of the Omani governors who lived in the fort, recalled joining these pickup games in his 1986 documentary *The Africans: A Triple Heritage*.[71]

More so than most historians, Ali Mazrui's articulation of the coast's "triple heritage" acknowledged the interplay of the European, Arab, and African schemas described in this chapter. He also emphasized accounts of Portuguese brutality, the disruption of commerce, and religious conflict between Christian rulers and their Muslim subjects. Though accurate, such accounts overlook how the clan confederations of littoral Kenya prospered despite successive foreign occupations. Regardless of the violence perpetrated by these invaders, local communities built up their numbers and succeeded in forming military alliances that fostered cis-oceanic networks of patronage between coastal brokers and their inland suppliers. Port towns adopted centralized methods of extracting customs. Town residents began to form markets instead of restricting business to the privacy of their coral homes. Ships from Arabia and India came to the coast less frequently after the Portuguese conquests, but they returned alongside other European ships that carried novel goods.

Conventional histories of Portuguese brutality and Omani corruption in littoral Kenya sometimes overlook how speakers of Sabaki languages embroiled foreign officials in their local rivalries. At first glance, the discord among moieties and clan confederations enabled foreign officials from Portugal, the Ottoman Empire, and the Omani Sultanate to assert authority from the turn of the sixteenth century until the mid-eighteenth century. Yet the eighteenth-century rivalries among the Mvita and Kilindini of Mombasa Island, the Nabahani factions in Pate, and the Zena and Suudi of Lamu also show how moieties manipulated the Portuguese and Omani occupiers. One word for "moiety" in Kiswahili is *mkao* (those who sit together).[72] The leaders of these moieties occasionally mixed their pastimes with their politics by plotting intrigues in the "clubs" in which they sat to play games of bao and cards.[73]

Despite their rivalries, the dozens of conurbations that speakers of Sabaki languages formed in earlier times coalesced into just two domains in the eighteenth century: one led by Pate, north of the Sabaki River, and the other led by Mombasa to its south. Their rivalry promoted the notion that there should be a single political union that stretched from Pate in the north to Pemba in the south, and from these offshore islands to the *nyika* wilderness in the west. Notably, the routine inclusion of Chimijikenda speakers in these alliances shows that speakers of Sabaki languages considered religious fault lines irrelevant to their political communities in the eighteenth century, even if adherence to Islam was essential for political legitimacy among Kiswahili speakers. By 1813 Mombasa was on the verge of consolidating littoral Kenya into a single country when Lamu invited Oman back into the region; but other communities shared a similar vision of littoral unity. Far from floundering in the global political currents that followed in the wake of Portuguese ships, speakers of Sabaki languages responded by imagining a shared littoral identity that gave little heed to the boundaries of religion and language that would inscribe ethnic boundaries in the twentieth century.

FIVE

Practicing Muslims, Marginalized Pagans

*Accommodating Arab Orthodoxies
in the Zanzibar Sultanate, 1813–1895*

> Those who used to call the council
> are the ones to be called today.
>
> —Muyaka bin Haji al-Ghassany

EVERY YEAR POLICE close the streets at the edge of Old Town in Mombasa, where Mombasa Road intersects with Digo Road. Families line up for a few hours to watch the annual *zefe* (procession) to Makadara Grounds, where they celebrate Maulidi ya Nabi, the birth of the Prophet Muhammad. In 2010 Muslim Boy Scout troops marched ahead of young men representing different Qur'an schools. Most of these groups dressed in matching tunics and gathered behind a banner to show their affiliation with different sects or Sufi orders. Every few minutes, they paused to dance and sing. As each group arrived at Makadara Grounds, they sang into a microphone for all to hear. Then they dispersed to enjoy ice cream, catch up with friends, and mingle with spectators.

By sunset, a wedding business had set up a stage and a separate seating area in which women could view the proceedings on a projected screen without mingling with men at the park. Some men clustered beneath the trees, but most gathered as a single body in front of the stage. The organizers led them in reciting, singing, and praying in unison for two hours. The afternoon festivities showcased the diversity of Mombasa's Muslims, but the evening assembly celebrated their shared devotion and common membership in the Islamic *umma* (community).

The annual Maulidi ya Nabi celebration seems to unify for one day the Swahili, Somali, Arab, and Indian Muslims of Mombasa; but the celebration is controversial. Some Muslims in Kenya consider *maulidi* celebrations to be *bidaa* (from Arabic *bid'a*)—an illegitimate religious innovation.[1] Such rhetoric aligns these critics with Salafi reformers, whose diverse global movement seeks to renew the religious practices of the earliest Muslims. Defenders of maulidi celebrations and other local practices often castigate Salafi reformers as "Wahhabi" who receive intellectual and financial support from organizations in Saudi Arabia and elsewhere.[2] Kenyan Muslims thus frame their local controversies over maulidi celebrations as part of

FIGURE 5.1. Zefe procession, Mombasa. Photograph by author.

138   INNOVATING ETHNICITY

global Islamic debates, but also through anti-imperialist rhetoric that valorizes local autonomy.³

Though such debates over orthodox Islamic practice almost certainly began with the first Kiswahili speakers who began practicing Islam in the ninth century, this chapter focuses on the nineteenth-century debates that opened a rift in Kenya's littoral society between Muslim Kiswahili speakers and (mostly) non-Muslim Chimijikenda speakers. Scholars often presume that this division into Muslim and non-Muslim zones preceded the founding of the Zanzibar Sultanate.⁴ This chapter argues instead that Kiswahili speakers did not abandon long-standing associations with the "pagan" escarpment until they sought recognition in the Zanzibar Sultanate as orthodox Muslims. In response, Chimijikenda speakers distinguished categories of political practice from traditional religion (*dini ya kienyeji*) so they could accommodate Muslim converts within their communities. The integration of the coast's Kiswahili speakers, but not their inland allies, into the Zanzibar Sultanate led speakers of Sabaki languages to segregate into exclusionary communities of religious practice.⁵

Despite these countervailing commitments, speakers of Sabaki languages continued to imagine themselves as part of a single littoral society. Their presumption of unity is exemplified in their responses to a revolt in 1895, when the vanquished Mazrui clan reasserted its claims to rule Mombasa and opposed the transfer of Mombasa and littoral Kenya from the Zanzibar Sultanate to Great Britain. Instead of distancing themselves from Chimijikenda speakers, the Mazrui clan relied on them to challenge the sultan's sovereignty, thus demonstrating the enduring potential for collective action across linguistic and religious boundaries in littoral Kenya.

LITTORAL ALLIANCES ON THE EVE OF THE ZANZIBAR SULTANATE

When Seyyid Sa'id bin Sultan became the sultan of Oman in 1804, he largely ignored the East African coast until Lamu requested his protection against the combined forces of Mombasa, Pate, and Giriama in 1813. He then isolated Mombasa by taking control of Pemba, Pate, and other coastal towns. However, Mombasa's Mazrui *liwali* (governor) stalled for time by arranging an agreement of protection with a British captain who stopped at Mombasa in 1824.

Lieutenants Reitz and Emery, who oversaw British interests in the short-lived Mombasa Protectorate, recorded their observations of Kiswahili- and Chimijikenda-speaking communities, illustrating the scope of their alliances in the early nineteenth century. For example, Reitz reported that the Kiswahili-speaking residents of Wassin Island, forty-five miles south of Mombasa, fled to the mainland to escape Busaidi raids. However, they told him they returned home because they feared more "the treachery of the wahnyekah [Wanyika] tribes," who spoke Chimijikenda.[6] Yet when Reitz arrived at the mainland town of Pongwe, its Chimijikenda-speaking residents emphasized their strong alliance with Mombasa. They told him they had joined Mbaruk bin Hemed, a Mazrui war hero, in battle to defend Mombasa's claims over Pemba. They even performed songs for Reitz that praised Mbaruk's exploits. Despite Pongwe's alliance with Mombasa, the people of Wassin preferred to go back to their island home and risk Omani raids instead of settling near Chimijikenda speakers in Pongwe.

In contrast, Lieutenant Emery highlighted the strong economic and political bonds that united Kiswahili-speaking residents of Mombasa Island with Chimijikenda-speaking communities on the near mainland. Though he noted the resumption of the grain trade with Pemba and other parts of the coast as a positive development, he emphasized that the "Whanikas [Wanyika] are the whole support of the island."[7] This support extended beyond the tree resin, ivory, and grain that Chimijikenda speakers brokered to Mombasa's merchants almost daily. Emery described how they also returned enslaved runaways to slaveholders, sought Mazrui assistance to mediate disputes, and offered allegiance, or at least recognition, to the liwali of Mombasa.[8]

Emery described how the Chimijikenda- and Kiswahili-speaking communities formalized this recognition when Salim bin Hemed deposed and replaced his uncle as liwali in 1825. Shortly after his ascension, the liwali sent for "the tribes of the Whanika [Wanyika]" to inform them that "the country is now entirely governed by the English."[9] When representatives from twenty-three of their settlements then visited the island, Salim persuaded Emery to give them gifts of cloth to demonstrate Great Britain's authority.[10] Portuguese accounts suggest that Chimijikenda speakers had expected such largesse upon the installation of a new ruler in Mombasa since the seventeenth century. While Portuguese observers described these payments as tribute, the liwali characterized them as gifts. The liwali's assumption that the Protectorate of Mombasa extended to these Chimijikenda-speaking communities suggests he considered them part of his polity. Together, Emery and Reitz's observations show that this crosslinguistic alliance extended as far south as Pangani (in northern Tanzania), even if some Kiswahili-speaking communities, like the residents of Wassin Island, had more ambivalent relationships with Chimijikenda speakers.

Although Seyyid Sa'id persuaded Great Britain to abandon the Mombasa Protectorate in 1826, he failed to subdue Mombasa for another decade. In 1837 both the Miji Tatu and the Miji Tisa tired of the Mazrui clan's succession disputes over the position of liwali. The Miji Tatu, once a stalwart supporter of the Mazrui clan, secretly agreed to facilitate the occupation of Mombasa. Within a year, the sultan arranged the lifelong exile, imprisonment, and likely execution of the last Mazrui liwali Rashid bin Salim (r. 1836–1837). The surviving members of the Mazrui clan scattered—some to Takaungu (north of Mombasa) and others to Gazi (on the southern coast of Kenya).

Mombasa's patricians relinquished their ambitions for primacy along the coast to retain autonomy within their town. The sultan formalized their authority with written compacts that acknowledged the leaders of each clan as sheikhs and the leaders of the two clan confederations as a *tammim* (pl. *matammim*)—a political title borrowed from Omani Arabic for the leaders of *ṭā'ifa* (confederations) in Oman.[11] Kiswahili speakers also translated their political schema into Omani terms by renaming their clan confederations: the Miji Tatu became the Thalatha Taifa (Three Confederations), and the Miji Tisa became the Tissia Taifa (Nine Confederations).

The written compacts also acknowledged the patronage that each of Mombasa's clans held over Chimijikenda-speaking communities. As officially appointed *matammim* of the sultan, perhaps they felt confident they could manipulate these new Omani imperialists to counter local rivals, just as they had managed Mazrui governors and Portuguese captains. However, the councils that ruled Mombasa's clan confederations increasingly took place in Zanzibar. Muyaka, a renowned poet of Mombasa in the early nineteenth century, mourned:

O the world has come to ashes, blowing like dust,
The wise ones have died while they still had their bravado,
The young fruit no longer ripens, and the green dries up.
Those who used to call the council, are the ones to be called today.[12]

ACCOMMODATING ARAB ORTHODOXIES

Seyyid Sa'id permanently relocated in 1837 to Zanzibar, where he consolidated his sultanate as a network of mercenaries, financiers, and merchants beholden to his personal patronage. They imported enslaved laborers to establish a plantation economy, and they expanded the exports of spices, resin, and ivory beyond the Indian Ocean to markets in Europe and the United States.[13] The sultan had abandoned the title of imam because he legitimized his rule through extravagant political patronage instead of religious piety. However, debates among Muslim immigrants, whom the booming economy drew from across the Indian Ocean to East Africa, made adherence to Islamic practice an essential component for the political legitimacy of his successors. Though Sufi saints, Sunni scholars, and Ibadi clerics disagreed about the permissibility of various practices, their disputes prompted Muslims to embrace Islamic orthodoxy, however their respective spiritual leaders defined it.

After 1837 most speakers of Sabaki languages abandoned armed resistance against Oman's sultans. Instead, they worked to accommodate their shared schema to a more intensive form of imperial rule under the Zanzibar Sultanate than they had previously experienced. Like European imperialists, Omani Arabs supported their own efforts to extract resources with professional soldiers and rhetoric about their innate superiority, but they also relied on local intermediaries who shaped their imperial projects. John Wilkinson has argued that Oman's centuries-long contact with East Africa meant that these disruptions were minimal; he rejected the description of Omani activities along the coast as imperialism.[14] However, Anna Bang and other scholars better reflected the perspective of Kiswahili speakers by stressing that the introduction of "textual Islam" by Omani and Yemeni immigrants undercut the spiritual and political authority of Kiswahili-speaking patricians.[15] All of these scholars have focused narrowly on Muslim communities along the coast. The cis-oceanic perspective adopted in this chapter reveals how Kiswahili speakers' accommodations to the Zanzibar Sultanate strained relationships with their Chimijikenda-speaking allies in littoral Kenya.[16]

Diminishing Authority

Prior to the nineteenth century, few Kiswahili-speaking towns in East Africa accommodated more than one Islamic *madhhab* (legal tradition) in the same political community. Indian merchants and Omani Arabs who settled in East Africa did not convert from their original *madhhab*, but they often worshipped alongside Muslims following the local Shafii-Sunni tradition, which had prevailed since at least Ibn Battuta's fourteenth-century visit to Mombasa. So despite centuries of Arab immigration, Kiswahili-speaking patricians—the *waungwana*—presided confidently over town rituals and guarded Islamic knowledge as the proprietary *uganga* (esoteric knowledge) of their respective clans. Omani sultans threatened the status of these waungwana as they imposed a centralized patronage network based in Zanzibar, promoted Arab civilization as superior, and encouraged immigration that further diversified the Muslim community of East Africa.

Seyyid Sa'id preferred a flat organization over which he could offer personal patronage. He appointed customs agents to collect tariffs, a governor in each port to assert political authority, military commanders to punish rebels and criminals, and judges to resolve legal disputes.[17] All of these officials reported directly to him, as did the two *matammim* of Mombasa. The Thalatha Taifa and Tissia Taifa used the written compacts of their *matammim* to assert their right to choose whom the sultan would appoint as judges in Mombasa and to exempt their increasingly profitable grain exports from taxation.[18] However, after Seyyid Sa'id's death in 1856, his successors appointed governors who supplemented their personal investments in plantations with land seizures.[19] When Barghash bin Sa'id (r. 1870–1888) became sultan, he replaced Mombasa's judges with men who drew a salary from him and canceled the clan confederations' exemptions from taxes on grain exports.[20] By encouraging Kiswahili speakers to look beyond the patricians of their respective towns for support and patronage, the sultans of Zanzibar diminished waungwana influence in each town.

Integrating every coastal town of East Africa into a single polity also created a common field for debates over Islamic piety and political authority. Muslims along the coast regarded the *baraka* (blessing) of Arab ancestry as indicative of both. Instead of aspiring to build the reciprocal ties intimated by the word *uungwana*, coastal patricians began to value *ustaarabu*, a new Kiswahili word for "civilization" based on an Arabic word that meant "to Arabize."[21] In Zanzibar those who aspired to Arab status adopted the outward trappings of Arab civilization, such as clothing styles and musical preferences.[22] They also began to distinguish between local traditions (*desturi*) and a new word for culture (*utamaduni*) drawn from an Arabic word that emphasized urbanity. The proliferation of Omani Arabic loanwords into Kiswahili during the nineteenth century suggests speakers' increasing desire to distinguish local practices from Islamic ones—with Arab Muslims' practices held up as the standard for deciding which was which.[23]

Besides adopting Arab fashion and peppering their speech with Arabic words, Kiswahili-speaking patricians Arabized their clan names and written chronicles, a deliberate effort to distance themselves from outsiders' designation of them as "Swahili." Patricians in Pate, in Lamu, and on the Benadir coast presented Arab lineages for their town founders. Towns to the south of Mombasa, including those on Zanzibar Island, asserted that they were "Shirazi"—a name derived from the Persian port of Shiraz. Mombasa's patricians were outliers in claiming both Arab and Shirazi descent.[24] They coined Arabic correlates for their clan names (e.g., *al-Jaufy* for Jomvu) to claim ancestral homelands in Arabia. However, they also asserted that Shehe Mvita, the founder of Mombasa, was from Shiraz.[25] By describing themselves as Shirazi or "as Arab as the Arabs," the waungwana challenged the monopoly on Arab descent that Omani immigrants regarded as a prerequisite for political leadership in Muslim communities.[26]

Unfortunately for coastal patricians, Omani imperialists refused to accept their claims to Arab or Shirazi descent. Omani scholar Sulaiman bin Said bin Ahmed Essorami expressed this perspective in a legal treatise he wrote during Sultan Khalifa's reign (1888–1890). He noted that a "sensible man does not believe" that Washirazi were *ma'ajami* (Persian) because "they ... have mixed with all clans [*qabīla*]."[27] He also questioned the religious commitments of "those who pretend to be Muslims among the Arabs and Wasawahili [*sic*: Waswahili]."[28] The syntax of his statement in Kiswahili indicates that his slander applied only to some Arabs but to all "Waswahili"—indigenous Muslims who spoke Kiswahili. His extended descriptions of different subject populations in the Zanzibar Sultanate reveal that the Omani ruling class perceived indigenous communities as non-Arabs, unbelievers, and potential criminals.[29] They organized a hierarchical schema that set three classes of Omani Arabs above their Nubian and Baluchi mercenaries, whom they derided nearly as much as the indigenous Comorian and "Waswahili" populations. Though these latter communities at least "pretended" to be Muslim, Essorami disdained the speakers of the Chimijikenda, Chagga, Seuta, and Nyamwezi languages who visited and resided in Zanzibar throughout the nineteenth century. He ignored their differences by grouping them together as *washenzi*, a word for "barbarian" derived from the Omani pronunciation of "Zanj" (i.e., coastal East Africa). He also applied this word to *mateka*, captives from Mozambique whom British navy officers had freed and settled in Zanzibar.[30] At the bottom of Essorami's schema lay the *koko*, which can be glossed as "bush dog."[31] He made the canine connotations of the word clear by noting that Baluchi soldiers often kept an enslaved man with a chain around his neck with them while they performed their duties.

Though Essorami described many groups defined by ancestry, only groups indigenous to East Africa appear in his descriptions of criminal punishment. Beyond the Kiswahili-speaking Muslims who resided in the port towns of the coast, indigenous mainland communities only received the attention necessary to exact punishment. He collapsed their complexities into generic names with connotations of barbarism, slavery, and criminality.

In order to escape these stereotypes, many people classified as washenzi aspired to be recognized as Waswahili. This strategy only increased coastal patricians' dedication to seek recognition as Arabs or Persians, lest they be classified with other, lesser indigenous communities. Since Kiswahili speakers failed to convince Omanis of their Arab and Persian ancestry, their ambitions in the Zanzibar Sultanate depended entirely on their commitment to Islamic practices that immigrating Arabs recognized as orthodox.

Three Immigrant Orthodoxies

Omani Arabs weakened the influence of waungwana by questioning their ancestry and piety, but it was a surge of immigrants into the Zanzibar Sultanate that directly challenged their local authority.[32] These migrants ushered in a new, if not unprecedented, era of debate about Islam in East Africa by insisting on standards of Islamic orthodoxy developed in the Arabian centers of Yemen, Mecca, and Oman.[33]

Many immigrants to the Zanzibar Sultanate came unwillingly as enslaved non-Muslim laborers from southeast Africa. Slaving merchants first focused on supplying the sugar plantations of Mauritius and Reunion; but in the 1830s and 1840s they began selling large numbers of enslaved laborers in Zanzibar to investors in clove plantations, including Sa'id bin Sultan.[34] The enslaved laborers worked the spice plantations and hauled the ivory that propelled Zanzibar's booming economy. Omani Arabs also expelled Oromo pastoralists around Malindi, which they resettled to establish grain plantations. The patricians of Mombasa also profited by purchasing enslaved people to work their smaller farms on the mainland around Mombasa Island. Though coastal patricians around Mombasa and Malindi did not invest in cloves, they participated in the plantation economy by growing grain to provision ships, plantations, and caravans.[35] Some of them made ad hoc arrangements to cultivate land controlled by the confederations of Chimijikenda speakers. Enslaved immigrants also became a source of authority for slaveholders because they served as armed supporters in political disputes and guarantees for loans.

After 1840 many immigrants from the Hadhramaut region in Yemen also flocked to East Africa. Many of these Hadrami took menial jobs as laborers, soldiers, and small traders, which undercut the ability of slaveholders to hire out their enslaved laborers. More importantly, those who claimed descent from the Prophet Muhammad contested patricians' monopoly on religious knowledge.[36] Some Hadramis, such as the Jamal al-Layl clan, had lived in East Africa for generations and were associated with the Alawiyya Sufi order based in Yemen.[37] Others joined Somali immigrants in promoting the Qadiriyya Sufi order in East Africa.[38]

These two Sufi orders disrupted the religious authority of Kiswahili-speaking patricians in three ways. First, Sufi orders introduced ambitious proselytizing efforts. Whereas earlier generations of Kiswahili-speaking Muslims treated Islam as valuable uganga to be guarded rather than disseminated, Sufis had the temerity to offer this knowledge to anyone, including the enslaved dependents of patricians. Second, Sufi orders popularized new forms of communal worship (*dhikr* [chant] sessions) and maulidi celebrations that attracted Kiswahili-speaking adherents as well as new Chimijikenda- and Kipokomo-speaking converts to Islam. By participating in a Sufi order, enslaved and formerly enslaved adherents could gain influence outside of the historic lineages, clans, and clan confederations that previously served as the gatekeepers of status in coastal towns. Third, Sufi orders redefined Islamic knowledge as "a distinct set of literate tenets which could be checked, controlled and debated."[39] This textual orthodoxy challenged the authority of waungwana lineages, which previously dominated oral and practical knowledge of Islam.

For example, Habib Swaleh (1853–1936) of the Hadrami Jamal al-Layl clan stirred up one of the first debates about maulidi in East Africa, after moving from the Comoros Islands to Lamu in 1870. As one of his first provocations, he allowed enslaved palm-wine tappers to perform "pagan" dances at his annual maulidi celebration. He also replaced the traditional Kiswahili recitation performed during the celebration with an Arabic one and scandalized Lamu's patricians by playing drums in a mosque during the celebration.[40] The patricians' efforts to ostracize Swaleh further endeared him to the lower classes of Lamu, and he eventually won over his skeptics when Arab Muslim scholars in Yemen endorsed his practices.[41] Though Swaleh's personal efforts were focused on Lamu, the graduates of his Riyadh Mosque College challenged patrician authority in every community of East Africa by serving as imams and *ulama* (religious scholars). Many patricians responded by joining Sufi orders and sponsoring maulidi celebrations themselves to retain some influence.

For Omani immigrants, waungwana affiliations with Sufi orders merely confirmed their suspicions that Waswahili were only pretending to be Muslim. They probably would have agreed with an early twentieth-century Ibadi man who explained: "The Sunnis are people who have mixed much with savages. They mix religion with noisy play and make great show of it."[42]

Though few Omani Muslims sought membership in Sufi orders, many of them began to listen to members of the Mazrui clan who resurfaced to challenge the doctrinal foundations of Ibadism. Sheikh Ali bin Abdullah al-Mazrui and his father had sought refuge in Mecca when Seyyid Saʻid expelled the Mazrui clan from Mombasa in 1837. Like others of Omani descent, they had retained their commitment to Ibadi Islam; but Sheikh Ali converted to Shafii-Sunni Islam while studying with renowned scholar and later mufti of Mecca, Aḥmad Zaynī Daḥlān (1817–1886).[43] Though most of the Mazrui clan had scattered to Takaungu or Gazi, Sheikh Ali returned to Mombasa, became a prominent teacher, and formed a wide network of scholars who promoted Shafii Islam throughout the coast. Compared to the parochialism of earlier Muslim scholars in Mombasa, they engaged more in Pan-Islamic debates about theology and the alarming influence of Europeans. Sheikh Ali wrote apologist works to defend Shafii theology against Ibadi scholars, and he asserted that the Mazrui clan should regain control over Mombasa's former domains. His textualist approach to theology and the reputation of the Mazrui convinced many Omani Muslims to convert from Ibadism to Sunnism without joining Sufi orders, which they considered too ecstatic.[44] As Shafii Muslims, the Mazrui clan aligned themselves with Kiswahili speakers and Hadrami Arabs in a bid to counter the influence of the sultans.

When Barghash bin Saʻid became sultan in 1870, he treated Omani conversions to Sunni Islam as a threat to his authority. Indeed, Wilkinson has argued that many Omanis in East Africa abandoned Ibadism in order to deny Barghash his "'constitutional' legitimacy as 'Defender of the Faith.'"[45] They were dissatisfied with his leadership because he increasingly depended on non-Muslim Europeans for his position. Great Britain and France had partitioned Seyyid Saʻid's domains into two sultanates following his death in 1856 to prevent a succession conflict. So the legitimacy of his successors in both Oman and Zanzibar depended on non-Muslim Europeans instead of Ibadi stakeholders in Oman. Barghash confirmed his weakness by failing to prevent Germany's unilateral declaration of a protectorate over the coast of Tanzania.

Barghash attempted to elevate his standing by aligning with the Omani Nahda, a movement that aimed to resuscitate the imamate of Oman in order to restore peace among its warring factions, thwart European imperialism, and offer an Ibadi alternative to the Sunni Wahhabi reform movement in Arabia.[46] He supported the movement by acting as a "pseudo-*da'if* Imam"—not necessarily a pious leader but one who heeded the counsel of Ibadi *ulama*.[47] Barghash consulted with advisers from various Omani factions, Kiswahili-speaking judges, and even a Shia Muslim. However, he also imprisoned Sheikh Ali bin Abdullah al-Mazrui and others for proselytizing to Omanis in Mombasa and Pemba.[48]

Despite his intolerance for conversion, Barghash's support for the Nahda ironically promoted Islamic pluralism in Zanzibar. For instance, he established a printing press for Nahda scholars to raise the profile of Ibadism within the emerging Pan-Islamic movement. This approach provided a foundation for debates among Muslims who disagreed about theology and practice but also recognized each other's faith as valid, in deliberate contrast to Wahhabis, who categorized Sufis and the followers of other Islamic sects as unbelievers. Rejecting "puritanical" logic allowed East Africans to accommodate many different Muslim communities.

Yet this tolerance for diversity in the Zanzibar Sultanate stemmed in part from Omanis' refusal to assimilate other Muslims. Few Kiswahili speakers converted to Ibadism, which involved a multigenerational process of intermarriage that Omani Arabs were loath to offer to those with questionable Arab ancestry.[49] Since assimilation into Omani communities was out of reach for most Kiswahili speakers, they tried to overcome Omani derision by adopting Arab orthodoxies offered by Hadrami Sufis and the students of a Meccan mufti. Omani Ibadis regarded these Sunni traditions as too ecstatic or theologically deficient, but they at least acknowledged their adherents as practicing Muslims.

Despite their initial success in retaining control of local offices after 1837, making claims to Arab and Persian pedigrees and accepting the textualist orthodoxies of Arab immigrants, coastal patricians lost control over local affairs. Sufi orders offered alternative paths to respectability for enslaved laborers, and Omani sultans used imprisonment and patronage to redirect waungwana and their potential followers to Omani patrons in Zanzibar. However, by aligning themselves with Sunni scholars trained in Mecca, and particularly Sheikh Ali bin Abdallah al- Mazrui, Mombasa's patricians challenged the influence of Sufi orders led by Hadrami immigrants and the preeminence of Omani Ibadism along the coast. These debates over orthodoxy required Muslim sects to tolerate one another, but they also encouraged Kiswahili speakers to sever their relationships with non-Muslim Chimijikenda-speaking allies.

DERIDING THE *WANYIKA WASHENZI*

Both the waungwana who claimed Arab status and the enslaved immigrants who claimed belonging as Waswahili in the nineteenth century strove to distinguish themselves from washenzi, a derogative stereotype used to refer both to newly imported captives and to willing, but non-Muslim, immigrants from the African interior. The waungwana and the Waswahili also applied the term to the Chimijikenda-speaking Wanyika (bush people) in nearby settlements.

For centuries, the name Wanyika had been simply descriptive: it indicated, from the perspective of coastal dwellers, their inland neighbors' mastery over the nyika environments, whose resources sustained the littoral economy. However, the stereotype acquired increasingly negative connotations under the Zanzibar Sultanate. In addition to being *kafiri* (unbelievers), the members of inland clan confederations had mostly relocated to rural homesteads, preserving their ancestral towns (*makaya*, sg. *kaya*) only for ritual observances. As coastal patricians joined an *umma* defined by urban living and adherence to Arab orthodoxies, they abandoned their political alliances with the patricians who led inland makaya. To the townspeople of the coast, the dispersed residents of the Wanyika became country bumpkins who lacked *utamaduni* (urbanity) and *ustaarabu* (civilization). Chimijikenda speakers accommodated the political regime of the Zanzibar Sultanate by adopting a bitter rhetoric of betrayal against their former allies, marshaling economic resources to join in the booming economy, and experimenting with ways to retain the loyalty of Muslim converts to their respective makaya.

Rhetoric of Betrayal

Zanzibar's sultans occasionally received Chimijikenda-speaking visitors while visiting Mombasa, but they had little interest in securing clients beyond the port towns, except along the coast of Tanzania.[50] Their disinterest made it difficult for Chimijikenda-speaking communities to exchange their goods directly at the coast. Chimijikenda speakers in the 1840s feared entering Mombasa because "the 'twelve sheikhs' who pay to represent the Wanyika in Mombasa [were] no longer able to provide protection and Wanyika [were] sometimes jailed for the debts of other Wanyika."[51] In Mombasa affiliation with an inland clan confederation became a liability.

For the duration of the Zanzibar Sultanate, inland confederations northwest of Mombasa included Giriama, Jibana, Chonyi, Kambe, Ribe, Kauma, and Rabai. The Duruma confederation south of Rabai started to disperse as its members extended southward, and at least five confederations south of Mombasa (Mtaye, Shimba, Longo, Digo, and Jombo) began consolidating into the Digo confederation.[52] The Giriama and Digo populations were the most populous by far; each of the other confederations included only a handful of settlements and hamlets. Each confederation considered its own dialect to be unique, but modern linguists group them into just two dialects: Northern and Southern Chimijikenda.[53] The missionary-linguist John Ludwig Krapf, who lived at Rabai from 1846 to 1853, treated the dialects of Giriama and Digo as variants of Kinyika, the language shared by the smaller confederations between them.[54] Krapf's grouping reflects how Chimijikenda speakers understood the relationships among their confederations at the time.

In addition to documenting languages, Krapf recorded some of the tensions between Mombasa and its former inland allies. He emphasized the haughtiness of Mombasa's residents toward the Wanyika, even as he noted their mutual interests: "The secular interests of the Wanicas [Wanyika] are intimately connected with those of the people of Mombas[a]. Both live in peace with each other, except that the latter according to the usual Mohamedan haughtiness look on the Wanicas as obstinate Koffas [*sic:* kafiri (unbelievers)] or infidels."[55] Krapf also described a mixed Muslim-Wanyika village (Kidutani) in which a well-marked physical boundary separated the two polarized communities "lest quarrels arise amongst the mixed population."[56] Krapf's reports indicate that speakers of these Sabaki languages had begun to emphasize contrasting elements in their schemas rather than the elements they shared. Instead of organizing complementary relationships between inland and coastal clan confederations, their respective accommodations to the political demands of the Zanzibar Sultanate led Kiswahili speakers to adopt contrastive stereotyping. The derogatory labels "Wanyika" and "kafiri" both implied the other.

Krapf described how Wanyika confederations drew together—as the outsiders they had been declared—to complain that their wards had been sold to slaving dhows headed for Arabia. He noted that "the Wanicas always take vengeance on the delinquents by closing their chief market places to the Mombassians."[57] By "delinquents," Krapf meant creditors in Mombasa who did not allow Chimijikenda speakers to redeem dependents whom they had pawned for grain during three major famines in the nineteenth century. Closing markets to all "Mombassians" inverted the collective punishment that Chimijikenda speakers suffered in Mombasa when imprisoned for debts incurred by members of their confederations. Their complaints about abduction demonstrate how inland patricians reciprocated the epithets of barbarism leveled against them in Mombasa with accusations of treachery. Although such rhetoric cultivated a negative stereotype of Mombasa's Muslim merchants throughout the escarpment, Chimijikenda speakers' shared resentment did not coalesce into political unity.

The Escarpment Economy

As in previous centuries, inland patricians attempted to draw on the collective strength of their confederations, title societies, and age-sets to ensure viable terms of exchange. Though Chimijikenda speakers never coordinated their interests as a single political community during the era of the Zanzibar Sultanate, each confederation developed regionally valued commodities and capitalized on the increased demand for grain exports. Most inland patricians organized their efforts at the clan or homestead level. For example, Rabai's patricians increased their investments in producing palm wine.[58] While tapping palm trees was an old technique, they began producing the alcohol in large enough quantities to supply increasing regional demand. In addition to recreational use, Chimijikenda speakers considered palm wine essential to rituals at their makaya. Still, mobilizing an entire clan confederation for one's personal interests was beyond the capacity of most people because the heterarchical organizations that led clan confederations usually diffused individual wealth and power.

Besides making products for consumption along the escarpment, clan confederations participated in the expanding caravan trade. Many of their young men served as porters, but they also intercepted Kamba and Nyamwezi ivory caravans that passed through their territory.[59] They could then sell the ivory at the regional seasonal markets that Krapf described or take them to the coast.[60] Also available at such markets would be local provisions for porters and tree resin destined for markets as distant as Boston, Massachusetts. Participating in the provisioning and caravan economy as producers, porters, and brokers connected inland confederations to the economy of the Zanzibar Sultanate, though their involvement in political matters at Mombasa greatly diminished.

The Giriama confederation was the most successful of the inland clan confederations in the nineteenth century. Many Giriama partnered with Mazrui investors who had founded Takaungu before their clan's expulsion from Mombasa.[61] The Mazrui purchased enslaved people to cultivate grain along the coastal plain, which Omani planters had made safe by driving off Oromo pastoralists.[62] Giriama men also participated in the grain trade that provisioned slave ships, caravans, and enslaved laborers in Zanzibar and Pemba. Meanwhile other Giriama, and Duruma, raised cattle in numbers large enough to support extravagant feasts at maulidi celebrations and *ngoma* (dance) competitions.[63]

The Giriama confederation grew in population as well as extent by receiving *watoro* (refugees from slavery, sg. *mtoro*) and some of the excess population from smaller confederations, whose opportunities for expansion were more constrained.[64] Giriama relationships with watoro varied. Slaveholders could often persuade Giriama to return watoro, but Giriama men also valued them as dependents who bolstered their own influence. When slaveholders in Takaungu raided the watoro community of Fuladoyo in 1882, the displaced watoro even convinced some Giriama to join them on a punitive raid against the Mazrui town of Takaungu.[65]

Mijikenda-speaking communities welcomed watoro in part because they needed dependents to clear land, haul ivory, and tap palm wine; and many of their youth sought brighter opportunities at the coast. For example, many of those who cultivated grain near Takaungu aligned themselves with coastal patrons through conversion to Islam and adoption into coastal lineages.[66] The influx of watoro fleeing the coast made up for this loss to some degree. Yet many inland parents and other kin described the new affiliations of their children as brazen betrayals.[67]

Inland patricians responded to the hemorrhage of their dependents to the coast by trying to reinforce the collective strength of their age-sets. Missionary Charles New noted the wide participation in age-sets in 1873: "Every adult expects to become a member of the Kambi [the eldest age-grade], and there are not many who do not attain the honour. Thus it becomes a parliament composed of almost the entire people."[68] If more youth were advanced to the elder *kambi* age-grade and given authority in the community, perhaps they would be more likely to contribute to the well-being of the patricians. The patricians' exclusion from direct participation in coastal commerce made the organizations associated with the makaya their principal path to political prominence. Inland patricians thus continued organizing title societies from which they derived their remaining (but declining) authority and prestige relative to Muslim patricians.

Accommodating Chimijikenda-Speaking Muslims

Chimijikenda speakers' accommodations of Islam in the nineteenth century reflect the competition among clan confederations over dependents and land. Chimijikenda speakers initially called converts to Islam *adzomba,* the same word they used to refer to Kiswahili speakers. This word is the Chimijikenda pronunciation of the Kiswahili word *mjomba* (maternal uncle) and thus reflects a long history of arranging marriages between Chimijikenda-speaking women and Kiswahili-speaking men.[69] Using the word *adzomba* to refer to Muslim converts from Chimijikenda-speaking communities suggests that the assimilation of individual men into coastal society was not uncommon before the middle of the nineteenth century.[70]

As historian David Sperling has argued, this "urban Islamization" of individuals increased as Chimijikenda speakers realized their interests in Mombasa and other coastal towns would be more secure if they converted to Islam and joined a town clan.[71] Sperling distinguished this pattern of individualistic conversion experiences from the establishment of entire communities of Muslim Chimijikenda speakers in the latter half of the nineteenth century. Although Sperling focused on tracing this major change in the pattern of Muslim conversion in East Africa, the community histories he compiled from oral histories also illustrate distinctive ways that Chimijikenda speakers accommodated Muslim religious practices. The integration of Muslim converts within Chimijikenda communities largely depended on how each community categorized religious or political practices in the schemas of their respective clan confederations.

After 1850 some Muslim converts began to establish independent Muslim settlements near the Mazrui town of Takaungu instead of living in coastal towns. Their founders were often successful traders who chafed at the idea of being someone else's dependent. Since these new settlements were independent of any Arab or Kiswahili-speaking Muslims, they signaled a novel enough change that Chimijikenda speakers adopted a new word for Muslim converts: *mahaji* (sg. *haji*).[72] It is derived from hajj, meaning the pilgrimage to Mecca that all Muslims are enjoined to perform once in their life. Though few Chimijikenda speakers had the means to perform hajj, the name symbolized their journey away from their kafiri past.

"Mahaji" was an appropriate reference for Muslim converts because they visibly and physically separated themselves from other Chimijikenda speakers. They adopted clothing styles of the coast (*kanzu* tunics for men and *kaniki* wraps in place of *hando* skirts for women), and they began speaking Kiswahili. But first and foremost, they left the escarpment. As Sperling's informant Ali Abdallah Tsori explained, "In those days, Muslims couldn't live with pagans. . . . When a pagan became a Muslim, the first thing he had to ask himself was, 'Now, where can I live?'"[73] Of course, in many cases, people emigrated away from the escarpment first and only converted afterward to ease their assimilation. They nevertheless made a conscious effort to maintain physical and social distance from old relations. Ribe converts in Mombasa, for instance, would not eat in the same room as non-Muslim relatives when they visited, and one early Digo convert is said to have used two sets of utensils when preparing food for herself and her non-Muslim husband.[74] Those who insisted on eating separately did so to follow Islamic prohibitions against meat that was not butchered by a Muslim in the prescribed (halal) way.

Patricians in most clan confederations tried to accommodate mahaji in a new schema that distinguished the religious elements associated with the makaya from its judicial or political functions. Some Chimijikenda-speaking communities accommodated mahaji by inviting them to butcher the animals so they could all eat together. Mahaji often fulfilled their familial obligation to attend and contribute to funerals, even when held in the ritual centers of the makaya.[75] However, many mahaji refused to live in their confederation's kaya or drink palm wine, which was an expected element in ceremonies that unified clan confederations.

Patricians sometimes responded to the religious taboos of Muslim (and Christian) converts with hostility. For example, missionary Thomas Rebmann reported that a Digo convert to Islam was killed for refusing to participate in traditional customs. He also described how the Giriama ostracized and exiled a Christian convert because he would not join the Wanika in the observance of their ancient customs.[76] Yet these examples of overt hostility were rare. The patricians of Rabai and Ribe usually tolerated the presence of Muslim and Christian converts in the nineteenth century—particularly if they participated in the confederations' ceremonies and feasts. For example, Krapf observed that a Muslim from the coast who had inherited land from a Rabai man gained membership in the community "by accommodation to their superstitious practices."[77]

So although there is some evidence for hostility against mahaji from Chimijikenda speakers, inland patricians more often aimed to retain their loyalty. Sperling's account of the mahaji community of Mtanganyiko, for example, illustrates how clan confederations maintained close relationships with Muslim converts.[78] Mtanganyiko was founded in the 1850s or 1860s by Swalehe Lenga, a Ribe man who married a Kauma woman and moved near her family, about an hour's walk from Takaungu, north of Mombasa. (Ribe and Kauma are two of the smaller Chimijikenda-speaking confederations.) He became a prosperous trader, converted to Islam, and married a Mazrui woman. Though this second marriage demonstrated his full integration into the Muslim community of Takaungu, disputes with Mazrui Arabs led him to move to the head of Kilifi Creek. There, he established Mtanganyiko with at least five other Kauma mahaji. Since the new town was more conveniently located for trade with inland clan confederations, it surpassed the trade volume of Takaungu. Chimijikenda speakers from the Kauma, the Giriama, and even the distant Digo confederations flocked to the town. Many of them converted to Islam, if they had not already. Swalehe and other Muslims in the community erected the first Friday Mosque to be built in the region without any aid from Kiswahili or Arab speakers. They called it Kauma Mosque, obviously proud of their affiliations with that confederation. They also established a Qur'an school led by mahaji who had studied in Mombasa.

In contrast to the *adzomba* converts in coastal towns, the mahaji of Mtanganyiko continued participating in many of their clan confederations' customs. As people moved to Mtanganyiko, Swalehe directed them to cluster in different areas of the town according to their respective clan confederations. Then each of these clusters formed their own council of elders.[79] Sperling's informant Ali Abdallah Tsori recalled that the council members of Kaya Kauma would even invite Kauma Muslims from Mtanganyiko to sit with them and discuss important matters. However, the refusal of mahaji to drink palm wine or eat meat slaughtered by the non-Muslim kaya elders set them apart. The kaya elders were also reticent to travel "to the Muslim zone" of Mtanganyiko because "they were afraid of coming under Muslim influence."[80]

The boundaries between Islam and what came to be called *dini ya kienyeji* (traditional religion) thus began coming into focus. Non-Muslim patricians along the escarpment had to deal with Muslims who valued some elements of their schema, like organizing councils, but would not participate in others, like drinking palm wine. The relationship between Kauma and Mtanganyiko demonstrated the tolerance of Islam among Chimijikenda-speaking patricians. However, their accommodations also showed that the mahaji required Chimijikenda speakers to articulate which elements of their shared schema were "religious" (and therefore anathema to Muslims) and which were not. Such distinctions created a social boundary between Kauma and Mtanganyiko that increased with each passing generation.

In contrast, distinguishing between religious and political activities in the makaya facilitated wider conversion to Islam within the five Digo confederations. Several of the most prominent converts to Islam south of Mombasa even became *wanatsi* (sons of the soil)—the elders who performed ceremonies in makaya, such as prayers and sacrifices for rain.[81] Many of these men had converted to Islam after building business relationships with Baluchi soldiers stationed at Fort Jesus. Others became Muslim through their associations with the Tangana clan in the Miji Tatu (i.e., Thalatha Taifa) of Mombasa or with residents in the Digo settlement of Mtongwe, half of whom were Muslim by 1875.[82] Some family histories emphasize the role that the Mazrui lineages exiled in Gazi played in facilitating conversion.

While the mahaji who associated with the Kauma confederation maintained a strict distance from the "religious" ceremonies of the kaya, the Digo *wanatsi* continued to participate and lead them. For instance, Muslim convert Kivoyero Mwapodzo sacrificed animals in kaya ceremonies and was particularly admired for his effective prayers for rain. Several of Sperling's informants, speaking as second- and third-generation Muslims, explained the involvement of early Muslim converts in kaya ceremonies as evidence of their half-hearted or shallow conversion.[83] However, since Mwapodzo was both Muslim and a kaya elder, there was no impediment for mahaji to partake of the animals he offered in sacrifice.

Though the Muslim status of the kaya leaders in Digo communities sidestepped the specific problem of eating unclean (haram) meat, the widespread conversion of Digo communities between 1880 and 1920 presented other incongruities. Regarding marriage, Shafii legal principles required a dowry paid to the bride rather than bridewealth to her family. At funerals, Muslim customs at the coast preferred a shorter three-day mourning period rather than week-long ceremonies with dances that marked communities as washenzi. Most disruptive of all, the Qur'an set forth guidelines for patrilineal inheritance that contrasted with Digo matrilineal customs.[84] Debates about how to reconcile these contradictions reverberated through the colonial era and into the twenty-first century. Since the

Muslim converts in Digo communities included the leaders of their makaya, they maintained the coherence of their clan confederations. However, as Muslims insisted on remaining inland, rather than absconding to the coast, they motivated their communities to recategorize the elements of their shared schema so that they could separate Islam from customs, like inheritance, that they considered beyond the purview of religion.

Wanyika Conversions to Islam

The relationship between clans and knowledge detailed in part 1 of this book and the political accommodations of the nineteenth century explain why Chimijikenda-speaking communities, as opposed to individuals, rarely converted to Islam until the late nineteenth century. Prior to the enthusiastic proselytization efforts of Sufi orders in that era, speakers of Sabaki languages regarded Islamic knowledge as a kind of uganga—the specialized, esoteric knowledge of clans—that Muslims protected by not teaching it to members of other clans. At the same time, any inland clan confederation could benefit from this uganga by allying with a Muslim clan or seeking the aid of a Muslim healer, just as they could commission carpenters along the coast to carve the gates of a kaya. *Adzomba* could also learn Islamic knowledge if they joined a Muslim clan. The communal ownership of knowledge and the value that non-Muslims placed on their own uganga discouraged conversion efforts but also encouraged complementary relationships among littoral communities.

After the establishment of the Zanzibar Sultanate, Kiswahili speakers' commitment to orthodox forms of Arab Islam made their alliances with washenzi communities untenable. However, proselytizing to potential partners allowed them to overcome this barrier to business relationships. For example, according to a tradition related to Sperling by Mwapodzo's son, Mwapodzo's business partner made their trading relationship contingent on conversion by saying, "You are a Nyika, become a Muslim and then we will eat together, and I will buy from you."[85] The exclusion of the Wanyika from Muslim communities, both in communal eating and in trading partnerships, is clear. Yet it was only after Muslims in the Zanzibar Sultanate committed to the exclusionary religious identities of Arab orthodoxy that Chimijikenda-speaking Wanyika became marginalized enough that patricians who aspired to lead inland communities, rather than escape them, sought conversion to Islam.

Many of the Chimijikenda speakers who converted to Islam wanted to retain the strength of their clan confederations and salvage profitable alliances with Muslims along the coast. However, for Chimijikenda speakers who were hostile or indifferent to Islam, the Mazrui lineages at Takaungu and Gazi offered another option. Once the Mazrui converted from Ibadi to Sunni Islam, they often sponsored the conversion of Chimijikenda individuals. However, in contrast to Thalatha Taifa and Tissia Taifa, Mazrui claims to Omani Arab and orthodox Muslim identity were indisputable; so they could partner with non-Muslims without worrying about their reputations for piety. In addition, from their new settlements at Takaungu and Gazi they maintained autonomy within the Zanzibar Sultanate. As the orthodox accommodations of Mombasa's Thalatha Taifa and Tissia Taifa strained relationships with so-called Wanyika confederations, Chimijikenda speakers built closer ties with the Mazrui clan than ever before.

DEFENDING THE FAITHFUL

Mbaruk bin Rashid al-Mazrui (1830–1912) was around seven years old in 1837, when Seyyid Sa'id ordered the abduction of his father, the last Mazrui liwali of Mombasa. By the 1850s Mbaruk had assumed leadership of his exiled lineage in Gazi and embarked on a quixotic quest to reunify the coast under Mazrui rule. Relying on over a thousand armed fighters, including many mahaji (Muslim converts) and watoro (runaways), he launched armed campaigns against coastal towns in the 1850s as well as in 1871–1874 and 1882–1887. His raids forced sultans to reassert their sovereignty over littoral Kenya at the price of annual subsidies that recognized Mazrui autonomy in Gazi. However, his final uprising in 1895–1896 targeted the British government, which had agreed to administer the coast on behalf of the Zanzibar Sultanate. Once he started fighting the imposition of non-Muslim rule, Mbaruk claimed a title that the sultans had reserved for themselves: Commander of the Faithful.

As British reports of the 1895–1896 conflict attest, the authority of the Zanzibar Sultanate in those territories that eventually became

Kenya hardly extended beyond the cities of Lamu, Malindi, and Mombasa. The hinterland between the Ozi River and Malindi was scarcely populated. South of Malindi, from Kilifi to Takaungu, Mazrui sheikhs acted as patrons of inland communities to profit from grain exports. The Mazrui lineages in Gazi did the same south of Mombasa. So while British reports describe Mbaruk as a rebel, littoral communities' efforts to hamper Great Britain's campaign against Mbaruk's "rebellion" indicate their tacit recognition of Mazrui sovereignty.[86]

However, the fertile stretch of coast between Mombasa and Takaungu avoided Mazrui influence. The towns there were presided over by Hamis bin Kombo al-Mutwafy, the *tammim* (administrator) of Mombasa's Tissia Taifa (Miji Tisa) confederation, which had habitually undermined Mazrui initiatives in the previous century. Though he and the leaders of the other clan confederations were rewarded for their help in ejecting the Mazrui from Mombasa in 1837, they lost influence when the sultan's officials and soldiers promoted their own commercial interests. After learning in 1887 that Sultan Barghash planned to lease the coast's administration to the privately held Imperial British East Africa Company, al-Mutwafy was incensed that the sultan would allow Christians to rule over Muslims; he left Mombasa for good and settled thirteen miles north in Mtwapa.[87]

British observers presented al-Mutwafy's position as bigotry, but the lease violated basic parameters of the decades-long debate among Sunni and Ibadi Muslims about religious orthodoxy and political legitimacy. Both Sunni reformers and proponents of the Ibadi Nahda movement emphasized that a just Islamic society was necessary to combat European imperialism. The Zanzibar Sultanate had already lost the coast of Tanzania, Kilwa, and the Witu Sultanate to Germany; relinquishing direct control of the coasts around Mombasa further deteriorated the legitimacy of Sultan Barghash, who died in 1887. When the British Foreign Office arranged to manage Mombasa and the surrounding coasts from his successor in 1895, officials assured the sultan's Muslim subjects that they would uphold Islamic law, but only within the ten-mile-wide strip of coast that British and German negotiators had arbitrarily set as the effective dominions of the Zanzibar Sultanate.

The formalities on which British officials insisted to maintain the sultan's "quasi-sovereignty" fooled no one on the coast. In a letter Arthur Hardinge, consul-general to Zanzibar, dismissed the disgruntled attitudes of Mombasa's leading Muslims as inevitable whenever "a once-dominant Moslem race or class, is under the rule of a non-Moslem Government."[88] He also belittled "the ignorant Wanyika" who did "not distinguish the English Government from that of the Sultan." He continued, "They know of it only as the white power in the coast towns."[89] However, for coastal and inland communities in littoral Kenya, the situation was clear enough. The Zanzibar Sultanate had withdrawn, and Great Britain was yet another foreign empire that intended to take its place.

A few months before the official transition between the Imperial British East Africa Company and the British government, the Mazrui sheikh of Takaungu died, prompting a succession dispute. Though Mbaruk bin Rashid initially stayed out of the conflict, both the rival parties forced his hand by demanding his support. When the anti-British claimant sought refuge with Mbaruk, British messengers insisted that he turn over the rebel. Mbaruk stalled for time, took up the flag of war, and adopted the "title of Commander of the Faithful (Emir-el-Mumenin), which in the Zanzibar dominions belongs to the [sultan] alone."[90]

Mbaruk's final uprising lasted from June 1895 until April 1896, with hostilities stretching from Vanga near the border with German East Africa to the Arabuko-Sokoke forest northwest of Takaungu. The latter's satellite communities, including the mahaji town of Mtanganyiko, were the primary targets of Mbaruk's three thousand fighters. Meanwhile, the new British East Africa Protectorate tried to hold a dozen towns with seven hundred irregular soldiers seconded from Zanzibar.[91]

Besides being outnumbered, British officials had to counter support for Mbaruk in Mombasa and inland communities. Hardinge complained that a "party at Mombasa" sympathized with Mbaruk "as Moslems resisting Christians" and offered him "supplies and information."[92] Muslim mutineers refused to muster once the holy month of Ramadan commenced at the end of February. Inland confederations and patricians also withheld support from the British officials.[93] At the height of the uprising, Mbaruk could count allies and friends among the Ribe, the Duruma, the Digo, and several allied mahaji communities near Mombasa Island. In October 1895, Mbaruk also gained the support of Hamis bin Kombo al-Mutwafy, who abandoned his confederation's long-standing enmity with the Mazrui clan on the chance that together they could throw off British authority.[94]

Unfortunately for Mbaruk's supporters, the British army received reinforcements from an Indian regiment of about three hundred troops with experience suppressing insurrections in South Asia. They swept through the escarpment, pushing Mbaruk and his followers south to German East Africa. By previous arrangement, German officials took them into custody as they crossed the border. Within a few months, Mbaruk was retired in Dar es Salaam, where he remained in exile until his peaceful death.

Though scholars have hesitated to describe Mbaruk's final rising as a jihad, he shrewdly built a wider alliance than in his previous risings by tapping into Muslim anxiety about the prospect of Christian rule.[95] Hardinge reported, "From the moment he really broke with us he assumed the title of 'Commander of the Faithful' and made a point of always speaking of us and even of our Moslem adherents as the 'Kafirs.'"[96] Mbaruk thus reflected a consensus that Arab immigrants and Kiswahili-speaking communities had developed over the past half century. The Omani Nahda movement, the Pan-Islamic sympathies of Shafii Muslims, and the Sufi orders had together promoted the idea that society would be more just and politics more legitimate if founded on Islam. The protectorate threatened that consensus by imposing non-Muslim rulers. Rather than a critique of their theology or religious practices, Mbaruk's description of Britain's Muslim supporters as kafiri castigated them for choosing political expediency over commitment to Muslim rule. He could not have employed this exclusionary religious rhetoric in his earlier rebellions because the sultans of Zanzibar had already claimed legitimacy as Muslim rulers. Against British officials who routinely sided with Christian missions and harangued coastal communities about the immorality of slavery, Mbaruk's claims to be the "Commander of the Faithful" garnered much support.

There is no evidence that adopting this Islamic title cost him support among Chimijikenda-speaking communities, perhaps because they were trying to accommodate mahaji converts in their communities rather than exile them. If anything, Mbaruk's status as a leader in the most prestigious Muslim family in the region accentuated his appeal as a person with powerful uganga and *baraka* (blessing). Besides obtaining an endorsement for his cause from his cousin Sheikh Ali al-Mazrui, Mbarak had already outwitted and outlasted several sultans. He received strong support from many watoro and mahaji communities who fought for him. And even members of the Giriama, the Digo, the Duruma, and the Ribe lent support and fought alongside Mbaruk, notwithstanding the fact that these confederations' leaders claimed neutrality to avoid collective retribution. Mbaruk ignored the boundaries between the "Muslim coastal towns" and the "pagan hinterlands" to resuscitate his clan's sovereign claims over all kinds of communities who supported his vision of an autonomous, unified littoral polity.

It is probably coincidental that Mombasa's annual maulidi procession begins at the corner of Mombasa Road and Digo Road, an intersection that unintentionally testifies of the cis-oceanic connections between Mombasa and the Mijikenda communities that surround it. However, it is no accident that the procession skirts the edge of Mji wa Kale (the "Old Town" neighborhoods of Mombasa's indigenous clan confederations) and does not approach Fort Jesus (the old Mazrui residence). Some of the old waungwana lineages and Mazrui families have found new avenues of influence as businessmen, scholars, Sufi leaders, and judges, but their claims to lead the Muslim communities of Mombasa Island faded under the Zanzibar Sultanate.

This chapter has examined how Kiswahili and Chimijikenda speakers accommodated Arab imperialism in the nineteenth century by articulating exclusionary religious identities. Debates among Arabs and Kiswahili speakers about who counted as a practicing Muslim raised the stakes of piety and marginalized inland neighbors who did not practice Islam. At Mombasa, the Muslims who accommodated Arab standards of Islamic orthodoxy abandoned centuries of close political alliance with their neighbors. They not only derided their Chimijikenda-speaking neighbors as *Wanyika washenzi* (barbarian hillbillies) but they also excluded non-Muslims from trade, withdrew traditional protections from them, and encroached on their territory. The clan confederations of Chimijikenda speakers adjusted to their exclusion from Mombasa's Islamic *umma* by increasing production of palm wine, grain, and cattle for regional markets. Yet an increasing number of them converted to Islam so they could regain access to the commercial networks of the Zanzibar Sultanate. The growing vigilance among waungwana over legitimate Muslim identities prompted enslaved laborers and youth from the escarpment to present themselves as Waswahili to coastal communities. Inland clan confederations reacted to their youths' exodus to the coast and the derision of *dini ya kienyeji* (traditional religion) by accommodating Muslim converts within their confederations. Digo communities even allowed Muslim converts to administer key rituals in their makaya. While the coastal *umma* demanded exclusive devotion to the Muslim faith, inland communities accepted multiple and flexible strategies of affiliation. Muslims could belong to an inland confederation if they participated in what struck Christian missionaries as "superstitious practices"; but doing so risked their Muslim affiliations on the coast.

The criteria of religious practice thus marked the coast as homogeneously Muslim and the coastal escarpment as kafiri. The discourses contrasting town with wilderness, Muslim with kafiri, waungwana with washenzi, and Arab with Wanyika laid the foundation for a new schema—shared throughout littoral Kenya—that separated the inland confederations of Chimijikenda speakers from the Kiswahili-speaking confederations of coastal Muslims. Despite Mbaruk bin Rashid's efforts to draw these communities back together under his banner, these novel boundaries of politics and religion endured to shape the "tribal" categories that the next generation would articulate to officials of the British East Africa Protectorate.

SIX

Gazetting Identity

Assembling Tribes and Demarcating Districts in the British East Africa Protectorate, 1895–1920

> They form an alien community with ... different history ... from any other component part of the district.
>
> —J. M. Pearson, district commissioner, Rabai

A FEW TARMAC roads cut through Rabai's hilly terrain, but most of the rural homesteads are connected by footpaths. *Voro watsa!* (Hello, friends!) is the customary greeting when meeting someone along the path. However, when entering a homestead, visitors call out, *Enye?* The word means "owner," as in the phrase *enye ntsi* (owners of land); the Kiswahili equivalent is *wenyeji*.[1] These greetings acknowledge the claims that residents make to the homesteads between the footpaths.

My research associate William Tsaka emphasized the importance of these daily interactions as he took me around the land of his lineage. During one of our walks, we came across one of his neighbors, who was weeding. She was suspicious of me and asked who I was. After I answered her and we took our leave, William said she was trespassing to farm on his family's land. I saw no obvious boundaries, but William explained that his father had walked him around the boundaries many times—a routine with no formal ceremonies but plenty of practicality. Land disputes are common in Rabai. Many plots have never been surveyed or registered with the government, so knowledge of which plots of land belong to whom is embodied in the community.

When British officials established the British East Africa Protectorate in 1895, they introduced new techniques of governance developed in India. The British government in India had jurisdiction over the British consulate in the Zanzibar Sultanate and heard legal disputes among Britain's Indian subjects who lived there. This subimperial government's influence continued when officials promulgated the Indian Penal Code in the British East Africa Protectorate in 1897, promoted Indian immigration, and stipulated that the protectorate should be treated as a "district of a presidency in India" for the purposes of various statutes.[2] One of the governing techniques that officials transferred from India was the surveying of territory. Instead of daily walks, they erected cement beacons, whose marks indexed an abstract, imaginary grid of latitudes and longitudes that officials could reference when they transferred to a new station.[3] They used surveyors to organize districts that divided their subjects according to British perceptions of their differences.[4] British officials published—or "gazetted"—district boundaries in the *Official Gazette of the British East Africa Protectorate*. As the repository of government acts, the *Gazette* recorded legal ordinances, the assignments of government officials, and the territorial boundaries of administrative units. They also gazetted the names of African men who were recognized as the "headmen" of specific locations.

As British officials demarcated the interior boundaries of their colony, they leaned heavily on the embodied knowledge of their colonial subjects. Speakers of Sabaki languages took these opportunities to align administrative boundaries and official categories with their own schemas for organizing communities in littoral Kenya. These districts— and the new tribes they circumscribed— have set the contexts of political engagement for speakers of Sabaki languages and their neighbors ever since the formative years of the British

East Africa Protectorate.[5] Colonial officials discouraged Africans from forming organizations that crossed these boundaries, but their inability to keep people in place demonstrates how the mobilities inherent to littoral societies challenged British efforts to impose territorial sovereignty in the Indian Ocean.

THE LIMITS OF DESCENT

Previous research on the invention of Swahili and Mijikenda as tribal identities has focused narrowly on the criteria of descent and kinship as instruments for acquiring government benefits in urban contexts. A. I. Salim's political history of the "Swahili-speaking" people of the Kenyan coast, for instance, detailed how being classified as Arab (or not) determined government benefits and legal rights.[6] Justin Willis elaborated on these debates over Swahili and Arab identity by showing that Mombasa's clan confederations strengthened their claims to Arab or Persian descent by ostracizing Chimijikenda speakers in Mombasa. Kiswahili speakers begrudgingly accepted their classification as "Swahili," but only after they partnered with officials to remove other Africans from that category through the principle of patrilineal descent. After those hailing from Chimijikenda speakers' inland confederations could no longer be classified as "Swahili," they organized urban labor gangs affiliated with their natal clan confederations so they could claim property and burial rights "back home" in the escarpment. Whereas historians previously presented Swahili and Mijikenda communities as centuries-old identities, Willis carefully traced how these two ethnic groups developed in tandem with each other in the colonial era.[7]

However, these instrumentalist explanations for the invention of ethnicity in the protectorate fail to account for continuities between the new rhetoric of tribalism and the ways that speakers of Sabaki languages organized earlier communities. For Willis the fixed, permanent boundaries that British officials erected between tribes contrasted sharply with precolonial communities that he described as loose, ephemeral networks. This analytical contrast is difficult to sustain given both the flexibility of modern ethnicity and the resilience of precolonial collective identities associated with clan confederations. In addition, this approach cannot account for the vernacular criteria that speakers of Sabaki languages compiled over previous centuries to distinguish one another in their littoral society, such as why Kiswahili speakers demanded recognition of their Arab and Persian descent while Chimijikenda speakers mobilized labor via natal membership in clan confederations.

Willis's primary focus on urban contexts also overlooked the importance of territorial imagination, as opposed to ancestral origins, in debates over tribal identities. Conflating descent claims with ethnicity showed how tribal identities formed and functioned in the urban contexts of Mombasa, but it only hinted at the ways Chimijikenda speakers created the corresponding communities that made laborers' strategy of seeking rural patrons viable. While Willis emphasized the motivations for Mombasa's laborers to seek patronage from headmen in the escarpment, this chapter explores the negotiations among district commissioners and headmen over the physical and cultural boundaries that established who had jurisdiction in specific locations and territories throughout the protectorate's "coastal strip."

INVENTING TRIBALISM

Examining how speakers of Sabaki languages shaped the internal district boundaries of the protectorate shows that neither they nor the British officials to whom they presented potential tribes controlled this process entirely. In theory, protectorate officials wanted administrative districts to align with the homeland of a tribe—a discrete, culturally homogenous group of inmarrying kin led by a chief. Coincidentally, this colonial definition of *tribe* coalesced strategies of affiliation that Sabaki speakers had kept logically distinct. Lineages reproduced themselves through exclusionary marriage alliances, clans claimed rights over town quarters and other locations, and the increasing commitment to religious identities in the nineteenth century gave rise to blocs of communities that regarded themselves as culturally homogeneous, especially in terms of religious practice. As British officials looked for tribes, Sabaki speakers obliged by combining smaller communities. One result of assembling and nesting these communities into one another was that lineages and clans stopped straddling boundaries among clan confederations.

Although speakers of Sabaki languages had often grouped lineages and clans into clan confederations, the invention of tribes introduced at least three changes to the previous schema. First, British officials pressured the leaders of tribes to forbid people from moving among confederations because mobile people disrupted administrative practices that sorted populations (and their territories) into different legal jurisdictions and systems of adjudication.[8] Second, Sabaki speakers continued to consider themselves members of clan confederations anchored to prominent settlements, but British policies encouraged them to also imagine themselves as members of tribes, whose homelands extended across bounded spaces. Third, their novel tribal boundaries responded to British officials' perspectives about which groups were culturally similar enough to coalesce.

The governing strategies of the British Empire, in contrast to its Portuguese, Omani, and Zanzibari predecessors, required subjects to present their communal identities to state authorities routinely for approval and official recognition in law and policy. So speakers of Sabaki languages formed tribes, for the first time, not only through negotiations among one another but with an imperial government that limited their options. Still, negotiations over the elements of Swahili and Wanyika identities, district boundaries, the authority of Islamic judges (qadis) and councils, and the mobility of individuals and communities show that the complex relationships among Sabaki speakers and their neighbors could not be contained within the tribal schema they helped create.

DEMARCATING MUSLIM ZONES ALONG THE COASTAL STRIP

In Mombasa ancestry determined the tribal identities of Kiswahili speakers, while geographical origin identified the tribal affiliation of Chimijikenda speakers. Outside of Mombasa the precise shape of territories from which the speakers of these two Sabaki languages were supposed to have originated emerged through debates that conflated religion with culture. The treaty of protection that Great Britain signed with the sultan of Zanzibar granted British officials control of a strip of coast that extended ten miles inland and stretched southward from Witu (north of Malindi) to the border with German East Africa (later Tanzania). As part of the treaty, Great Britain agreed to maintain Islamic law for the sultan of Zanzibar's subjects. However, they interpreted this provision to apply only to Arab and Swahili communities, all of which identified as Muslim. For everyone else in the strip, British officials relied on "native customs" to adjudicate disputes. Even Wanyika who identified as Muslims and resided outside of native reserves were judged according to the customs of their designated homeland. British officials thus linked the demarcation of territories with efforts to appoint "Arab administrators" and native headman who would govern them.

Officials consulted extensively with local communities because they wanted to avoid lawsuits in the protectorate's own courts. For example, in 1913 Charles Hobley asked a district commissioner to revise a map of a proposed reserve west of Mombasa: "A boundary... bounded by lines of Latitute [sic] and Longitude is undefinable on the ground and *it would be impossible for anyone to prove in Court* whether any person was inside or outside of the Reserve boundary."[9] In response the district commissioner noted that he would need to "make a tour round the respective areas with natives having local knowledge" since government maps did not include names of streams and hills.[10] So officials' ignorance gave littoral communities extensive influence over the protectorate's internal boundaries.

However, British officials' schema for organizing territory also limited indigenous input. They divided protectorate territory into different categories: titled private land, Crown (i.e., public) Land, land trusts (waqfs) for Muslim mosques and cemeteries, and reserves for forests, game, and tribes. The latter grouping betrayed their assumptions that tribal populations could be managed along the same principles as wildlife and trees. As early as 1908 the government provisionally marked out a single large "Nyika Native Reserve" that stretched from the border with German East Africa to the Sabaki River. However, its officials found it difficult to separate Muslim and non-Muslim communities in the areas between the reserve and the coast, as well as along the coasts north and south of Mombasa.

It proved impossible to align legal jurisdictions defined by a person's status as a Muslim or a "pagan" with territories defined by uniform legal codes. First, officials could not rely on the notional ten-mile limit to separate Muslims from Wanyika communities anywhere in the protectorate. Northwest of Mombasa an official drew the "Osborne line" (named for himself) on a map to keep the "lands of the pagan Jibana on the west and of the Mohemedans whether Arabs or converts to the East," even though the Jibana confederation lay fully within the ten-mile strip.[11] Officials marked out a similar "Watkins line" south of Mombasa to keep the Thalatha Taifa from encroaching on Digo land and a "Baratum line" inland from Malindi to prevent Muslim encroachment on Giriama land.[12] They then attempted, with limited success, to convince people to resettle themselves on the side of the line assigned to their presumed religion.

South of Mombasa several Digo confederations occupied territory from the Shimba Hills right up to the coast, where their settlements intermingled with a half-dozen Arab and Swahili settlements.[13] In addition, the government granted a concession there to a European company called the East African Estates. One district commissioner divided the area into seventeen locations that he felt reflected "racial, political and Geographical consideration." Most locations were uniformly Digo or Duruma; but Pongwe contained a mix of Swahili, Segeju, and Digo residents. He figured they could get along because the latter two groups had "lost all traces of their old tribal organization."[14] He also described the Mwera location as a mixture of Kamba and Duruma residents, who were impossible to separate.

Officials faced a similar issue west of Mombasa: if they measured the ten-mile strip from the high-water mark of the ocean tides (as stipulated by treaty), several non-Muslim settlements, including Rabai, would have been included because they nestled against tidal, salt-water creeks that extended several miles inland.[15] Marking distance from the shore instead of the creeks had the opposite effect: it placed Jomvu within the territory planned for the "Nyika Reserve."[16] Although Jomvu was settled by members of Mombasa's Tissia Taifa, its three mainland settlements were closer to the district station at Rabai than Mombasa. By placing Jomvu in Rabai District, administrative convenience took precedence over the official policy of isolating Muslims from pagans.

A second challenge to separating Muslim and non-Muslim jurisdictions was a shortage of administrators. Officials placed Mombasa, the coastal escarpment, and the Taita Hills into the Seyyidie Province, named for an honorific title of the sultan of Zanzibar. As officials carved it up into reserves and districts, they often drew boundaries that cut across the western limit of the "ten-mile strip" so that a single official could administer territories from a more convenient station. When Great Britain distinguished (but still did not demarcate) the area of the ten- mile strip as the Kenya Protectorate in 1920, district boundaries crossed the notional boundary between it and the Kenya Colony so often that no one could positively identify where they divided.[17]

Administrative vestiges of the Zanzibar regime also disrupted efforts to restrict Islamic law to the coast. When Arthur Hardinge, consul-general of Zanzibar, assumed control of the new protectorate in 1895, he asked officials appointed by the sultan to stay on in a subordinate "Arab Administration" to oversee the courts that administered Islamic law.[18] But British officials complained that their Arab colleagues promoted conversion to Islam in a bid to increase their personal influence.[19] So as a limitation on Muslim officials' authority, an 1897 ordinance required that a Muslim judge (qadi) could only serve as an assessor in cases involving Muslims in the "Mohammedan Coast Region," while "an elder . . . of the tribe to which the . . . defendant belongs" would be chosen as the assessor in "non-Mohammedan"regions.[20]

The requirement that assessors should share the tribal affiliation of defendants highlights a final administrative challenge to the neat division of the protectorate's indigenous population. This imperial classification project was hampered by the mismatch between the protectorate's inflexible tribal schema—which acknowledged two major indigenous categories (Swahili and Wanyika) in the ten-mile strip—and the organization of many clan confederations. Kiswahili speakers maintained their affiliations to the Tissia Taifa or Thalatha Taifa of Mombasa, as well as confederations in Lamu, Siyu, Pate, Faza, and the Bajun coast, while Chimijikenda speakers belonged to one of (at least) nine clan confederations in 1895—Giriama, Jibana, Ribe, Chonyi, Kauma, Kambe, Rabai, Duruma, or Digo.[21] In addition, the retention of the Omani schema made it difficult to accommodate Chimijikenda speakers who converted to Islam, particularly if they decided to remain in "non-Muslim" territories. Dividing districts according to religious criteria along the coast required a far greater commitment to re-sorting and relocating communities than colonial officials could manage.

British officials imagined that traditional chiefs would be the key to managing non-Muslim indigenous communities in the protectorate.[22] However, the deliberate diffusion of authority by Chimijikenda speakers among title societies, councils, age-sets, clans, and lineages made the search for chiefs fruitless.[23] Officials tried to elevate men from patrician lineages as tax collectors, labor recruiters, and judicial arbiters. Few showed any interest, in part because the 1902 ordinance that granted authority to headmen also subjected them to fines if they failed to maintain good behavior in their locations.[24]

To attract more headmen, officials expanded the position's authority and resources in the Native Tribunal Rules of 1911 and the Native Authority Ordinance of 1912. These reforms organized headmen into government councils similar to the *kambi* (councils) that led Chimijikenda-speaking confederations. Kambi councils were assemblies of patrician elders who had (ideally) assumed the authority of age by advancing to the eldest age-grade and sharing their wealth in feasts. Their composition balanced the interests of all clans in the confederation. In contrast, the government councils were intended as centralized instruments of colonial control.

District officials often complained about the ineffectiveness of government councils.[25] However, Charles Hobley, who became provincial commissioner of the coast in 1912, deemed them an overall success. He argued that the "Nyika tribes . . . were much more happy . . . obtaining justice from the councils than in the district courts under the old regime."[26] In his view the government councils were simply kambi councils whose authority had been gazetted and co-opted by the government. However, British officials often appointed as headmen junior members of the kambi age-grade who lacked influence.[27] The members of some government councils managed to reframe imperial demands as opportunities to establish themselves as patrons for urban laborers. However, most Chimijikenda speakers tended to view government councils as poor imitations of kambi councils that nevertheless helped mediate relationships with the government.[28]

Councils often claimed stewardship over *makaya* to frame their authority in religious terms that British officials would honor. As historian David Bresnahan observed, British officials were initially indifferent to makaya, which they regarded as insignificant abandoned settlements.[29] However, once British officials were persuaded that the makaya ceremonies were essential to the councils' authority, they began protecting makaya as sacred sites.[30] One official, for example, expressed his outrage about unauthorized logging near a Duruma *kaya* by suggesting there was "no reason why the Kayas should not be entitled to the same respect as a Church or Mosque."[31]

British officials interpreted the common orientation to makaya among the "Nyika tribes" as a shared religious commitment that culturally distinguished their population from other tribes, and particularly from Muslims at the coast.[32] Bresnahan argued that this acknowledgment emboldened headmen to claim not only the clearings and ceremonial sites in the makaya but also the territories that surrounded them.[33] Once recognized as the trustees of these communal lands, the council members could offer them as assets to laborers in Mombasa who would eventually return home to retire. Instead of seeking authority by building consensus, these aspiring leaders joined the governing hierarchy of the British Empire. Getting recognized as a headman or a council member in the "Official Gazette" gave men (but never women) control over the distribution of territory in "tribal" homelands that the government made artificially scarce through imperial fiat.

As Hobley expanded the use of government councils after 1912, he emphasized the need to separate Muslim and "tribal" jurisdictions. "Mixed" populations interfered with officials' ability to form government councils that could resolve disputes without close oversight. District commissioner Charles Dundas spoke in praise of Bombo: "[Where] all the inhabitants are Wadigo, there is no alien settlement, nor alien shambas [farms]."[34] At Mtongwe, just across the creek from Mombasa's southwest shore, he complained that a council of six Wanyika and six Swahili elders disputed often about "Nyika custom" and "Mohamedan Law."[35] Dundas also reported on Miritini, a railroad junction south of Rabai: "People consist of a jumble of all tribes and the land all belongs to aliens. There is no Council and there can be none as the people are too mixed."[36] Gazetting "native reserves" and the jurisdictions of government councils was supposed to resolve such inconsistencies.

THE JOMVU PETITION

As speakers of Sabaki languages realized that British officials used religious criteria to separate them into administrative categories, they began to manipulate that logic in their disputes with one another. An argument over Jomvu's inclusion in Rabai District shows how the Tissia Taifa of Mombasa manipulated officials' notions of religion and culture to revise district boundaries and increase their influence in the protectorate.[37]

In a letter dated May 2, 1913, Assistant Commissioner J. M. Pearson expressed the desire to make Mombasa's subdistrict of Rabai into an independent district. Since Jomvu was administered from Rabai, he noted, "No Arabs live in Jomvu . . . , so it should not be difficult but for the contrary influence of the Tissia Taifa."[38] The Tissia Taifa supported a faction in Jomvu that opposed the government council there.

Before Pearson could finalize his plans, the government council at Jomvu faced an existential crisis. In late August 1913 they ordered the eviction of Mfaki bin Salim, whom they accused of insubordination and immoral behaviors related to gambling and prostitution.[39] Instead of accepting the council's authority, Mfaki sought help from members of the Tissia Taifa in Mombasa, who convinced Provincial Commissioner Charles Hobley to halt the eviction order. Mfaki also hired a European lawyer to contest his eviction on the grounds that the people of Jomvu ought to be subject to Islamic law since they were Muslims. Part of his petition reads as follows:

> 3rd Recently the Government Mzee [headman] of Maunguja with *a so called council* have taken upon themselves to decide cases and have caused much dissatisfaction among the rest of the people of Jomvu and the powers exercised by this Mzee going even to the extent of expulsion from the Village are entirely illegal and even if such Powers *are in accord with Wanyika custom they cannot be legally exercised over Mohamedans* [Muslims] such as the Petitioners. The *Wajomvu are similar to the Wachangamwe* and in Changamwe there is a duly appointed Mudir who decides cases according to the Mohamedan Law.

4th The Petitioners very strongly *object to any return to Paganism and pagan customs* such as is implied in a grant of new Powers to the Mzee and a council.[40]

Mfaki's petition expressly associated the Jomvu council with paganism and Wanyika custom. To argue for the placement of Jomvu within an Islamic jurisdiction, Mfaki even went so far as to compare Jomvu favorably with Changamwe, a confederation affiliated with the rival Thalatha Taifa.[41]

At first Pearson disputed the petitioner's characterization of councils as pagan, noting that Jomvu's council enforced Islamic law as far as they understood it.[42] However, his claim that councils could administer Islamic law was undercut by the official policy that distinguished the system of councils among Chimijikenda speakers with the Islamic courts overseen by the Arab administration in the "Mohamedan zone." In response to the petition, the provincial commissioner, district officials, and a *liwali* met at Jomvu on October 25. They reaffirmed the authority of the council, but they rescinded the eviction order.[43]

In the midst of this dispute, Pearson submitted a new recommendation for the formation of the "Nyika Reserve and Rabai District" that expressly excised Jomvu on the grounds of cultural and religious difference:

> By this boundary it is noted that Jomvu is cut out from the Rabai District. This has been done because *Rabai is to be a Nyika District with tribal organization of local councils* to be supervised from the District Office, whereas the Wa Jomvu are Mohammedans *alleged Arabs from Shirazi* with no innate tribal organization, whose interests are with the Coast and not in the Nyika country. . . . *As it is they form an alien community with different customs, different religion, different standards of morals and conduct, different history, different temperament, from any other component part of the district.*[44]

Mfaki and his supporters in Jomvu thus used the government's administrative categories to support the Tissia Taifa's ongoing campaign to assert Arab identity. Though Pearson described them as "alleged Arabs," he also affirmed that they were "alien" rather than indigenous. For Mfaki bin Salim the immediate result was freedom from the authority of a local council in return for lax oversight from more distant Islamic judges. For cattle traders and women potters at Jomvu, confusion over pass laws that regulated movements across the district boundary created new burdens.[45] British authorities thus accepted the arguments of the Tissia Taifa and realigned the district boundaries accordingly. This adjustment is illustrative of other efforts to transform districts into tribal homelands distinguished by cultural criteria.[46]

Jomvu's excision from the Nyika Native Reserve shows how the Tissia Taifa used the rhetoric of religious and cultural difference, which they had articulated under Omani rule, to persuade British officials that Muslims should be subject to Islamic courts instead of "pagan" councils, regardless of where they lived. Specifically, British officials followed the lead of the Tissia Taifa in recategorizing councils as "innate tribal organizations" ill-suited to the administration of Muslims. Yet the government councils they instituted did not precisely replicate the councils organized by speakers of Sabaki languages, who thus discounted their authority. For every man who deigned to become a tax collector, there were many more who learned to hide from him in the forest.[47]

THE GIRIAMA UPRISING AND REMOVALS

While many Chimijikenda speakers contributed to official projects for reserving homelands and appointing headmen, the Giriama clan confederation defied British authority with determination. Most of the Giriama lived inland from Takaungu and Malindi, where the fertile coastal plain was widest. British officials considered these territories, which were beyond the ten-mile strip, to be part of the Nyika Native Reserve, though they did not officially gazette the reserve until March 1916.[48] Their failure to corral Giriama communities into this reserve reflects Sabaki speakers' continued mobility across the protectorate's internal boundaries.

Instead of seeking work at Mombasa, many young Giriama men established independent homesteads along the coastal plain in partnership with Omani Arabs in the mid-nineteenth century. The abolition of slavery had devastated the productivity of plantations at the coast, but Giriama farmers revived exports by recruiting clients from among those who were emancipated. As early as 1891 a quarter of the Giriama population had moved north of the Sabaki River, and others were encouraged by the protectorate's administration to move there after 1895.

As historian Cynthia Brantley argued, the Giriama's experiments with commercial agriculture diminished the influence of the kambi council at Kaya Fungo, the main Giriama kaya, which was located a few miles north of Rabai.[49] However, Hobley inadvertently revived the influence of the kaya elders in 1913 by promoting government councils. His demands for allegiance to his appointees unified two categories of Giriama men who had grown apart: Big Men (who exported grain and ivory) and the patrician kaya elders (who derived influence from managing the ceremonies of Kaya Fungo).

Hobley tasked the district commissioner, Arthur Champion, to bring Giriama communities under closer control because he wanted to recruit laborers to Mombasa and push down wages. After Champion set up a station at Mwangea, south of the Sabaki River, he established government councils and required young men to work as government porters. He also encouraged them to seek work in Mombasa. After facing much opposition, he instead recommended that the government focus on the Giriama communities' obvious potential in reinvigorating the agricultural sector.[50]

Provincial Commissioner Hobley dismissed this recommendation. In June 1913 he visited the region and threatened to remove Giriama households living on "Crown Land" north of the Sabaki River if they did not honor the government councils and provide wage labor. Though earlier administrators had supported these Giriama settlements, Hobley wanted to lease large blocks of the land north of the river to European companies without worrying about the patchwork of indigenous land claims that thwarted development closer to Mombasa.

Hobley's June tour directly precipitated the Giriama Uprising of 1913–1914, which proceeded in two phases. A woman named Mekatilili wa Mwenza (ca. 1860–1924) prompted the first phase. Though she was not even a member of the women's *kifudu* society, she gained prominence by serving as a crucial bridge between the kambi council and Big Men like Ngoyo wa Mwavuo—the son of a Digo immigrant who prospered in the ivory and grain trade but showed no interest in joining title societies at Kaya Fungo.[51] She traveled to communities on both sides of the river to rally against British efforts to employ young men.[52]

In August 1913 many of the Giriama responded to Mekatilili's call to attend a meeting at Kaya Fungo, where the leaders of the men's and women's title societies administered new oaths. As with oathing and revival movements that emerged later in central Kenya, the leaders first called for a restoration of moral behavior.[53] They forbade doing laundry in reservoirs of drinking water or arranging marriages with strangers, as well as adopting Western styles of clothing, like trousers for men. Soiled water could corrupt the body; unions with outsiders threatened the multigenerational reciprocities that bound the clans of the Giriama confederation together. According to Brantley's informants in the early 1970s, these oaths did not compel the Giriama to fight the British government; rather they enjoined them to stop cooperating with British demands for information about the (illicit) ivory trade, guides to help police and hut-counters, and labor. Mekatilili claimed that British labor demands amounted to slavery, regardless of any wages earned, because sending young men to work at the coast removed them from participation in Giriama life. It also threatened the livelihood of women like her, who depended on male relatives for access to land.[54] Crucially, the oath forbade anyone from appearing before government councils.[55]

For two months, no Giriama dared present a case to a government council. When Champion returned from a medical leave, he found all his work establishing government councils ruined and began urging the government to compel Giriama respect for British authority. In November 1913, Hobley ordered the kambi elders at Kaya Fungo to establish a new kaya closer to Champion's station. He then deported Mekatilili and Wanje (a member of Kaya Fungo's *vaya* society and kambi council) to Kisii near Lake Victoria (Nyanza).[56] Hobley also secured permission from Governor Belfield to "evacuate" the Giriama from the area north of the Sabaki River, but he took a leave of absence before it could start.

In July 1914, Mekatilili and Wanje returned after hiking overland for more than two months and four hundred miles to find that the resistance had carried on in their absence. Unfortunately, they arrived just in time to witness officials dynamite Kaya Fungo on August 4 because the kambi council would not relocate their kaya. The destruction of the kaya was demoralizing to Giriama communities, and officials exiled Wanje and Mekatilili again so they would not stir up trouble.

The second phase of the uprising began despite these leaders' absence when the protectorate resumed its demands for laborers. Champion, who had returned to his station at Mwangea, misinterpreted an informational telegram about the need for porters to serve in World War I as an official order. Determined to meet an impossible quota of one thousand men in six days, he permitted his recruiters to use force. One of them raped a Giriama woman to provoke men out of hiding. The Giriama responded by besieging the station on August 17 and killing the rapist.[57] In response to further rumors of unrest, the acting provincial commissioner, Charles Hemsted, arranged for the government to dispatch a company of the King's African Rifles to put down the Giriama Rebellion.

So it was the King's African Rifles who fulfilled Hobley's earlier threat to displace Giriama settlers from the north bank of the Sabaki River. They burned Giriama villages in several campaigns between September 1914 and January 1915. District commissioner F. S. F. Traill then continued the removal with government police until British officials launched a final punitive expedition in August 1915. Officials even forbade other communities in Malindi District from offering sanctuary to Giriama refugees in an effort to corral them into the Nyika Native Reserve. They sorted Giriama out from "friendly Wanyika" refugees and moved them to the proposed reserve.[58] Though the government claimed success, many Giriama households evaded the evacuation. This prompted Arthur Gibson, district commissioner of Malindi District, to initiate removal operations of all Giriama who had settled east of the Baratum line in 1916, including those who had lived there since before the uprising. Hobley approved the project, thinking that Gibson was only planning to remove Giriama vagrants without employment or residence agreements with landowners. It was left to the Malindi Commission of Inquiry of 1916, appointed to investigate a complaint about another set of improper evictions, to uncover the miscommunication and stop the Giriama removals. The Giriama Uprising demonstrated both the potential and limitation of Britain's military capacity. They could coerce an entire population to relocate their homes to a reserve; yet doing so endangered any semblance of legitimacy for their government councils.

THE MALINDI COMMISSION OF INQUIRY

During the Giriama Uprising, the British army and colonial police displaced thousands of Giriama, some of whom had no idea what the war was about.[59] The removal also swept up "friendly" Chimijikenda speakers from other confederations who had settled among the Giriama. The government probably would have ignored these plights if the violent evacuations had not also disrupted the work of the Land Arbitration Board in Malindi. William de Lacy, a British magistrate who adjudicated land claims in Malindi, accused the provincial administration of illegally intimidating Muslim claimants into withdrawing their title applications by burning homes during the Giriama Uprising. He also condemned the government for relying on Arab administration officials to persuade applicants to drop their claims.[60] De Lacy called the Malindi Commission of Inquiry of 1916 "the commission of camouflage" because it substantiated most of his claims but disguised their severity: the final report euphemized evictions as "moves," discounted the traumas of state-sponsored arson, and blamed the weather instead of forced evacuations for widespread famine.[61]

At least the commission gave displaced refugees an opportunity to speak. Their testimonies demonstrate that the rural areas of the protectorate were nearly as cosmopolitan and diverse as the urban coast. Speakers of Sabaki languages from various confederations, immigrants from beyond the protectorate, *mahaji* converts to Islam, and *watoro* (refugees from enslavement) disrupted British officials' neat territorial categories as they asserted their freedom to move about the country.

Many of the testimonies to the commission demonstrate that Chimijikenda speakers maintained their affiliations to confederations elsewhere despite their settlement among the Giriama. For instance,

FIGURE 6.1. Paziani borderland, from "Map of Gaji Hill and Neighborhood," MPG 1/1099, National Archives of the United Kingdom. Reprinted with permission.

Kaura wa Ndoro's community of five villages "went to Malindi and signed a paper [indicating] that [they] had nothing to do with the war." Though Kaura lived among the Giriama for thirty-three years, he identified himself and two of these villages as Kauma and the other three as "Wanyika . . . *not Giriama*."[62] For their demonstration of loyalty, the gvovernment told them to head south to the territory of the Kauma confederation, but they could get no food there. A different Kauma community eventually took them in at Paziani—a place within the ten-mile strip that was south of the Sabaki River, east of the Nyika Native Reserve and west of the Baratum line (see figure 6.1). Displaced watoro communities also scrambled to find new places to live south of the Sabaki River, without the benefit of a homeland or

Gazetting Identity   183

confederates to offer relief. They had to squat on private or Crown Land, where they were subject to rent.

The testimonies of these watoro revealed a confused colonial administration working at cross-purposes with itself in what the Malindi Commission labeled the "ex-slaves move." In 1895 a government official encouraged the watoro community to move to Bure, north of the Sabaki River.[63] There they lived until the Giriama Uprising, when Harold Montgomery, district commissioner of Malindi, instructed them to move south to Paziani because he was planning to launch indiscriminate removal operations.[64] Unbeknownst to Montgomery, Governor Belfield had already approved Paziani for inclusion in a land concession to the Magarini Syndicate, a European company. So when Montgomery's successor, Ralph Skene, became aware of the watoro at Paziani in late 1914, he told them to move to Pumwani, an area north of the river but east of the evacuation zone. He wanted to "clear natives off of it for Europeans."[65] Instead, the watoro community made an arrangement to move to Maangani, which was east of the Baratum line, to land owned by the father of Liwali Seif bin Salim, an Arab administrator in Lamu. This arrangement contradicted the provincial commissioner's directive to settle squatters on European land (where they could be induced to labor) rather than on Arab land (where they usually just paid rent). Skene could not object to the watoro's private arrangements with the liwali, but he burned the watoro's homes in Paziani in January 1915 to dissuade them from returning. This demolition happened to coincide with a Kenya African Rifles campaign to burn homes and eject Giriama from north of the Sabaki River. The watoro community's movements show the inconsistencies in official classifications that led administrators to make contradictory decisions about who belonged where.

These dislocations only came to light because the Land Arbitration Board in Malindi was trying to make sense of claims to private land in Paziani and other locations between the Nyika Native Reserve and the Baratum line from which the watoro and other communities were evicted. The owners of these plots had disregarded a personal request from Liwali Ali bin Salim at a public meeting in 1908 to stay east of the provisional boundary. A map of the Baratum line was confirmed and signed by the colonial governor in 1908 and visibly cut by another liwali, Seif bin Salim, in 1911. But since it was never officially gazetted, de Lacy noted that "the line had no legal signification, and [he] should have heard the applications to the West of the line if they had not been withdrawn."[66]

De Lacy was particularly incensed when a claimant, Omar bin Athman bin Shehe, reported during arbitration in February 1915 that the government burned down his grandmother's house the previous month on property he was claiming west of the Baratum line.[67] This destruction occurred in the same time frame that Skene directed police to burn down the watoro homes in Paziani. De Lacy immediately sent a servant to make inquiries that confirmed the charge. Another claimant, Fathil bin Omar, revealed that the government had threatened to burn his dwellings if he did not withdraw his claim. His tenants told him, "An *askari* [colonial policeman] told them to leave, they wouldn't, they saw burning 5–700 yards away, so they pulled down their roofs, took their doors and moved."[68] These reports of house burning prompted de Lacy's complaints of government misconduct; but the commission treated the reports of arson as hearsay from people who mistook Skene's burning of abandoned watoro huts at Paziani as a threat against those with bona fide land claims.

De Lacy's efforts to combat these abuses were weakened when both Omar bin Athman and Fathil bin Omar withdrew their title applications after speaking with Liwali Ali bin Salim; they also denied that the liwali or the threat of arson induced them to do so. Even though the commissioners noted with concern that Fathil bin Omar regarded a personal request from the liwali as a government order, none of the claimants were willing to admit to the commission that they felt compelled to withdraw their applications.[69] The only hint of dissatisfaction among Muslim claimants actually came from John Jones, the administrator of the Magarini Syndicate concession, who had heard "one or two complaints [in 1915] that it was unfair they (Arab landholders) should lose their lands which were given to a Wanyika Chief"—probably a reference to the Nyika Native Reserve, whose proposed territory extended into the ten-mile strip.[70]

The government was also taking land away from Chimijikenda speakers. Mzungu wa Kiasi, the Kauma headman who had taken in the Kauma refugees at Paziani, complained to the commission, "Some of my tribe's land was being taken [by the Magarini Syndicate]. None of my people have yet been told to move[,] but I am afraid they will be."[71] In addition, Abdulla Jefa, a Giriama convert to Islam, testified that Skene evicted him to make room for the Magarini Syndicate.[72] The eviction forced this former headman into tenancy. For "unoccupied" Crown Land, Paziani certainly hosted many people.

The correspondence and reports collected by the Malindi Commission also show that residents in both Malindi and its hinterland affiliated with many overlapping and intersecting communities, even as the government insisted on standard naming conventions to facilitate simple categorization. Since land claimants could identify themselves as they wished on application forms, the several hundred names compiled in lists for the benefit of the Malindi Commission offer a convenient survey of how residents imagined their communities in Malindi District.

For example, one list contained the names of "Mahaji [Muslim converts], Mazrui, Swahilis, ex slaves, [and] Beluchi . . . Mohamedans" who claimed land west of the Baratum Line; another list included these groups as well as the names of Muslim and Hindu Indians, Somalis, and Nubians who claimed land north of the Sabaki River near the coast.[73] Individuals emphasized their group affiliation in these applications. As the "Children of Sheikh Pate Arab" apparently knew, the names that applicants placed on official documents could claim patrician status, indigeneity, and foreign descent all at once. Applicants who identified themselves as the children of a particular person expressed the logic that the land belonged to them by virtue of unilineal descent. Many applicants decided it was important to include their racial classification and town of residence like "Azizi bin Mohamed Arab Malindi" and "Sefu bin Amrani Arab of Malindi," probably because of the ongoing dispute in the protectorate about whether non-Arabs could claim land. Seven applicants identified explicitly as Swahili, including "Mambruk, Mswahili, Mambrui" and "Fundi Juhudhi Swahili." Mambrui is a town north of Malindi; "Fundi" can be a name but is also a title designating a skilled craftsman. The lack of surnames may suggest these two men had been enslaved, while the format adopted by "Thaib Nuhu bin Thakure, Swahili" suggests he claimed membership in a lineage.

As in Mombasa, those who identified as Swahili on land claims likely did so because they could not substantiate claims to Arab status but did not want to be categorized as Wanyika or reveal their past enslavement. However, several applicants identified openly as emancipated slaves by naming their former slaveholder, such as "Baruti free slave of Serenge Feruzi," or adopting a euphemism, like "Baka Makame servant of Shamaun." Others continued to identify as enslaved, like "Akmani (Hadimu) slave of Abdulla Kombo." These applicants may have been tenants on the land of former slaveholders, an arrangement that gave them access to land; but a successful claim to the land would have given them ownership. The calculations of the risk inherent in claiming land from a patron illustrates how the precarity of formerly enslaved people persisted after emancipation.

The naming variations that land claimants chose for themselves contrast with the uniform naming conventions in government lists that presented individuals as members of homogenous tribes. For example, Merwyn Beech, district commissioner of Malindi, organized a list of male tenants on Crown Land into two sections.[74] The first section included over a hundred men identified simply as Giriama; but the second "Nyika" section was divided into thirty-three Mduruma, three Nduruma, twenty-seven Mchonyi, ten Mjibana, and twenty-three Mkambi (i.e., Kambe) individuals. Beech also standardized these names to distinguish more easily among individual renters. All but seventeen of the named men are listed in standard format: their given name followed by their father's name, as in "Lewa wa Kilumo." Beech settled these people into two separate locations, one for the Giriama section and another for the "Nyika" section because he said "the populations [of each section were] homogeneous."[75] Beech omitted clan affiliations that would have provide a clearer picture of the complex relationships among the tenants.

Beech's omission concealed that Chimijikenda speakers in Malindi District, like those who submitted applications for land titles at the coast, lived in a cosmopolitan society whose complexities officials could barely perceive. For instance, when an official presented a plan for expelling the Giriama from the northern bank of the Sabaki River, he referenced oral traditions elicited from government headmen to suggest that "areas should be allocated to clans just as it was done by the tribe in the past."[76] Yet just the next month, a different official reported, "The different clans are very mixed up now and there is no chance of each clan living together so it is next to impossible to follow the migrations of each 'lalo' [location]."[77] The clans intermingled so much that it was impossible (for officials) to separate them out from each other. In addition to living in a patchwork manner, clans continued changing names, dividing, and combining—bedeviling decades of efforts to compile a standard list of all Chimijikenda-speaking clans. Besides the Kauma, Jibana, Kambe, Chonyi, Duruma, and watoro communities who lived with the Giriama north of the Sabaki, there were a number of Wa-Shambara, originally from German East Africa, who had their own headmen because they would "have nothing to do with the Nyika Headman nor the Wa-Nyika with the Mshambara Headman."[78] The colonial schema that divided littoral peoples into the categories of Arab, Swahili, and Wanyika was simply incapable of capturing all the entanglements among speakers of Sabaki languages and the immigrants who joined their littoral society.

Despite documenting administrative irregularities, the Malindi Commission of Inquiry in 1916 satisfied itself that claimants west of the Baratum line withdrew their applications voluntarily and that government officials had acted in good faith. They found five distinct "moves" of people around the district to be disordered because of unclear policy but that most colonial officials operated appropriately in each case.[79] They also recommended compensation for some of the displaced communities and wrote that the watoro should be allowed to return to the north bank of the Sabaki River, along with any of the Giriama and other Wanyika who wished to do so.

The negotiations over internal boundaries in the British East Africa Protectorate illustrate how littoral societies in the Indian Ocean bedeviled the imposition of territorial sovereignty. The creeks extending inland from Mombasa to Rabai raised practical questions like where to begin measuring the coastline, and the variegated landscape made the imaginary grid of latitude and longitude impractical. Yet the greatest challenge to British officials was the mobility to which littoral communities were accustomed. Aside from the anchor towns claimed on behalf of clan confederations, speakers of Sabaki languages and their neighbors largely claimed land on behalf of their respective clans. These practices formed mosaics of communities in urban and rural areas throughout littoral Kenya that complicated its division into Muslim and non-Muslim zones.

The three episodes described in this chapter also demonstrate a range of outcomes in the negotiations between speakers of Sabaki languages and the officials of th e British East Af rica Protectorate. The dispute over Jomvu's boundaries showed Kiswahili speakers' proficiency in using the protectorate's official dis tin ction between Islamic and customary law to realign district boundaries. The devastation of the Giriama Uprising illustrated the limits of challenging British authority to draw territorial boundaries; yet the Giriama ultimately gained the right to settle north of the Sabaki River anyway. The Malindi Inquiry of 1916 documented the commitment of British officials to keep Muslims and pagans separate; but it also highlighted inconsistencies in the social and territorial categories the government tried to impose. The ambiguous status of Paziani between the ten-mile strip and the Native Nyika Reserve attracted ambiguously categorized peoples like watoro and Muslim members of the Giriama, as well as members of other Chimijikenda-speaking confederations who lived among them. Though colonial officials partitioned the British East Africa Protectorate into territories defined by religious adherence— either to Islam or to the institutions of sacralized makaya—they could not make people stay in place.

Yet the official project of associating homogenous tribes with district boundaries was largely successful because speakers of Sabaki languages also found it useful. British officials thought that they were aligning district boundaries with preexisting tribal homelands; but the headmen who invented tribes were busy enlarging their constituencies. Instead of relying only on the narrow criteria of lineage, they used territorial claims to unify communities within homelands gazetted by the colonial government. By drawing a few district boundaries around dozens of local communities, British officials induced speakers of Sabaki languages to assemble the largest possible alliance of communities that they could convince officials to recognize as culturally homogenous.

Recasting clan confederations, age-sets, title societies, clans, and lineages as the components of tribes helped recruit members by making the novel category of "tribe" a repository for these smaller groups' ancestral traditions. These incipient tribes grew as communities realized that recognition in the colony's *Official Gazette* made tribes effective at making claims on the British government. Thus, in the British East Africa Protectorate, districts and tribes formed in tandem as speakers of Sabaki languages nested the ancestors of ethnicity into new tribal identities and assembled their disparate heritages. The interventions of imperial governments from Oman and Great Britain motivated Chimijikenda speakers and Kiswahili speakers to draw sharp boundaries between their respective confederations. Yet many speakers of Sabaki languages in the twenty-first century continue offering their loyalty to tribes, partly because their forebears ensured that the district boundaries which defined tribes largely reflected their vernacular understanding of communal boundaries.

SEVEN

Historicizing Tribalism

A Kaleidoscope of Communities in the Colony and Protectorate of Kenya, 1921–1953

> This coast of Mombasa has nine tribes.... All of them are Swahili.... These days they call themselves "Mijikenda."
>
> —William Frank

WHEN THE INTERIM Independent Boundaries Review Commission (IIBRC) arrived at Lamu in February 2010 to solicit public comments on the boundaries of electoral constituencies, the commissioners asked attendees to sit in sections that corresponded with their current constituencies. One man placed his chair in the aisle between the two seating areas. He looked around to make sure everyone saw his joke and waited for some chuckles before moving. His witty disruption evoked many Kenyans' frustration with, confusion about, and occasional defiance of administrative boundaries that divided them. He also exposed the forum as a bureaucratic performance. Like colonial-era commissions, the IIBRC made a great show of soliciting opinions from the public, which it was later accused of disregarding.

Many participants in the IIBRC forum at Lamu criticized the national government for marginalizing communities indigenous to Kenya's coast. For instance, they noted that the government had not dredged the waterways necessary for local industries in decades; but it had invested in resettlement schemes near the coast for the benefit of upcountry Kenyans. Some petitioners urged the commission to draw boundaries that would isolate newcomers, whom they considered intrusive immigrants. Though some speakers blamed immigrants for a perceived rise in crime in Lamu, most feared being outvoted more than suffering physical violence.[1]

As at Lamu, citizens throughout Kenya complained to the IIBRC about immigrants from other parts of Kenya. After the commission made its recommendations, a parliamentary committee criticized it for adhering to an algorithm that balanced population instead of favoring historical and cultural ties. Issack Hassan (whose Independent Electoral Boundaries Commission continued the work of the IIBRC) defended the recommendations by describing the detractors' focus on history and culture as tribalism: "It is not possible to carve out pure breed zones. Kenyans must learn to tolerate and accommodate each other."[2] British officials had used (presumed) biological ancestry to form districts, but the commissioners rejected this criterion for forming electoral constituencies. However, in doing so, the IIBRC and its successor also disregarded decades of cultural and historiological reasoning by ethnic patriots who had integrated tribalism into vernacular schemas throughout Kenya.

This chapter explores how ethnic patriots who spoke Sabaki languages articulated tribal criteria to government officials and their respective communities in the Colony and Protectorate of Kenya from 1921 to 1953. They aimed to make their new tribes seem ancestral and primordial by recasting their leaders as stewards of tradition, morality, and communal interests. To participate in the British Empire's political framework, they formed associations and crafted petitions to claim ancestral land. Their writings made it possible for disparate peoples to see themselves as unified tribes with shared heritages.[3] Many people in littoral Kenya committed to this vision of their past and present. However, they often transgressed the tribal boundaries promoted by ethnic patriots and officials, just as Kenyans have continued to cross (and sit between) such boundaries in the twenty-first century.

TRIBAL TERMINOLOGIES AND PATRIOT DREAMS

When historians refer to tribes as "ethnic groups" (to dissociate Africans from tribalism), they obscure how and why the speakers of Sabaki languages who articulated Swahili and Mijikenda identities embraced the criteria that British officials associated with tribes. The Standard Kiswahili word for "tribe" is *kabila* (pl. *makabila*). Kiswahili speakers borrowed *qabīla* from Arabic, in which the word means "kind, specimen, species, or sort" but also groups with reciprocal obligations related to the paying of blood money.[4] Speakers of the Mombasa dialect of Kiswahili (Kimvita) originally used *kabila* to denote an intermediate grouping of communities between clan (*mbari*) and confederation (*miji* or *taifa*). British officials adopted *kabila* as a translation for the English word "tribe," which they had used in India to denote societies that (they thought) resembled primitive Germanic tribes in European history.[5] Speakers of most Sabaki languages joined British officials in treating *makabila* as exclusionary communities defined by ancestry, occupation of contiguous territory, and shared culture.[6] Conflating these three criteria helped them articulate and defend their claims to the British government. Yet tribal boundaries also limited their ability to integrate people from other communities and confined them to the territories of gazetted "homelands."

Scholars have sometimes called the founders of tribes "ethnic entrepreneurs" to emphasize their ingenuity and agency compared to colonial officials, whom earlier scholars blamed for inventing tribes. However, the title of "entrepreneur" also suggests they formed tribes for their own profit and self-interest.[7] Referring to these founders as "ethnic patriots" instead emphasizes positive values of patriotism that align more closely with tribal founders' self-perception: loyalty to a homeland, commitment to a moral order, and service to one's community.[8]

In order to promote tribal identities, ethnic patriots reinterpreted numerous myths about the founding of clans and settlements as oral traditions about the origins of their new tribes. These traditions also drew on the physical and cultural boundaries that Chimijikenda and Kiswahili speakers had already negotiated with British officials before 1920. By committing these traditions to writing in new historical genres, ethnic patriots reimagined littoral Kenya as a society composed of biologically self-reproducing, historically isolated communities—the "pure breed zones" Issack Hassan disparaged.

Ethnic patriots' efforts to recategorize their communities as tribes faced some opposition. As Derek Peterson and Giacomo Macola noted, these histories were not "affirmations of an existing locality" but "interventions in a field of argument."[9] Thus, the ethnic patriots' work was hampered when colonial officials rejected their recommendations or when they disagreed over who belonged to which tribe. Tribes also competed for allegiance with other kinds of communities. Lineages and clans continued to organize most intimate familial relationships. Converts to Christian revivalist movements and Sufi orders rejected past traditions, a direct challenge to the moral authority of aspiring tribal elders. Speakers of Sabaki languages also joined labor unions, cultural and educational associations, and sports teams. Few people reoriented their entire lives around tribes. Despite these competing loyalties, testimonies to government commissions and the writings of ethnic patriots show that a consensus was emerging among speakers of Sabaki languages that littoral Kenya was, and had always been, a society of tribes.

THE POLITICS OF ASSOCIATION

Ethnic groups rarely act as a collective whole. Rather, people form smaller organizations that purport to act on behalf of their ethnic groups.[10] Many of the organizations that speakers of Sabaki languages formed after 1921 struggled to convince government officials that they could legitimately speak for a specific constituency. Government officials also declined to acknowledge African associations that would compete with the officially gazetted Local Native Councils (LNCs) and Arab administrators. Several historians have traced the development of these associations among Kiswahili and Chimijikenda speakers separately.[11] By adopting a cis-oceanic framework that examines the associational politics of these speech communities in tandem, this chapter illustrates how ethnic patriots articulated the Swahili and the Mijikenda as mutually exclusive tribes; that is, "Mijikenda" patriots transcended administrative, religious, cultural, and ancestral divisions among Chimijikenda speakers by defining their tribe as "not Swahili." Kiswahili-speaking patriots similarly defined their ethnicity in contradistinction to Chimijikenda speakers.

After World War I, Great Britain introduced reforms to make colonial administrations more responsive to both European settlers and colonial subjects. As part of this effort, the Colonial Office renamed the British East Africa Protectorate the Colony and Protectorate of Kenya in 1921. The new administration forbade political parties but allowed Europeans to elect voting members to the colony's Legislative Council. Nonvoting representatives for Indians and Arabs were selected by the governor of Kenya; but the governor designated the Chief Native Commissioner and Christian missionaries to advocate for Africans.[12] The government intended European settlers to lead under its watchful eye, but it also assumed colonial subjects would gain suffrage in the far-off future.[13]

Asian and African leaders in Kenya pushed against these limitations by organizing associations to lobby for additional rights. The East African Indian National Congress organized just before World War I; in 1921 the rural Kikuyu Association and the urban East African Association in Nairobi became the first associations of Africans in Kenya.[14] A few months later Arabs in Mombasa organized the Coast Arab Association (CAA). In order to assemble a larger constituency, its organizers invited Mombasa's Thalatha Taifa and Tissia Taifa—recently renamed in English as the Three Tribes and Nine Tribes, respectively—to join them. The CAA promised to help make their "status . . . equal to that of the Arabs."[15]

However, this alliance foundered when some members of the CAA derided the members of the Mombasa confederations as indistinguishable from Chimijikenda-speaking Africans. For instance, after calling a town meeting for the election of a new Arab adviser to Kenya's Legislative Council, Liwali Ali bin Salim pointedly told members of the Three Tribes and the Nine Tribes to exit the building. He said they could not elect an Arab representative because they were not Arab.[16]

Members of the Three Tribes and the Nine Tribes were furious. Not only did they leave the CAA but they also stopped praying at mosques built by immigrant Arabs and ceased socializing with them. Hyder al-Kindy, a member of the Three Tribes who later gained prominence as a respected civil servant, reported that the rival parties held meetings in which they "assessed . . . their chances of annihilating one another." Al-Kindy, then a young man, even assaulted an elderly Arab man who had equated the Three Tribes with Chimijikenda-speaking confederations in a letter to the *Mombasa Times*. In al-Kindy's view, by writing that the "Wakilindini are the Wadigos . . . Wachangamwe are the Waduruma," the man had called al-Kindy's people savages.[17] The violent response of al-Kindy illustrates how far the Three Tribes and Nine Tribes had distanced themselves from Chimijikenda speakers, despite their historical alliances. Conversely, Arabs' consistent denial of this distinction shows why erecting a boundary between Chimijikenda and Kiswahili speakers was integral to vernacular understandings of Swahili ethnicity in Kenya.

Once the Three Tribes and the Nine Tribes realized the CAA would not support their interests, they allied their confederations as the "Twelve Tribes," or Thenashara Taifa.[18] They also organized the Afro-Asian Association (AAA), whose name evoked their claims to foreign descent as well as their status as the original settlers of littoral Kenya with inviolable land rights. They explained that this association "was formed many years ago, before the Europeans came. It was the Three Tribes and the Nine Tribes Association before that time. . . . They joined up together when there was any question concerning them all, even before 1926."[19] Portraying the AAA as a continuation of historical clan confederations granted it historical legitimacy. Legally registering their association was yet another incremental step in adapting the confederations that had organized littoral Kenya for centuries to the changing polities of the Indian Ocean. It also severed their connection with the CAA.

Nevertheless, when the CAA sent a petition to a British House of Commons' committee in 1931, they still claimed to represent the Twelve Tribes. The delegation discussed at length the ambiguities of Arab classification in Kenya. They reported, for instance, that Arabs in Kenya spoke Kiswahili almost exclusively. Among those "enumerated in the census as Arabs were Swahilis, . . . call[ed] the Twelve Tribes, [who] mostly have Arab blood in them." When asked if the Swahili were African, the CAA delegation replied in the negative, but its members affirmed that the Swahili were a "mixed race" with an "African element." Pressed on the meaning of "Swahili," they claimed it meant "Coastal inhabitants" and conflated the term with the Twelve Tribes by indicating that the latter were "scattered all over the coast" rather than just around Mombasa. They also distinguished the Swahili from the Chimijikenda-speaking "Wanikas and others [who] are the proper natives of the coast itself."[20]

If members of the AAA had been present, they might have chafed at the claims that they were a mixed race, that they encompassed all the coast's Kiswahili-speaking confederations, and that Wanyika settled the coast before them. Although they did not manage to send a delegation to this joint committee in London, they sent their own petition in the care of a European settler delegation. It differed little from the CAA petition, except that the Twelve Tribes requested that they, like Arabs, be excluded from the legal definition of "native."[21]

The House of Commons committee referred the issue of the Twelve Tribes' native status back to Kenya's governor, who met with ten members of the AAA on April 22, 1932. The governor reminded them that Arab status was defined by Islamic law through direct patrilineal descent and said it was difficult to distinguish among those who "might undoubtedly be recognized" as Arab and those who were "purely natives." He rejected their renewed offer to "point out who was a real member of the 12 tribes and who was a follower," and he encouraged them to approach "the Arabs" and come to an understanding. The AAA responded that "mischief mongers" had already spoiled their earlier compact to seek interests in common.[22] These deep divisions among Kiswahili speakers over Arab classification made it impossible to rally behind a single association to represent their interests.

As Kiswahili speakers continued their debates over who could be considered Arab, Chimijikenda speakers started in the 1930s to explore the possibilities of concerted action across district boundaries. They did not yet identify as Mijikenda; so those who wanted to refer to all Chimijikenda speakers used the collective name "Nyika"— despite its pejorative connotations. For example, three members of the Giriama LNC formed the Young Nyika Association in 1931. They planned to send a delegation to represent all "Nyika tribes" at the same House of Commons committee meeting in London that the CAA attended. However, as soon as they started collecting funds to go, the district commissioner of Kilifi arrested them. He then pressed the other members of the LNC to eject them and "ban any future associations of Africans outside of the [local native] council."[23] Some LNC members agitated unsuccessfully in the 1930s to elect chiefs and forbid government vetoes over their decisions; but most LNC members defended British policies to protect their limited authority within their respective districts. Meanwhile, the thousands of Chimijikenda speakers who lived in Mombasa District turned to labor unions to support them, despite systematic exclusion from leadership positions.[24]

Since the government suppressed political organizations, Chimijikenda speakers focused their collaborations on cultural revival projects instead. These projects' names and activities detail the cultural elements that Chimijikenda speakers started to regard as common to them all. The Mbodzi-Matsezi Union in 1941 was the first association to try unifying all Chimijikenda speakers.[25] The name asserted common descent for all Chimijikenda speakers by referencing two maternal ancestors from their mythical Shungwaya homeland. The union, organized at Rabai, operated in Mombasa, Kilifi, and Kwale Districts, with meetings on the coast at Mombasa and Malindi as well as inland towns. They garnered excitement for restoring the ancestral *makaya* and even convinced the government to redirect communal labor requirements toward that goal. The organization drew on the intricacies of Sabaki kinship by asserting that all Chimijikenda speakers shared biological, unilineal descent from two founding women; they also highlighted their orientation around the now ceremonial makaya settlements as evidence for their shared identity. Despite the modest success of this union, Chimijikenda speakers remained politically and socially fragmented.

This rural effort to unite Chimijikenda speakers through claims of common culture and shared descent was revived in 1945 by middle-aged "youth" living in Nairobi who formed the Mijikenda Union. *Mijikenda* literally means "nine towns" and came to refer to nine makaya, one from each of the nine inland confederations that was operative during colonial rule. As historian Justin Willis noted, a Digo LNC first used the word (as *Midzichenda*) in 1924, when the name referred collectively to nine localities in their jurisdiction.[26]

The following year, Digo residents from two different reserves both told British officials that their respective territories should be called Midzichenda. The director of surveys distinguished them by adding the names of nearby locations as prefixes: Waa-Midzichenda and Pungu-Midzichenda.[27] The Mijikenda Union in 1945 appears to be the first association to promote the name as a reference to all Chimijikenda speakers.

The first meeting of the Mijikenda Union attracted over one thousand people to Rabai from all nine confederations in Kilifi and Kwale Districts. Notably, the administration granted special permission for official chiefs and LNC members to cross district boundaries to attend the meeting. According to the meeting minutes, the founders first came together to solve the problems of Chimijikenda speakers in Nairobi. However, after a visit to Mombasa, they decided to "create a party in our country ... to revive the original kinship of our tribes."[28] That is, they self-consciously sought to unify disparate tribes into a political association; and they framed this innovation as a revival of ancestral ties.

As with the Mbodzi-Matsezi Union, the Mijikenda Union took pains to identify common cultural elements that could serve as a foundation for collaboration among all Chimijikenda speakers. Edward K. Binns, who spoke for the young organizers, opened the organization's first meeting with rituals that acknowledged the authority of elders in the *kambi* age-grade over the union. First, he asked representatives from each of the confederations to delegate an elder to sit in one of nine chairs. Then he announced that the union needed to pay an *ada* (traditional fee) to the men who constituted the *kambi ya Mijikenda* (Mijikenda council). He led these elders to a separate area in which they placed their hands on a live bull, gave permission for it to be slaughtered, and made a covenant to revive the kinship of the Mijikenda and improve the condition of their people and country.[29] Attendees voted on only one item: an authorization for the new union to collect funds for the benefit of all Mijikenda. However, these rituals of submission to patrician elders were at least as important: they connected the modern association—with its executive committee, post office savings account, typed minutes, and registered bylaws—to an imagined past in which elders upheld customary law as they presided over a community of kin.[30]

In the preamble to the bylaws registered with the government, organizers asserted that they had "learnt from history" that the "these nine tribes (known as Wanyika) were once one and of the same origin."[31] As evidence, they noted the similarity in their languages and the rituals that accompanied stages in life, mourning, celebration, and public meetings. They also pointed to the clan names shared among different confederations as proof that they were "of the same blood and brothers without a doubt."[32] In the words of Canon Samuel Kuri, the meeting at Rabai was "for brothers of one blood," and he confidently asserted that "this day is the founding day for awakening the bright knowledge that will light our country and awaken those who sleep."[33] The Mijikenda Union thus recast its project to unify disparate communities into a new tribe by describing its actions as a revival of slumbering kinship obligations.

The Mijikenda Union also drew on the intricacies of its inherited kinship schema to distinguish its community from foreigners, especially Kiswahili speakers. It accused foreigners of "illwill and avarice . . . who stirred up frictions that caused them to separate into groups."[34] Not only did this historical claim assert its members' rights as the indigenous people of the coast, but it identified Asians (including Arabs) and Europeans as the cause of their disunion and weakness. In order to defend against divided loyalties, a clause in their bylaws limited membership to those whose fathers belonged to one of nine listed confederations. They required anyone with solely matrilineal ties to these confederations to wait until the union was stronger to join.[35] This provision specifically targeted those with Swahili fathers.

While Arabs and the Twelve Tribes espoused exclusionary religious identities, the Mijikenda Union actively recruited Muslims, Christians, and followers of *dini ya kienyeji* (traditional religion). Ali bin Salim (not the *liwali* of the same name) later became the union's president. At the union's inaugural conference, he requested that "if a Christian prays for this union, or a Muslim prays for this union, or a Pagan prays for this union to God," then everyone should respond "Amen, because all prayers are directed to God, for God is One, though the manner of giving prayers is different indeed." He then recited the *fatiha*—an Islamic prayer used to inaugurate an act—to which all in attendance responded "Amen."[36]

He thus presented loyalty to the Mijikenda tribe as a solution for religious divisions.

While the Mijikenda Union appealed to its members' common history as the *wenyeji wa pwani* (the owners of the coast), it competed for members and funds with the Digo Welfare Association, the Digo Association, the Rabai Association, the Young Duruma Association, and others. These associations worked within district boundaries and aimed to form smaller tribes based on the boundaries of each historical clan confederation. The Mijikenda Union also competed with the Coast African Association established in 1943. Its founders were descended from freed captives whom the British navy had resettled in littoral Kenya. Since they lacked ancestral ties to any clan confederation, they organized an association to represent the interests of all Africans residing in the Coast Province, regardless of indigeneity.[37] By the end of the 1950s there were over sixty "tribal" associations registered in Mombasa alone, including many that claimed to represent different Chimijikenda-speaking confederations.[38]

Although the Mijikenda Union ultimately failed as a labor organization and a cultural revival movement, both Chimijikenda-speaking laborers in Mombasa and their inland associates adopted "Mijikenda" as a respectable alternative to the pejorative "Wanyika."[39] One reason the name may have captured their imagination is its correspondence to naming conventions of Kiswahili-speaking confederations like the Seven Tribes of Pate and the Twelve Tribes of Mombasa. Claiming a Mijikenda identity inverted a negative stereotype into a positive affirmation of common interests, culture, and history among the residents of the escarpment.

HISTORICIZING TRIBES IN THE 1932 LAND COMMISSION

Besides organizing tribal associations to serve as the stewards of culture and history, ethnic patriots presented arguments to government officials for formal validation of their claims over territory. In 1932 the Kenya Land Commission convened to resolve Kikuyu complaints that the British government had stolen Kikuyu land in central Kenya for European settlers.[40] Since the commission's mandate extended to the entire colony, many communities in littoral Kenya also sought to redress their grievances at the forum. Though the commissioners refused to reconsider claims on which colonial courts had previously ruled, the historical claims that speakers of Sabaki languages presented in their memoranda, petitions, and speeches to the commission illustrate enduring fractures that unsettled the tribal categories of Swahili and Mijikenda.[41]

Kiswahili speakers crafted claims that isolated themselves from Africans in the past as well as in the present. The "people of Lamu" disassociated themselves from Africans by questioning whether their petition was even receivable by a commission concerned with "land questions affecting Africans only."[42] They submitted one anyway. When petitioners from Wassin Island (south of Mombasa) pressed for exclusive use of territory on the mainland nearby, they objected "strongly against the idea of a Native Communal Reserve, with all that implies."[43] As Arabs, they feared that designating the land as a reserve would prevent them from claiming individual land tenure and allow non-Arabs to settle among them.

Yet Kiswahili speakers also claimed prerogatives reserved for indigenous communities. The Afro-Asian Association of Mombasa argued that its claims were equal to those of "Natives in respect of land. . . . The Arab land should be defined and considered as *sacred* to the Tribes . . . , in exactly the same way as Natives' reserves."[44] This claim appealed to Kenyan High Court precedents that entrusted the makaya of inland confederations to gazetted elders and equated the "tribal authority to prevent strangers from cultivating" in an area with ownership.[45] The association's memoranda and testimonies also asserted that its members' were the rightful inheritors of the Arab settlers who had colonized empty land.

The Twelve Tribes of Mombasa based their right to exclude strangers from their territory on four historical claims that affirmed their Arab and Persian ancestors settled the coast before any Africans. First, they described the geographical limits of their settlements as extending a full seventy miles from the seashore. Second, they asserted that Chimijikenda speakers all came as refugees from Tanaland District—a reference to the Shungwaya myth—and thereafter remained "confined in their reserved villages." Third, they pointed to abandoned coastal stone towns as proof that their ancestors' occupation extended from time immemorial. Fourth, they claimed that "no one, not even the Sultan of Zanzibar, nor the Crown" could buy coastal land without their permission because they owned it prior to the fifteenth-century Portuguese invasions.[46] The timing of different waves of immigrants to the coast both dated and substantiated their territorial claims.[47] These historical narratives thus presented unambiguous myths of empty land—contradicting some of their own oral traditions that emphasize intermarriage between Arab or Persian immigrants and indigenous communities.

While all Kiswahili-speaking petitioners claimed Arab or Persian ancestry, those who distanced themselves from the emerging Swahili tribe had a difficult time making territorial claims. For example, since the Kiswahili-speaking Arabs in the Coast Arab Association had disclaimed a Swahili identity, they could not appropriate the Twelve Tribes' claim to indigeneity. They simply pleaded for "some land to be reserved for them . . . because they had 'nowhere else to go.'"[48] Members of the Afro-Asian Association of the Twelve Tribes presented themselves as a mixture of settlers from "Arabia, Persia, and even farther afield" but omitted even a hint of African origins (despite the allusion to African origins in the organization's name).[49]

The petition from Lamu's residents presented the most ambiguities. Instead of claiming a homogenous Arab identity, they confused the commissioners by claiming joint ownership of the mainland as a single tribe, yet they also claimed membership in seven different tribes: three Arab tribes of Lamu Town, the Arab tribes of Shella, Matondoni, and Kipungani (also on Lamu Island), and the Swahili (i.e., non-Arab) residents of Lamu Island.[50] Separating the coastal population into Arabs and Swahili groups made it impossible for Kiswahili-speaking petitioners to present a united front to demand a rehearing of claims previously presented to British courts, even though commissioners accepted the historical theory of Arab colonization.

Chimijikenda speakers had their own stories to tell, but only petitioners from the Digo and Duruma confederations could represent themselves to the Kenya Land Commission because the commissioners received coastal delegations only at Mombasa. Like Kiswahili speakers, the petitioners from these clan confederations focused on specific problems that affected narrowly defined communities rather than claiming to speak for all Chimijikenda speakers. A delegation from Likoni (south of Mombasa) claimed territory in a European concession because they "were living there before the Europeans came."[51] Digo petitioners from Mtongwe submitted a more complex historical survey that contradicted Swahili narratives of isolation. Their memorandum emphasized their historical "amiabilities" with the Watangana clan of Mombasa's Three Tribes from before the Portuguese arrival to the end of the sultan's reign in Mombasa.[52] They also credited the Watangana for introducing them to Islam. Like the Twelve Tribes, their representatives to the commission noted that the sultan of Zanzibar "was only ruling the country, but the land did not belong to him."[53]

It is no accident that the Digo of Mtongwe mentioned the Kiswahili-speaking Tangana clans in their request. The Mtongwe spokesman confirmed during his interview with the commission that the memorandum was prepared by an Arab of "The African Association"—that is, the Afro-Asian Association. Although no Watangana signed the petition, they seem to have partnered with the Mtongwe Digo to claim a narrower reserve near Mombasa in the likely event that the expansive claims of the Twelve Tribes failed. Despite the prejudices that Arab petitioners expressed against Africans, this partnership shows that speakers of Sabaki languages continued to trespass the tribal, racial, and linguistic boundaries that were supposed to contain them.

The single Duruma petition to the Kenya Land Commission also demonstrates the ever-shifting kaleidoscope of communities that occupied the rural districts around Mombasa. It dealt with Lucas Mgande, a Duruma man who began selling plots near the Mwache River. The petitioners asked the commissioners to forbid him or any Duruma from selling land. They emphasized that Lucas's buyers included a "Duruma Mission boy," a "Kikuyu working for Wireless, Mombasa," and "Delle an Mchonyi (Giriama)."[54] Presumably they wanted to forbid the sale of land to outsiders (including Duruma converts to Christianity), whose exclusion from customary Duruma marriage alliances would permanently alienate land sold to them outside the clan confederation.[55] The commission testimonies of Kiswahili and Chimijikenda speakers show that they did not yet imagine themselves as single tribes. However, ethnic patriots were already repurposing the historiological reasoning they used to defend territorial claims to imagine and write unified tribes into existence.

CONCEPTUALIZING COMMUNITY IN SHEIKH AL-AMIN'S NEWSPAPERS

The most prominent ethnic patriot among Kiswahili speakers was a member of the Mazrui clan named Sheikh al-Amin bin Ali al-Mazrui (1891–1947). As the rift between the CAA and AAA intensified in the late 1920s, he reprised his family's historic role as Mombasa's mediator. The Mazrui clan still maintained close relationships with the Twelve Tribes, and as the son of Ali bin Abdallah al-Mazrui, he was heir to the most prestigious network of scholars in East Africa. He studied in Zanzibar with Sufi sheikhs as well as the scholars of his own clan in Mombasa. Though he did not move through the Indian Ocean himself, he benefited from his mentors' overseas training and the accelerated current of ideas that accompanied steamships, telegrams, and newspapers.

Sheikh al-Amin was particularly drawn to the work of Islamic modernists like Rashid Rida and Mohamed Abduh in Egypt.[56] Their publications inspired him to publish the first local newspaper in Kiswahili, called *Sahifa* (Page), in January 1930.[57] It was a one-page, double-sided broadside of editorial opinions that railed against Western vices, called for education reforms, and encouraged greater commitment to Islam and the local community. Though Sheikh al-Amin emphasized that Islam could transcend the tribal divisions of coastal people, he nevertheless insisted on a clear boundary between his people and Chimijikenda speakers, including Digo converts to Islam. Their exclusion from his imagined community demonstrates how tribalism, especially the rift between Kiswahili and Chimijikenda speakers, constrained the possibilities of Muslim solidarity in littoral Kenya.

Sheikh al-Amin's *Sahifa* reflected (and consciously aimed to shape) how Kiswahili speakers in Kenya imagined their positions relative to other groups in the colony.[58] In his paper he noted, "We have left all the meaningful work to the Chagga and Taita and Kikuyu and Kamba" who ran the trains, repaired telegraphs and telephones, and raised communal funds for education.[59] He even warned, "If ever slavery were to return, it would be us who would be sold by the Kikuyu and bought by the Kavirondo!"[60] He also used caricatures of other tribes to encourage his readers to embrace thrift, hard work, and education. For instance, he discouraged his audience from being foolish enough to patronize Bamuhoho, a stereotype for a Giriama *mganga* (i.e., "healer," but in this context a "witch doctor").

Sheikh al-Amin's message reprised the *uungwana* ethic—celebrating communal solidarity—that the appeal of *ustaarabu* (Arabization) had upended by linking high status to being a foreigner from elsewhere.[61] However, his patrician ideology also validated class divisions by elevating the *wana chuoni* (scholars) and *watu wakuu wa mji* (town leaders). In his view, these leaders were patriots who showed their love for their country (*watan*) by educating and leading; everyone else showed patriotism by following their commands.[62] Using the Arabic word *watan* also mirrored the evolving vocabulary of Arab and Islamic nationalists.[63] His dream of an ideal community also corresponded to the vision of other ethnic patriots in Kenya who held up elderly men as moral guardians.[64]

The issues of *Sahifa* show the painstaking process of elaborating a working vocabulary that could express a novel sense of community, one that did not map neatly onto the word *kabila* (tribe). For instance, in the December 15, 1930, issue of *Sahifa*, he wrote, "People differ in terms of their *kabila, miji*, or *dini*. Now, the signs indicating to people to which *taifa* they belong are these customs and traditions of theirs."[65] Here he juxtaposed the words *kabila, miji*, and *dini*—"tribes," "towns," and "religion"—as different categories of belonging.[66] *Taifa* in the Mombasa dialect of Kiswahili meant "clan confederation," but it was then gaining wider currency in Standard Kiswahili as the word for "nation." In one issue Sheikh al-Amin specifically identified his community as the twelve thousand "Arabs and Swahilis" of Mombasa, but he usually referred to it as *sisi wapwani* (us coastal people).[67] He called for the Arabs and the Twelve Tribes to unify as one people so they could better compete with other tribes in the colony.

As Sheikh al-Amin reworked the political vocabulary of Kiswahili to forge a single Wapwani community, he drew inspiration from Islamic modernists who were elaborating Arabic terms to unite Muslims against European domination.[68] In his article "The

Muslim Community," he clarified Arabic terms for his Kiswahili-speaking readers to explain what kind of community the Wapwani should be: "In the Arabic language 'JAMIA' means something that unites people, cooperating with each other in a specific manner. A *Watan* for example, is a form of 'JAMIA,' it requires of people who live in one *mji* to cooperate in the interests of the *mji*, without differences between *kabila* and *kabila* or *dini* and *dini*."[69] Here again he distinguished *mji*, *kabila*, and *dini* as different categories, but instead of placing *mji* alongside *kabila* and *dini* as subcomponents of a *taifa*, he equated *mji* with *watan* as another type of *jamia*. As Kai Kresse and Hassan Mwakimako observed, Sheikh al-Amin used *watan* "interchangeably [in *Sahifa*] to mean either country or town or city, referring to one's home community."[70] By equating *mji* with *watan*, he reframed Mombasa's Kiswahili speakers (including its Arabs) as a single community. He then praised Islam as the key to overcoming their differences since it "requires every Muslim to be a brother to a fellow Muslim, without differentiating between an Indian and a Swahili, nor between an Arab and a Kikuyu, nor between a European and a Javanese."[71] Whereas Ali bin Salim of the Mijikenda Union presented tribalism as the solution to religious divisions, Sheikh al-Amin presented Muslim solidarity as a way to transcend tribalism.[72]

In February 1932, Sheikh al-Amin launched a larger, more ambitious newspaper in Arabic and Kiswahili that sought to bring together Muslims throughout littoral Kenya. He called it *al-Islah* (Reform). Besides his weekly editorials, he included local, regional, and foreign news items; guest columns; interviews; letters from readers; and translations of a serialized column from Rashid Rida's journal *al-Manar* about how to reverse the decline of Islam.[73] He also published the population of Natives, Whites, Indians, Goans, and Arabs from census data for the Coast Province. Enumerating these populations showed that his imagined community would be large enough to secure their rights if they stood together as coastal Muslims. The masthead of *al-Islah*'s first issue declared it "The Only Muslim Newspaper Published in Kenya." The tenor of *al-Islah* was best summed up by a reader who was disappointed by Sheikh al-Amin's single effort to report on a soccer tournament.[74] The reader wrote that "al-Islah journal is a guardian of our religion Islam and the World and learning Knowledge of Politics and other such things. Sir, please stop allowing Football [soccer] to appear in Islah."[75]

Al-Islah also differed from Sheikh al-Amin's first paper in its audience and message. In *Sahifa*, he called his community *sisi wapwani*; in the pages of *al-Islah* he referred to them exclusively as *Waarabu* (Arabs). This deliberate rephrasing promoted the Twelve Tribes' claims to Arab status by refusing to isolate them as a separate population. Indeed, he only acknowledged the Twelve Tribes as a distinct community once, in an editorial that refuted a "rotten" claim in a *Mombasa Times* article that the Twelve Tribes were not Arab.[76]

He still used the word *pwani*, however, to reference the *miji ya pwani* (towns of the coast) outside of Mombasa. *Sahifa* was a one-town newspaper, but the subscribers to *al-Islah* extended beyond Mombasa to many Kiswahili-speaking towns along the coast. The reach of his readership is indicated by the letters, *maulidi* celebration announcements, and petitions to the government he published. In addition to broadening his audience, he helped his readers identify with the wider Arab world by including news items from Iraq, Yemen, and Egypt. These news sections helped his readers imagine their political struggles as part of a movement to reinvigorate a universal Islamic society for which he most often used the word *umma*. Yet Sheikh al-Amin settled on the familiar Kiswahili word *miji* rather than *taifa*, *watan*, or *umma* as the most appropriate term for denoting the communities to which Arabs belonged. For instance, he translated the phrase "land of the Arabs" as *Miji ya Arabuni*.[77] *Watan* was a problematic alternative because he routinely used the Arabic word *wataniyya* to translate the hated term "native." Though committed to a universal Islamic *umma*, he insisted on building a strong regional community.

Sheikh al-Amin sometimes reprinted his moralizing essays from *Sahifa*; but his second newspaper also taught readers to demand rights from the colonial government. One article educated his audience on the three rights of freedom, equality, and representation.[78] Another condemned the colonial government for dividing its citizens into *daraja* (ranks) and placing Arabs between categories: they were subject to both the tax obligations of Indian immigrants and the indignities imposed on natives.[79] Exasperated, he asked, "How is that we are told that we are barbarians in everything except taxes?"[80]

Although both *Sahifa* and *al-Islah* distinguished coastal Muslims from upcountry tribes and Indian immigrants, Sheikh al-Amin's later publication also took closer notice of the fraught relationship between Kiswahili and Chimijikenda speakers. Though Sheikh al-Amin dismissed the Giriama as superstitious barbarians, he took a paternalistic approach to the Digo. He wrote that the Digo were the "biggest receivers of the Islamic religion" among all the African people. However, he expressed sorrow that they "do not know a thing about their religion," especially in regard to marriage and inheritance customs. Sheikh al-Amin wrote that his own ancestors had worked hard to bring the Digo into the Islamic faith, but Muslims in Kenya struggled to maintain the integrity and prestige of the Islamic *umma* because the British legal system elevated customary law as a legal tradition equal to Islamic law. Thus, as historian Nathaniel Matthews has noted, Sheikh al-Amin viewed Digo Muslims' ambivalence toward Islamic law as a danger to Mombasa's Muslim community.[81] However, instead of ostracizing Digo converts, he called for his community to "teach our Digo brethren matters of religion and proper behavior."[82] To assist in this effort, he prepared pamphlets on inheritance, marriage, and dietary restriction in Kiswahili to make people more familiar with Islamic law.[83] He thus inaugurated yet another genre of Kiswahili literature: accessible, didactic pamphlets that promoted Islamic orthodoxy.

Sheikh al-Amin's discussions about Digo Muslims suggest the limits of Islamic solidarity among Kenya's Waarabu. He accepted the Twelve Tribes of Mombasa and other Kiswahili speakers from the *miji wa pwani* as Arab; and adding their thousands to the Arab constituency put it on par with the European population in Kenya. At thirty thousand strong, the Digo population could have helped the Arabs assemble a constituency that rivaled even the Indian community—but the unambiguous classification of the Digo as African made them more of a liability than an asset for those seeking nonnative status. Besides the political considerations of the colony's racialized schema, Sheikh al-Amin's plea for Islamic unity could not overcome prejudices that the Digo were uncivilized barbarians. Thus, even Muslim affiliations along the coast privileged tribal identities defined by descent and culture over religious solidarity. Despite Sheikh al-Amin's efforts, his dream of reconciling the Twelve Tribes and the Arab community also faltered. In 1932, when he passed on the editorship of *al-Islah* to serve as the qadi of Mombasa, the Afro-Asian Association of the Twelve Tribes opposed his appointment.[84]

AUTOETHNOGRAPHIES AS TRIBAL HISTORIES

No Chimijikenda speakers experimented with serial publications comparable to Sheikh al-Amin's newspapers before independence. However, in the 1940s, Ronald Ngala (a Giriama) and William Frank (a Ribe) wrote autoethnographies that reveal some of the ways that Chimijikenda speakers were imagining their relationships to one another. Both men agreed that there was something that united Chimijikenda speakers, but they disagreed with each other, as well as with the organizers of the Mijikenda Union, about how to describe their commonalities.[85] Both Ngala and Frank recognized the term *Mijikenda* as a reference to nine Chimijikenda-speaking confederations but preferred other formulas.

Ngala's book *Nchi na Desturi za Wagiryama* (The country and customs of the Giriama) is better known than Frank's work because he became the foremost proponent of Mijikenda claims to coastal territories. Ngala followed a format first established in Kenya by Paul Mboya's 1938 book *Luo Kitgi gi Timbegi* (The Luo, their cultures and traditions).[86] Ngala's 1949 book started with a historical account followed by a survey of customs. He described these elements as distinctive to his Giriama tribe rather than all of the Nyika tribes of the Coast Province, which he said "now have joined in one by the name of Miji-Kenda."[87] He routinely distinguished the Giriama from other Chimijikenda speakers, even when he noted that they had started "mixing with tribes in the south like Kambe, Ribe, and Rabai" after fleeing from Shungwaya and settling along the escarpment.[88] Taking a cue from Kenya's *Official Gazette,* he used latitude and longitude, with distances in miles, to document the perimeter around Giriama territory. Contradicting the claims of the Twelve Tribes that their territory extended seventy miles inland, Ngala described Giriama territory as reaching from thirty-five miles inland to very near the coast at Malindi. From north to south, he wrote, the country reached from the Sabaki River to the Uganda Railway. However, he slightly modified this boundary by noting that the Giriama bordered Rabai territory in the south (which was north of the railway) and three other confederations to the east. The remainder of the book detailed customs of the Giriama relating to marriage, raising children, farming, food, music, and religion, without noting how they compared to those of other Chimijikenda speakers.

Frank's 1953 book *Habari na Desturi za Ribe* (The history and customs of the Ribe) organized his account in the same way: he provided a brief historical account of the migration from Shungwaya tradition followed by descriptions of tribal customs relating to marriage, inheritance, religion, and other categories. Like Ngala, he seemed uninterested in comparing Ribe customs to those of other Chimijikenda speakers. He also rejected the idea of a Mijikenda tribe. He used both *taifa* and *kabila* interchangeably to refer to each of "those nine" confederations, but he did not apply either word to the collection of them that "these days call themselves 'Miji Kenda.'"[89] Rather, in a direct inversion of the formula that Sheikh al-Amin used to treat the *miji ya pwani* as Arabs, Frank referred to the *kabila ya pwani* (tribes of the coast) as Waswahili. To clarify his meaning, he listed the nine confederations whose members spoke Chimijikenda and then wrote, "All these are Waswahili, meaning they live at the coast. . . . [Their] pronunciation of words is a little different but they hear each other as a person who speaks in the manner of Kiswahili."[90]

Frank also downplayed the divisions of the confederations in the escarpment as archaic by noting regular trespasses among tribal boundaries: "Even now if you look among the Waribe you will find many tribes of the coast and they usually call themselves Waribe, but they are not pure Waribe[;] rather they have assimilated. . . . In the past, there were not these changes, but now . . . a Mribe can marry a Mdigo and bring the clan of Wadigo into the Ribe tribe. . . . Many of those tribes . . . are made like this."[91] Aligning the Mijikenda clan confederations with the littoral Swahili identity was Frank's way of transcending parochial attachments to more localized tribes.

Sheikh al-Amin also composed a history of his community in the 1940s. Instead of an autoethnography of Omani Arabs, he organized his *Tarikh al-Mazrui* (History of the Mazrui) as a chronicle, using his clan's oral traditions to detail the major conflicts and personalities of each Mazrui liwali from 1698 until 1835.[92] Writing in

Arabic, he cited (and disputed) European accounts of Mombasa's history and weighed the veracity of different oral traditions against each other and written accounts. His account of the communities of Mombasa was more like his description of them in *Sahifa* than in *al-Islah*: his family's Omani Arab community was considered distinct from, but allied to, the Twelve Tribes of Mombasa, while the confederations of Chimijikenda speakers featured as useful but sometimes treacherous outsiders.

Sheikh al-Amin did not finish the chronicle before his death in 1947, and publication of his manuscript was delayed until 1995. Like the tribal histories included in the autoethnographies of Ngala and Frank, his chronicle circulated among a much more limited readership than his newspaper *al-Islah*. So it is unlikely that any of these histories shaped the collective imagination of the Coast Province to any great degree. However, they reflected conversations and debates among speakers of Sabaki languages about how to arrange the kaleidoscope of their communities in colonial Kenya, at least until a new political cycle conspired to reconfigure them again.

The tension described in this chapter between the interests of local communities and a distant, but not disinterested, state—whether headquartered in Zanzibar, London, or Nairobi—distinguishes tribal identities like Swahili and Mijikenda from the ancestors of ethnicity. Confederations, clans, and lineages came together to collaborate with and against other confederations, clans, and lineages. Some speakers of Sabaki languages were more prosperous than others because of their proximity to the sea or cattle ranges—or because they developed other kinds of valuable *uganga* (esoteric knowledge). They shared a common schema with organizations like title societies, age-sets, and marriage alliances that could cut across these divisions while maintaining the coherence of each speech community. In contrast, centralized governments, starting first with the Portuguese captains of the sixteenth century, engaged with speakers of Sabaki languages as subordinates whom they could coerce with violence. Though the Zanzibar government promoted Islamic orthodoxies that introduced religious divisions in littoral Kenya, it was not until British colonial rule that imperial governance became intrusive enough to motivate speakers of Sabaki languages to embrace tactics of political tribalism against one another.

Just after World War I speakers of Sabaki languages formed tribal organizations like the Afro-Asian Association and the Young Nyika Association to present their interests to the government. Their testimonies to the Kenya Land Commission of 1932 revealed how these groups experimented with different ways of narrating the past to justify their territorial claims. Yet their arguments also complicate the illusion of homogenous tribes by offering glimpses of the ever-shifting kaleidoscope of communities (and alliances among them) that speakers of Sabaki languages continued to assemble in the colonial era. In the interwar period, ethnic patriots focused on persuading their (distinct) audiences to imagine themselves as tribes so they could collectively compete with other tribes in Kenya. Despite ethnic patriots' dreams of tribal unity, many speakers of Sabaki languages continued to entertain alternative imaginaries like those of William Frank, who challenged the basic premise that the Swahili and Mijikenda were distinct peoples. Yet even Frank conceptualized relationships among speakers of Sabaki languages through an overarching schema that sorted distinct histories and cultural practices into tribal categories.

When these ethnic patriots wrote about their collective identities, they wrote for audiences who shared their languages and interests but also for imperial audiences who had appointed themselves the arbiters over land, finite resources, and associational politics. Many Chimijikenda and Kiswahili speakers found refuge in millenarian Christianity or Sufi orders that allowed them to leave behind embarrassing origins or break ancestral obligations—but the colonial government frowned on these movements as disruptive.[93] In contrast, the British officials lent support to tribal associations by legitimizing their authority on Local Native Councils and in the Arab administration.

As speakers of Sabaki languages became familiar with British governance, they assembled larger coalitions of confederations into tribes. Yet there were limits to the kinds of associations they could imagine. Hyder al-Kindy's assault of an Arab man paradoxically demonstrated the antagonism he and other members of the Twelve Tribes held for Chimijikenda speakers. Sheikh al-Amin's writings papered over the hostility between Arabs like himself and the Twelve Tribes with appeals to Islamic brotherhood, but he held the line against including Muslim members of the Digo confederation. This aversion to assimilation went both ways: the bylaws of the Mijikenda Union drew on the intricacies of their inherited kinship schema to exclude Swahili individuals from membership. They turned coastal Muslims' refusal to marry their daughters to Chimijikenda-speaking men into a bulwark against infiltration of their own tribe.

However, setting the boundaries of political tribalism was not enough to imagine a community. Ethnic patriots also needed to persuade British officials that they genuinely represented the interests of their new tribes. So they aligned their new alliances with the category of "tribe" as understood by British officials: a kin-based, culturally homogenous population that occupies contiguous territory. Shared clan names became a sign of shared blood, religious practices transformed into cultural demarcations, and ruins and cemeteries marked territories. Instead of proclaiming their association to be a novel alliance, the Mijikenda Union historicized their tribal traditions by describing its movement as an awakening of forgotten family ties; meanwhile, Swahili petitioners claimed their direct ancestors had settled in empty land centuries before the Mijikenda had even arrived. The previous generation of residents in littoral Kenya had demarcated the territorial boundaries of tribes who spoke Sabaki languages in the British East Africa Protectorate, but it was ethnic patriots like al-Mazrui, Ngala, and Frank who articulated the cultural, religious, and historical memories around which their respective tribes came together in the Colony and Protectorate of Kenya.

PART III

Transcending Ethnicity?

EIGHT

Transcending Ethnicity?

Nationalist Sentiments and the Appeal of Autonomy during Kenyan Decolonization, 1953–1962

> We want to have the Coast for the Coastals. No question of race or religion here.
>
> —Abdilahi Nassir

RAILA ODINGA CALLED for street demonstrations after Kenya's election in October 2017. Kenya's Supreme Court had invalidated the previous month's election because of irregularities, but Odinga insisted that the electoral commission had failed to follow the reforms that the Supreme Court required for the fresh election. So he withdrew as a candidate for the president of Kenya and called his supporters to join in protests. The demonstrations ended quickly once incumbent president Uhuru Kenyatta banned protests, but not before police killed at least thirty-three protestors. In the following weeks, some of Odinga's supporters started to promote secession as the only possible solution to the impasse.

Twitter served as a forum for considering the possibilities. Ndung'u Wainaina saw two possibilities: "There will be a full blown secession struggle from different fronts or completely different negotiated autonomy devolved system in #Kenya." Moses Kite connected the election dispute to other crises: "FACT—There is the option of secession when the KENYA experiment fails, just like #Catalonia said enough is enough in Spain." Emmanuel construed it as a reaction to Kikuyu dominance: "40+ Tribes turning against Kikuyu Hegemony isn't Tribalism, Its the end of it." Retired Comrade saw only one outcome: "secession is inevitable."[1] Some Kenyans put their speculation and hopes into more visual formats. Odinga supporters designed maps for a People's Republic of Kenya that isolated counties that supported Kenyatta's party in a landlocked "Central Republic of Kenya."[2]

None of these secessionists mentioned the proposals of the Mombasa Republican Council (MRC), which had been calling for the former Coast Province to secede as an independent nation for years. Their slogan is *Pwani si Kenya* (The Coast Is Not Kenya). Kenya's interior secretary banned the MRC as a terrorist group because of its separatist rhetoric, but Kenya's Supreme Court overturned the ban in 2015 because the new 2010 constitution guaranteed its freedom of speech and association.[3] Police banned the MRC again in 2016. However, MRC's open calls for secession, and the Supreme Court's support for the group's right to do so, suggested that the 2010 constitution, the newfound independence of the judiciary, and the open critique of centralized government were reopening debates about the future of Kenya's polity.

Kenya's electoral crises since 2007 have often echoed the debates of decolonization in the 1960s, when Kenya's future—and particularly that of Coast Province—seemed open for negotiation. Then, too, visions of the future were saddled by colonial legacies that encouraged Kenyans to claim membership in mutually exclusive tribes. This chapter examines how speakers of Sabaki languages sought to transcend ethnicity as they joined competing nationalist movements. Many joined KANU (Kenya African National Union) nationalists and KADU (Kenya African Democratic Union) regionalists that touched all of Kenya. Others supported Arab nationalism and reunification with Zanzibar, or they joined the Mwambao United Front to press for the Protectorate of Kenya's independent sovereignty. Each of these nationalist movements strived to transcend ethnicity;

but even KANU nationalists embraced political tribalism as the de facto system for divvying up the spoils of decolonization after they secured victory. Once Kenyans' tribes were carved into the landscape, printed in gazettes, and granted stewardship of ancestral heritages, they proved difficult to uproot.

Like the maps that circulated on Twitter, communities throughout the Kenya Colony and Protectorate created maps to propose alternative cartographies to British decolonization commissions. In littoral Kenya residents offered contradictory visions of the future and the past: sovereign claims by the Digo National Union and the Three Tribes, calls for the expulsion of long-established Kamba residents, and even alliances between White settlers and Arab associations to establish Coast Province as a separate nation-state. Instead, as the prospect of an independent nation faded, speakers of Sabaki languages learned to reimagine their ethnic groups as communities within the national community of Kenya.

MAU MAU AT THE COAST

Nationalist aspirations in Kenya sharpened in the wake of the Mau Mau Emergency (1952–1957). Injustices following World War II compounded grievances from the half measures of the 1932 Kenya Land Commission. Kenyan soldiers who served in the war returned to unemployment, racial segregation in urban areas, and few opportunities for land tenure in rural areas. The "Second Colonial Occupation" of the British Empire promised increased investments and political participation for African Kenyans, but only in the far-off future. Jomo Kenyatta's Kenya African Union (KAU) and several other African associations pushed for faster reform. The Kikuyu who organized the Land and Freedom Army refused to wait.

The Land and Freedom Army (demeaned as the barbaric "Mau Mau" in the British press) aimed to oust settlers and the colonial government from the highlands of central Kenya. They horrified British settlers with grotesque spectacles of violence; and the British Empire responded with disproportionate reprisals from its military and police.[4] Kikuyu communities bore the brunt of forced internment and indiscriminate screenings that officials used to root out sympathizers. However, colonial police also targeted Embu, Meru, and Kamba communities because they spoke Central Kenya Bantu languages related to the Kikuyu language.[5] The government deemed them especially susceptible to Mau Mau propaganda.

In 1953 a screening team visited Mombasa to identify Mau Mau sympathizers among the large population of Kamba who lived there. Authorities then established a Kamba Investigation Centre at the coast the following year.[6] Though Kamba communities had resided on the coast for generations, the government response to the Mau Mau Emergency endorsed the notion that Kamba were perpetual alien immigrants to the coast.

The attitudes of littoral communities toward the government crackdown were contradictory. Intelligence officers noted that Africans and Arabs in Coast Province seemed pleased that screening operations would "result in the speedy removal of Kikuyu" from their region.[7] However, they also opposed the government's ban on the KAU.[8] When officials arrested the leader of KAU's branch in Coast Province, political organizations throughout the region paused many of their activities. Tribal associations, especially, narrowed their focus to welfare issues and seemed "determined not to become involved in up-country politics."[9]

Although few, if any, coastal people joined the Land and Freedom Army, many offered support to activists who would press for land and freedom in other ways. For example, Wilson Amumo, a Pokomo man, encouraged people to oppose the construction of Hola, a detention center for Mau Mau suspects in Tana District, and warned that the government was going to seize coastal land.[10] On the opposite end of Coast Province, in the Shimba Hills of Kwale District, three Digo men organized a secret society called Utsi. Intelligence officers reported that it was a vestige of the banned KAU.[11] Yet they also described Utsi as "an old tribal association, its name in the Mdigo language meaning 'unity.'"[12] Since this name derived from *ntsi* (land), more accurate glosses might include "patriotism," "nativism," or even "nationalism." Fearful of another insurgence, the government arrested and exiled the organizers to Kipini District near Lamu. As Kenya's intelligence officers concluded in 1954, there was "no sympathy for Mau Mau terrorism" in the Coast Province, but "tribal communities residing in Mombasa [were] passively in sympathy with African nationalism."[13]

In 1955 the government lifted the ban on political organizations to undercut support for the Land and Freedom Army. African politicians quickly formed political unions.[14] However, they were still forbidden from operating outside the districts in which they registered. So when Kenyan politicians entered negotiations for independence with Great Britain in 1960, the tribal associations who drew members from district-demarcated populations were already primed to speak in the forums that determined the form of the postcolonial state in Kenya. Ethnic patriots worked to ensure that their tribes became the building blocks of district, provincial, and national political parties.

INCOMPATIBLE NATIONALISMS

Though the government's crackdown on the Land and Freedom Army and its sympathizers had made it more dangerous to criticize the colonial government, African nationalists felt free to sharpen their rhetoric against Arabs at the coast. As Chimijikenda-speaking politicians like Ronald Ngala articulated grievances against Arabs, they made African nationalism irreconcilable with the Arab nationalist movements that attracted Kiswahili speakers.[15] A colonial intelligence report from September 1955 noted a "noticeable increase in the open antagonism between Arab and Giriama in the Malindi sub-district, provided mainly by African bush-lawyers who encourage[d] African cultivators to break agreements made with their Arab employers."[16] Historian Joseph Caruso has noted that Chimijikenda speakers' new antagonism toward Arabs was a shift from earlier decades when their associations focused on curtailing Indian merchants' trading privileges.[17] In addition to breaking rental agreements, cultivators boycotted Arab shops and refused to share profitable cashew crops with landowners. One politician even called for the Kilifi African Peoples Union to stockpile bows and arrows so they could kill "any Arab who attempted to interfere in any way" with these harvests.[18]

Cooler heads prevailed against these violent proposals, but the Kilifi African Peoples Union continued to translate these grievances into political demands. In particular, they echoed calls for the ten-mile strip of the protectorate to be "abolished and converted into an African Land Unit."[19] They offered a historical claim as justification: "Arabs had originally come to the country for the purpose of slave trading and the Europeans to steal land. . . . These two races had conspired together and intended to steal the Coastal Strip."[20] Such rhetoric, which echoed the charter of the Mijikenda Union, left little wiggle room for cooperation with Arabs or the members of the Twelve Tribes, who had finally secured legal status as Arabs in 1952.[21]

Ngala had claimed land for the Giriama "very near the coast at Malindi" in his 1949 autoethnography, but his political fortunes improved when he began claiming that every square inch of the coastal strip belonged to the Mijikenda. After Ngala's election to the office of African elected member in the Legislative Council in 1956, he encouraged supporters to organize district-wide political associations in Kilifi and Kwale Districts, allied with Luo labor activist Tom Mboya to rally trade unions in Mombasa, and revived the Mijikenda Union as a cultural association. Associating with the *kaya* elders of this union granted him legitimacy while allowing him to evade restrictions against political activity that crossed district boundaries. Colonial intelligence offices mocked Ngala for giving speeches on parochial issues like agricultural development and education. However, when the government finally allowed African political associations to organize across district lines in 1961, his position as the patron of the Mijikenda was unassailable because he had demonstrated his concern for these everyday issues. He quickly formed a provincial organization—the Coast African People's Union—as an umbrella group for the nominally independent district associations he had helped promote.

While Ngala was busy consolidating his influence, factionalism among Kiswahili speakers hindered their engagement with Arab nationalist movements. Earlier generations of Kiswahili speakers had argued over who should be regarded as Arab; in the 1950s they disputed how to guarantee Arabs' autonomy as Africans gained political influence. The foremost Arab nationalist in Kenya, Mafudh Mackawi, beat Shariff Muhammad Shatry in the 1952 election as the Arab representative to the Legislative Council, but much of his support came from Arabs in Nairobi. The Coast Arab Association in Mombasa remained under the sway of his rival. So as the election of 1956 approached, Mackawi mobilized support for reaffirming the sovereignty of Zanzibar's sultan over the Kenya Protectorate. He traveled often to Zanzibar and even applied (without success) for permission to recruit protectorate residents as members of the Zanzibar Nationalist Party.[22] Meanwhile, Shatry argued that Arabs could only hope to retain their privileges if they propped up British rule against African nationalists. His faction even supported a proposal to build a British naval base at Mombasa. Members of the Twelve Tribes split their votes in the 1956 election to the Legislative Council between one of Shatry's allies and Mackawi, who won.

Intelligence officers ascribed Mackawi's win in 1956 to "incipient Arab nationalism."[23] However, when the Afro-Shirazi Party (which espoused African nationalism) defeated the Zanzibari Nationalist Party in Zanzibar's 1957 election, Mackawi lost resources as well as a coherent political agenda. With African nationalists ascendant in Zanzibar, hope for reunification vanished. Arab nationalism in Kenya faced another dead end once Gamal Abdel Nassir withdrew Egypt's support for Arab nationalist organizations south of the Sahara.[24] Turning to "Islamic nationalism" as an alternative, Mackawi reached out to Kenya's Somali community (which had no representative on the Legislative Council) to offer his advocacy in return for their support. They said no because they preferred unification with Somalia.[25] As with earlier Muslim politicians in Kenya, Mackawi failed to reconcile or transcend the racial, sectarian, and tribal divisions among Indian, Arab, and African Muslims.[26]

The factionalism among Arab politicians in Mombasa opened the door for a new generation of leadership, which organized as the Afro-Arab Youth League (AAYL) in 1958. Abdilahi Nassir, a member of the Twelve Tribes, became their most effective spokesman. Though intelligence reports initially characterized the AAYL as Arab nationalists, Nassir and his associates also sought support from Chimijikenda speakers. They blamed Mackawi and Shatry for sowing disunity and losing "the Baluchi and African Muslim communities as a pro-Arab voting bloc."[27] Later intelligence reports noted that the AAYL leaders were "mainly of African blood and believe it to be in their best interests to side with the Africans."[28] Colonial officials' fascination with bloodlines aside, the AAYL reversed half a century of associational politics when they sought both African and Arab support.

When the African elected members of Kenya's Legislative Council pressed for constitutional reforms by boycotting their first legislative sessions in spring 1959, the AAYL pressured Mackawi and Shatry to follow suit. They also presented more radical constitutional reforms than the Arab representatives. Instead of increasing the number of Coast Province representatives, the AAYL proposed that "all Protectorate people, regardless of ethnic origin," be given a "Protectorate national status" and enrolled in a common electoral list for "all nationals willing to pay allegiance to a Protectorate government."[29] Whereas Ronald Ngala called for African nationalism and Mahfudh Mackawi embraced Arab nationalism, Nassir argued for a national identity based solely on allegiance to an expanded coastal strip. Instead of narrow tribes or races defined by descent, they elevated residence in Kenya's littoral territories and patriotic devotion to its people as the primary criteria for belonging.

MWAMBAO NEVER WAS KENYA

Nassir called his proposed nation Mwambao. Previously, the word had the meaning of "shoreline."[30] By 1960 Nassir transformed it into a unifying emblem that could bring together all the people of littoral Kenya, regardless of their religion, language, tribe, race, or origin. Coastal politicians who had built their constituencies through tribalism offered no support to this agenda. So Nassir worked to replace them.

In January and February 1960 representatives to Kenya's Legislative Council gathered with the British secretary of state for the colonies in London to negotiate independence. Although not invited to this conference, Nassir managed to eclipse both Mackawi and Shatry. He had resigned from the AAYL to become the secretary of the reinvigorated Afro-Arab Association that represented Mombasa's Twelve Tribes. In that capacity, he sent a telegram and a memorandum to the British officials and Kenya's African Elected Members who attended the conference. These messages rejected the right of the Arab representative to speak on behalf of the "indigenous" people of the coastal strip (meaning the Twelve Tribes).[31] Nassir's very public rift with the Arab representatives made it impossible for them to speak with any authority for their constituents' wishes. To settle the matter, the secretary of state for the colonies promised to organize a commission to gather opinions about how to reconcile the protectorate's technical legal status as the sovereign territory of Zanzibar's sultan with the imminent independence of Kenya.

Following the conference, the colonial administration finally expanded permission for political parties to form colony-wide alliances, instead of limiting them to provincial boundaries. Many European and Asian representatives joined multiracial parties and held out hope for a state that would affirm their rights to property and carve out protections for racially defined constituencies. The African representatives initially contemplated a single African party but split to pursue different approaches. Kikuyu and Luo politicians formed KANU to press for a strong, centralized government. Ronald Ngala, Daniel Arap Moi, and others created KADU to promote a system of regional autonomy called *majimboism* that would protect the interests of their smaller tribes. (*Majimbo* means "provinces" in Kiswahili.)

Nassir's telegram of protest against Arab representation paid off. By June 1960 intelligence officers reported that Hadhramy and Omani Arabs had lost their political influence to "those Arabs of mixed descent (i.e. 12 tribes) who have an affinity with the Coast African."[32] In 1961 Nassir was elected as the representative for the Mombasa Central constituency as an independent. Nassir allied with KANU at first; but he concluded that Kikuyu and Luo leaders intended to impose "upcountry imperialism" and would not support his argument that the residents of Coast Province needed to clarify their relationship to Zanzibar and Great Britain before they could consider a place within Kenya's polity.[33]

Nassir's writings in the following years called for coastal autonomy by disparaging tribal, racial, and religious schemas as irrelevant in Mwambao. He outlined these positions in speeches, letters to newspapers, and interviews. For example, in March 1961 Nassir fired off a telegram to the conference organizers of the All-Africa People's Conference in Egypt when KANU's representative managed to exclude his representatives from participating. In the telegram, Nassir complained that the Kenyan delegates "treat us as foreigners. . . . Please advise [them] to treat people of Mwambao brotherly and as good neighbors."[34] Mr. Msanifu Kombo of KANU responded by claiming that the "half-castes" who "call themselves Arabs" were claiming autonomy for the coastal strip "under the cloak of imperialists, colonists and capitalists . . . with the intention of creating another Katanga or Congo in Kenya."[35] The tragic violence in Central Africa seemed to provide clear warnings against entertaining secessionists.

However, Nassir parried accusations that he was fomenting secession by noting that the Colony and Protectorate of Kenya had never been together: "Our two countries . . . have been two nations all the time."[36] To counter KANU's claims that the coastal autonomy movement was led by Arabs, Nassir drafted a press release to declare his movement's African credentials: "We regard ourselves as Africans. . . . [It] is wrong for anyone, whose home is in Africa, to identify himself as non-African. . . . Mwambao is an African country."[37] Nassir's focus on residence and loyalty as criteria for inclusion offered Mwambao nationality to anyone who would offer undivided allegiance.

He also countered claims that the mwambaoists represented only the interests of his Twelve Tribes community in Mombasa. For instance, to the *Sunday Post* he wrote, "We, the so-called Arabs[,] have never sought autonomy for the Arabs exclusively. We want to have the Coast for the Coastals. No question of race or religion here."[38] After hearing rumors that the government was going to buy out European farms in central Kenya, he argued that the money should go instead to the coast: "Why not Bajunis or Pokomos instead of Kikuyus in the Tana River District?"[39] Taking a step further than the Coast African Association of the 1940s, he extended a welcome to non-Africans. To the *Daily Nation* he wrote, "The coast is developing toward nationhood and it is doing away with all racial compartments whether Asian, European, Arab or 'black' African. . . . The Strip existed long before nationalism was born, and that is why by now Mwambao is a national land unit by every consideration."[40] Nassir paradoxically categorized littoral Kenya as a nation because the unity of its people historically preceded the concept of nationalism.

Hyder al-Kindy dismissed the Mwambao movement as a "fiasco" in his memoirs.[41] The young man who had assaulted an Arab elder to defend the honor of the Twelve Tribes in 1927 had become a respected civil servant by 1960. He noted that supporters for Mwambao genuinely crossed racial lines, but they could never overcome their differences. Abdilahi Nassir invited seven political parties to join a Mwambao United Front and offered a clear vision of a purely territorial nation rather than an ethnic, national, or religious one. But the movement was hampered by mistrust. A Bajuni Swahili party in northeast Kenya and the autonomists in Malindi felt marginalized by those in Mombasa. Meanwhile, the membership of Europeans in some of the parties frustrated those who saw the recognition of Mwambao as an indigenous rights movement. The Mwambao United Front struggled to instill the same loyalty as district associations based on tribal membership.

Though a few Muslim Mijikenda joined the Mwambao movement, most Mijikenda remained committed to Ngala's KADU party. When the Robertson Commission, which was sent to evaluate the coastal strip's legal status, finally arrived in late 1961, Ngala and other nationalist politicians from both KANU and KADU had managed to turn *mwambao* into a byword for secession from Kenya rather than the name of an autonomous African nation.

COUNTER-MAPPING THE COAST AT DECOLONIZATION COMMISSIONS

The Robertson Commission was a farce. Even before it started collecting documents and testimonies, the British government had decided to pay the sultan of Zanzibar for the coastal strip and incorporate the former protectorate into Kenya. Yet the performances that accompanied the Robertson Commission provide a remarkable portrait of the fissures in coastal society.[42] The petitions and memoranda—as well as street demonstrations and boycotts timed to disrupt the commission—showed how speakers of Sabaki languages repurposed history to make judgments about who should be excluded from Kenya's future polity. They and other Kenyans also offered these visions—this time with maps—to two commissions led by Sir Foster-Sutton: the Regional Boundaries Commission and the Constituencies Delimitation Commission of 1962. The testimonies to each of these commissions show that speakers of Sabaki languages supported national parties, but only if their tribal interests would be protected. However, they also promoted coastal solidarity within the framework of a Kenyan nation.

The Robertson Commission

Petitioners often defined the coastal strip in ways that surprised the Robertson Commission. Some called for the restoration of ancient polities. For example, the Coastal League—which boasted Mijikenda, Arab, Asian, and European members—called for the "re-establishment of the state of Azania" mentioned in the *Periplus of the Erythraean Sea* on behalf of the *Wenyeji Wa Mwambao* (owners of the coast).[43] Similarly, Yahya Ali Omar asked Great Britain to recognize the sultan of Zanzibar as the sovereign over "the Sultanate of Swahilini." Recognizing the sultan's claims to the coastal strip and its islands, he said, would rectify the harm caused by colonial partition. The commissioners suggested that he was "thinking too much of the past and was not thinking enough about the realities of the future."[44]

Other petitioners wanted the coastal strip to be an autonomous region in a larger East African federation. Abdurahman Mohamed and three associates recommended a slower pace. Only after a new coast legislature could function as the voice of the people could they decide to remain independent, join with Kenya, or take a place within an East African federation.[45] Sheikh Ali Muhamad bin Yunus also supported a federation; but he added the wrinkle that if the British government abrogated their treaty with the sultan of Zanzibar, they would need to make a new one with him. With the help of Hyder al-Kindy, he had recently revived and claimed the office of *tammim* (administrator) over the Three Tribes section of the Twelve Tribes. He helpfully translated his new title as "king of Mombasa."[46]

While Swahilis, Arabs, Europeans, some South Asians, and even fewer of the Mijikenda opposed consolidation with Kenya, petitions from most Mijikenda and Pokomo communities, as well as labor unions dominated by upcountry migrants, argued for unity with Kenya. In contrast to the diverse proposals of mwambaoists, they converged on common points: the strip was economically unviable on its own, many Africans from elsewhere in Kenya had resided in the strip for generations, and secessionists were Arabs.[47] The latter identification was meant to disqualify secessionists as foreigners whose ancestors engaged in the slave trade. They also argued that the sovereignty of Zanzibar's sultan only extended to coastal cities since Seyyid Sa'id had never conquered the rural territories around them. As a result, the negotiations that turned their land over to British rule were illegitimate because the rightful owners (their forebears) had been excluded. To avoid compounding this tragedy, a delegation from the Mijikenda Union headed by Ronald Ngala provocatively asked the Robertson Commission to amend its itinerary so that they would visit towns along the escarpment to hear the testimonies of "indigenous" Africans instead of focusing on areas along the coast dominated by "Arab slave traders."[48]

Robertson's final report made no mention of Swahilini, the king of Mombasa, or Azania. He expressed a preference for turning the coastal strip into a federal territory and making Mombasa the capital of a wider East African federation. However, Kenya's nationalist politicians wanted to secure their own positions as heads of state before contemplating a larger union with Tanganyika and Uganda; and Great Britain arranged to keep these two countries out of the negotiations. Robertson's second preference—that the sultan retain nominal sovereignty over the coast—was unacceptable to the British government. In the end, the residents of the coast had to settle for Robertson's weakest option: no independence or autonomy, just basic protections in the constitution to retain treaty provisions that Muslims would be subject to Islamic law.[49]

After the Robertson Commission submitted its report, the representatives to Kenya's Legislative Council met once again in London. Most of the delegates represented KANU or KADU, but Abdilahi Nassir and another associate appeared for the Mwambao United Front to argue once more for coastal autonomy. The secretary of state for the colonies sidelined their efforts by sequestering discussions about the status of the coastal strip in a separate, concurrent conference. He offered the dubious rationale that coastal autonomy was a matter between the sultan of Zanzibar and the British government that did not concern Kenyans.[50]

The Foster-Sutton Commissions

After the second conference concluded, Foster-Sutton's Regional Boundaries Commission was instructed to recommend adjustments to regional boundaries that reflected "the desires of those people who wish to associate in one region"—verbiage designed to avoid mentioning the word *tribe*.[51] More to the point, the Constituencies Delimitation Commission was forbidden from creating constituencies for "particular tribes or particular sections of the community."[52] There was some debate about regional boundaries in western and central Kenya in the commissions' joint hearings, but most of the concern was focused on two provinces whose populations were threatening to secede. In Northern Frontier District, many Somali residents wanted to join Somalia. In the Coast Province, Mijikenda residents were among the most emphatic supporters of regional autonomy, but they contended with Swahili, Arab, and European residents who insisted on union with Zanzibar or outright independence for the coastal strip.

Petitioners offered more elaborate proposals for reorganizing the coast to the Foster-Sutton commissions than they gave the Robertson Commission. In support of their arguments, they turned to what historian Julie MacArthur has described in Western Kenya as "counter-mapping"— providing alternative visions of territoriality that use cartography to imagine political communities.[53] Their stenciled maps took earlier twentieth-century district maps as their templates. Though petitioners requested adjustments to some district boundaries, most of the memoranda proposed moving entire districts and native reserves between regions. There were two reasons their memoranda left district boundaries intact. First, the commissioners were empowered to recommend changes to Kenya's provincial boundaries, but they were instructed not to amend the underlying district boundaries. Second, many petitioners appeared satisfied that the district boundaries already aligned with their communities of interest.

Although the petitioners' maps did not challenge the official geography of the colonial government, they illustrated competing visions of who belonged to the coast. For instance, the Coast People's Party submitted a map of "Mwambao" (figure 8.1) that included all districts adjoining the Indian Ocean, the Northern Frontier District claimed by Pokomo speakers, and even a part of Somalia that Great Britain had previously ceded to Italy. (They added this last region to include settlements of Bajuni Swahili.)

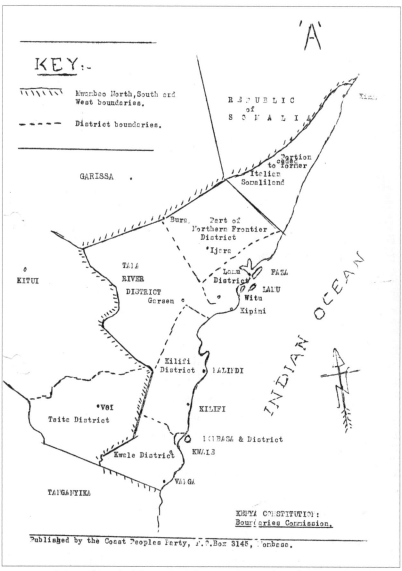

FIGURE 8.1. Mwambao, in "Coast People's Party Memorandum," Kenya Regional Boundaries (Foster-Sutton) Commission, Papers, CO 897/1, National Archives of the United Kingdom. Reprinted with permission.

While most maps included all the Sabaki-speaking communities of the coast (Pokomo, Mijikenda, and Swahili), they differed on whether to include Taita District. The Coast People's Party excluded Taita District because it was beyond the protectorate boundaries, even though it had been administered as part of Coast Province for decades. In contrast, the map submitted by the Coast United Front opted to include all of Northern Frontier District and Taita District. A separate petition from the "United Voice of the People of Taita District" argued, "[Their] traditions, cultural pattern and peace lovingness resemble and tend more towards those of the other coastal peoples than those of any up-country region."[54] The profession of "peace lovingness" by some of the Taita was likely intended to disclaim the Mau Mau violence that coastal peoples associated with people from central Kenya. The Coast People's Party opted not to include Taita District. When commissioners asked why, they explained, "that District did not have the same community of interests as others living in the Coast Province."[55] Taita District's elected representative, David Wanyumba, concurred: he warned that belonging to Coast Province would subject them to Mijikenda domination.[56]

The inclusion of Kamba communities in coastal society was even more controversial. Though most of the Kamba lived in central Kenya's Ukambani District, a large population lived in Kilifi and Kwale Districts. They requested the government to expand Ukambani District to include territory up to the coast and referenced a nineteenth-century meeting in Mombasa in support of their claim: "The Historical fact is that the Akamba Boundaries extended to right down the Coast or Mombasa Island[,] where Dr. Krapf met Mr. Kivui Munda, a prominent Akamba Leader."[57] Barring a contiguous extension of Kamba District's boundary, they hoped to form a satellite subdistrict of the Ukambani District because they worried that the Mijikenda would abuse them as foreigners.

This fear of Mijikenda abuse was no idle fear. Some of the Mijikenda memoranda argued for the expulsion of foreigners. These included obvious newcomers like the Luo and Kikuyu and old scapegoats like the Arab "slave traders," but they also portrayed the Kamba as alien outsiders.[58] For instance, a memorandum from the Mijikenda Union explained that no one was more closely related to them than the Pokomo and that the Bajuni were their nephews and nieces, but "the presence of the Kambas in our territory is . . . a great nuisance; and immediate steps should be taken to hasten their exodus."[59] Taita petitioners specifically disclaimed rumors that they wished to be in the same district as the Kamba.[60] The unfiltered rhetoric of these petitions and testimonies is particularly striking given the explicit denunciation of tribalism in Foster-Sutton's instructions.

Kamba petitioners replied to these calls for removal by stating that the only newcomers among them were those who had settled in the Shimba Hills of Kwale District. Mariakani and other areas were the "permanent places" of the Kamba, which "belong[ed] to them by right of achievement during the Great Bantu-Migratory period across Africa."[61] The Coast Akamba Advancement Association also noted that their members were being threatened "in public places like bars, football fields, and in the streets" because of their support for KANU's plan for a strong central government instead of KADU's *majimboism*.[62] The national debates over regionalism thus heightened commitments to tribal divisions but framed each tribe as either a community of the coast or upcountry. Members of the Mijikenda and the Swahili worried about being dominated by Kikuyu and Luo populations in a national government, while the Taita and the Kamba felt that only a strong national government could protect them from discrimination by regional governments.

Digo organizations were particularly active at the Foster-Sutton commissions. Instead of supporting the broader Mijikenda claims to the coast, they asserted that they alone were the original settlers, and thus owners, of the entire Coast Province, from Vanga on the border with Tanganyika to Lamu and inland from Mombasa to Taita. Though they also wanted the Kamba to be expelled, they surprisingly reserved their primary complaint for another Mijikenda confederation: the Duruma, with whom they shared Kwale District. On letterhead proclaiming the motto "Freedom and Unity," the Kwale Branch of the KANU wrote, "Waduruma can only be living peacefully if they . . . remember that they descend from the Wadigo tribe and if not[,] they are bound lawfully to pack and march south to Mozambique."[63] The memorandum from the Digo National Union offered additional context: it explained that the Duruma descended from enslaved people whom a Portuguese slaver brought from Mozambique in the mid-fifteenth century.[64] These enslaved people had intermarried with locals but had no "Sacred Settlement (KAYA)" other than what the Digo had given them. Thus, the Digo repurposed ancestry and affiliation with a sacred kaya to exclude even Chimijikenda speakers from the coastal community.

The Digo National Union also narrated a history of Arab settlement along the coast that offered a surprising revision of a pivotal moment in littoral history. They claimed that no Arabs had settled along Kenya's coast until after the Digo themselves had gone to Muscat and requested help in expelling the Portuguese. The Arabs sent by the sultan were successful. However, they refused his order to return home, so the sultan sent a governor to Zanzibar "to rule all the Arabs living in that island, and those living along the Coastal belt and in Mombasa withou[t] our knowledge."[65] The Digo Political Union proposed a Digo president for Mombasa as a remedy, while the "Wadigo of Shimba North Location" suggested that Digo representatives should constitute the majority in the proposed regional parliament.[66] These petitions thus demanded acknowledgment of exclusive Digo claims to the coast, a sharp contrast to the 1932 Kenya Land Commission petitions that emphasized close connections with the Three Tribes of Mombasa.

Most Digo organizations presumed that the boundaries of their territory were self-evident; only the Digo National Union submitted a map (figure 8.2). Using hand-drawn hatch marks and colored ink, they illustrated their ambitious claims and called attention in their memorandum to the following features on their map:

1. Kwale District should be renamed "Digoland"
2. Coastal Strip should be renamed Digoland Coast
3. Duruma Hinterland should be referred to as Digoland Hinterland
4. And Mombasa Island should be renamed Digo Island.[67]

Not content with claiming the entire coastal strip, they also recommended that Kenya's maritime claims should extend to the halfway point between East Africa and India and that their half of the sea should be called the "East African Ocean." The commissioners let them know that this was beyond their terms of reference.[68] Yet the demand emphasizes how closely the Digo defined themselves through their connection to the sea.

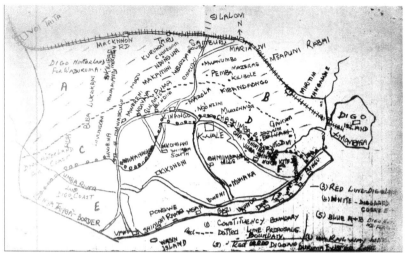

FIGURE 8.2. Map drawn by the Digo National Union, in "Digo Coast and Hinterland," Kenya Regional Boundaries (Foster-Sutton) Commission, Papers, CO 897/1, National Archives of the United Kingdom. Reprinted with permission.

These maps and the debates about immigrants, permanent places, and their history revealed the tension between national and tribal loyalties on the eve of Kenya's independence. The memorandum of the Tana River Inhabitants agreed, for instance, that the "country should not be separated tribalistically" but then argued that a fair representation would require separate constituencies for the three tribes of Tana District to ensure that "each tribe may not be ignored."[69] Though petitioners committed to a common electoral roll that would give every voter an equal voice, they tried to persuade commissioners to draw constituency boundaries that would ensure the influence of their respective tribes. Supporters of Mwambao and KADU both decided that forging a regional identity was essential to preserving these interests. However, the claims of the Digo organizations that they alone were the original Mijikenda owners of the coast suggest that commitments to clan confederations still offered alternative ways of imagining the past as well as the future—independent of the tribes that had superseded the confederations in the colonial era.

"I am not really a Kenyan; I'm just forced to pretend I'm a Kenyan. I'm a *mmwambao*."[70] In 2011 I was speaking with a highly educated Digo guide, who offered to show me around Kwale District. He explained that the Digo communities south of Mombasa were in turmoil because the Mombasa Republican Council (MRC) was competing for recruits with al-Shabaab, an armed insurgency in Somalia that aimed to form an Islamic state.[71] Al-Shabaab's message resonated with some members of the Somali community in Mombasa as well as with some other coastal Muslims. In contrast, the MRC was taking advantage of the freedoms guaranteed by the new constitution to organize a movement for Pwani (the coast) to secede from Kenya. My guide explained that the MRC appealed to patriots of the coastal community, whom upcountry immigrants exploited for personal gain. In Nairobi, he said, they believe in "*binafsi*, every man for himself"; but on the coast they have *ustaarabu* (civilization) and believe in *jumuiya*—the same word that Sheikh al-Amin had used to translate "association" in the 1930s.[72]

Incidentally, www.jumuiya.org is the internet domain name for the Jumuiya ya Kaunti za Pwani (Association of Coastal Counties). This umbrella organization was created to coordinate investment opportunities along the coast after the 2010 constitution divided Coast Province into five new counties. Though Coast Province and the Protectorate of Kenya are no more, county officials and autonomists both agree that the people of littoral Kenya are a single society that should forge their future together, regardless of their tribal origins.

Collaborations across county and tribal boundaries draw on the linguistic and cultural heritage shared by speakers of all Sabaki languages and by others who have made their homes along the coast. Although centuries old, this cis-oceanic heritage has never been static. Sabaki speakers accommodated and learned from Segeju and Oromo immigrants from the African interior as well as Portuguese, Omani, and British immigrants who arrived from the sea to elaborate the schema of their shared littoral society. Some of the military, commercial, and kinship alliances that had motivated collaboration among them for centuries gave way to tribal identities based on religious and cultural traits. British officials may have enshrined these distinctions in imperial law, administrative practice, and district boundaries, but residents drew on centuries of common experiences to organize and imagine themselves as members of the Swahili and

Mijikenda ethnic groups. The concept of ethnicity was no less a creation of the collective imagination than of its ancestors in the preceding millennia.

The invention of tribes in Kenya was a major inflection point in a centuries-long process of assembling and imagining ever more populous and extensive communities in littoral Kenya. Yet tribalism was not hegemonic in colonial Kenya. Speakers of Sabaki languages did not completely discard their former affiliations in favor of tribes, nor could the tribes that they assembled fully contain the "communities of interest" they brought together. Though proponents of tribalism pitted Chimijikenda- and Kiswahili-speaking communities against one another as Kenya moved toward independence, other voices consistently pressed for the shared interests of Mwambao wa Pwani, a territory for all *watu wa pwani* (the people of the coast).

Though Abdilahi Nassir and other Kiswahili speakers were the earliest proponents of a Mwambao state, some of Mwambao's most dedicated supporters in recent years live several miles inland and speak Chimijikenda. More felt than imagined, Mwambao gives little heed to the narrow boundaries of language and religion that inscribed ethnic boundaries in the twentieth century. Although Mwambao never achieved autonomy or recognition as a political community, it remains a tantalizing dream—an enduring alternative to the succession of imperial, religious, ethnic, and national identities that have engulfed and polarized littoral Kenya since the sixteenth century.

EPILOGUE

Reconciling Ethnicity and Nationalism

> *Sote raiya wapwani*
> *kheri tunakuombeya*
> . . . .
> *Sote ni raiya kwake*
> *pasiwa kubaguwana*
>
> All of us coast people are citizens
> blessings we pray for you
> . . . .
> All of us are its [Kenya's] citizens
> there is no cause for discrimination.
>
> —Nasor Said Riyamy, lyrics from "Harambee"

JUST AFTER DAYBREAK on Sunday, July 18, 2010, about sixty men, over a dozen women, and a handful of boys gathered in Old Town Mombasa to celebrate Siku ya Kibunzi, the Swahili New Year. The holiday also served as a reunion for the Wamiji who claim the island as their homeland. As participants arrived in *tuk-tuk* taxis, old friends greeted one another with a handshake accompanied by a kiss on the backs of their clasped hands. A videographer conducted spontaneous interviews for a promotional video about the holiday as he circulated through the small crowd. Most of the men and boys wore cylindrical *kofia* hats and gleaming white or brown *kanzu* tunics. A few men appeared in shorts or slacks and tattered shirts, dressed for labor. The women wore modest black *bui-bui* (coverings) that almost concealed their *kanga* wraps and blouses. The organizers intended to assemble everyone on a field facing the grave of Shehe Mvita, the sixteenth-century founder of the town of Mvita, whom Mombasa's indigenous communities celebrate as a martyr and claim as their ancestor. But a morning rain drove them inside the auditorium of Allidina Visram High School, whose campus surrounds the grave near Mombasa's creek. One participant told me they had celebrated Siku ya Kibunzi on the same site for a thousand years, maybe two.[1]

Despite celebrating on the grounds of a high school named for a prominent Indian immigrant, the Wamiji asserted their ownership of Mombasa Island by maintaining their ancestor's grave. Most attendees recited the Qur'an in Arabic and sang religious songs in Kiswahili in the auditorium. After an hour, a muezzin made the traditional Islamic call to prayer, which the workmen outside took as the signal to slaughter a cow, a goat, and a chicken. The meat from this *sadaqa* (sacrifice) went into a stew that they fed to the poor at midday—a public act of generosity and hospitality that sustained the Wamiji's status as *waungwana* (patricians) and *wenyeji* (owners of the town). After the feast, they placed the carcasses and leftovers in a rubber sack and paid a fisherman to heave it into the sea. One of the men explained that this symbolic act would cast out the pollution and evil that had accumulated in the town over the previous year. Some of the women offered a broader context for their ceremonies as they left. In response to my question about why they celebrate Swahili New Year, they said it was a prayer of peace for Kenya.

A few months after Swahili New Year, on the eve of Kenya's inaugural Mashujaa (Heroes) Day in October 2010, human rights lawyer Joseph Mwarandu knelt and bowed his head before a member of a Giriama *kambi* council. For hours he received instructions and blessings at the feet of the *kaya* elder. At dawn he dressed in the regalia of a Giriama council member: he wrapped a red cloth with blue stripes around his lower body and draped a white cloth around his shoulders, leaving his torso uncovered. He wore a headband decorated with tufts of monkey hair and cowry shells. In his hands he held a long fly whisk and a *fimbo* (a slender walking stick). As the sun rose, he walked a few miles to the museum at Malindi's waterfront with dozens of followers dressed in Mijikenda attire. Women in *hando* skirts or *kanga* wraps and men sporting *kaniki* wraps, fez hats, or turbans milled about—dancing, drumming, and chatting as they waited. When Mwarandu finally reappeared outside the museum, he was accompanied by Ruth Enkeseni, a Maasai woman. In honor of Mashujaa Day, the Giriama elders had bestowed on her the title Mekatilili wa Mwenza, the heroine who helped inspire the Giriama Uprising in 1913. Around midmorning they took their places in front of two companies: Mwarandu led a group of men with his *fimbo* stick and Enkeseni led a group of women as she wielded a thin sword in a silver scabbard.

When the two companies met in front of the museum, Mwarandu and Enkeseni ceremoniously clasped each other's right hands and raised them three times in the air for all to see. A man narrating the event to the crowd noted that joining the hands of the woman and the man "showed that our country sees peace, peace in our leadership, peace in our cities, peace in our whole society." He added that "wondrous celebrations" like these are how people cause their culture to continue.[2] Although Mwarandu and Enkeseni already enjoyed great respect in Kenya as activists, the Giriama council endorsed their leadership by bestowing on them regalia, secret knowledge, and access to the sacred places that preserve their ancestral heritage. After the ceremony, the media-savvy Mwarandu invited the press to attend the official installation of a statue in Malindi's Uhuru Park that depicted Mekatilili wa Mwenza. There, on national television, Mwarandu urged Kenyans to "live in peace" and to "respect each other's culture."[3] He said the organizers of the statue's public unveiling had asked Enkeseni, a Maasai women, to represent Mekatilili because the Mijikenda woman should be a heroine for all Kenyans.

These two celebrations exemplify how littoral Kenyans reconciled pride in their ethnic heritage with loyalty to their nation in the years following the 2007 election crisis. Immediately following the election, scholars had focused on parsing the political factions, crimes, and grievances that had nearly shattered Kenya's national cohesion. However, when I began my research in late 2009, Mijikenda and Swahili consultants focused on how their ethnic heritage could pull Kenya back together instead of worrying that it would drive the nation apart.

As my consultants directed my attention away from "negative ethnicity" to the aspects of their ethnic identities that they celebrated, they helped me explore elements of Kenya's past that historians have rarely analyzed together. The historiological arguments embodied in the intangible heritage of rituals and everyday activities offered unexpected perspectives on their shared past that complemented other sources about the past. A bridewealth negotiation for a Mijikenda couple from different clan confederations illustrated the historical intricacies of kinship. Pondering an impromptu blessing of a handful of medicinal twigs led me to consider how clans mediated collaborations among groups defined by knowledge. Sword dances and games of *bao* inspired research on the entanglements of warfare and commerce. Elaborate *zefe* processions showed how religious practices transformed not only public roads and parks but also entire territories into religious spaces. The daily greetings exchanged while visiting consultants in Rabai indicated how speakers of Sabaki languages embody communal claims to territory. Even the humorous placement of a chair at a civil forum prompted questions about how they imagined the boundaries that divided them. Consultants sat with me for dozens of hours to explain their respective ethnic group's history and culture; but their quotidian practices, intimate family traditions, and elaborate public ceremonies also offered insights into their vernacular understanding of ethnicity.

Instead of asserting diametric contrasts between modern and premodern identities, imagined communities and face-to-face communities, or ethnic and nonethnic groups, this book has drawn on linguistic, archaeological, oral, and documentary evidence to reconceptualize ethnicity as just one category in a series of collective identities that Africans have articulated over the past two millennia. In particular, it traced the ancestors of ethnicity as expressed in Sabaki languages. In the introduction, the genealogy of a single word—*miji*—illustrated how speakers of Sabaki languages elaborated the Proto-Bantu word for "village" to mean groups as diverse as clan confederations, tribes, and cultural associations. Here I summarize some of the criteria that speakers of Sabaki languages assembled over centuries before repurposing them in the twentieth century to define ethnicity on their own terms.

As is common throughout the world, speakers of Sabaki languages assert that their ethnic groups descend from founding lineages. However, the multiple foremothers and forefathers mentioned in their oral traditions blur the boundaries of unilineal descent by imagining the founding generations of these tribes as multiple sets of kin and kith rather than a single family. These traditions thus portray ethnicity as a gradient of intimacy that presumes some ethnic groups are distant relatives while others are strangers. Hence, even at their greatest strain, relationships among Mijikenda and Swahili communities tended to be more amicable than those with Kamba or Oromo communities, whom they excluded as perpetual immigrants to the coast.

Though kinship is a salient symbol of ethnic affiliation among speakers of Sabaki languages, they also emphasize the criteria of proprietary knowledge and shared, sacred space. Rituals in *makaya,* cemeteries, mosques, and other sacred spaces offer focal points for symbolizing ethnic affiliations that extend much farther in space. At various points in the history of littoral Kenya, speakers of Sabaki languages embodied this distinctive knowledge in clans, title societies, age-sets, and councils, whose membership often overlapped. Though several groups have claimed authority to speak on behalf of the Mijikenda in the twenty-first century, clans are the only one of these groups' categories that remains a major criterion for determining belonging in an ethnic group. The multiplicity of spaces that define ethnic affiliation also leads speakers of Sabaki languages to identify more as members of clan confederations that were founded as long ago as the sixteenth century (e.g., Rabai or Jomvu) than as members of the Mijikenda or Swahili ethnic group. Finally, they employ religious practice as a key criterion for determining ethnic belonging, despite the many Muslim Mijikenda who complicate presumptions that Islam is an exclusively Swahili characteristic.

The cis-oceanic approach that traced inland and overseas influences on littoral Kenya in this book revealed that the criteria that speakers of Sabaki languages have assembled over two millennia are not theirs alone. Rather, they managed to accommodate a stream of immigrants, interlopers, and imperial officials by incorporating their contributions into an ever-changing, littoral schema. Scholars can trace some elements back to the Proto-Sabaki speech community, or even the Proto–Mashariki Bantu speech community. Yet the schema through which people organized their communities in littoral Kenya does not derive solely from any one origin. Their shared concept of "tribe," for instance, conflates the experiences of British administrators in India and East Africa with nineteenth-century histories of Europe and Rome, Arabic connotations of the word *qabīla,* and the unique mix of kinship, political, linguistic, and religious criteria with which speakers of Sabaki languages differentiated their communities. So although this book has focused on the experiences of the Sabaki language group, reducing the array of elements they developed into a single "Sabaki culture" would mispresent their historical experiences. By investigating the history of ethnicity and its ancestors through the framework of a littoral society, this book has transcended the conventional organization of African (and Kenyan) history around ethnic identities and Indian Ocean history around diasporic communities.

Tracing the history of littoral Kenya over two millennia has also offered insights into the formation and transformation of littoral societies that could be compared with other regions of the Indian Ocean. Part 1 explored how speakers of Sabaki languages acquired "littoral" features: settlement on the coast, exploitation of marine resources for foodways and architecture, and engagements with commerce and Islam. Most importantly, the millennia-long timeframe demonstrated that speakers of Sabaki languages embraced the cosmopolitan ethic of living in diverse, complementary communities before they tied their economies to oceanic trade. They found prosperity in the transitional zones of littoral ecologies by establishing towns in the late first millennium CE that could accommodate people pursuing different subsistence strategies. This hospitality then increased their capacity to accelerate their investments in Indian Ocean commerce in the tenth century. The formation of Kenya's littoral society thus contrasted sharply with islands like Mauritius, whose littoral society was an amalgamation of many diasporic communities converging to engage in established systems of oceanic trade. Given the early development of overseas commerce throughout much of the Indian Ocean, scholars will likely need to engage in multidisciplinary analysis that considers archaeological and linguistic evidence to determine if other societies developed "littoral" characteristics before or after their integration into the Indian Ocean economy.

The centuries-long timeframe in part 2 similarly demonstrated how littoral societies transformed to accommodate changes in the "common fields" of Indian Ocean politics. Participating in the Dar al-Islam and the empires of Portugal, Oman, and Great Britain required speakers of Sabaki languages to repeatedly reconfigure their inherited schemas. These reimaginations eventually led speakers of Sabaki languages to see themselves as a "coastal people" defined by their residence in and mastery of a littoral zone stretching from the Lamu Archipelago to Pemba Island and inland to the edge of the *nyika* escarpment. This self-perception became even more salient in the decolonization era explored in part 3. As Kenya negotiated its independence, speakers of Sabaki languages struggled to remain separate from, and then reconcile themselves to, the interior communities of Kenya. Whether they claimed the name Wapwani, Mwambao, Sultanate of Swahilini, or Digoland, speakers of Sabaki languages in littoral Kenya used their connection to the seashore to distinguish themselves from other Kenyans. This perception was buttressed by treaties, administrative structures, and colonial boundary-making that made integration with the rest of Kenya difficult for some to imagine.

In addition to investigating the movements of diasporic communities or their integration into littoral host societies, this book has demonstrated how scholars of the Indian Ocean might investigate the ways in which littoral people consciously distinguished themselves and their territory from their interior neighbors. As in Kenya, a cis-oceanic analysis that attends equally to interior and oceanic influence may help explore this dynamic. For instance, understanding Sabaki speakers' perception of the Mau Mau Emergency in central Kenya helps explain why they were so eager to eject the Kamba communities who had lived alongside them at the coast for more than a century. This approach is especially important when considering early eras of East African history because information and research about developments in the Indian Ocean still outweigh scholarly knowledge about the African interior. Cis-oceanic approaches that destabilize conventional boundaries between internal and external communities, or national and subnational ones, could similarly reveal vernacular notions of ethnicity, caste, tribe, and religion along other frontiers in Africa and horizons of the Indian Ocean. As in littoral East Africa, scholars may find language families to be a useful scope for transcending their analyses of single groups like "the Mijikenda" or "the Swahili" without getting engulfed in the staggering scale of continents and oceans that make the intricacies of identity difficult to discern.

Speakers of Sabaki languages (and their Proto–NEC Bantu forebears) have made their homes in littoral East Africa since the beginning of the current era. Yet aside from chapter 1's grounding in the Great Lakes region, each chapter of this book has detailed how they navigated the complicated waters of innovation in the Indian Ocean without ever leaving their shore. After their initial settlement along the coastal frontier, they managed the extension of the western Indian Ocean's commercial zone into the coastal escarpment, learned to manipulate the incursion of Portugal into their corner of Dar al-Islam and accommodated the sectarian prejudices of the Zanzibar Sultanate even before they began to negotiate with the British Empire's extension from India into their territory. The institutional triumph of African nationalism—over Arab, Zanzibari, or Mwambaoist varieties—may have integrated them into the Republic of Kenya, but as the vignettes that opened this conclusion indicate, many of them still have their eyes fixed toward the sea.

The persistence of elements in language, ritual, and everyday practices over generations makes this past discernible to historians and other scholars, but it also makes nearly two thousand years of social innovation available to Kenyans. Disentangling ethnicity from its ancestors unmasks ethnicity in Africa as a modern novelty—but one rooted in elements that speakers of Sabaki languages have reinvigorated for centuries. Though Kenyans' electoral politics have demonstrated how politicians can use ethnic loyalties to exacerbate political violence, speakers of Sabaki languages affirm that their cultural heritage also offers models for reconciling ethnicity, nationality, and religion, as well as any other identity they might wish to imagine.

Notes

INTRODUCTION

1. Nic Cheeseman and Daniel Branch, eds., "Election Fever: Kenya's Crisis," special issue, *Journal of Eastern African Studies* 2, no. 2 (July 2008).
2. Abdullah Said Naji, "Informal Remarks at Malindi Cultural Festival Intellectual Session," Malindi, Kenya, April 4, 2010, digital audio and photographs, Ray Research Deposit E026A5. For "negative ethnicity" in Kenyan politics, see Koigi wa Wamwere, *Towards Genocide in Kenya: The Curse of Negative Ethnicity* (Nairobi: MvuleAfrica Publishers, 2008), 95.
3. E.g., Leif O. Manger, *The Hadrami Diaspora: Community-Building on the Indian Ocean Rim* (New York: Berghan Books, 2010), 9; Sureshi Jayawardene, "Racialized Casteism: Exposing the Relationship between Race, Caste, and Colorism through the Experiences of Africana People in India and Sri Lanka," *Journal of African American Studies* 20, nos. 3–4 (December 2016): 323–45; Michael C. Hawkins, *Making Moros: Imperial Historicism and American Military Rule in the Philippines' Muslim South* (Ithaca, NY: Cornell University Press, 2021).
4. Partha Chatterjee, *The Nation and Its Fragments: Colonial and Postcolonial Histories* (Princeton, NJ: Princeton University Press, 1993); M. Crawford Young, "Nationalism, Ethnicity, and Class in Africa: A Retrospective," *Cahiers d'Études Africaines* 26, no. 103 (January 1, 1986): 421–95.
5. Patrick Gathara, "What Is Your Tribe? The Invention of Kenya's Ethnic Communities," *The Elephant* (blog), March 5, 2018, www.theelephant.info.
6. Wamwere, *Towards Genocide in Kenya*, 95.
7. Pier M. Larson, *Ocean of Letters: Language and Creolization in an Indian Ocean Diaspora* (Cambridge: Cambridge University Press, 2009); Manger, *Hadrami Diaspora*.

8. Thomas Hylland Eriksen, *Common Denominators: Ethnicity, Nation-Building and Compromise in Mauritius* (New York: Berg, 1998).
9. Young, "Nationalism, Ethnicity, and Class in Africa"; Leroy Vail, "Introduction: Ethnicity in Southern African History," in *The Creation of Tribalism in Southern Africa*, ed. Leroy Vail (Berkeley: University of California Press, 1991), 1–20; Patrick Harries, "The Roots of Ethnicity: Discourse and the Politics of Language Construction in South-East Africa," *African Affairs* 87, no. 346 (January 1, 1988): 25–52.
10. Godfrey Muriuki, *A History of the Kikuyu: 1500–1900* (Oxford: Oxford University Press, 1974); William Robert Ochieng', *A Precolonial History of the Gusii of Western Kenya from c. A.D. 1500 to 1914* (Kampala: East African Literature Bureau, 1974); David William Cohen and E. S. Atieno Odhiambo, *Siaya: The Historical Anthropology of an African Landscape* (Athens: Ohio University Press, 1989); Thomas T. Spear and Richard Waller, eds., *Being Maasai: Ethnicity and Identity in East Africa* (Athens: Ohio University Press, 1993); Bill Bravman, *Making Ethnic Ways: Communities and Their Transformations in Taita, Kenya, 1800–1950* (Portsmouth, NH: Heinemann, 1998); Gabrielle Lynch, *I Say to You: Ethnic Politics and the Kalenjin in Kenya* (Chicago: University of Chicago Press, 2011); Myles Osborne, *Ethnicity and Empire in Kenya: Loyalty and Martial Race among the Kamba, c. 1800 to the Present* (New York: Cambridge University Press, 2014); Julie MacArthur, *Cartography and the Political Imagination: Mapping Community in Colonial Kenya* (Athens: Ohio University Press, 2016); Randall L. Pouwels, *Horn and Crescent: Cultural Change and Traditional Islam on the East African Coast, 800–1900* (Cambridge: Cambridge University Press, 1987); Justin Willis, *Mombasa, the Swahili, and the Making of the Mijikenda* (New York: Oxford University Press, 1993).
11. Allen F. Isaacman and Barbara Isaacman, *Slavery and Beyond: The Making of Men and Chikunda Ethnic Identities in the Unstable World of South-Central Africa, 1750–1920* (Portsmouth, NH: Heinemann, 2004), 9.
12. Elizabeth Tonkin, "Processes of Identity, Ethnicising and Morality," in *Ethnicity in Africa: Roots, Meanings, and Implications*, ed. Louisa de la Gorgendiere et al. (Edinburgh: Center of African Studies, University of Edinburgh, 1996), 242.
13. Paul Nugent, "Putting the History Back into Ethnicity: Enslavement, Religion, and Cultural Brokerage in the Construction of

Mandinka/Jola and Ewe/Agotime Identities in West Africa, c. 1650–1930," *Comparative Studies in Society and History* 50, no. 4 (October 1, 2008): 920–48; Alexander Keese, ed., *Ethnicity and the Long-Term Perspective: The African Experience* (New York: Peter Lang, 2010).

14. See, for example, Lynch, *I Say to You*.
15. K. N. Chaudhuri, *Trade and Civilisation in the Indian Ocean: An Economic History from the Rise of Islam to 1750* (Cambridge: Cambridge University Press, 1985); see further discussion below.
16. E.g., Jeremy Prestholdt, *Domesticating the World: African Consumerism and the Genealogies of Globalization* (Berkeley: University of California Press, 2008); Fahad Ahmad Bishara, *A Sea of Debt: Law and Economic Life in the Western Indian Ocean, 1780–1950* (New York: Cambridge University Press, 2017); Thomas Franklin McDow, *Buying Time: Debt and Mobility in the Western Indian Ocean* (Athens: Ohio University Press, 2018).
17. Young, "Nationalism, Ethnicity, and Class in Africa," 442–43.
18. Derek R. Peterson, *Ethnic Patriotism and the East African Revival: A History of Dissent, c. 1935–1972* (Cambridge: Cambridge University Press, 2013).
19. Terence O. Ranger, "The Invention of Tradition Revisited: The Case of Africa," in *Legitimacy and the State in Twentieth Century Africa,* ed. Terence Ranger and Olufemi Vaughan (London: Palgrave Macmillan, 1993), 82–101.
20. Curtis A. Keim, *Mistaking Africa: Curiosities and Inventions of the American Mind,* 3rd ed. (Boulder, CO: Westview, 2014).
21. E.g., Christopher Lowe, "Talking about 'Tribe': Moving from Stereotype to Analysis," Africa Policy Information Center, November 1997, http://www.africafocus.org/docs08/ethno801.php.
22. Young, "Nationalism, Ethnicity, and Class in Africa," 453; Donald L. Horowitz, *Ethnic Groups in Conflict* (Berkeley: University of California Press, 1985), 52–55; Rogers Brubaker and Frederick Cooper, "Beyond 'Identity,'" *Theory and Society* 29, no. 1 (February 1, 2000): 1–47.
23. Jonathon Glassman, "Ethnicity and Race in African Thought," in *A Companion to African History,* ed. William H. Worger, Charles Ambler, and Nwando Achebe (Hoboken, NJ: Wiley-Blackwell, 2018), 199–223; Louisa de la Gorgendiere, Kenneth King, and Sarah Vaughan, eds., *Ethnicity in Africa: Roots, Meanings and Implications* (Edinburgh: Center of African Studies, University of Edinburgh, 1996).
24. Eriksen, *Common Denominators,* 9.

25. Ananya Chakravarti, "Mapping 'Gabriel': Space, Identity and Slavery in the Late Sixteenth-Century Indian Ocean," *Past & Present* 243, no. 1 (May 1, 2019): 6.
26. Richard Jenkins, *Rethinking Ethnicity: Arguments and Explorations,* 2nd ed. (Los Angeles: Sage, 2008), 14.
27. Fredrik Barth, *Ethnic Groups and Boundaries: The Social Organization of Culture Difference,* 2nd ed. (Prospect Heights, IL: Waveland, 1998).
28. Thomas Hylland Eriksen, *Ethnicity and Nationalism: Anthropological Perspectives* (New York: Pluto Press, 2002), 27.
29. Tonkin, "Processes of Identity, Ethnicising and Morality," 237–59; Pier M. Larson, *History and Memory in the Age of Enslavement: Becoming Merina in Highland Madagascar, 1770–1822* (Portsmouth, NH: Heinemann, 2000), 29. Cf. Bernard S. Cohn, "The Census, Social Structure and Objectification in South Asia," in *An Anthropologist among the Historians and Other Essays* (New Delhi: Oxford University Press, 2006), 224–54.
30. Eriksen, *Ethnicity and Nationalism,* 20–22.
31. Horowitz, *Ethnic Groups in Conflict,* 68–70.
32. Jenkins, *Rethinking Ethnicity;* Rogers Brubaker, Mara Loveman, and Peter Stamatov, "Ethnicity as Cognition," *Theory and Society* 33, no. 1 (February 1, 2004): 31–64.
33. Benedict Anderson, *Imagined Communities: Reflections on the Origin and Spread of Nationalism,* 2nd ed. (London: Verso, 1991); Ernest Gellner and John Breuilly, *Nations and Nationalism,* 2nd ed. (Ithaca, NY: Cornell University Press, 2009); Eric Hobsbawm and Terence O. Ranger, *The Invention of Tradition* (New York: Cambridge University Press, 1983).
34. Vail, "Introduction," 10–16.
35. Glassman, "Ethnicity and Race," 202–6.
36. Horowitz, *Ethnic Groups in Conflict.*
37. John Lonsdale, "The Moral Economy of Mau Mau: Wealth, Poverty, and Civic Virtue in Kikuyu Political Thought," in *Unhappy Valley: Conflict in Kenya and Africa,* ed. Bruce Berman and John Lonsdale, vol. 2 (London: James Currey, 1992).
38. Lynch, *I Say to You.*
39. MacArthur, *Cartography and the Political Imagination.*
40. John Lonsdale, "When Did the Gusii (or Any Other Group) Become a Tribe?," *Kenya Historical Review* 5, no. 1 (1977): 123–33; Charles H. Ambler, *Kenyan Communities in the Age of Imperialism: The Central Region in the Late Nineteenth Century* (New Haven, CT: Yale University Press, 1988).

41. See Daren E. Ray, "Disentangling Ethnicity in East Africa ca. 1–2010 CE: Past Communities in Present Practices" (PhD diss., University of Virginia, 2014), 354–58.
42. Larson, *Becoming Merina,* 30–31; Eriksen, *Ethnicity and Nationalism,* 87–89.
43. Nugent, "Putting the History Back into Ethnicity," 926.
44. Thomas T. Spear, *The Kaya Complex: A History of the Mijikenda Peoples of the Kenya Coast to 1900* (Nairobi: Kenya Literature Bureau, 1978); Derek Nurse and Thomas T. Spear, *The Swahili: Reconstructing the History and Language of an African Society, 800–1500* (Philadelphia: University of Pennsylvania Press, 1984).
45. Willis, *Making of the Mijikenda.*
46. Thomas T. Spear, "Neo-traditionalism and the Limits of Invention in British Colonial Africa," *Journal of African History* 44, no. 1 (January 1, 2003): 20, 23–24.
47. Ronald Cohen, "Ethnicity: Problem and Focus in Anthropology," *Annual Review of Anthropology* 7 (1978): 387.
48. Cohen, 393–95.
49. Abdul Sheriff and Engseng Ho, *The Indian Ocean: Oceanic Connections and the Creation of New Societies* (London: Hurst, 2014), 2.
50. Chaudhuri, *Trade and Civilisation;* Janet L. Abu-Lughod, *Before European Hegemony: The World System A.D. 1250–1350* (New York: Oxford University Press, 1991).
51. Kenneth McPherson, *The Indian Ocean: A History of People and the Sea* (New Delhi: Oxford University Press, 1998); Himanshu Prabha Ray and Edward A. Alpers, eds., *Cross Currents and Community Networks: The History of the Indian Ocean World* (Oxford: Oxford University Press, 2007), 2.
52. Michael N. Pearson, *The Indian Ocean* (London: Routledge, 2003), 38.
53. E.g., Edward A. Alpers, "Littoral Society in the Mozambique Channel," in *East Africa and the Indian Ocean* (Princeton, NJ: Markus Wiener Publishers, 2009); Abdul Sheriff, *Dhow Cultures of the Indian Ocean: Cosmopolitanism, Commerce, and Islam* (New York: Columbia University Press, 2010).
54. Sheriff, *Dhow Cultures;* Edward Simpson and Kai Kresse, *Struggling with History: Islam and Cosmopolitanism in the Western Indian Ocean* (New York: Columbia University Press, 2008).
55. See "Project," SEALINKS Project, Max Planck Institute for the Science of Human History, accessed July 10, 2023, https://sealinksproject.com/?page_id=9. Also see Himanshu Prabha Ray, *The*

Archaeology of Knowledge Traditions of the Indian Ocean World (Abingdon, UK: Routledge, 2020).
56. Michael N. Pearson, "Littoral Society: The Case for the Coast," *Great Circle* 7, no. 1 (1985): 6.
57. David Armitage, "Three Concepts of Atlantic History," in *The British Atlantic World, 1500–1800*, ed. David Armitage and Michael J. Braddick (New York: Palgrave Macmillan, 2002), 22.
58. Sebastian R. Prange, *Monsoon Islam: Trade and Faith on the Medieval Malabar Coast* (Cambridge: Cambridge University Press, 2018); Pedro Machado, *Ocean of Trade: South Asian Merchants, Africa and the Indian Ocean, c. 1750–1850* (Cambridge: Cambridge University Press, 2014).
59. Armitage, "Three Concepts," 23.
60. Jeremy Prestholdt, "Portuguese Conceptual Categories and the 'Other' Encounter on the Swahili Coast," *Journal of Asian & African Studies* 36, no. 4 (November 2001): 383–406.
61. Lionel Casson, *The Periplus Maris Erythraei: Text with Introduction, Translation, and Commentary* (Princeton, NJ: Princeton University Press, 1989), 61; Esther S. Brielle et al., "Entwined African and Asian Genetic Roots of Medieval Peoples of the Swahili Coast," *Nature* 615, no. 7954 (March 2023): 869.
62. Derek Nurse and Thomas Hinnebusch, *Swahili and Sabaki: A Linguistic History* (Berkeley: University of California Press, 1993).
63. Hamo Sassoon, "Excavations at the Site of Early Mombasa," *Azania* 15, no. 1 (January 1, 1980): 1–42; Colin Breen and Paul Lane, "Archaeological Approaches to East Africa's Changing Seascapes," *World Archaeology* 35, no. 3 (2003): 469–89.
64. Richard Helm, "Conflicting Histories: The Archeology of the Iron-Working, Farming Communities in the Central and Southern Coast Region of Kenya" (PhD diss., University of Bristol, 2000), 54.
65. Henry W. Mutoro, "An Archaeological Study of the Mijikenda 'Kaya' Settlements on Hinterland Kenya Coast" (PhD diss., University of California, Los Angeles, 1987).
66. Mark Horton and John Middleton, *The Swahili: The Social Landscape of a Mercantile Society* (Malden, MA: Blackwell Publishers, 2000); Prita Meier, *Swahili Port Cities: The Architecture of Elsewhere* (Bloomington: Indiana University Press, 2016).
67. Peter Garlake, *The Early Islamic Architecture of the East African Coast* (Nairobi: Oxford University Press, 1966).
68. F. J. Berg and B. J. Walter, "Mosques, Population, and Urban Development in Mombasa," *Hadith* 1 (1968): 47–100.

69. Spear, *Kaya Complex*.
70. See J. Strandes, *The Portuguese Period in East Africa*, ed. James Kirkman, trans. J. F. Wallwork (Nairobi: East African Literature Bureau, 1961).
71. David Parkin, *Sacred Void: Spatial Images of Work and Ritual among the Giriama of Kenya* (Cambridge: Cambridge University Press, 1991).
72. John Middleton, *The World of the Swahili: An African Mercantile Civilization* (New Haven, CT: Yale University Press, 1992). A comprehensive DNA study of over eighty individuals who lived between 1250 and 1800 CE (and a few dozen living individuals) confirms that modern Swahili populations are descended from populations of Persian men and African women. Esther S. Brielle et al., "Entwined African and Asian Genetic Roots." See discussion below for the longevity of Mijikenda forebears in the region.
73. Richard Helm, "Re-evaluating Traditional Histories on the Coast of Kenya: An Archaeological Perspective," in *African Historical Archaeologies*, ed. Andres M. Reid and Paul J. Lane (New York: Kluwer Academic / Plenum Publishers, 2004).
74. Thomas T. Spear, *Traditions of Origin and Their Interpretation: The Mijikenda of Kenya* (Athens: Ohio University Center for International Studies, 1981); James de Vere Allen, *Swahili Origins: Swahili Culture and the Shungwaya Phenomenon* (Athens: Ohio University Press, 1993).
75. Thomas T. Spear, "Traditional Myths and Historian's Myths: Variations on the Singwaya Theme of Mijikenda Origins," *History in Africa* 1 (1974): 67–84.
76. Spear, *Kaya Complex*; Nurse and Spear, *Swahili*.
77. Willis, *Making of the Mijikenda*; Martin Walsh, "Mijikenda Origins: A Review of the Evidence," *Transafrican Journal of History* 21 (1992): 1–18.
78. David Parkin, "Swahili Mijikenda: Facing Both Ways in Kenya," *Africa* 59, no. 2 (1989): 161–75.
79. Janet McIntosh, *The Edge of Islam: Power, Personhood, and Ethnoreligious Boundaries on the Kenya Coast* (Durham, NC: Duke University Press, 2009).
80. Thomas T. Spear, "Swahili History and Society to 1900: A Classified Bibliography," *History in Africa* 27 (2000): 339–73. Besides works by Spear and Willis cited above, major works on Mijikenda history and culture include Parkin, *Sacred Void*; Cynthia Brantley, *The Giriama and Colonial Resistance in Kenya, 1800–1920* (Berkeley: University of California Press, 1981); McIntosh, *Edge*

of Islam; Rebecca Gearhart and Linda L. Giles, eds., *Contesting Identities: The Mijikenda and Their Neighbors in Kenyan Coastal Society* (Trenton, NJ: Africa World Press, 2014).
81. Alamin M. Mazrui, *Kayas of Deprivation, Kayas of Blood: Violence, Ethnicity and the State in Coastal Kenya* (Nairobi: Kenya Human Rights Commission, 1998).
82. Sheriff, *Dhow Cultures.*
83. Michael N. Pearson, *Port Cities and Intruders: The Swahili Coast, India, and Portugal in the Early Modern Era* (Baltimore: Johns Hopkins University Press, 1998), 40; Thomas Vernet, "East African Travelers and Traders in the Indian Ocean: Swahili Ships, Swahili Mobilities, 1500–1800," in *Trade, Circulation, and Flow in the Indian Ocean World,* ed. Michael N. Pearson (New York: Palgrave Macmillan, 2015), 167–203.
84. Erik O. Gilbert, "Oman and Zanzibar: The Historical Roots of a Global Community," in *Cross Currents and Community Networks: The History of the Indian Ocean World,* ed. Himanshu Prabha Ray and Edward A. Alpers (New York: Oxford, 2007).
85. Shihan de S. Jayasuriya, *African Identity in Asia: Cultural Effects of Forced Migration* (Princeton, NJ: Markus Wiener Publishers, 2009); Abdulaziz Y. Lodhi, "African Settlements in India," *Nordic Journal of African Studies* 1, no. 1 (1992): 83–86.
86. K. N. Chaudhuri, *Asia before Europe: Economy and Civilisation of the Indian Ocean from the Rise of Islam to 1750* (New York: Cambridge University Press, 1990), 36.
87. Engseng Ho, *The Graves of Tarim: Genealogy and Mobility across the Indian Ocean* (Berkeley: University of California Press, 2006); Anne K. Bang, *Sufis and Scholars of the Sea: Family Networks in East Africa, 1860–1925* (New York: Routledge, 2003); Machado, *Ocean of Trade;* Bishara, *Sea of Debt;* McDow, *Buying Time;* Edward A. Alpers, "Soldiers, Slaves, and Saints: An Overview of the African Presence in India," *Kenya Past and Present* 34 (2003): 47–54; Prestholdt, *Domesticating the World;* Pearson, *Port Cities and Intruders.*
88. Jonathon Glassman, *War of Words, War of Stones: Racial Thought and Violence in Colonial Zanzibar* (Bloomington: Indiana University Press, 2011).
89. Ronald Raymond Atkinson, *The Roots of Ethnicity: The Origins of the Acholi of Uganda before 1800* (Philadelphia: University of Pennsylvania Press, 1994).
90. Jan Bender Shetler, *Imagining Serengeti: A History of Landscape Memory in Tanzania from Earliest Times to the Present* (Athens:

Ohio University Press, 2007); Kathryn M. de Luna, Jeffrey B. Fleisher, and Susan Keech McIntosh, "Thinking across the African Past: Interdisciplinarity and Early History," *African Archaeological Review* 29, nos. 2–3 (September 18, 2012): 75–94.
91. Brubaker, Loveman, and Stamatov, "Ethnicity as Cognition," 77.
92. Cf. *habitus* in Pierre Bourdieu, *Outline of a Theory of Practice* (Cambridge: Cambridge University Press, 1977); and *tradition* in Jan Vansina, *Paths in the Rainforests: Toward a History of Political Tradition in Equatorial Africa* (Madison: University of Wisconsin Press, 1990).
93. Glassman, "Ethnicity and Race," 211.
94. Smriti Srinivas, Bettina Ng'weno, and Neelima Jeychandran, "Introduction: Many Worlds, Many Oceans," in *Reimagining Indian Ocean Worlds,* ed. Smriti Srinivas, Bettina Ng'weno, and Neelima Jeychandran (New York: Routledge, 2020), 15.
95. Christopher Ehret, *History and the Testimony of Language* (Berkeley: University of California Press, 2011).
96. Harries, "Roots of Ethnicity."
97. Kenya National Bureau of Statistics, "Census 2009 Summary of Results: Ethnic Affiliation," updated March 22, 2013, www.knbs .or.ke.
98. Spear, *Traditions.*

CHAPTER 1: ANCESTORS IN THE DOORWAY

1. See "Rabai Malozi Ceremony," April 17, 2010, digital photograph, video, and audio, Ray Research Deposit E014.
2. Marshall Sahlins, *What Kinship Is—and Is Not* (Chicago: University of Chicago Press, 2014). For Swahili kinship, see Marc J. Swartz, *The Way the World Is: Cultural Processes and Social Relations among the Mombasa Swahili* (Berkeley: University of California Press, 1991); for Mijikenda kinship, see David Parkin, *Sacred Void: Spatial Images of Work and Ritual among the Giriama of Kenya* (Cambridge: Cambridge University Press, 1991).
3. E.g., Donald L. Horowitz, *Ethnic Groups in Conflict* (Berkeley: University of California Press, 1985), 55; Justin Willis, "The Makings of a Tribe: Bondei Identities and Histories," *Journal of African History* 33, no. 2 (1992): 191–208.
4. E.g., David L. Schoenbrun, *A Green Place, a Good Place: Agrarian Change, Gender, and Social Identity in the Great Lakes Region to the 15th Century* (Portsmouth, NH: Heinemann, 1998); Jeff Marck and Koen Bostoen, "Proto Oceanic Society (Austronesian) and Proto East Bantu Society (Niger-Congo), Residence, Descent

and Kin Terms ca. 1000 BC," in *Kinship, Language, and Prehistory: Per Hage and the Renaissance in Kinship Studies*, ed. Doug Jones and Bojka Milicic (Salt Lake City: University of Utah Press, 2011), 83–94.
5. See Lyle Campbell, *Historical Linguistics: An Introduction*, 2nd ed. (Cambridge, MA: MIT Press, 2004).
6. Christopher Ehret, *An African Classical Age: Eastern and Southern Africa in World History, 1000 BC to AD 400* (Charlottesville: University of Virginia Press, 1998), 36.
7. See Kathryn M. de Luna, Jeffrey B. Fleisher, and Susan Keech McIntosh, "Thinking across the African Past: Interdisciplinarity and Early History," *African Archaeological Review* 29, nos. 2–3 (September 18, 2012): 75–94; and Christopher Ehret, *History and the Testimony of Language* (Berkeley: University of California Press, 2011), chap. 5. For examples of probabilistic modeling, see Thomas E. Currie et al., "Cultural Phylogeography of the Bantu Languages of Sub-Saharan Africa," *Proceedings: Biological Sciences* 280, no. 1762 (2013): 1–8; and Thembi Russell, Fabio Silva, and James Steele, "Modelling the Spread of Farming in the Bantu-Speaking Regions of Africa: An Archaeology-Based Phylogeography," *PLOS ONE* 9, no. 1 (January 31, 2014): e87854.
8. Currie et al., "Cultural Phylogeography."
9. E.g., Clare Janaki Holden and Ruth Mace, "Spread of Cattle Led to the Loss of Matrilineal Descent in Africa: A Coevolutionary Analysis," *Proceedings: Biological Sciences* 270, no. 1532 (December 7, 2003): 2425–33; Marck and Bostoen, "Kin Terms."
10. Wyatt Macgaffey, "Changing Representations in Central African History," *Journal of African History* 46, no. 2 (2005): 198.
11. Arthur Mortimer Champion, *The Agiryama of Kenya*, ed. John Middleton (London: Royal Anthropological Institute of Great Britain and Ireland, 1967), 55n17.
12. Both phrases are from the Giriama dialect of Chimijikenda. For the Swahili "outdooring" ceremony, see Mbarak Ali Hinawy, "Notes on Customs in Mombasa," *Swahili (Kiswahili)* 34 (1964): 29; and Mtoro bin Mwinyi Bakari, *The Customs of the Swahili People: The Desturi Za Waswahili of Mtoro Bin Mwinyi Bakari and Other Swahili Persons*, trans. J. W. T. Allen (Berkeley: University of California Press, 1981), 9.
13. Champion, *Agiryama of Kenya*, 55n17. For Pokomo naming conventions, see Alice Werner, *The Bantu Coast Tribes of the East Africa Protectorate* (London: Royal Anthropological Institute of Great Britain and Ireland, 1915), 340.

14. Linda Donley, "House Power: Swahili Space and Symbolic Markers," in *Symbolic and Structural Archaeology*, ed. Ian Hodder (Cambridge: Cambridge University Press, 1982), 70–72.
15. Bakari, *Customs*, 8–9; Hinawy, "Notes," 29.
16. Champion, *Agiryama of Kenya*, 55n17.
17. See R. F. Morton, *Children of Ham: Freed Slaves and Fugitive Slaves on the Kenya Coast, 1873 to 1907* (Boulder, CO: Westview, 1990).
18. Mark Horton and John Middleton, *The Swahili: The Social Landscape of a Mercantile Society* (Malden, MA: Blackwell Publishers, 2000), 101; Patricia Caplan, *Choice and Constraint in a Swahili Community: Property, Hierarchy and Cognatic Descent on the East African Coast* (London: Oxford, 1975).
19. A. H. J. Prins, *The Swahili-Speaking Peoples of Zanzibar and the East African Coast: Arabs, Shirazi and Swahili* (London: International African Institute, 1967), 80.
20. Cf. Cymone Fourshey, Rhonda M. Gonzales, and Christine Saidi, *Bantu Africa* (New York: Oxford University Press, 2017); Ehret, *African Classical Age;* Jan Vansina, *How Societies Are Born: Governance in West Central Africa before 1600* (Charlottesville: University of Virginia Press, 2004).
21. John Middleton, *The World of the Swahili: An African Mercantile Civilization* (New Haven, CT: Yale University Press, 1992), 101.
22. Derek Nurse and Thomas Hinnebusch, *Swahili and Sabaki: A Linguistic History* (Berkeley: University of California Press, 1993), 187–96.
23. Proto–Mashariki Bantu includes zones E, F, G, L, M, N, P, and S, as well as the J zone proposed by linguists at Tervuren. See Malcolm Guthrie, *Comparative Bantu: An Introduction to the Comparative Linguistics and Prehistory of the Bantu Languages* (Farnborough, UK: Gregg, 1967); Jouni Maho, "A Classification of the Bantu Languages: An Update of Guthrie's Referential System," in *The Bantu Languages*, ed. Derek Nurse and Gérard Philippson (London: Routledge, 2003), 639–51.
24. I use Ehret's Proto–Mashariki Bantu classification because it is conventional among linguistic historians of Africa. See Christopher Ehret, "Bantu Expansions: Re-envisioning a Central Problem of Early African History," *IJAHS* 34, no. 1 (2001): 35; Derek Nurse and Gérard Philippson, *The Bantu Languages* (London: Routledge, 2003); Colin Flight, "Malcolm Guthrie and the Reconstruction of Bantu Prehistory," *History in Africa* 7 (1980): 81–118.

25. Fourshey, Gonzales, and Saidi, *Bantu Africa*, 86–87. Yvonne Bastin et al., *Bantu Lexical Reconstructions 3* [hereafter *BLR3*] (Leiden, Netherlands: Leiden University, 2003), Main 2140, 2806, 1050, www.africamuseum.be/en.
26. Schoenbrun, *Green Place*, 96; see also Ehret, *African Classical Age*, 149–50. Bastin et al., *BLR3*, Main 1120, DER 1133, 1135.
27. Kathryn de Luna, *Collecting Food, Cultivating People: Subsistence and Society in Central Africa* (New Haven, CT: Yale University Press, 2016), 252.
28. Marck and Bostoen, "Kin Terms," 86, 93.
29. Bastin et al., *BLR3*, Main 1997, 3435.
30. Malcolm Ruel, "The Structural Articulation of Generations in Africa (L'articulation Structurelle des Générations En Afrique)," *Cahiers d'Études Africaines* 42, no. 165 (January 1, 2002): 73.
31. Bastin et al., *BLR3*, Main 3493. The relict distribution of *jípùà* in all East Bantu Zones plus Zone C suggests Bantu speakers innovated the term before the divergence of Mashariki Bantu languages but after Proto-Bantu times.
32. Schoenbrun, *Green Place*, 97; David L. Schoenbrun, *The Historical Reconstruction of Great Lakes Bantu Cultural Vocabulary: Etymologies and Distributions*, Sprache und Geschichte in Afrika, Supplement 9 (Cologne, Germany: Rüdiger Köppe Verlag, 1997), 86–87; Janice Irvine, "Exploring the Limits of Structural Semantics" (PhD diss., University of Rochester, 1980).
33. Cf. Ruel, "Articulation of Generations"; and Iain Walker, *Becoming the Other, Being Oneself: Constructing Identities in a Connected World* (Newcastle upon Tyne, UK: Cambridge Scholars Publishers, 2010), 118. Rhiannon Stephens, *A History of African Motherhood: The Case of Uganda, 700–1900* (New York: Cambridge University Press, 2015) 57.
34. Marck and Bostoen, "Kin Terms," 88.
35. Cf. de Luna, *Collecting Food, Cultivating People*, 15–17.
36. Ehret, *African Classical Age*. These two language groups are from different branches of the Nilo-Saharan language family; see Christopher Ehret, *Southern Nilotic History: Linguistic Approaches to the Study of the Past* (Evanston, IL: Northwestern University Press, 1971).
37. Ehret, *African Classical Age*, 301–5.
38. E.g., *-bágá* (livestock pen) and *kòló* (sheep) from Eastern Sahelian. Ehret, *African Classical Age*, 302, 305.
39. Jan Vansina, *Paths in the Rainforests: Toward a History of Political Tradition in Equatorial Africa* (Madison: University of Wisconsin Press, 1990), 58–61.

40. Schoenbrun, *Historical Reconstruction*, 84; Schoenbrun, *Green Place*, 94.
41. For descendant languages of Kusi and Kaskazi areal groups, see Ehret, *African Classical Age*, 36, 55.
42. Schoenbrun, *Green Place*, 100.
43. For *ñàngò*, see Ehret, *African Classical Age*, 150; and Schoenbrun, *Historical Reconstruction*, 74–75. Ehret suggests *umba is a loanword from Central Sudanic *omba*, from the verb *mba* "to sit, stay." Ehret, *African Classical Age*, 141n17. Schoenbrun considers *yùmbá an original innovation in Mashariki. Schoenbrun, *Historical Reconstruction*, 108.
44. Schoenbrun, *Historical Reconstruction*, 54, 89.
45. Ehret, *African Classical Age*, 143–46, 160–64.
46. Cf. Schoenbrun, *Green Place*, 93.
47. Ehret, *African Classical Age*, 149–51.
48. Ehret, 115.
49. Reflexes of *yùmbá (house) in Lakes Bantu languages emphasize maternal ties. Schoenbrun, *Historical Reconstruction*, 108.
50. Ruel, "Articulation of Generations," 70.
51. Cf. Stephens, *African Motherhood*, 56; and Ehret, *African Classical Age*, 154.
52. Irvine, "Limits of Structural Semantics," 299, 345.
53. Schoenbrun, *Green Place*, 100.
54. Ehret, *African Classical Age*, 165; Fourshey, Gonzales, and Saidi place the emphasis on matrilineal reckoning for *lukólò (*Bantu Africa*, 87).
55. Ehret, *African Classical Age*, 67–68, 325–28.
56. Ehret's "Upland Bantu" includes Central Kenya Bantu languages as well as the Kilimanjaro-Taita classification in Nurse and Philippson, *Bantu Languages*, 475–500. Ehret, *African Classical Age*, 246–48.
57. The Proto-Sabaki word *ilumbu (cosibling, of one mother) is most likely derived from the Proto–Savanna Bantu word *dùmbù* (his sis-ter, her brother). Nurse and Hinnebusch, *Swahili and Sabaki*, 628.
58. Johann Ludwig Krapf, *A Dictionary of the Suahili Language* (London: Trübner, 1882), s.v. "*enza*."
59. Hassan O. Ali, "Kanga Writings," Swahili Language & Culture, 2004, http://www.glcom.com/hassan/kanga.html.
60. Ali.
61. Thomas T. Spear, *Traditions of Origin and Their Interpretation: The Mijikenda of Kenya* (Athens: Ohio University Center for International Studies, 1981), 35, 42.
62. Middleton, *World of the Swahili*, 184–88.

63. Middleton, 30–35.
64. Randall L. Pouwels, *Horn and Crescent: Cultural Change and Traditional Islam on the East African Coast, 800–1900* (Cambridge: Cambridge University Press, 1987), 28.
65. Wycliff Tinga, interview by author, April 17, 2010, digital audio, Ray Research Deposit C013.

CHAPTER 2: MAKING A PEACEFUL HOME

1. Gona Dzoka, interview by author, August 16, 2010, digital video and audio, trans. William Tsaka, Ray Research Deposit C045.
2. Thomas T. Spear, *Traditions of Origin and Their Interpretation: The Mijikenda of Kenya* (Athens: Ohio University Center for International Studies, 1981), 75.
3. Yvonne Bastin et al., *Bantu Lexical Reconstructions 3* (Leiden, Netherlands: Leiden University, 2003), Main 1332, www.africamuseum.be/en.
4. This chapter draws on material previously published as Daren E. Ray, "Recycling Interdisciplinary Evidence: Abandoned Hypotheses and African Historiologies in the Settlement History of Littoral East Africa," *History in Africa* 49 (December 23, 2022): 97–130.
5. Each of the following terms means "named clan" in modern Sabaki dialects: *ukoo* (Kiswahili), *gosa* (Kielwana from Oromo), *sindo* (Kipokomo), *dzuwo* (Shicomorian), *mbari* (Chimijikenda, Kimvita Kiswahili from Central Kenya Bantu), *k'amasi* (Bajuni Kiswahili), and *taifa* (Mombasa Kiswahili from Arabic). See Derek Nurse, "South Meets North: Ilwana = Bantu + Cushitic on Kenya's Tana River," in *Mixed Languages,* ed. Peter Bakker and Maarten Mous (Amsterdam: IFOTF, 1994), 213–22; Norman Townsend, "Age, Descent and Elders among Pokomo," *Africa* 47, no. 4 (December 1977): 386; Iain Walker, *Becoming the Other, Being Oneself: Constructing Identities in a Connected World* (Newcastle upon Tyne, UK: Cambridge Scholars Publishers, 2010); Johann Ludwig Krapf, *A Dictionary of the Suahili Language* (London: Trübner, 1882); Johann Ludwig Krapf and Johannes Rebmann, *A Nika-English Dictionary* (London: Society for Promoting Christian Knowledge, 1887); Derek Nurse, "Historical Texts from the Swahili Coast Part II," *Afrikanistische Arbeitspapiere* 42 (1995): 41–72; A. H. J. Prins, *The Coastal Tribes of the North-Eastern Bantu (Pokomo, Nyika, Teita)* (London: International African Institute, 1952).
6. Kai Kresse, *Philosophizing in Mombasa: Knowledge, Islam, and Intellectual Practice on the Swahili Coast* (Edinburgh: Edinburgh University Press, 2007), 4–5, 26–27.

7. George H. O. Abungu and H. W. Mutoro, "Coast-Interior Settlements and Social Relations in the Kenya Coastal Hinterland," in *Archaeology of Africa: Foods, Metals, and Towns*, ed. T. Shaw et al. (London: Routledge, 1993), 694–704; C. Shipton et al., "Intersections, Networks and the Genesis of Social Complexity on the Nyali Coast of East Africa," *African Archaeological Review* 30, no. 4 (December 1, 2013): 427–53.
8. Neil Kodesh, *Beyond the Royal Gaze: Clanship and Public Healing in Buganda* (Charlottesville: University of Virginia Press, 2010).
9. Kodesh, 192.
10. Rhonda M. Gonzales, *Societies, Religion, and History: Central-East Tanzanians and the World They Created, c. 200 BCE to 1800 CE* (New York: Columbia University Press, 2009).
11. Sarah Croucher and Stephanie Wynne-Jones, "People, Not Pots: Locally Produced Ceramics and Identity on the Nineteenth-Century East African Coast," *IJAHS* 39, no. 1 (February 2006): 107–24; Herman Ogoti Kiriama, "Iron-Using Communities in Kenya," in *Archaeology of Africa: Foods, Metals, and Towns*, ed. T. Shaw et al. (London: Routledge, 1993), 485–98.
12. David Wright, "Environment, Chronology and Resource Exploitation of the Pastoral Neolithic in Tsavo Kenya" (PhD diss., University of Illinois, 2005), 76, 100.
13. E.g., Chapurukha M. Kusimba, "Social Context of Iron Forging on the Kenya Coast," *Africa* 63 (1996): 194–210; Sibel Kusimba, "What Is a Hunter-Gatherer? Variation in the Archaeological Record of Eastern and Southern Africa," *Journal of Archaeological Research* 13, no. 4 (2005): 337–66.
14. Jeffrey Fleisher and Stephanie Wynne-Jones, "Ceramics and the Early Swahili: Deconstructing the Early Tana Tradition," *African Archaeological Review* 28, no. 4 (2011): 245–78.
15. Lionel Casson, *The Periplus Maris Erythraei: Text with Introduction, Translation, and Commentary* (Princeton, NJ: Princeton University Press, 1989), 61.
16. David Wright, "New Perspectives on Early Regional Interaction Networks of East African Trade: A View from Tsavo National Park, Kenya," *African Archaeological Review* 22, no. 3 (2005): 111–40.
17. G. S. P. Freeman-Grenville, *The East African Coast: Select Documents from the First to the Nineteenth Century*, 2nd ed. (Oxford: Clarendon, 1975), 8.
18. Robert C. Soper, "Kwale: An Early Iron Age Site in Southeastern Kenya," *Azania* 2 (1967): 1–17.

19. Fleisher and Wynne-Jones, "Ceramics," 252. See Mark Horton and Felix Chami, "Swahili Origins," in *The Swahili World*, ed. Stephanie Wynne-Jones and Adria Jean LaViolette (New York: Routledge, 2017), 139–40. For a contrary interpretation that involves multiple Bantu language groups, see Christopher Ehret, *An African Classical Age: Eastern and Southern Africa in World History, 1000 BC to AD 400* (Charlottesville: University of Virginia Press, 1998); and Gonzales, *Societies, Religion, and History*, 61–65.
20. Thomas Hinnebusch, "The Shungwaya Hypothesis: A Linguistic Reappraisal," in *East African Cultural History*, ed. Joseph T. Gallagher, Foreign and Comparative Studies / Eastern Africa Series 25 (Syracuse, NY: Maxwell School of Citizenship and Public Affairs, Syracuse University, 1976), 17, 36.
21. Spear, *Traditions*, 45.
22. Richard Helm, "Conflicting Histories: The Archeology of the Iron-Working, Farming Communities in the Central and Southern Coast Region of Kenya" (PhD diss., University of Bristol, 2000), 136.
23. Shipton et al., "Genesis of Social Complexity," 438.
24. Derek Nurse and Thomas Hinnebusch, *Swahili and Sabaki: A Linguistic History* (Berkeley: University of California Press, 1993), 670, 621.
25. Wright, "New Perspectives," 123.
26. Nurse and Hinnebusch, *Swahili and Sabaki*, 449–60.
27. For support of a homeland nearer Mombasa, see Martin T. Walsh, "The Segeju Complex? Linguistic Evidence for the Precolonial Making of the Mijikenda," in *Contesting Identities: The Mijikenda and Their Neighbors in Kenyan Coastal Society*, ed. Rebecca Gearhart and Linda Giles (Trenton, NJ: Africa World Press, 2013), 25–51.
28. Helm, "Conflicting Histories," 115.
29. Nurse and Hinnebusch, *Swahili and Sabaki*, 618, 645, 647.
30. Richard Helm et al., "Exploring Agriculture, Interaction and Trade on the Eastern African Littoral: Preliminary Results from Kenya," *Azania* 47, no. 1 (March 1, 2012): 55.
31. Nurse and Hinnebusch, *Swahili and Sabaki*, 662.
32. Randall L. Pouwels, *Horn and Crescent: Cultural Change and Traditional Islam on the East African Coast, 800–1900* (Cambridge: Cambridge University Press, 1987), 91.
33. Spear, *Traditions*, 65.
34. Spear, 34.
35. Shipton et al., "Genesis of Social Complexity."
36. Helm, "Conflicting Histories," 227; Fleisher and Wynne-Jones, "Ceramics," 265.

37. Helm, "Conflicting Histories," 282–88.
38. George H. O. Abungu, "Communities on the River Tana, Kenya: An Archaeological Study of Relations between the Delta and the River Basin, 700–1890 A.D." (PhD diss., Cambridge University, 1989), cited in Helm, "Conflicting Histories," 56–57.
39. Middle Proto-Sabaki can be positively identified by at least seven shared sound changes. Nurse and Hinnebusch, *Swahili and Sabaki*, 477, 533, chap. 4.
40. Nurse and Hinnebusch, 412. E.g., Proto-Kiswahili speakers made a new past tense (*ali*) and a new future tense from their verb for "to want" (*caka*).
41. Nurse and Hinnebusch, 501.
42. Nurse and Hinnebusch, 533.
43. Nurse and Hinnebusch, 481–87. Shicomorian and Southern Kiswahili both share "Class 5 Strengthening" and a verbal suffix for a "negative habitual" state.
44. Nurse and Hinnebusch, 135, 495.
45. Nurse and Hinnebusch, 531. On Comorian settlements, see Henry T. Wright, "The Comoros and Their Early History," in Wynne-Jones and LaViolette, *Swahili World*, 266–76. Walker suggests that Comorian-speaking communities may have encountered a previously established Bantu community from the coasts of Tanzania and Mozambique. Walker, *Becoming the Other*, 44.
46. Nurse and Hinnebusch, *Swahili and Sabaki*, 487–96.
47. Proto-Chimijikenda speakers distinguished their speech from other Late Proto-Sabaki speakers by pronouncing the phoneme *l* as the sound *r* in front of vowels and replacing the sound *i* at the beginning of word stems with the sounds *a* or *e*. Nurse and Hinnebusch, *Swahili and Sabaki*, 536.
48. Richard Helm, "Re-evaluating Traditional Histories on the Coast of Kenya: An Archaeological Perspective," in *African Historical Archaeologies*, ed. Andres M. Reid and Paul J. Lane (New York: Kluwer Academic / Plenum Publishers, 2004), 75.
49. Roderick J. McIntosh, *Ancient Middle Niger: Urbanism and the Self-Organizing Landscape* (New York: Cambridge University Press, 2005); also see Susan Keech McIntosh, *Beyond Chiefdoms: Pathways to Complexity in Africa* (Cambridge: Cambridge University Press, 2005).
50. Nurse and Hinnebusch, *Swahili and Sabaki*, 619, 621, 646.
51. Jeffrey Fleisher and Stephanie Wynne-Jones, "Finding Meaning in Ancient Swahili Spatial Practices," *African Archaeological Review* 29, nos. 2–3 (September 1, 2012): 171–207.

52. Mark Horton, Helen W. Brown, and Nina Mudida, *Shanga: The Archaeology of a Muslim Trading Community on the Coast of East Africa* (London: British Institute in Eastern Africa, 1996), 394–406.
53. Horton, Brown, and Mudida, 398.
54. Horton, Brown, and Mudida, 118, 398.
55. Christopher Ehret, *The Civilizations of Africa: A History to 1800* (Charlottesville: University of Virginia Press, 2002), 50.
56. Philip F. Kennedy et al., *Two Arabic Travel Books: Accounts of China and India and Mission to the Volga* (New York: New York University Press, 2014), 121.
57. Freeman-Grenville, *Select Documents*, 16.
58. Bernard Lewis, *Islam: From the Prophet Muhammad to the Capture of Constantinople*, vol. 2, *Religion and Society* (New York: Harper and Row, 1974), 118; Freeman-Grenville mistakenly records this word as *al-Musnafu* in *Select Documents*, 20.
59. Freeman-Grenville, *Select Documents*, 11–12.
60. For a discussion on relationships between Islamic knowledge and uganga among Kiswahili speakers, see Pouwels, *Horn and Crescent*, chaps. 3–5.
61. Horton, Brown, and Mudida, *Shanga*, 399.
62. Freeman-Grenville, *Select Documents*, 20.
63. Horton, Brown, and Mudida, *Shanga*, 400–401.
64. Horton, Brown, and Mudida, 400.
65. Horton, Brown, and Mudida, 75.
66. Horton, Brown, and Mudida, 425.
67. Freeman-Grenville, *Select Documents*, 8. Also see Gwyn Campbell, "East Africa in the Early Indian Ocean World Slave Trade: The Zanj Revolt Reconsidered," in *Early Exchange between Africa and the Wider Indian Ocean World* (London: Palgrave Macmillan, 2016), 275–304.
68. Horton, Brown, and Mudida, *Shanga*, 31, 46–48.
69. Helm, "Re-evaluating Traditional Histories."
70. Thomas H. Wilson, "Spatial Analysis and Settlement Patterns on the East African Coast," *Paideuma: Mitteilungen zur Kulturekunde* 28 (1982): 215.

CHAPTER 3: DANCING WITH SWORDS

1. See "Lamu Maulid Activities, Sponsored by Riyadha Mosque," digital photographs and video, Ray Research Deposit E010.
2. See "Pate Island Tour," digital photographs and video, May 29–31, 2010, Ray Research Deposit E016; Ulrich Rinn, "Mwaka Koga: The Development of Syncretistic Rituals in a Globalising World,"

in *Unpacking the New: Critical Perspectives on Cultural Syncretization in Africa and Beyond,* ed. Afe Adogame, Magnus Echtler, and Ulf Vierke (Berlin: LIT Verlag, 2008), 349–67; Sarah Mirza and Margaret Strobel, *Three Swahili Women: Life Histories from Mombasa, Kenya* (Bloomington: Indiana University Press, 1989), 58; and Marc J. Swartz, *The Way the World Is: Cultural Processes and Social Relations among the Mombasa Swahili* (Berkeley: University of California Press, 1991), 47.
3. John Ludwig Krapf, "Section IV, Africa Missions," in *Revd Dr. Krapf's Journal* (Marlborough, UK: Adam Matthew Publications, 1997), 500, microfilm, part 16, reel 317, Church Missionary Society. Also see Charles New, *Life, Wanderings, and Labours in Eastern Africa,* 3rd ed. (London: Cass, 1971), 79.
4. Krapf, "Africa Missions," 497.
5. J. Strandes, *The Portuguese Period in East Africa,* ed. James Kirkman, trans. J. F. Wallwork (Nairobi: East African Literature Bureau, 1961), 20.
6. Adria LaViolette and Stephanie Wynne-Jones, "The Swahili World," in *The Swahili World,* ed. Stephanie Wynne-Jones and Adria Jean LaViolette (New York: Routledge, 2017), 1–14.
7. Thomas T. Spear, *Traditions of Origin and Their Interpretation: The Mijikenda of Kenya* (Athens: Ohio University Center for International Studies, 1981), 4–5.
8. Thomas T. Spear, *The Kaya Complex: A History of the Mijikenda Peoples of the Kenya Coast to 1900* (Nairobi: Kenya Literature Bureau, 1978), 24.
9. R. F. Morton, "The Shungwaya Myth of Mijikenda Origins: A Problem of Late Nineteenth-Century Kenya Coastal History," *IJAHS* 5, no. 3 (1972): 397–423.
10. Richard Helm, "Re-evaluating Traditional Histories on the Coast of Kenya: An Archaeological Perspective," in *African Historical Archaeologies,* ed. Andres M. Reid and Paul J. Lane (New York: Kluwer Academic / Plenum Publishers, 2004).
11. Cf. Jan Bender Shetler, *Imagining Serengeti: A History of Landscape Memory in Tanzania from Earliest Times to the Present* (Athens: Ohio University Press, 2007), 18–25.
12. Joseph Calder Miller, "Introduction: Listening for the African Past," in *The African Past Speaks: Essays on Oral Tradition and History* (Hamden, CT: Archon, 1980), 1–59.
13. G. S. P. Freeman-Grenville, *The East African Coast: Select Documents from the First to the Nineteenth Century,* 2nd ed. (Oxford: Clarendon, 1975), 9–13.
14. Spear, *Traditions,* 52; emphasis added.

15. For conurbations, see Mark Horton and John Middleton, *The Swahili: The Social Landscape of a Mercantile Society* (Malden, MA: Blackwell Publishers, 2000), 136–37. Also see Henry Mutoro, *A Nearest Neighbour Analysis of the Mijikenda Makaya on the Kenya Coastal Hinterland* (Nairobi: Department of History, University of Nairobi, 1985); Thomas H. Wilson, "Spatial Analysis and Settlement Patterns on the East African Coast," *Paideuma: Mitteilungen zur Kulturekunde* 28 (1982): 201–19.
16. Portuguese sources mention Chonyi and Arabaja (i.e., Rabai). George McCall Theal, *Records of South Eastern Africa*, 7 vols. (London: William Clowes and Sons, 1899); Johann Ludwig Krapf, *Travels, Researches, and Missionary Labours, during an Eighteen Years' Residence in Eastern Africa*, 2nd ed. (London: Frank Cass, 1968).
17. Matthew Christopher Pawlowicz, "Finding Their Place in the Swahili World: An Archaeological Exploration of Southern Tanzania" (PhD diss., University of Virginia, 2011).
18. Archaeologists also label country towns "commoner towns" or "secondary towns." Horton and Middleton, *Swahili: Social Landscape*, 126.
19. Adria LaViolette, "Craft and Industry," in Wynne-Jones and LaViolette, *Swahili World*, 319–34.
20. Thomas Gensheimer, "At the Boundaries of Dar-al-Islam: Cities of the East African Coast in the Late Middle Ages" (PhD diss., University of California, Berkeley, 1997), 306.
21. Cf. the four-tier settlement pattern of Comorians in Iain Walker, *Becoming the Other, Being Oneself: Constructing Identities in a Connected World* (Newcastle upon Tyne, UK: Cambridge Scholars Publishers, 2010), 84.
22. Sarah C. Walshaw, "Converting to Rice: Urbanization, Islamization and Crops on Pemba Island, Tanzania, AD 700–1500," *World Archaeology* 42, no. 1 (March 2010): 137–54.
23. Abdallah Ali (head of antiquities, government of Zanzibar), personal communication, March 18, 2018.
24. Jeffrey Fleisher, "Rituals of Consumption and the Politics of Feasting on the Eastern African Coast, AD 700–1500," *Journal of World Prehistory* 23, no. 4 (2010): 210–13.
25. Adria LaViolette and Jeffrey Fleisher, "The Urban History of a Rural Place: Swahili Archaeology on Pemba Island, Tanzania, 700–1500 AD," *IJAHS* 42, no. 3 (October 2009): 433–55.
26. W. J. G. Mohlig and Bernd Heine, *Historical Phonological Atlas of the Bantu Languages of Kenya*, Language and Dialect Atlas of Kenya 6 (Berlin: Dietrich Reimer, 1980).

27. Johann Ludwig Krapf and Johannes Rebmann, *A Nika-English Dictionary* (London: Society for Promoting Christian Knowledge, 1887), s.v. "*Mutzi Mwiru.*"
28. Derek Nurse and Thomas Hinnebusch, *Swahili and Sabaki: A Linguistic History* (Berkeley: University of California Press, 1993), 560.
29. Nurse and Hinnebusch, 560.
30. Nurse and Hinnebusch, 564.
31. Frederick Johnson, *A Standard English-Swahili Dictionary* (London: Oxford University Press, 1939), s.v. "*kongowea.*"
32. Hassan Muhammad, author's field notes, May 6, 2010.
33. Taasisi ya Uchunguzi wa Kiswahili [Institute of Kiswahili Research], *Kamusi ya Kiswahili-Kiingereza* (Dar es Salaam: Institute of Kiswahili Research, 2001), s.v. "*konga¹*," "*konga²*," "*konga³*."
34. Gensheimer, "Boundaries of Dar-al-Islam," 102.
35. Gensheimer, 198.
36. Freeman-Grenville, *Select Documents*, 108–9.
37. Freeman-Grenville, 109–11.
38. Freeman-Grenville, 27–28.
39. Horton and Middleton, *Swahili: Social Landscape*, 116–17.
40. Jeffrey Fleisher and Adria LaViolette, "Elusive Wattle-and-Daub: Finding the Hidden Majority in the Archaeology of the Swahili," *Azania* 34, no. 1 (1999): 87–108; Jeffrey Fleisher and Stephanie Wynne-Jones, "Finding Meaning in Ancient Swahili Spatial Practices," *African Archaeological Review* 29, nos. 2–3 (September 1, 2012): 171–207.
41. Jeffrey Fleisher and Adria LaViolette, "The Changing Power of Swahili Houses, AD Fourteenth to Nineteenth Centuries," in *The Durable House: House Society Models in Archaeology*, ed. Robin A. Beck (Carbondale, IL: Center for Archaeological Investigations, Southern Illinois University, 2007), 175–97.
42. Marina Tolmacheva, trans., *The Pate Chronicle* (East Lansing: Michigan State University Press, 1993), 40.
43. Cf. Randall L. Pouwels, *Horn and Crescent: Cultural Change and Traditional Islam on the East African Coast, 800–1900* (Cambridge: Cambridge University Press, 1987), chap. 3.
44. Jeremy Prestholdt, "Portuguese Conceptual Categories and the 'Other' Encounter on the Swahili Coast," *Journal of Asian & African Studies* 36, no. 4 (November 2001): 390.
45. Tolmacheva, *Pate Chronicle*, 169.
46. Pouwels associated the building of town walls with the Oromo incursions of the fifteenth century (*Horn and Crescent*, 29). But

Sabaki-speaking clan confederations also conducted raids against one another. See V. Gona Kazungu, "The Agiryama: The Rise of a Tribe and Its Traditions" (senior thesis, University of Nairobi, 1973), 75–83.

47. Horton and Middleton, *Swahili: Social Landscape*, 175–78.
48. See Kelly M. Askew, "Female Circles and Male Lines: Gender Dynamics along the Swahili Coast," *Africa Today* 46, nos. 3–4 (1999): 67–102.
49. Johnson, *English-Swahili Dictionary*, s.v. "*kisi.*"
50. Cymone Fourshey, Rhonda M. Gonzales, and Christine Saidi, *Bantu Africa* (New York: Oxford University Press, 2017), chap. 2.
51. Pouwels, *Horn and Crescent*, 91.
52. Norman Townsend, "Age, Descent and Elders among Pokomo," *Africa* 47, no. 4 (December 1977): 386–97; Walker, *Becoming the Other*; Elizabeth Orchardson-Mazrui, "Expressing Power and Status through Aesthetics in Mijikenda Society," *Journal of African Cultural Studies* 11, no. 1 (June 1998): 85–102; Jonathon Glassman, *Feasts and Riot: Revelry and Rebellion on the Swahili Coast, 1856–88* (Portsmouth, NH: Heinemann, 1995).
53. Johann Ludwig Krapf, *A Dictionary of the Suahili Language* (London: Trübner, 1882), s.v. "*Muunguana.*"
54. Spear, *Traditions*, 104.
55. Orchardson-Mazrui, "Aesthetics," 91.
56. Cf. Pouwels, *Horn and Crescent*, chap. 5.
57. Mirza and Strobel, *Three Swahili Women*; Cynthia Brantley, "Mekatalili and the Role of Women in Giriama Resistance," in *Banditry, Rebellion, and Social Protest in Africa*, ed. Donald Crummey (London: James Currey, 1986), 333–50.
58. Orchardson-Mazrui, "Aesthetics," 91.
59. Krapf, "Africa Missions," March 25, 1845, 571.
60. New, *Life, Wanderings, and Labours*, 108.
61. Cynthia Brantley, "An Historical Perspective of the Giriama and Witchcraft Control," *Africa* 49, no. 2 (1979): 112–33.
62. Orchardson-Mazrui, "Aesthetics," 91; Cynthia Brantley, "Gerontocratic Government: Age-Sets in Pre-colonial Giriama," *Africa* 48, no. 3 (1978): 253; Spear, *Kaya Complex*, 66.
63. Spear, *Traditions*, 66; Kate Parsons, "The Aesthetic and Spiritual Contexts of Giriama Vigango in Kenya and Their Relationship to Contemporary Sculptural Form," *Azania* 35 (2000): 226–30.
64. Yvonne Bastin et al., *Bantu Lexical Reconstructions 3* (Leiden, Netherlands: Leiden University, 2003), Main 8861, www.africamuseum.be/en. The *BLR3* database shows cognates of the Sabaki words for "witchcraft" (*utsai*, Chimijikenda; *uchawi*, Kiswahili) in the Congo River Basin but not in intervening territories, suggesting a very old provenance.

65. Spear, *Traditions*, 64.
66. Spear, 89.
67. Fourshey, Gonzales, and Saidi, *Bantu Africa*, chap. 2.
68. Krapf and Rebmann, *Nika-English Dictionary*, s.v. "*kiravo*"; emphasis mine.
69. Orchardson-Mazrui, "Aesthetics," 90–91; Brantley, "Gerontocratic Government," 255–56.
70. Fleisher, "Rituals of Consumption," 207.
71. Jeffrey Fleisher, "On the Mimetic Qualities of Bowls on the Medieval Swahili Coast," in *World on the Horizon: Swahili Arts across the Indian Ocean*, ed. Allyson Purpura and Prita Meier (Urbana-Champaign: Krannert Art Museum and the University of Illinois, 2018). Also see Kathryn M. de Luna and Jeffrey B. Fleisher, *Speaking with Substance* (Cham, Switzerland: Springer, 2019).
72. Stephanie Wynne-Jones, *A Material Culture: Consumption and Materiality on the Coast of Precolonial East Africa* (Oxford: Oxford University Press, 2016), 100–104.
73. Krapf and Rebmann, *Nika-English Dictionary*, s.v. "*kihendo*."
74. Hassan Muhammad, author's field notes, May 6, 2010.
75. Martin T. Walsh, "The Segeju Complex? Linguistic Evidence for the Precolonial Making of the Mijikenda," in *Contesting Identities: The Mijikenda and Their Neighbors in Kenyan Coastal Society*, ed. Rebecca Gearhart and Linda Giles (Trenton, NJ: Africa World Press, 2013), 25–51.
76. Derek Nurse, "South Meets North: Ilwana = Bantu + Cushitic on Kenya's Tana River," in *Mixed Languages*, ed. Peter Bakker and Maarten Mous (Amsterdam: IFOTF, 1994), 213–22.
77. James Kirkman, "The Muzungulos of Mombasa," *IJAHS* 16, no. 1 (January 1, 1983): 75.
78. Derek Nurse, "Segeju and Daisū: A Case Study of Evidence from Oral Tradition and Comparative Linguistics," *History in Africa* 9 (1982): 175–208.
79. Thomas Vernet, "Re-considering the Swahili City-States in the Early Modern Era: New Evidences and Renewed Paradigms" (paper presented at the Zanzibar Indian Ocean Research Institute Inaugural Conference, Zanzibar, Tanzania, 2008), 18.
80. Walsh, "Segeju Complex."
81. Walsh, 33–34.
82. Helm, "Re-evaluating Traditional Histories," 75.
83. Freeman-Grenville, *Select Documents*, 141.
84. Kirkman, "Muzungulos," 73.
85. Midani bin Mwidad, "The Founding of Rabai: A Swahili Chronicle," trans. Lyndon Harries, *Swahili* 30 (1960): 140–49.

86. Freeman-Grenville, *Select Documents*, 141.
87. New, *Life, Wanderings, and Labours*, 108; William Tsaka, author's field notes, May 27, 2011.
88. Walsh, "Segeju Complex," 42–45.
89. Fourshey, Gonzales, and Saidi, *Bantu Africa*, 82.
90. Christopher Ehret, *An African Classical Age: Eastern and Southern Africa in World History, 1000 BC to AD 400* (Charlottesville: University of Virginia Press, 1998), 329.
91. A. H. J. Prins, *East African Age Class Systems* (Groningen, Netherlands: J. B. Wolters, 1953).
92. Walsh, "Segeju Complex," 38–39.
93. Orchardson-Mazrui, "Aesthetics," 89.
94. Compare Krapf and Rebmann, *Nika-English Dictionary*, s.v. "*kirimusha* (to entertain or treat hospitably)" with Hans Wehr, *A Dictionary of Modern Written Arabic*, ed. J. Milton Cowan, 3rd ed. (London: MacDonald & Evans, 1980), s.v. "*karīm* (noble, generous)."
95. Spear, *Traditions*, 73.
96. Spear, 111.
97. Spear, 69–70.
98. Spear, 59, 111, 142.
99. See "Proceedings of Duruma Baraza (Kambi)," November 16, 1923, DC/KWL/3/1/196–7, KNA.
100. Quoted in Kirkman, "Muzungulos," 76; Freeman-Grenville, *Selected Documents*, 180, 185.
101. Spear, *Traditions*, 70, 75.
102. See Krapf, *Travels*.
103. Gona Kazungu records four wars among inland clan confederations. Gona Kazungu, "Agiryama," 75–83.
104. Spear, *Traditions*, 75.
105. Krapf and Rebmann, *Nika-English Dictionary*, s.v. "*dendana*" and "*fomorera*."
106. Janet McIntosh, "Elders and 'Frauds': Commodified Expertise and Politicized Authenticity among Mijikenda," *Africa* 79, no. 1 (2009): 35–52.
107. Richard Waller, "Age and Ethnography," *Azania* 34, no. 1 (January 1, 1999): 140.

CHAPTER 4: POLARIZING POLITICS

1. Andrie Meyer and Chris Cloete, "Architectural Traditions of Mapungubwe and Bambandyanalo (K2)," *Journal for Transdisciplinary Research in Southern Africa* 6, no. 1 (April 4, 2010): 241–70.

2. For full rules, see Ralf Gering, "Bao la Kiswahili," Fandom, Mancala World, accessed June 26, 2023, https://mancala.fandom.com/wiki/Bao_la_Kiswahili; Nino Vesella, "Kanuni za kucheza [rules]," Bao, Klubo Internacia de Bao, accessed June 26, 2023, https://www.kibao.org/kanuni.php?lng=en; or Alex de Voogt, "Limits of the Mind: Towards a Characterisation of Bao Mastership" (PhD diss., University of Leiden, 1995).
3. John Iliffe, *Africans: The History of a Continent,* 2nd ed. (New York: Cambridge University Press, 2007), 99.
4. Alex de Voogt, "Muyaka's Poetry in the History of Bao," *Bulletin of the School of Oriental and African Studies* 66, no. 1 (February 1, 2003): 61.
5. John Laband, *Bringers of War: The Portuguese in Africa during the Age of Gunpowder and Sail from the Fifteenth to the Eighteenth Century* (London: Frontline Books, 2013).
6. For example, Giancarlo Casale, "Global Politics in the 1580s: One Canal, Twenty Thousand Cannibals, and an Ottoman Plot to Rule the World," *Journal of World History* 18, no. 3 (2007): 267–96.
7. Mark Horton and John Middleton, *The Swahili: The Social Landscape of a Mercantile Society* (Malden, MA: Blackwell Publishers, 2000), 80–81.
8. Jeremy Prestholdt, "Portuguese Conceptual Categories and the 'Other' Encounter on the Swahili Coast," *Journal of Asian & African Studies* 36, no. 4 (November 2001): 383–406.
9. Michael N. Pearson, *The Portuguese in India* (Cambridge: Cambridge University Press, 2006), 95.
10. G. S. P. Freeman-Grenville, *The East African Coast: Select Documents from the First to the Nineteenth Century,* 2nd ed. (Oxford: Clarendon, 1975), 42.
11. Casale, "Global Politics," 277.
12. Abdul Sheriff, *Dhow Cultures of the Indian Ocean: Cosmopolitanism, Commerce, and Islam* (New York: Columbia University Press, 2010), 291–314.
13. Pearson, *Portuguese in India.*
14. Casale, "Global Politics," 289.
15. Casale, 281–82.
16. Eric Allina, "The Zimba, the Portuguese, and Other Cannibals in Late Sixteenth-Century Southeast Africa," *Journal of Southern African Studies* 37, no. 2 (June 1, 2011): 211–27.
17. J. Strandes, *The Portuguese Period in East Africa,* ed. James Kirkman, trans. J. F. Wallwork (Nairobi: East African Literature Bureau, 1961), 140.

18. Casale, "Global Politics," 276.
19. Reginald Coupland, *East Africa and Its Invaders: From Earliest Times to the Death of Seyyid Said* (Oxford: Clarendon, 1938), 57–59.
20. Jomvu elders, group interview by author, digital audio recording, Ray Research Deposit C052; Mohamed Shalo, interview by author, June 18, 2010, digital video and audio, Ray Research Deposit C024.
21. F. J. Berg, "The Swahili Community of Mombasa, 1500–1900," *Journal of African History* 9, no. 1 (1968): 47.
22. F. J. Berg, "Mombasa under the Busaidi Sultanate: The City and Its Hinterlands in the Nineteenth Century" (PhD diss., University of Wisconsin, 1971), 69–73; Mohamed Hassan Abdulaziz, *Muyaka, 19th Century Swahili Popular Poetry* (Nairobi: Kenya Literature Bureau, 1979), 154–55.
23. Michael N. Pearson, *Port Cities and Intruders: The Swahili Coast, India, and Portugal in the Early Modern Era* (Baltimore: Johns Hopkins University Press, 1998), 113.
24. Strandes, *Portuguese Period*, 169.
25. Strandes, chap. 14.
26. Strandes, 175.
27. Tome N. Mbuia-Joao, "The Revolt of Don Jeronimo Chingulia of Mombasa, 1590–1637: An African Episode in the Portuguese Century of Decline" (PhD diss., Catholic University, 1990); C. R. Boxer and C. de Azevedo, *Fort Jesus and the Portuguese in Mombasa, 1593–1729* (London: Hollis and Carter, 1960).
28. Freeman-Grenville, *Select Documents*, 218–19.
29. Strandes, *Portuguese Period*, 175.
30. Freeman-Grenville, *Select Documents*, 219.
31. Strandes, *Portuguese Period*, 189.
32. James Kirkman, "The Muzungulos of Mombasa," *IJAHS* 16, no. 1 (January 1, 1983): 80.
33. Strandes, *Portuguese Period*, 239–42.
34. Freeman-Grenville, *Select Documents*, 216.
35. Berg, "Mombasa under the Busaidi Sultanate," 51, 55. Here I follow the convention of referring to named groups of intermarrying lineages in Arab communities as *clans;* but see ch. 3 for a discussion of *clans* as conceptualized by Sabaki Bantu speakers.
36. Patricia Risso, *Oman and Muscat: An Early Modern History* (New York: St. Martin's Press, 1986), 30.
37. Derek Nurse and Thomas Hinnebusch, *Swahili and Sabaki: A Linguistic History* (Berkeley: University of California Press, 1993), 328.

38. Sheikh al- Amin Bin Ali al- Mazrui, *The History of the Mazru'i Dy-nasty of Mombasa*, trans. J. McL. Ritchie (Oxford: Oxford Uni-versity Press, 1995).
39. Risso, *Oman and Muscat*, 82.
40. Marina Tolmacheva, trans., *The Pate Chronicle* (East Lansing: Michigan State University Press, 1993), 69.
41. A mile was defined as 810 by 200 paces. Charles Guillain, *Documents Sur l'Historie, La Géographie, et Le Commerce de La Côte Orientale d'Afrique* [Documents on the history, geography, and economy of the East Coast of Africa] (Paris: Arthus Bertrand, 1856), 3:260n1.
42. Tolmacheva, *Pate Chronicle*, 54.
43. Al-Mazrui, *Mazru'i Dynasty*, 31–32.
44. Al-Mazrui, 32–33.
45. Freeman-Grenville, *Select Documents*, 215.
46. Freeman-Grenville, 216.
47. Freeman-Grenville, 216.
48. Berg, "Swahili Community," 52.
49. Al-Mazrui, *Mazru'i Dynasty*, 60.
50. Al-Mazrui, 43–48.
51. Guillain, *Documents*, 3:259.
52. Al-Mazrui, *Mazru'i Dynasty*, 40–41.
53. Johann Ludwig Krapf and Johannes Rebmann, *A Nika-English Dictionary* (London: Society for Promoting Christian Knowledge, 1887), s.v. "*ensi, aensi.*"
54. Abdulaziz, *Muyaka*, 11.
55. In this context *Rika Nguli* was "the name adopted by all who were circumcised [sic: initiated] at the same time." Taylor, quoted in Abdulaziz, *Muyaka*, 26n16.
56. Al-Mazrui, *Mazru'i Dynasty*, 55.
57. Randall L. Pouwels, "The Battle of Shela: The Climax of an Era and a Point of Departure in the Modern History of the Kenya Coast," *Cahiers d'Études Africaines* 31, no. 123 (January 1, 1991): 377n50.
58. Alice Werner, "Swahili History of Pate," *Journal of the African Society* 14 (1914): 291.
59. Abdulaziz, *Muyaka*, 117.
60. Abdul Sheriff, *Slaves, Spices, and Ivory in Zanzibar: Integration of an East African Commercial Empire into the World Economy, 1770–1873* (London: James Currey, 1987), 87–101.
61. Pouwels, "Battle of Shela," 371.
62. Ann Biersteker and Ibrahim Noor Shariff, eds., *Mashairi Ya Vita Vya Kuduhu: War Poetry in Kiswahili Exchanged at the Time of*

the Battle of Kuduhu (East Lansing: Michigan State University Press, 1995).
63. My translation, adapted from Abdulaziz, *Muyaka*, 118.
64. Pouwels, "Battle of Shela," 379.
65. Pouwels, 379n59.
66. Risso, *Oman and Muscat*, 13–14.
67. Sheriff, *Slaves, Spices, and Ivory*, 41.
68. Cynthia Brantley and V. Gona Kazungu, "Giriama Historical Texts," 1971, University of Nairobi Research Project Archives.
69. Abdulaziz, *Muyaka*, 117.
70. Thomas H. Wilson, "Swahili Funerary Architecture of the North Kenya Coast," in *Swahili Houses and Tombs of the Coast of Kenya*, ed. James de Vere Allen and Thomas H. Wilson (London: Art and Archaeology Research Papers, 1979), 33–36.
71. Ali A. Mazrui, presenter and writer, "The Nature of a Continent," in *The Africans: A Triple Heritage*, 1986, BBC TV, 1 hr.
72. John Middleton, *The World of the Swahili: An African Mercantile Civilization* (New Haven, CT: Yale University Press, 1992), 81.
73. Al-Mazrui, *Mazru'i Dynasty*, 68–70.

CHAPTER 5: PRACTICING MUSLIMS, MARGINALIZED PAGANS

1. Kai Kresse, "Debating Maulidi: Ambiguities and Transformations of Muslim Identity on the Swahili Coast," in *The Global Worlds of the Swahili: Interfaces of Islam, Identity, and Space in 19th and 20th-Century East Africa*, ed. Roman Loimeier and Rudiger Seesemann (Berlin: LIT Verlag, 2006), 209–28.
2. Roman Loimeier, "Traditions of Reform, Reformers of Tradition: Case Studies from Senegal and Zanzibar/Tanzania," in *Diversity and Pluralism in Islam Historical and Contemporary Discourses amongst Muslims*, ed. Zulfikar Hirji (London: IB Tauris, 2010), 135–62; Mohamed Bakari, "The New 'Ulama of Kenya," in *Islam in Kenya* (Nairobi: MEWA Publications, 1995), 168–93.
3. Kresse, "Debating Maulidi"; Jeremy Prestholdt, "Politics of the Soil: Separatism, Autochthony, and Decolonization at the Kenyan Coast," *Journal of African History* 55, no. 2 (July 2014): 249–70.
4. Thomas T. Spear, *The Kaya Complex: A History of the Mijikenda Peoples of the Kenya Coast to 1900* (Nairobi: Kenya Literature Bureau, 1978); John Middleton, *The World of the Swahili: An African Mercantile Civilization* (New Haven, CT: Yale University Press, 1992), 1; Janet McIntosh, *The Edge of Islam: Power, Personhood, and Ethnoreligious Boundaries on the Kenya Coast* (Durham, NC: Duke University Press, 2009), 51–54.

5. McIntosh, *Edge of Islam*.
6. W. F. W. Owen, *Narrative of Voyages to Explore the Shores of Africa, Arabia and Madagascar* (London: R. Bentley, 1833), 2:141.
7. James Emery, "Early 19th Century Trade and Politics at Mombasa: Lieutenant James Emery's Diary 1824–1826," August 16, 1825, 2:3, D/4/3, University of Nairobi Research Project Archives.
8. David Colton Sperling, "The Growth of Islam among the Mijikenda of the Kenya Coast, 1826–1930" (PhD diss., University of London, 1988), 40.
9. Emery, "Emery's Diary," October 14, 1825, 2:6.
10. Emery, 2:6.
11. *Tammims* in Oman were leaders of "major tribal-cum-regional confederations." John Wilkinson, *The Arabs and the Scramble for Africa* (Bristol, CT: Equinox Publishing, 2014), 7.
12. Mohamed Hassan Abdulaziz, *Muyaka, 19th Century Swahili Popular Poetry* (Nairobi: Kenya Literature Bureau, 1979), 153–54.
13. Abdul Sheriff, *Slaves, Spices, and Ivory in Zanzibar: Integration of an East African Commercial Empire into the World Econ-omy, 1770–1873* (London: James Currey, 1987), 87– 101; Marek Pawełczak, *The State and the Stateless: The Sultanate of Zanzibar and the East African Mainland; Politics, Economy and Society, 1837–1888* (Warsaw: SOWA, 2010).
14. Wilkinson, *Scramble for Africa*, 12.
15. Randall L. Pouwels, *Horn and Crescent: Cultural Change and Traditional Islam on the East African Coast, 800–1900* (Cambridge: Cambridge University Press, 1987); Anne K. Bang, *Sufis and Scholars of the Sea: Family Networks in East Africa, 1860–1925* (New York: Routledge, 2003).
16. David Robinson, *Paths of Accommodation: Muslim Societies and French Colonial Authorities in Senegal and Mauritania, 1880–1920* (Athens: Ohio University Press, 2000).
17. Pawełczak, *State and the Stateless;* F. J. Berg, "The Swahili Community of Mombasa, 1500–1900," *Journal of African History* 9, no. 1 (1968): 35– 36.
18. Peter L. Koffsky, "History of Takaungu, East Africa, 1830–1896" (PhD diss., University of Wisconsin, 1977), 97.
19. Pouwels, *Horn and Crescent*, 110–11, 123.
20. Pouwels, 151; Pawełczak, *State and the Stateless*, 277.
21. Elisabeth McMahon, "'A Solitary Tree Builds Not': Heshima, Community, and Shifting Identity in Post-emancipation Pemba Island," *IJAHS* 39, no. 2 (June 2006): 200; Pouwels, *Horn and Crescent*, 72–73.

22. Sulaiman bin Said bin Ahmed Essorami, *The Jurisdiction of the Sultan of Zanzibar and the Subjects of Foreign Nations*, trans. Katrin Bromber (Würzburg, Germany: Ergon-Verl, 2001), 27.
23. Derek Nurse and Thomas Hinnebusch, *Swahili and Sabaki: A Linguistic History* (Berkeley: University of California Press, 1993), 321–31.
24. Scholars often treated such claims to Persian ancestry on the East African coast as fanciful or exaggerated, but they have been confirmed by DNA evidence. Esther S. Brielle et al., "Entwined African and Asian Genetic Roots of Medieval Peoples of the Swahili Coast," *Nature* 615, no. 7954 (March 2023): 866–73.
25. Mohamed Shalo, interview by author, June 18, 2010, digital video and audio, Ray Research Deposit C024.
26. Randall L. Pouwels, "Oral Historiography and the Problem of the Shirazi of the East African Coast," *History in Africa* 11 (1984): 240.
27. Essorami, *Jurisdiction*, 71. It is unclear why Bromber translates *qabīla* as "clan" instead of "tribe" in this context.
28. Essorami, 19.
29. Essorami, 80–85.
30. Essorami, 21.
31. A subentry of *mbwa* (dog) lists *mbwa koko* (bush dog) in Frederick Johnson, *A Standard English-Swahili Dictionary* (London: Oxford University Press, 1939), s.v. "*mbwa*."
32. Bradford G. Martin, "Arab Migrations to East Africa in Medieval Times," *IJAHS* 7, no. 3 (1974): 371.
33. For twentieth-century examples, see Kai Kresse, "The Uses of History: Rhetorics of Muslim Unity and Difference on the Kenyan Swahili Coast," in *Struggling with History: Islam and Cosmopolitanism in the Western Indian Ocean*, ed. Edward Simpson and Kai Kresse (New York: Columbia University Press, 2008), 223–60.
34. Sheriff, *Slaves, Spices, and Ivory*, 60–61.
35. Frederick Cooper, *Plantation Slavery on the East Coast of Africa* (Portsmouth, NH: Heinemann, 1997).
36. Bang, *Sufis and Scholars of the Sea*, 128–29, 146–52.
37. Engseng Ho, *The Graves of Tarim: Genealogy and Mobility across the Indian Ocean* (Berkeley: University of California Press, 2006), chap. 6.
38. August Nimitz, *Islam and Politics in East Africa: The Sufi Order in Tanzania* (Minneapolis: University of Minnesota Press, 1980), 70–71.
39. Bang, *Sufis and Scholars of the Sea*, 128.

40. Abdul Hamid el-Zein, *The Sacred Meadows: A Structural Analysis of Religious Symbolism in an East African Town* (Evanston, IL: Northwestern University Press, 1974).
41. Mohsein Sayyid Ali Said Ahmed Badawy (mudir of Lamu College), interview by author, February 17, 2010, digital video and audio, trans. Mohammed Hassen, Ray Research Deposit C010.
42. Wilkinson, *Scramble for Africa*, 77.
43. Wilkinson, 153.
44. Pouwels, *Horn and Crescent*, 146.
45. Wilkinson, *Scramble for Africa*, 148–49.
46. Wilkinson, 54–55.
47. Wilkinson, 148–49.
48. Wilkinson, 151.
49. Wilkinson, 9.
50. Pawełczak, *State and the Stateless*; Wilkinson, *Scramble for Africa*.
51. John Ludwig Krapf, "Section IV, Africa Missions," in *Revd Dr. Krapf's Journal* (Marlborough, UK: Adam Matthew Publications, 1997), 585, microfilm, part 16, reel 317, Church Missionary Society.
52. Sperling, "Growth of Islam," 31, 101n3.
53. Nurse and Hinnebusch, *Swahili and Sabaki*, 17.
54. Johann Ludwig Krapf and Johannes Rebmann, *A Nika-English Dictionary* (London: Society for Promoting Christian Knowledge, 1887).
55. Krapf, "Africa Missions," September 15, 1844, 491.
56. Krapf, May 23, 1845, 543.
57. Krapf, September 25, 1845, 506.
58. Thomas J. Herlehy, "An Economic History of the Kenya Coast: The Mijikenda Coconut Palm Economy, ca. 1800–1980" (PhD diss., Boston University, 1985).
59. Krapf, "Africa Missions," February 17, 1845, 598.
60. Krapf, 586; Pawełczak, *State and the Stateless*, chap. 3.
61. Cynthia Brantley, *The Giriama and Colonial Resistance in Kenya, 1800–1920* (Berkeley: University of California Press, 1981), 19.
62. Cooper, *Plantation Slavery*, 83.
63. el-Zein, *Sacred Meadows*.
64. Brantley, *Giriama and Colonial Resistance*, 49.
65. Pawełczak, *State and the Stateless*, 150–51. See R. F. Morton, *Children of Ham: Freed Slaves and Fugitive Slaves on the Kenya Coast, 1873 to 1907* (Boulder, CO: Westview, 1990).
66. Brantley, *Giriama and Colonial Resistance*, 19–25.
67. Willis, *Making of the Mijikenda*, 55.

68. Charles New, *Life, Wanderings, and Labours in Eastern Africa,* 3rd ed. (London: Cass, 1971), 108.
69. Carol M. Eastman, "Waungwana Na Wanawake: Muslim Ethnicity and Sexual Segregation in Coastal Kenya," *Journal of Multilingual and Multicultural Development* 5 (1984): 97–112.
70. Sperling, "Growth of Islam," 66.
71. Sperling, 66.
72. Sperling, 71n153.
73. Sperling, 92.
74. Sperling, 148, 66.
75. Sperling, 92.
76. Thomas Rebmann to Henry Venn, May 2, 1863, CMS CA5/024/42, cited in Sperling, "Growth of Islam," 71n152.
77. Krapf, "Africa Missions," March 23, 1845, 554.
78. Sperling, "Growth of Islam," 60–61.
79. Sperling, 90.
80. Sperling, 92.
81. Sperling, 106–55.
82. Sperling, 103.
83. Sperling, 156.
84. Sperling, "Growth of Islam," 135–43; Bettina Ng'weno, "Inheriting Disputes: The Digo Negotiation of Meaning and Power through Land," *African Economic History,* no. 25 (1997): 59–77.
85. Sperling, "Growth of Islam," 110.
86. C. E. Gissing, "Report of a Journey from Mombasa to Mambrui," September 14, 1884, AA/10/1, Zanzibar National Archives.
87. S. Chiraghdin, "Maisha Ya Sheikh Mbaruk Bin Rashid al-Mazrui" [The life of Sheikh Mbaruk bin Rashid al-Mazrui], *Swahili* 31 (1960): 150–79.
88. *Africa,* no. 6 (1896): *Correspondence Respecting the Recent Rebellion in British East Africa,* vol. 59 (London: House of Commons, 1896), 56, ProQuest.
89. "Recent Rebellion," 61.
90. "Recent Rebellion," 98.
91. "Recent Rebellion," 50, 105.
92. "Recent Rebellion," 53.
93. "Recent Rebellion," 55.
94. Chiraghdin, "Maisha Ya Sheikh Mbaruk."
95. Sperling, "Growth of Islam," 95–96.
96. "Recent Rebellion," 89.

CHAPTER 6: GAZETTING IDENTITY

1. Frederick Johnson, *A Standard English-Swahili Dictionary* (London: Oxford University Press, 1939), s.v. "*enye.*"

2. Order-in-Council of July 7, 1897, LPJ/6/451, file 138, Oriental and India Office Collections, British Library, London, quoted in Thomas R. Metcalf, *Imperial Connections: India in the Indian Ocean Arena, 1860–1920* (Berkeley: University of California Press, 2008), 23.
3. Kapil Raj, "Circulation and the Emergence of Modern Mapping: Great Britain and Early Colonial India, 1764–1820," in *Society and Circulation: Mobile People and Itinerant Cultures in South Asia, 1750–1950*, ed. Claude Markovits, Jacques Pouchepadass, and Sanjay Subrahmanyam (Delhi: Permanent Black, 2003), 23–54.
4. Thomas R. Metcalf, *Ideologies of the Raj* (Cambridge: Cambridge University Press, 1997), chap. 4.
5. "Seyidie Province: District Boundaries," *Official Gazette of the East Africa Protectorate* 14, no. 298 (April 1, 1912): 207; Simeon H. Ominde, *Land and Population Movements in Kenya* (London: Heinemann, 1968), 7–11. Cf. David M. Anderson, "'Yours in Struggle for Majimbo': Nationalism and the Party Politics of Decolonization in Kenya, 1955–64," *Journal of Contemporary History* 40, no. 3 (July 1, 2005): 558.
6. Ahmed Idha Salim, *The Swahili-Speaking Peoples of Kenya's Coast, 1895–1965* (Nairobi: East African Publishing House, 1973).
7. Justin Willis, *Mombasa, the Swahili, and the Making of the Mijikenda* (New York: Oxford University Press, 1993).
8. Metcalf, *Imperial Connections*, 17–19.
9. Charles Hobley to R. G. Fanant, July 25, 1913, PC/Coast/1/11/101, Kenya National Archives (KNA); emphasis added.
10. R. G. Fanant to Charles Hobley, July 26, 1913, PC/Coast/1/11/101, KNA.
11. David Colton Sperling, "The Growth of Islam among the Mijikenda of the Kenya Coast, 1826–1930" (PhD diss., University of London, 1988), 132n139.
12. Hamidin Abdullah Hamid, "Unfinished Business: The Implementation of the Land Titles Ordinance in Coastal Kenya, 1908–1940s" (PhD diss., University of London, 2000), 158.
13. See Hamid, 116–18. Johann Ludwig Krapf noted five Digo groups a few decades earlier in his book, *Travels, Researches, and Missionary Labours, during an Eighteen Years' Residence in Eastern Africa*, 2nd ed. (London: Frank Cass, 1968), 91, 97–100.
14. E. V. Hemmant, "Memorandum Re Vanga District Locations," June 18, 1913, DC/KWL/4/1, KNA.
15. O. F. Watkins, "Memorandum on Waste Lands in the Zanzibar Dominions of the Mombasa District," November 11, 1909, CY/2/22, KNA Mombasa Branch.

16. "Notice Re: Boundary of Wa-Nyika Native Reserve," *Official Gazette of the East Africa Protectorate* 10, no. 204 (May 1, 1908): 271.
17. Kenya Land Commission, *Evidence and Memoranda* (London: His/Her Majesty's Stationary Office, 1934), 2630.
18. Hassan Mwakimako, "The Historical Development of Muslim Courts: The Kadhi, Mudir and Liwali Courts and the Civil Procedure Code and Criminal Procedure Ordinance, c. 1963," *Journal of Eastern African Studies* 5, no. 2 (May 1, 2011): 329–43.
19. Sperling, "Growth of Islam," 117n73.
20. "Native Courts Regulation of August 12, 1897," quoted in "Circular, Chief Native Court, Mombasa," December 18, 1900, AG/11/16, KNA.
21. See Hamid, "Unfinished Business," 124.
22. C. W. Hobley, "Native Administration," October 8, 1912, DC/KWL/4/1, KNA.
23. Hemmant, "Memorandum"; E. V. Hemmant to Charles Hobley, November 26, 1913, DC/KWL/4/1, KNA; and W. Marchant (district commissioner, Kwale) to senior commissioner (Coast), "Intercolonial Boundaries," March 8, 1926, CC/12/15, KNA. On the Zumbe, see C. S. Hemsted (district commissioner, Mombasa) to provincial commissioner (Mombasa), August 1, 1917, DC/MSA/5/1, KNA.
24. "Village Headmen Ordinance 1902," in *East Africa Protectorate Ordinances and Regulations, 1901–1902* (Mombasa: Government Printing Press, 1903), 4:58.
25. See a sampling of unfavorable evaluations in "Takaungu Annual Report 1913–1914," 1914, DC/KFI/1/1, KNA.
26. Hobley, "Native Administration."
27. Cynthia Brantley, *The Giriama and Colonial Resistance in Kenya, 1800–1920* (Berkeley: University of California Press, 1981), 79–80.
28. Bresnahan labels government councils as judiciary councils, but Ciekawy suggests older Chimijikenda speakers associate the word "kambi" with those appointed by the government. David Bresnahan, "Forest Imageries and Political Practice in Colonial Coastal Kenya," *Journal of Eastern African Studies* 12, no. 4 (October 2, 2018): 660, 660n38; Diane Marie Ciekawy, "Witchcraft Eradication as Political Process in Kilifi District, Kenya, 1955–1988" (PhD diss., Columbia University, 1992), 71–73.
29. Bresnahan, "Forest Imageries," 664.
30. H. L. Mood, "Duruma Kambi," 1917, DC/MSA/5/1, KNA; H. L. Mood, "Notes on the Wa-Duruma, Kayas, Kambis, Customs &c.," n.d., DC/KWL/1/3/5, KNA.

31. H. L. Mood (assistant district commissioner, Rabai) to provincial commissioner (Mombasa), November 2, 1917, PC/Coast/1/7/11, KNA.
32. David Parkin, *Sacred Void: Spatial Images of Work and Ritual among the Giriama of Kenya* (Cambridge: Cambridge University Press, 1991).
33. Bresnahan, "Forest Imageries."
34. "Tour by C. Dundas, Changamwe, 12th–15th March 1915," 1915, PC/Coast/1/1/400, KNA.
35. "Tour by C. Dundas, Mtongwe, 13th–14th February 1915," 1915, PC/Coast/1/1/400, KNA.
36. "Tour by C. Dundas, Changamwe, 17th–20th Febr[u]ary 1915," 1915, PC/Coast/1/1/400, KNA.
37. This section revises an analysis first published in Daren Ray, "From Constituting Communities to Dividing Districts: The Formalization of a Cultural Border between Mombasa and Its Hinterland," in *Borderlands in World History*, ed. Paul Readman, Cynthia Radding, and Chad Bryant (London: Palgrave Macmillan, 2014), 109–14.
38. J. M. Pearson to Charles Hobley, "Wa Jomvu Community," May 2, 1913, PC/Coast/1/3/62, KNA.
39. J. M. Pearson to Charles Hobley, September 8, 1913, PC/Coast/1/3/62, KNA.
40. "Petition of Wajomvu of Maunguja to the Provincial Commissioner, Mombasa," n.d., PC/Coast/1/3/62, KNA; emphasis added.
41. See Pearson to Hobley, "Wa Jomvu Community." Cf. Jomvu elders, group interview by author, May 20, 2011, digital audio, Ray Research Deposit Co52.
42. Pearson to Hobley, September 8, 1913.
43. "Meeting Held at Jomvu," October 25, 1913, DC/KFI/3/2, KNA.
44. J. M. Pearson, "Rabai District Boundaries," September 1, 1913, DC/KFI/3/2, KNA; emphasis added.
45. P. L. Deacon (district commissioner, Mombasa) to R. W. Lambert (assistant district commissioner, Rabai), September 2, 1918, DC/MSA/5/1, KNA.
46. Ominde, *Land and Population*, 4–7.
47. Pekeshe Ndeje, interview by author, May 23, 2011, trans. William Tsaka, digital video and audio, Ray Research Deposit Co53; Henry Ndune Mkando, interview by author, May 24, 2011, trans. William Tsaka, digital video and audio, Ray Research Deposit Co55.
48. This provisional boundary was formalized March 15, 1916. See "Boundaries of the [Takaungu] Sub-district," n.d., DC/KFI/1/1, KNA.

49. Cynthia Brantley, "Mekatalili and the Role of Women in Giriama Resistance," in *Banditry, Rebellion, and Social Protest in Africa*, ed. Donald Crummey (London: James Currey, 1986), 333–50.
50. Brantley, *Giriama and Colonial Resistance*, 81.
51. Brantley, *Giriama and Colonial Resistance*, 47; Brantley, "Mekatalili."
52. "Takaungu Annual Report," 1914, p. 3, DC/KFI/1/1, KNA.
53. Derek R. Peterson, *Ethnic Patriotism and the East African Revival: A History of Dissent, c. 1935–1972* (Cambridge: Cambridge University Press, 2013); Matthew Carotenuto, "Riwruok E Teko: Cultivating Identity in Colonial and Postcolonial Kenya," *Africa Today* 53, no. 2 (2006): 53–73; John Lonsdale, "The Moral Economy of Mau Mau: Wealth, Poverty, and Civic Virtue in Kikuyu Political Thought," in *Unhappy Valley: Conflict in Kenya and Africa*, ed. Bruce Berman and John Lonsdale, vol. 2 (London: James Currey, 1992).
54. Brantley, "Mekatalili," 345.
55. Brantley, 341–42.
56. "Report of the Malindi Commission of Inquiry Part II, Appendix VI" (henceforth "MCI App. VI"), December 22, 1916, item 18, CO/533/180, TNA.
57. Brantley, *Giriama and Colonial Resistance*, 112–13.
58. Ralph Skene, in "Report of the Malindi Commission of Inquiry Part II, Appendix VII" (henceforth "MCI App. VII"), December 22, 1916, p. 55, CO/533/180, TNA.
59. Jefa wa Kikutha and Ziro wa Njezali, in "MCI App. VII," 31, 34.
60. W. E. F. de Lacy, in "MCI App. VII," 21.
61. W. E. F. de Lacy, *The Forcible Stoppage of Native Food Production, Illegal Evictions, Persecution of Natives in Seyedie Province and the Commission of Camouflage* (Nairobi: East African Standard, 1918), 77.
62. Kaura wa Ndoro, in "MCI App. VII," 37; emphasis added.
63. Mzee Baruti bin Suleman bin Shanoon, in "MCI App. VII," 32; Sef bin Salim, in "Report of the Malindi Commission of Inquiry Part II," December 22, 1916, p. 15, item 18, CO/533/180, TNA.
64. Mzee Baruti bin wa Suleman bin Shenoon, in "MCI App. VII," 32. Officials disputed this account. See H. Montgomery and R. Skene, in "MCI App. VII," 9, 57.
65. John Jones and R. Skene, in "MCI App. VII," 48, 57.
66. De Lacy, in "MCI App. VII," 5.
67. "Report of the Malindi Commission of Inquiry, Part I," December 22, 1916, pp. 15–16, CO/533/180, TNA; "Application Cause

No. 18 D of 1915," in "Report of the Malindi Commission of Inquiry, Appendix V," December 22, 1916, CO/533/180, TNA; de Lacy, in "MCI App. VII," 3, 20–21; Omar Bin Athman bin Shehe, in "MCI App. VII," 25.
68. Fathil bin Omar, in "MCI App. VII," 29.
69. Fathil bin Omar, in "MCI App. VII," 28. Cf. Sperling, "Growth of Islam," 132–35.
70. Jones, in "MCI App. VII," 27.
71. Mzungu wa Kiasi, in "MCI App. VII," 34.
72. Abdulla Jefa, in "MCI App. VII," 38.
73. All names listed in the following discussion come from "MCI App. VI," items 2 and 11.
74. "MCI App. VI," item 7.
75. Report appended to Merwyn Beech to Charles Hobley, April 13, 1915, in "MCI App. VI," item 14, p. 2.
76. Arthur Mortimer Champion, "The Movement of the Wa Giriama from the North to the South Bank of the Sabaki," February 11, 1914, in "MCI App. VI," item 15.
77. G. M. Hazlerigg to Charles Hobley, "Native Affairs, Giriama: Move from North Bank of Sabaki," March 7, 1914, in "MCI App. VI," item 15.
78. Hazlerigg to Hobley.
79. "Malindi Commission of Inquiry, Part I," 3–20.

CHAPTER 7: HISTORICIZING TRIBALISM

1. "IIBRC Hearing," Lamu, February 16, 2010, notes and digital audio, Ray Research Deposit E002.
2. "IEBC Notably Alters Ligale Proposals," *Capital News*, February 9, 2012.
3. Cf. Derek R. Peterson and Giacomo Macola, "Introduction: Homespun Historiography and the Academic Profession," in *Recasting the Past: History Writing and Political Work in Modern Africa*, ed. Derek R. Peterson and Giacomo Macola (Athens: Ohio University Press, 2009), 9.
4. Hans Wehr, *A Dictionary of Modern Written Arabic*, ed. J. Milton Cowan, 3rd ed. (London: MacDonald & Evans, 1980), s.v. "*qabīl*"; Richard Tapper, "Anthropologists, Historians, and Tribespeople on Tribe and State Formation in the Middle East," in *Tribes and State Formation in the Middle East*, ed. Philip S. Khoury and Joseph Kostiner (Berkeley: University of California Press, 1990), 48– 73.
5. Thomas R. Metcalf, *Ideologies of the Raj* (Cambridge: Cambridge University Press, 1997), 68–80.

6. F. J. Berg, "The Swahili Community of Mombasa, 1500–1900," *Journal of African History* 9, no. 1 (1968): 41.
7. Rogers Brubaker, "Ethnicity without Groups," *European Journal of Sociology* 43, no. 2 (2002): 166–67.
8. Julie MacArthur, *Cartography and the Political Imagination: Mapping Community in Colonial Kenya* (Athens: Ohio University Press, 2016), 9; John Lonsdale, "Writing Competitive Patriotisms in Eastern Africa," in Peterson and Macola, *Recasting the Past*, 251.
9. Peterson and Macola, "Homespun Historiography," 15.
10. Brubaker, "Ethnicity without Groups," 172–73.
11. Ahmed Idha Salim, *The Swahili-Speaking Peoples of Kenya's Coast, 1895–1965* (Nairobi: East African Publishing House, 1973); Joseph Samuel Caruso, "Politics in Colonial Kenya, 1929–1963: A History of Kilifi District" (PhD diss., Columbia University, 1993); Justin Willis and George Gona, "Tradition, Tribe, and State in Kenya: The Mijikenda Union, 1945–1980," *Comparative Studies in Society and History* 55, no. 2 (March 2013): 448–73.
12. David Anderson, *Histories of the Hanged: The Dirty War in Kenya and the End of Empire* (New York: W. W. Norton, 2005), 15.
13. For example, see O. F. Watkins, "The Report of the Kenya Land Commission, September 1933," *Journal of the Royal African Society* 33, no. 132 (July 1934): 207–16.
14. Derek R. Peterson, "Colonial Rule and the Rise of African Politics (1930–1964)," in *The Oxford Handbook of Kenyan Politics*, ed. Nic Cheeseman, Karuti Kanyinga, and Gabrielle Lynch (New York: Oxford University Press, 2020).
15. Hyder al-Kindy, *Life and Politics in Mombasa* (Nairobi: East African Publishing House, 1972), 28.
16. Al-Kindy, 30.
17. Al-Kindy, 32.
18. Alternate names include Ithanashera Taifa, Ithna'ashera Taifa, Miji Ithnashera, and Miji Kumi na miwili. See al-Kindy, 47.
19. *Kenya Land Commission, Evidence and Memoranda* (London: His/Her Majesty's Stationary Office, 1934), 2573.
20. "Minutes of Evidence," May 1, 1931, pp. 426–28, CO/533/411/6, The National Archives of the United Kingdom (hereafter TNA); "Representations of the Arab Delegates (Joint Committee on Closer Union in E.A.)," n.d., CO/533/411/6, TNA.
21. "Note on the Question of Status of Arabs, Swahilis and Somalis in Kenya," p. 2, in "Afro-Asian Association Petition: Status of Arabs," n.d., CO/533/425/20, TNA.

22. "Interview between His Excellency the Governor and the Members of the Afro-Asian Association on 22.4.32 at Government House, Mombasa," in "Afro-Asian Association Petition," CO/533/425/20, TNA.
23. Caruso, "Politics in Colonial Kenya," 136–37.
24. Caruso, 141–42.
25. Caruso, 181.
26. Justin Willis, *Mombasa, the Swahili, and the Making of the Mijikenda* (New York: Oxford University Press, 1993), 192.
27. A. G. Baker (director of land surveys) to district commissioner (Kwale), "Re—Digo Reserve Boundaries," September 28, 1925, CC/12/15, Kenya National Archives (hereafter KNA).
28. "Miji Kenda Union General Meeting—Kisulutini, Rabai, 28th/29th, December 1945," 1945, p. 2, CC/1/49, KNA; my translation.
29. "Miji Kenda Union General Meeting," 1.
30. "Miji Kenda Union General Meeting," 1; Willis and Gona, "Tradition, Tribe, and State," 455.
31. "The Foregoing," November 1944, CC/1/49, KNA.
32. "The Foregoing."
33. "Miji Kenda Union General Meeting," 2.
34. "The Foregoing." For Mijikenda boundary disputes, see Caruso, "Politics in Colonial Kenya," 193n57.
35. "Miji Kenda Union—Rules and Regulation," November 1944, CC/1/49, 2.
36. "Miji Kenda Union General Meeting," 4.
37. Joseph E. Harris, *Repatriates and Refugees in a Colonial Society: The Case of Kenya* (Washington, DC: Howard University Press, 1987), 87.
38. Derek R. Peterson, *Ethnic Patriotism and the East African Revival: A History of Dissent, c. 1935–1972* (Cambridge: Cambridge University Press, 2013), 16; George Muwawa, interview by author, September 30, 2010, digital video and audio, trans. William Tsaka, Ray Research Deposit C051.
39. Willis and Gona, "Tradition, Tribe, and State," 461.
40. *Report of the Kenya Land Commission, September, 1933* (London: His/Her Majesty's Stationary Office, 1934), Cmnd 4556; John Overton, "The Origins of the Kikuyu Land Problem: Land Alienation and Land Use in Kiambu, Kenya, 1895–1920," *African Studies Review* 31, no. 2 (September 1988): 109–26.
41. Kenya Land Commission, "Precis and Memoranda for the Land Enquiry Commission," November 17, 1932, film 1925, Africana Microfilms, E. S. Byrd Library, Syracuse University.

42. *Kenya Land Commission: Evidence and Memoranda*, 2610.
43. *Kenya Land Commission: Evidence and Memoranda*, 2532. Colonial officials often looked to the coast to solve overcrowding issues in central Kenya. For example, *Kenya Land Commission: Evidence and Memoranda*, 2613.
44. *Kenya Land Commission: Evidence and Memoranda*, 2565.
45. *Kenya Land Commission: Evidence and Memoranda*, 2635.
46. C. G. Fannin summarized the claims of the Afro-Arab Association in a letter to the commission. See *Kenya Land Commission: Evidence and Memoranda*, 2568.
47. Also see the Wassin Petition, which quotes a European research article to make similar claims. A. C. Hollis, "Notes on the History of Vumba, East Africa," *Journal of the Anthropological Institute of Great Britain and Ireland* 30 (1900): 281–83.
48. *Kenya Land Commission: Evidence and Memoranda*, 2712.
49. *Kenya Land Commission: Evidence and Memoranda*, 2565.
50. *Kenya Land Commission: Evidence and Memoranda*, 2611.
51. *Kenya Land Commission: Evidence and Memoranda*, 2651.
52. *Kenya Land Commission: Evidence and Memoranda*, 2559.
53. *Kenya Land Commission: Evidence and Memoranda*, 2562.
54. *Kenya Land Commission: Evidence and Memoranda*, 2605.
55. Cf. Giriama prohibitions on marrying their daughters to Duruma during the Giriama Uprising. Cynthia Brantley, "Mekatalili and the Role of Women in Giriama Resistance," in *Banditry, Rebellion, and Social Protest in Africa*, ed. Donald Crummey (London: James Currey, 1986), 346.
56. For a biographical summary of Sheikh al-Amin, see al-Amin Bin Ali al-Mazrui, *Guidance (Uwongozi) by Sheikh al-Amin Mazrui: Selections from the First Swahili Islamic Newspaper: A Swahili-English Edition*, ed. Kai Kresse and Hassan Mwakimako (Boston: Brill, 2016), 15–17.
57. Previous newspapers in Kiswahili were published by the German and British colonial governments. See al-Mazrui, *Guidance,* 2n5. A critical edition of reprints of al-Mazrui's newspaper is available in al-Mazrui, *Guidance.*
58. Al-Mazrui, *Guidance*, 7.
59. Al-Mazrui, 61.
60. Al-Mazrui, 133.
61. Elisabeth McMahon, "'A Solitary Tree Builds Not': Heshima, Community, and Shifting Identity in Post-emancipation Pemba Island," *IJAHS* 39, no. 2 (June 2006): 197–219. See my discussion on *uungwana* and *ustaarabu* in ch. 5 of this book.

62. Al-Mazrui, *Guidance*, 137.
63. Ami Ayalon, *Language and Change in the Arab Middle East: The Evolution of Modern Arabic Political Discourse* (Oxford: Oxford University Press, 1987), 51–53.
64. John Lonsdale, "The Moral Economy of Mau Mau: Wealth, Poverty, and Civic Virtue in Kikuyu Political Thought," in *Unhappy Valley: Conflict in Kenya and Africa*, ed. Bruce Berman and John Lonsdale, vol. 2 (London: James Currey, 1992), 465; Brantley, "Mekatalili," 340–43.
65. Al-Mazrui, *Guidance*, 60–61.
66. Al-Mazrui's examples include both tribes and races (e.g., Kikuyu, Indians, Europeans); Kresse translates *kabila* in this context as "communal descent" in al-Mazrui, *Guidance*, 60–61.
67. Al-Mazrui, *Guidance*, 171.
68. Charles Kurzman, ed., *Modernist Islam, 1840–1940: A Sourcebook* (New York: Oxford University Press, 2002). Sheikh al-Amin often conflated Arab and Muslim identities.
69. Al-Mazrui, *Guidance*, 81.
70. Al-Mazrui, 137n1.
71. Al-Mazrui, 81.
72. Al-Mazrui, 83.
73. The column was written by Lebanese scholar Amir Shakib Arslan, republished in English as *Our Decline: Its Causes and Remedies* (Kuala Lumpur: Islamic Book Trust, 2004).
74. See al-Kindy, *Life and Politics*, chap. 9.
75. Vumbama, "Kongo mwezi andamia kwaheri" [Welcome the month, prepare for goodbyes], *al-Islah*, October 31, 1932.
76. "Khabari Mbovu Zilizotoka katika *Mombasa Times* hivi juzi" [Rotten news from a recent *Mombasa Times*], *al-Islah*, Octo-ber 24, 1932.
77. "Khabari ya Miji ya Arabuni: Wafdi wa El-Yaman" [News from Arab lands: The Yemen delegation], *al-Islah*, June 6, 1932.
78. "Maneno Machache ya Ilmu ya Siyasa [A Few Words on Political Knowledge]," *al-Islah*, June 6, 1932.
79. "Ulingamanifu Katika Dini ya Islamu: Siyasa ya kupambanuwa na Madhara yake juu ya Watu, Sababu ya Mikao ya Taifa" [Equality in the religion of Islam: The politics of being divided and its violence over people; the cause of factions among communities], *al-Islah*, September 5, 1932.
80. "Kodi! Kodi! Kodi!" [Taxes! Taxes! Taxes!], *al-Islah*, July 25, 1932, Africana Microfilms, E. S. Byrd Library, Syracuse University.

81. Nathaniel Mathews, "Imagining Arab Communities: Colonialism, Islamic Reform, and Arab Identity in Mombasa, Kenya, 1897–1933," *Islamic Africa* 4, no. 2 (2013): 147–51.
82. "Katika ndia ya ulingano wa Mwinyi-ezi-M'ngu" [In Almighty God's path of harmony], *al-Islah*, April 11, 1932. For a discussion of this article and the views expressed in readers' letters in later issues of *al-Islah*, see Mathews's discussion in "Imagining Arab Communities," 151–56.
83. Al-Mazrui, *Guidance*, 19–20.
84. Al-Mazrui, 14.
85. On Ngala's initial reticence to embrace the Mijikenda instead of the Giriama, see Caruso, "Politics in Colonial Kenya," 193.
86. Peterson and Macola, "Homespun Historiography," 5.
87. Ronald G. Ngala, *Nchi na Desturi za Wagiriama* [The country and customs of the Giriama] (Nairobi: Eagle Press, 1949), 1.
88. Ngala, 2.
89. William Frank, *Habari na Desturi za Waribe* [The history and customs of the Ribe] (London: Macmillan, 1953), 9.
90. Frank, 6–7.
91. Frank, 6–7.
92. Sheikh al- Amin Bin Ali al- Mazrui, *The History of the Mazru'i Dynasty of Mombasa*, trans. J. McL. Ritchie (Oxford: Oxford University Press, 1995).
93. Cf. Peterson, *Ethnic Patriotism*; and August Nimitz, *Islam and Politics in East Africa: The Sufi Order in Tanzania* (Minneapolis: University of Minnesota Press, 1980).

CHAPTER 8: TRANSCENDING ETHNICITY?

1. Ndung'u Wainaina (@NdunguWainaina), Twitter, October 4, 2017, https://twitter.com/NdunguWainaina/status/915623005795110912; Moses Kite (@naghmoo), Twitter, October 7, 2017, https://twitter.com/naghmoo/status/916896260677914625; Emmanuel (@manu_PNB), Twitter, October 17, 2017, https://twitter.com/manu_PNB/status/920348144243748865; Retired Comrade (@retiredcomrade), Twitter, October 15, 2017, https://twitter.com/retired_comrade /status/919558108959182850.
2. Kenya West (@KinyanBoy), Twitter, August 24, 2017, https://twitter.com/kinyanboy/status/900630648515420160.
3. "Miscellaneous Application 468 of 2010: Randu Nzai Ruwa, Robert Charo Tukwatukwa, and Nyae Ngao v. the Internal Security Minister and the Attorney General," Kenya Law, para. 72, accessed December 22, 2019, http://kenyalaw.org/caselaw/cases

/view/81426/. Decision confirmed on appeal "Civil Appeal 275 of 2012: Attorney General and Ministry of Internal Security v. Randu Nzai Ruwa, Robert Charo Tukwatukwa, and Nyae Ngao," Kenya Law, accessed December 22, 2019, http://kenyalaw.org/caselaw/cases/view/123880/.
4. David Anderson, *Histories of the Hanged: The Dirty War in Kenya and the End of Empire* (New York: W. W. Norton, 2005).
5. Mickie Mwanzia Koster, *The Power of the Oath* (Rochester, NY: University of Rochester Press, 2016).
6. "Summary for February 1956," Coast Provincial Intelligence Committee (hereafter CPIC), March 1956, Minute 82/56, p. 6, FCO/141/5855, The National Archives of the United Kingdom (hereafter TNA); "Summary for the Month of November 1955," CPIC, December 1955, Minutes 297/55 and 298/55, FCO/141/5854, TNA.
7. "Summary for 8th July 1953," CPIC, July 23, 1953, Minute 149/53, pp. 1–2, FCO/141/5854, TNA. This antipathy extended to all upcountry immigrants, not just Kikuyu. See "Summary for Fortnight Ending 12th October 1953," CPIC, October 13, 1954, Minute 442/54, p. 1, FCO/141/5854, TNA.
8. "Summary for 24th June 1953," CPIC, June 25, 1953, Minute 125/53, p. 3, FCO/141/5854, TNA.
9. "Extract from Summary for 11th March 1953," CPIC, April 16, 1953, FCO/141/5854, TNA.
10. "Summary for December 1955," CPIC, December 28, 1955, Minute 340/55, p. 5, FCO/141/5854, TNA.
11. "Summary for 5th August 1953," CPIC, August 5, 1953, Minute 149/53, p. 1, FCO/141/5854, TNA.
12. "Summary for 5th August 1953," Minute 161/53, p. 4.
13. "Summary for 3rd August 1954," CPIC, August 1954, Minute 285/54, p. 1, FCO/141/5854, TNA.
14. Keith Kyle, *The Politics of the Independence of Kenya* (Basingstoke, UK: Palgrave Macmillan, 1999); Ahmed Idha Salim, *The Swahili-Speaking Peoples of Kenya's Coast, 1895–1965* (Nairobi: East African Publishing House, 1973); Joseph E. Harris, *Repatriates and Refugees in a Colonial Society: The Case of Kenya* (Washington, DC: Howard University Press, 1987).
15. Jonathon Glassman, *War of Words, War of Stones: Racial Thought and Violence in Colonial Zanzibar* (Bloomington: Indiana University Press, 2011); Nathaniel Mathews, "The Zinjibari Diaspora, 1698–2014: Citizenship, Migration and Revolution in Zanzibar, Oman and the Post-war Indian Ocean" (PhD diss., Northwestern University, 2016).

16. "Summary for September 1955," CPIC, September 27, 1955, Minute 222/55, p. 3, FCO/141/5854, TNA.
17. Joseph Samuel Caruso, "Politics in Colonial Kenya, 1929–1963: A History of Kilifi District" (PhD diss., Columbia University, 1993), 201.
18. "Summary for April 1960," CPIC, May 4, 1960, Minute 61/60, p. 3, FCO/141/5856, TNA.
19. "Summary for August 1956," CPIC, September 8, 1956, Minute 439/56, p. 9, FCO/141/5855, TNA.
20. "Summary for August 1958," CPIC, September 5, 1958, Minute 149/58, p. 4, FCO/141/5856, TNA.
21. Ahmed Idha Salim, "The Movement for 'Mwambao' or Coast Autonomy in Kenya, 1956–63," in *Hadith*, ed. Bethwell A. Ogot (Nairobi: East African Publishing House, 1970), 2:220.
22. "Summary for March 1957," CPIC, April 1957, Minute 37–39/57, p. 3, FCO/141/5855, TNA. On the Zanzibar Nationalist Party, see Jonathon Glassman, "Sorting Out the Tribes: The Creation of Racial Identities in Colonial Zanzibar's Newspaper Wars," *Journal of African History* 41, no. 3 (2000): 395–428.
23. "Summary for October 1956," CPIC, November 1956, Minute 499/56, p. 1, FCO/141/5855, TNA.
24. "Summary for March 1960," CPIC, March 4, 1960, appendix, p. 3, FCO/141/5856, TNA.
25. See Keren Weitzberg, *We Do Not Have Borders: Greater Somalia and the Predicaments of Belonging in Kenya* (Athens: Ohio University Press, 2017).
26. "Summary for 22nd December 1953," CPIC, December 30, 1953, Minute 317/53, p. 1, FCO/141/5854, TNA.
27. "Summary for October 1958," CPIC, November 5, 1958, Minute 181/58, p. 3, FCO/141/5856, TNA.
28. "Summary for March 1959," CPIC, April 5, 1959, Minute 37/59, p. 3, FCO/141/5856, TNA.
29. Salim, "Movement for 'Mwambao,'" 2:220.
30. "Khabari ya Mji," *al-Islah,* May 16, 1932, Africana Microfilms, E. S. Byrd Library, Syracuse University; Frederick Johnson, *A Standard English-Swahili Dictionary* (London: Oxford University Press, 1939), s.v. "*ambaa.*"
31. "Summary for February 1960," CPIC, March 3, 1960, Minute 32/60, p. 3, FCO/141/5856, TNA.
32. "Summary for June 1960," CPIC, July 6, 1960, Minute 107/60, p. 3, FCO/141/5856, TNA.
33. Abdilahi Nassir, unpublished letter to the *Daily Nation,* April 18, 1961, Stambuli Nassir Media Articles Collection (hereafter

Stambuli Collection). For Nassir's account of why he left KANU, see Jeremy Prestholdt, "Politics of the Soil: Separatism, Autochthony, and Decolonization at the Kenyan Coast," *Journal of African History* 55, no. 2 (July 2014): 262.
34. "Mombasa Protest to Cairo Talks," *Mombasa Times*, March 25, 1961, Stambuli Collection.
35. "An Appeal to Nasser on Coastal Strip," *Daily Nation*, March 27, 1961, Stambuli Collection.
36. "We Dispute 10-Mile Boundary," *Daily Nation*, March 24, 1961, Stambuli Collection.
37. Abdilahi Nassir, "Mr. Chokwe's Statement," *Daily Nation*, April 15, 1961, Stambuli Collection.
38. Abdilahi Nassir, "Coast for Coastals," *Sunday Post*, March 19, 1961, Stambuli Collection.
39. Abdilahi Nassir, untitled press release, April 9, 1961, Stambuli Collection.
40. Abdilahi Nassir, "Coastal Strip" [unpublished letter to *Daily Nation*], March 13, 1961, Stambuli Collection.
41. Hyder al-Kindy, *Life and Politics in Mombasa* (Nairobi: East African Publishing House, 1972), 185.
42. Prestholdt, "Politics of the Soil," 263; James R. Brennan, "Lowering the Sultan's Flag: Sovereignty and Decolonization in Coastal Kenya," *Comparative Studies in Society and History* 50, no. 4 (October 2008): 831–61.
43. "Coastal League Deputation," October 16, 1961, in "Robertson Commission: Reports of Meetings in Mombasa" (henceforth "Robertson Commission: Meetings"), CO/894/4, TNA.
44. "Mr. Yahya Ali Omar," October 21, 1961, in "Robertson Commission: Meetings," CO/894/4, TNA.
45. "Note of a Meeting [with Abdurahman Mohamed]," October 21, 1961, in "Robertson Commission: Meetings," CO/894/4, TNA.
46. "Delegation Led by the Tamim and His Elders," October 20, 1961, in "Robertson Commission: Meetings," CO/894/4, TNA. See al-Kindy, *Life and Politics*, chap. 6.
47. Cf. a similar Pokomo petition by Masuluti Simeon, "Memorandum against the Coastal Belt," October 11, 1961, in "Robertson Commission: Written Evidence," vol. B, CO/894/12, TNA.
48. "Delegation from the Miji Kenda Union, Headed by the Hon. R. Ngala," October 11, 1961, in "Robertson Commission: Meetings," CO/894/4, TNA.
49. James W. Robertson, *The Kenya Coastal Strip, Report of the Commissioner* (London: His/Her Majesty's Stationary Office, 1961), Cmnd. 1585, 37.

50. Kyle, *Politics of the Independence of Kenya*.
51. *Report of the Regional Boundaries Commission [Kenya]* (London: His/Her Majesty's Stationary Office, 1962), Cmnd. 1899, 1.
52. E.g., "Meeting with the Tamin Thalatha Twaifa and Sheikh Ahmed Salim (Deputy Tamin)," August 20, 1962, in "Kenya Constituencies Delimitation (Foster-Sutton) Commission: Oral Testimony" (henceforth "Kenya Delimitation Commission: Oral Testimony"), CO/895/5, TNA.
53. Julie MacArthur, *Cartography and the Political Imagination: Mapping Community in Colonial Kenya* (Athens: Ohio University Press, 2016), 15–23.
54. "Memorandum of the United Voice of the People of Taita District," August 4, 1962, in "Kenya Constituencies Delimitation (Foster-Sutton) Commission: Papers and Memoranda" (henceforth "Kenya Delimitation Commission: Papers"), CO/895/2, TNA.
55. "A Delegation from the Coast Peoples' Party," August 16, 1962, in "Kenya Delimitation Commission: Oral Testimony," CO/895/5, TNA.
56. "Memorandum Submitted by David M. Wanyumba," August 21, 1962, in "Kenya Regional Boundaries (Foster-Sutton) Commission: Papers" (henceforth "Kenya Boundaries Commission: Papers"), CO/897/1, TNA.
57. B. J. Mutua, S. N. Katwa, and D. I. Nzou, "Re: Wakamba Living in the Coast Region," August 10, 1962, in "Kenya Delimitation Commission: Papers," CO/895/2, TNA.
58. Digo Political Union—Coast Region, "Memorandum of Boundaries (Coast)," September 18, 1962, in "Kenya Boundaries Commission: Papers," CO/897/1, TNA.
59. "A Memorandum from the People of Miji-Kenda," September 18, 1962, in "Kenya Boundaries Commission: Papers," CO/897/1, TNA. The author is identified as the Miji Kenda Union in "A Meeting with a Delegation of the Miji Kenda Union," September 18, 1962, in "Kenya Regional Boundaries (Foster-Sutton) Commission: Record of the Oral Representations" (henceforth "Kenya Boundaries Commission: Oral Representations"), CO/897/8, TNA.
60. Taita/Taveta Tribe, "Memorandum," July 25, 1962, in "Kenya Delimitation Commission: Papers," CO/895/2, TNA.
61. Mutua, Katwa, and Nzou, "Re: Wakamba."
62. Coast Akamba Advancement Association, "RE: Akamba Living in the Coast Region," August 28, 1962, in "Kenya Delimitation Commission: Papers," CO/895/2, TNA.

63. Kenya African National Union, Kwale Branch, "Memorandum to Constitutional Commissioner," August 18, 1962, in "Kenya Delimitation Commission: Papers," CO/895/2, TNA.
64. "Digo National Union," August 13, 1962, in "Kenya Boundaries Commission: Papers," pp. 2–3, CO/897/1, TNA.
65. "Digo National Union," 3.
66. "Wadigo of Shimba North Location," memorandum, September 15, 1962, in "Kenya Boundaries Commission: Papers," CO/897/1, TNA.
67. "Digo National Union."
68. "Delegation from the Digo National Union," September 18, 1962, "Kenya Boundaries Commission: Oral Representations," CO/897/8, TNA.
69. Tana River Inhabitants, "Memorandum to the Constituency Commission from Tana River," August 18, 1962, in "Kenya Delimitation Commission: Papers," CO/895/2, TNA.
70. Author's field notes, May 17, 2011. Consultant declined to be identified.
71. David M. Anderson and Jacob McKnight, "Understanding al-Shabaab: Clan, Islam and Insurgency in Kenya," *Journal of Eastern African Studies* 9, no. 3 (July 3, 2015): 536–57; Paul Goldsmith, *The Mombasa Republican Council Conflict Assessment: Threats and Opportunities for Engagement* (Nairobi: USAID, 2011).
72. Author's field notes, May 17, 2011. Consultant declined to be identified.

EPILOGUE

1. See "Siku ya Kibunzi," July 18, 2010, digital photograph, video, and audio, Ray Research Deposit E020.
2. "MVI_3533," in "Mekatalili Celebration," October 20, 2010, digital video, Ray Research Deposit E026.
3. "MVI_3546," in "Mekatalili Celebration," October 20, 2010, digital video, Ray Research Deposit E026.

Bibliography

ABBREVIATIONS

Africa *Africa: Journal of the International African Institute*
Azania *Azania: Archaeological Research in Africa*
IJAHS *International Journal of African Historical Studies*
KNA Kenya National Archives
TNA The National Archives of the United Kingdom

RECORDINGS

Fort Jesus Museum, Audio-Visual Department, Mombasa, Kenya.
Ray Research Deposit, Consultations.
> *Note:* The following list includes only cited consultations. Additional recordings are available in the deposit or from the author.
> C010 Mohsein Sayyid Ali Said Ahmed Badawy. Lamu, February 17, 2010.
> C013 Wycliffe Tinga. Rabai, April 17, 2010.
> C024 Mohamed Shalo. Mombasa, June 18, 2010.
> C045 Gona Dzoka. Rabai, August 16, 2010.
> C051 George Muwawa. Mombasa, September 30, 2010.
> C052 Jomvu elders (group interview). Jomvu, May 20, 2011.
> C053 Pekeshe Ndeje. Rabai, May 23, 2011.
> C055 Henry Ndune Mkando. Rabai, May 24, 2011.

Ray Research Deposit, Cultural and Civic Events.

ARCHIVES

Kenya National Archives.
> Mombasa: CY/2/22.
> Nairobi: AG/11/16, CC/1/49, CC/12/15, DC/KFI/1/1, DC/KFI/3/2, DC/KWL/1/3/5, DC/KWL/3/1, DC/KWL/4/1,

DC/MSA/5/1, PC/Coast/1/1/400, PC/Coast/1/3/62, PC/Coast/1/7/11, PC/Coast/1/11/10.
National Archives of the United Kingdom.
CO/533/180, CO/533/411/6, CO/533/425/20, CO/894, CO/895, CO/897, FCO/141/5854, FCO/141/5855, FCO/141/5856.
Research Project Archives. Department of History, University of Nairobi.
Brantley, Cynthia, and V. Gona Kazungu. "Giriama Historical Texts." 1971.
Emery, James. "Early 19th Century Trade and Politics at Mombasa: Lieutenant James Emery's Diary 1824–1826." Mombasa, n.d., D/4/3, typewritten transcript.
Stambuli Nassir. Media Articles Collection, Mombasa, Kenya.
Clippings of Abdilahi Nassir's writings from *Mombasa Times, Sunday Post, and Daily Nation*
de Lacy, W. E. F. *The Forcible Stoppage of Native Food Production, Illegal Evictions, Persecution of Natives in Seyedie Province and the Commission of Camouflage*. Nairobi: East African Standard, 1918.
Zanzibar National Archives.
AA/10.

NEWSPAPERS AND JOURNALS

al-Islah (Mombasa, Kenya)
Capital News (Nairobi, Kenya)

MICROFILMS

Africana Microfilms. E. S. Byrd Library, Syracuse University.
Church Missionary Society. Marlborough, Wiltshire: Adam Matthew Publications, 1997.

PUBLISHED GOVERNMENT DOCUMENTS

Africa no. 6 (1896): Correspondence Respecting the Recent Rebellion in British East Africa. Vol. 59. London: House of Commons, 1896. ProQuest.
East Africa Protectorate: Ordinances and Regulations, 1901–1902. Vol. 4. Mombasa: Government Printing Press, 1903.
Kenya Land Commission: Evidence and Memoranda. London: His/Her Majesty's Stationary Office, 1934.
Kenya National Bureau of Statistics. "Census 2009 Summary of Results: Ethnic Affiliation." Updated March 22, 2013. www.knbs.or.ke.
Official Gazette of the East Africa Protectorate [1899–1920].

Report of the Kenya Land Commission, September, 1933. Cmd. 4556. London: His/Her Majesty's Stationary Office, 1934.
Report of the Regional Boundaries Commission [Kenya]. Cmnd. 1899. London: His/Her Majesty's Stationary Office, 1962.
Robertson, James W. *The Kenya Coastal Strip, Report of the Commissioner.* Cmnd. 1585. London: His/Her Majesty's Stationary Office, 1961.

DISSERTATIONS AND THESES

Abungu, George H. O. "Communities on the River Tana, Kenya: An Archaeological Study of Relations between the Delta and the River Basin, 700–1890 A.D." PhD diss., Cambridge University, 1989.

Berg, F. J. "Mombasa under the Busaidi Sultanate: The City and Its Hinterlands in the Nineteenth Century." PhD diss., University of Wisconsin, 1971.

Caruso, Joseph Samuel. "Politics in Colonial Kenya, 1929–1963: A History of Kilifi District." PhD diss., Columbia University, 1993.

Ciekawy, Diane Marie. "Witchcraft Eradication as Political Process in Kilifi District, Kenya, 1955–1988." PhD diss., Columbia University, 1992.

de Voogt, Alex. "Limits of the Mind: Towards a Characterisation of Bao Mastership." PhD diss., University of Leiden, 1995.

Gensheimer, Thomas. "At the Boundaries of Dar-al-Islam: Cities of the East African Coast in the Late Middle Ages." PhD diss., University of California, Berkeley, 1997.

Gona Kazungu, V. "The Agiryama: The Rise of a Tribe and Its Traditions." Senior thesis, University of Nairobi, 1973.

Hamid, Hamidin Abdullah. "Unfinished Business: The Implementation of the Land Titles Ordinance in Coastal Kenya, 1908–1940s." PhD diss., School of Oriental and African Studies, University of London, 2000.

Helm, Richard. "Conflicting Histories: The Archeology of the Iron-Working, Farming Communities in the Central and Southern Coast Region of Kenya." PhD diss., University of Bristol, 2000.

Herlehy, Thomas J. "An Economic History of the Kenya Coast: The Mijikenda Coconut Palm Economy, ca. 1800–1980." PhD diss., Boston University, 1985.

Irvine, Janice. "Exploring the Limits of Structural Semantics." PhD diss., University of Rochester, 1980.

Koffsky, Peter L. "History of Takaungu, East Africa, 1830–1896." PhD diss., University of Wisconsin, 1977.

Mathews, Nathaniel. "The Zinjibari Diaspora, 1698–2014: Citizenship, Migration and Revolution in Zanzibar, Oman and the Postwar Indian Ocean." PhD diss., Northwestern University, 2016.

Mbuia-Joao, Tome N. "The Revolt of Don Jeronimo Chingulia of Mombasa, 1590–1637: An African Episode in the Portuguese Century of Decline." PhD diss., Catholic University, 1990.

Mutoro, Henry W. "An Archaeological Study of the Mijikenda 'Kaya' Settlements on Hinterland Kenya Coast." PhD diss., University of California, Los Angeles, 1987.

Pawlowicz, Matthew Christopher. "Finding Their Place in the Swahili World: An Archaeological Exploration of Southern Tanzania." PhD diss., University of Virginia, 2011.

Ray, Daren E. "Disentangling Ethnicity in East Africa, ca. 1–2010 CE: Past Communities in Present Practices." PhD diss., University of Virginia, 2014.

Sperling, David Colton. "The Growth of Islam among the Mijikenda of the Kenya Coast, 1826–1930." PhD diss., University of London, 1988.

Wright, David K. "Environment, Chronology and Resource Exploitation of the Pastoral Neolithic in Tsavo Kenya." PhD diss., University of Illinois, 2005.

PUBLISHED WORKS

Abdulaziz, Mohamed Hassan. *Muyaka, 19th Century Swahili Popular Poetry*. Nairobi: Kenya Literature Bureau, 1979.

Abu-Lughod, Janet L. *Before European Hegemony: The World System A.D. 1250–1350*. New York: Oxford University Press, 1991.

Abungu, George H. O., and H. W. Mutoro. "Coast-Interior Settlements and Social Relations in the Kenya Coastal Hinterland." In *Archaeology of Africa: Foods, Metals, and Towns*, edited by T. Shaw, P. J. J. Sinclair, B. Andah, and A. Okpoko, 694–704. London: Routledge, 1993.

Allina, Eric. "The Zimba, the Portuguese, and Other Cannibals in Late Sixteenth-Century Southeast Africa." *Journal of Southern African Studies* 37, no. 2 (June 1, 2011): 211–27.

Alpers, Edward A. "Littoral Society in the Mozambique Channel." In *East Africa and the Indian Ocean*. Princeton, NJ: Markus Wiener Publishers, 2009.

———. "Soldiers, Slaves, and Saints: An Overview of the African Presence in India." *Kenya Past and Present* 34 (2003): 47–54.

Ambler, Charles H. *Kenyan Communities in the Age of Imperialism: The Central Region in the Late Nineteenth Century*. New Haven, CT: Yale University Press, 1988.

Anderson, Benedict. *Imagined Communities: Reflections on the Origin and Spread of Nationalism.* 2nd ed. London: Verso, 1991.

Anderson, David M. *Histories of the Hanged: The Dirty War in Kenya and the End of Empire.* New York: W. W. Norton, 2005.

———. "'Yours in Struggle for Majimbo': Nationalism and the Party Politics of Decolonization in Kenya, 1955–64." *Journal of Contemporary History* 40, no. 3 (July 1, 2005): 547–64.

Anderson, David M., and Jacob McKnight. "Understanding Al-Shabaab: Clan, Islam and Insurgency in Kenya." *Journal of Eastern African Studies* 9, no. 3 (July 3, 2015): 536–57.

Armitage, David. "Three Concepts of Atlantic History." In *The British Atlantic World, 1500–1800,* edited by David Armitage and Michael J. Braddick, 11–27. New York: Palgrave Macmillan, 2002.

Arslan, Amir Shakib. *Our Decline: Its Causes and Remedies.* Kuala Lumpur: Islamic Book Trust, 2004.

Askew, Kelly M. "Female Circles and Male Lines: Gender Dynamics along the Swahili Coast." *Africa Today* 46, nos. 3–4 (1999): 67–102.

Atkinson, Ronald Raymond. *The Roots of Ethnicity: The Origins of the Acholi of Uganda before 1800.* Philadelphia: University of Pennsylvania Press, 1994.

Ayalon, Ami. *Language and Change in the Arab Middle East: The Evolution of Modern Arabic Political Discourse.* Oxford: Oxford University Press, 1987.

Bakari, Mohamed. "The New 'Ulama of Kenya." In *Islam in Kenya,* edited by Mohamed Bakari, 168–93. Nairobi, Kenya: MEWA Publications, 1995.

Bakari, Mtoro bin Mwinyi. *The Customs of the Swahili People: The Desturi Za Waswahili of Mtoro Bin Mwinyi Bakari and Other Swahili Persons.* Translated by J. W. T. Allen. Berkeley: University of California Press, 1981.

Bang, Anne K. *Sufis and Scholars of the Sea: Family Networks in East Africa, 1860–1925.* New York: Routledge, 2003.

Barth, Fredrik. *Ethnic Groups and Boundaries: The Social Organization of Culture Difference.* 2nd ed. Prospect Heights, IL: Waveland, 1998.

Bastin, Yvonne, André Coupez, Evariste Mumba, and Thilo C. Schadeberg. *Bantu Lexical Reconstructions 3.* Leiden: Leiden University, 2003. www.africamuseum.be.

Berg, F. J. "The Swahili Community of Mombasa, 1500–1900." *Journal of African History* 9, no. 1 (1968): 35–56.

Berg, F. J., and B. J. Walter. "Mosques, Population, and Urban Development in Mombasa." *Hadith* 1 (1968): 47–100.

Biersteker, Ann, and Ibrahim Noor Shariff, eds. *Mashairi Ya Vita Vya Kuduhu: War Poetry in Kiswahili Exchanged at the Time of the Battle of Kuduhu*. East Lansing: Michigan State University Press, 1995.

bin Mwidad, Midani. "The Founding of Rabai: A Swahili Chronicle." Translated by Lyndon Harries. *Swahili* 30 (1960): 140–49.

Bishara, Fahad Ahmad. *A Sea of Debt: Law and Economic Life in the Western Indian Ocean, 1780–1950*. New York: Cambridge University Press, 2017.

Bourdieu, Pierre. *Outline of a Theory of Practice*. Cambridge: Cambridge University Press, 1977.

Boxer, C. R., and C. de Azevedo. *Fort Jesus and the Portuguese in Mombasa, 1593–1729*. London: Hollis and Carter, 1960.

Brantley, Cynthia. "Gerontocratic Government: Age-Sets in Precolonial Giriama." *Africa* 48, no. 3 (1978): 248–64.

———. *The Giriama and Colonial Resistance in Kenya, 1800–1920*. Berkeley: University of California Press, 1981.

———. "An Historical Perspective of the Giriama and Witchcraft Control." *Africa* 49, no. 2 (1979): 112–33.

———. "Mekatalili and the Role of Women in Giriama Resistance." In *Banditry, Rebellion, and Social Protest in Africa*, edited by Donald Crummey, 333–50. London: James Currey, 1986.

Bravman, Bill. *Making Ethnic Ways: Communities and Their Transformations in Taita, Kenya, 1800–1950*. Portsmouth, NH: Heinemann, 1998.

Breen, Colin, and Paul Lane. "Archaeological Approaches to East Africa's Changing Seascapes." *World Archaeology* 35, no. 3 (2003): 469–89.

Brennan, James R. "Lowering the Sultan's Flag: Sovereignty and Decolonization in Coastal Kenya." *Comparative Studies in Society and History* 50, no. 4 (October 2008): 831–61.

Bresnahan, David. "Forest Imageries and Political Practice in Colonial Coastal Kenya." *Journal of Eastern African Studies* 12, no. 4 (October 2, 2018): 655–73.

Brielle, Esther S., Jeffrey Fleisher, Stephanie Wynne-Jones, Kendra Sirak, Nasreen Broomandkhoshbacht, Kim Callan, Elizabeth Curtis et al. "Entwined African and Asian Genetic Roots of Medieval Peoples of the Swahili Coast." *Nature* 615, no. 7954 (March 2023): 866–73.

Brubaker, Rogers. "Ethnicity without Groups." *European Journal of Sociology* 43, no. 2 (2002): 163–89.

Brubaker, Rogers, and Frederick Cooper. "Beyond 'Identity.'" *Theory and Society* 29, no. 1 (February 1, 2000): 1–47.

Brubaker, Rogers, Mara Loveman, and Peter Stamatov. "Ethnicity as Cognition." *Theory and Society* 33, no. 1 (February 1, 2004): 31–64.

Campbell, Gwyn. "East Africa in the Early Indian Ocean World Slave Trade: The Zanj Revolt Reconsidered." In *Early Exchange between Africa and the Wider Indian Ocean World*, edited by Gwyn Campbell, 275–304. London: Palgrave Macmillan, 2016.

Campbell, Lyle. *Historical Linguistics: An Introduction*. 2nd ed. Cambridge, MA: MIT Press, 2004.

Caplan, Patricia. *Choice and Constraint in a Swahili Community: Property, Hierarchy and Cognatic Descent on the East African Coast*. London: Oxford, 1975.

Carotenuto, Matthew. "Riwruok E Teko: Cultivating Identity in Colonial and Postcolonial Kenya." *Africa Today* 53, no. 2 (2006): 53–73.

Casale, Giancarlo. "Global Politics in the 1580s: One Canal, Twenty Thousand Cannibals, and an Ottoman Plot to Rule the World." *Journal of World History* 18, no. 3 (2007): 267–96.

Casson, Lionel. *The Periplus Maris Erythraei: Text with Introduction, Translation, and Commentary*. Princeton, NJ: Princeton University Press, 1989.

Chakravarti, Ananya. "Mapping 'Gabriel': Space, Identity and Slavery in the Late Sixteenth-Century Indian Ocean." *Past & Present* 243, no. 1 (May 1, 2019): 5–34.

Champion, Arthur Mortimer. *The Agiryama of Kenya*. Edited by John Middleton. London: Royal Anthropological Institute of Great Britain and Ireland, 1967.

Chatterjee, Partha. *The Nation and Its Fragments: Colonial and Postcolonial Histories*. Princeton, NJ: Princeton University Press, 1993.

Chaudhuri, K. N. *Asia before Europe: Economy and Civilisation of the Indian Ocean from the Rise of Islam to 1750*. New York: Cambridge University Press, 1990.

———. *Trade and Civilisation in the Indian Ocean: An Economic History from the Rise of Islam to 1750*. Cambridge: Cambridge University Press, 1985.

Cheeseman, Nic, and Daniel Branch, eds. "Election Fever: Kenya's Crisis." Special issue, *Journal of Eastern African Studies* 2, no. 2 (July 2008).

Chiraghdin, S. "Maisha Ya Sheikh Mbaruk Bin Rashid Al-Mazrui." *Swahili* 31 (1960): 150–79.

Cohen, David William, and E. S. Atieno Odhiambo. *Siaya: The Historical Anthropology of an African Landscape*. Athens: Ohio University Press, 1989.

Cohen, Ronald. "Ethnicity: Problem and Focus in Anthropology." *Annual Review of Anthropology* 7 (1978): 379–403.
Cohn, Bernard S. "The Census, Social Structure and Objectification in South Asia." In *An Anthropologist among the Historians and Other Essays*, 224–54. New Delhi: Oxford University Press, 2006.
Cooper, Frederick. *Plantation Slavery on the East Coast of Africa.* Portsmouth, NH: Heinemann, 1997.
Coupland, Reginald. *East Africa and Its Invaders: From Earliest Times to the Death of Seyyid Said in 1856.* Oxford: Clarendon, 1938.
Croucher, Sarah, and Stephanie Wynne-Jones. "People, Not Pots: Locally Produced Ceramics and Identity on the Nineteenth-Century East African Coast." *IJAHS* 39, no. 1 (February 2006): 107–24.
Currie, Thomas E., Andrew Meade, Myrtille Guillon, and Ruth Mace. "Cultural Phylogeography of the Bantu Languages of Sub-Saharan Africa." *Proceedings: Biological Sciences* 280, no. 1762 (2013): 1–8.
de la Gorgendiere, Louisa, Kenneth King, and Sarah Vaughan, eds. *Ethnicity in Africa: Roots, Meanings and Implications.* Edinburgh: Center of African Studies, University of Edinburgh, 1996.
de Luna, Kathryn Michelle. *Collecting Food, Cultivating People: Subsistence and Society in Central Africa.* New Haven, CT: Yale University Press, 2016.
de Luna, Kathryn Michelle, and Jeffrey B. Fleisher. *Speaking with Substance.* Cham, Switzerland: Springer, 2019.
de Luna, Kathryn Michelle, Jeffrey B. Fleisher, and Susan Keech McIntosh. "Thinking across the African Past: Interdisciplinarity and Early History." *African Archaeological Review* 29, nos. 2–3 (September 18, 2012): 75–94.
de Vere Allen, James. *Swahili Origins: Swahili Culture and the Shungwaya Phenomenon.* Eastern African Studies 11. Athens: Ohio University Press, 1993.
de Voogt, Alex. "Muyaka's Poetry in the History of Bao." *Bulletin of the School of Oriental and African Studies* 66, no. 1 (February 1, 2003): 61–65.
Donley, Linda. "House Power: Swahili Space and Symbolic Markers." In *Symbolic and Structural Archaeology,* edited by Ian Hodder, 63–73. Cambridge: Cambridge University Press, 1982.
Eastman, Carol M. "Waungwana Na Wanawake: Muslim Ethnicity and Sexual Segregation in Coastal Kenya." *Journal of Multilingual and Multicultural Development* 5 (1984): 97–112.
Eberhard, David M., Gary F. Simons, and Charles D. Fennig, eds. *Ethnologue: Languages of the World.* Dallas: SIL International, 2022.

Ehret, Christopher. *An African Classical Age: Eastern and Southern Africa in World History, 1000 BC to AD 400.* Charlottesville: University Press of Virginia, 1998.

———. "Bantu Expansions: Re-envisioning a Central Problem of Early African History." *IJAHS* 34, no. 1 (2001): 5–41.

———. *The Civilizations of Africa: A History to 1800.* Charlottesville: University of Virginia Press, 2002.

———. *History and the Testimony of Language.* Berkeley: University of California Press, 2011.

———. *Southern Nilotic History: Linguistic Approaches to the Study of the Past.* Evanston, IL: Northwestern University Press, 1971.

Eriksen, Thomas Hylland. *Common Denominators: Ethnicity, Nation-Building and Compromise in Mauritius.* New York: Berg, 1998.

———. *Ethnicity and Nationalism: Anthropological Perspectives.* New York: Pluto Press, 2002.

Essorami, Sulaiman bin Said bin Ahmed. *The Jurisdiction of the Sultan of Zanzibar and the Subjects of Foreign Nations.* Translated by Katrin Bromber. Bibliotheca Academica (Reihe Orientalistik) 8. Würzburg, Germany: Ergon-Verl, 2001.

Fleisher, Jeffrey. "On the Mimetic Qualities of Bowls on the Medieval Swahili Coast." In *World on the Horizon: Swahili Arts across the Indian Ocean,* edited by Allyson Purpura and Prita Meier, 235–48. Urbana-Champaign, IL: Krannert Art Museum and the University of Illinois, 2018.

———. "Rituals of Consumption and the Politics of Feasting on the Eastern African Coast, AD 700–1500." *Journal of World Prehistory* 23, no. 4 (2010): 195–217.

Fleisher, Jeffrey, and Adria LaViolette. "The Changing Power of Swahili Houses, AD Fourteenth to Nineteenth Centuries." In *The Durable House: House Society Models in Archaeology,* edited by Robin A. Beck, 175–97. Carbondale, IL: Center for Archaeological Investigations, Southern Illinois University, 2007.

———. "Elusive Wattle-and-Daub: Finding the Hidden Majority in the Archaeology of the Swahili." *Azania* 34, no. 1 (1999): 87–108.

Fleisher, Jeffrey, and Stephanie Wynne-Jones. "Ceramics and the Early Swahili: Deconstructing the Early Tana Tradition." *African Archaeological Review* 28, no. 4 (2011): 245–78.

———. "Finding Meaning in Ancient Swahili Spatial Practices." *African Archaeological Review* 29, nos. 2–3 (September 1, 2012): 171–207.

Flight, Colin. "Malcolm Guthrie and the Reconstruction of Bantu Prehistory." *History in Africa* 7 (1980): 81–118.

Fourshey, Cymone, Rhonda M. Gonzales, and Christine Saidi. *Bantu Africa*. New York: Oxford University Press, 2017.

Frank, William. *Habari na Desturi za Waribe* [The history and customs of the Ribe]. London: Macmillan, 1953.

Freeman-Grenville, G. S. P. *The East African Coast: Select Documents from the First to the Nineteenth Century*. 2nd ed. Oxford: Clarendon, 1975.

Garlake, Peter. *The Early Islamic Architecture of the East African Coast*. Nairobi: Oxford University Press, 1966.

Gathara, Patrick. "What Is Your Tribe? The Invention of Kenya's Ethnic Communities." *The Elephant* (blog), March 5, 2018. www.theelephant.info.

Gearhart, Rebecca, and Linda L. Giles, eds. *Contesting Identities: The Mijikenda and Their Neighbors in Kenyan Coastal Society*. Trenton, NJ: Africa World Press, 2014.

Gellner, Ernest, and John Breuilly. *Nations and Nationalism*. 2nd ed. Ithaca, NY: Cornell University Press, 2009.

Gilbert, Erik O. "Oman and Zanzibar: The Historical Roots of a Global Community." In *Cross Currents and Community Networks: The History of the Indian Ocean World*, edited by Himanshu Prabha Ray and Edward A. Alpers, 163–180. New York: Oxford, 2007.

Glassman, Jonathon. "Ethnicity and Race in African Thought." In *A Companion to African History*, edited by William H. Worger, Charles Ambler, and Nwando Achebe, 199–223. Hoboken, NJ: Wiley-Blackwell, 2018.

———. *Feasts and Riot: Revelry and Rebellion on the Swahili Coast, 1856–88*. Portsmouth, NH: Heinemann, 1995.

———. "Sorting Out the Tribes: The Creation of Racial Identities in Colonial Zanzibar's Newspaper Wars." *Journal of African History* 41, no. 3 (2000): 395–428.

———. *War of Words, War of Stones: Racial Thought and Violence in Colonial Zanzibar*. Bloomington: Indiana University Press, 2011.

Goldsmith, Paul. *The Mombasa Republican Council Conflict Assessment: Threats and Opportunities for Engagement*. Nairobi: USAID, 2011.

Gonzales, Rhonda M. *Societies, Religion, and History: Central-East Tanzanians and the World They Created, c. 200 BCE to 1800 CE*. New York: Columbia University Press, 2009.

Guillain, Charles. *Documents Sur l'Historie, La Géographie, et Le Commerce de La Côte Orientale d'Afrique* [Documents on the history, geography and commerce of the East Coast of Africa]. 3 vols. Paris: Arthus Bertrand, 1856.

Guthrie, Malcolm. *Comparative Bantu: An Introduction to the Comparative Linguistics and Prehistory of the Bantu Languages*. Farnborough, UK: Gregg, 1967.

Harries, Patrick. "The Roots of Ethnicity: Discourse and the Politics of Language Construction in South-East Africa." *African Affairs* 87, no. 346 (January 1, 1988): 25–52.

Harris, Joseph E. *Repatriates and Refugees in a Colonial Society: The Case of Kenya*. Washington, DC: Howard University Press, 1987.

Hawkins, Michael C. *Making Moros: Imperial Historicism and American Military Rule in the Philippines' Muslim South*. Ithaca, NY: Cornell University Press, 2021.

Helm, Richard. "Re-evaluating Traditional Histories on the Coast of Kenya: An Archaeological Perspective." In *African Historical Archaeologies*, edited by Andres M. Reid and Paul J. Lane, 59–89. New York: Kluwer Academic / Plenum Publishers, 2004.

Helm, Richard, Alison Crowther, Ceri Shipton, Amini Tengeza, Dorian Fuller, and Nicole Boivin. "Exploring Agriculture, Interaction and Trade on the Eastern African Littoral: Preliminary Results from Kenya." *Azania* 47, no. 1 (March 1, 2012): 39–63.

Hinawy, Mbarak Ali. "Notes on Customs in Mombasa." *Swahili (Kiswahili)* 34 (1964): 17–35.

Hinnebusch, Thomas. "The Shungwaya Hypothesis: A Linguistic Reappraisal." In *East African Cultural History*, edited by Joseph T. Gallagher, 1–42. Foreign and Comparative Studies / Eastern Africa Series 25. Syracuse, NY: Maxwell School of Citizenship and Public Affairs, Syracuse University, 1976.

Ho, Engseng. *The Graves of Tarim: Genealogy and Mobility across the Indian Ocean*. Berkeley: University of California Press, 2006.

Hobsbawm, Eric, and Terence O. Ranger. *The Invention of Tradition*. New York: Cambridge University Press, 1983.

Holden, Clare Janaki, and Ruth Mace. "Spread of Cattle Led to the Loss of Matrilineal Descent in Africa: A Coevolutionary Analysis." *Proceedings: Biological Sciences* 270, no. 1532 (December 7, 2003): 2425–33.

Hollis, A. C. "Notes on the History of Vumba, East Africa." *Journal of the Anthropological Institute of Great Britain and Ireland* 30 (1900): 275–97.

Horowitz, Donald L. *Ethnic Groups in Conflict*. Berkeley: University of California Press, 1985.

Horton, Mark, Helen W. Brown, and Nina Mudida. *Shanga: The Archaeology of a Muslim Trading Community on the Coast of East Africa*. London: British Institute in Eastern Africa, 1996.

Horton, Mark, and Felix Chami. "Swahili Origins." In *The Swahili World*, edited by Stephanie Wynne-Jones and Adria Jean LaViolette, 135–46. New York: Routledge, 2017.
Horton, Mark, and John Middleton. *The Swahili: The Social Landscape of a Mercantile Society*. Malden, MA: Blackwell Publishers, 2000.
Iliffe, John. *Africans: The History of a Continent*. 2nd ed. Cambridge: New York, 2007.
Isaacman, Allen F., and Barbara Isaacman. *Slavery and Beyond: The Making of Men and Chikunda Ethnic Identities in the Unstable World of South-Central Africa, 1750–1920*. Portsmouth, NH: Heinemann, 2004.
Jayasuriya, Shihan de S. *African Identity in Asia: Cultural Effects of Forced Migration*. Princeton, NJ: Markus Wiener Publishers, 2009.
Jayawardene, Sureshi. "Racialized Casteism: Exposing the Relationship between Race, Caste, and Colorism through the Experiences of Africana People in India and Sri Lanka." *Journal of African American Studies* 20, nos. 3–4 (December 2016): 323–45.
Jenkins, Richard. *Rethinking Ethnicity: Arguments and Explorations*. 2nd ed. Los Angeles: Sage, 2008.
Johnson, Frederick. *A Standard English-Swahili Dictionary*. London: Oxford University Press, 1939.
Keese, Alexander, ed. *Ethnicity and the Long-Term Perspective: The African Experience*. CEAUP Studies in Africa 1. New York: Peter Lang, 2010.
Keim, Curtis A. *Mistaking Africa: Curiosities and Inventions of the American Mind*. 3rd ed. Boulder, CO: Westview, 2014.
Kennedy, Philip F., Shawkat M. Toorawa, Tim Mackintosh-Smith, and James E. Montgomery. *Two Arabic Travel Books: Accounts of China and India and Mission to the Volga*. New York: New York University Press, 2014.
Kindy, Hyder al-. *Life and Politics in Mombasa*. Nairobi: East African Publishing House, 1972.
Kiriama, Herman Ogoti. "Iron-Using Communities in Kenya." In *Archaeology of Africa: Foods, Metals, and Towns*, edited by T. Shaw, P. J. J. Sinclair, B. Andah, and A. Okpoko, 485–98. London: Routledge, 1993.
Kirkman, James. "The Muzungulos of Mombasa." *IJAHS* 16, no. 1 (January 1, 1983): 73–82.
Kodesh, Neil. *Beyond the Royal Gaze: Clanship and Public Healing in Buganda*. Charlottesville: University of Virginia Press, 2010.
Koster, Mickie Mwanzia. *The Power of the Oath*. Rochester, NY: University of Rochester Press, 2016.

Krapf, Johann Ludwig. *A Dictionary of the Suahili Language.* London: Trübner, 1882.

———. *Travels, Researches, and Missionary Labours, during an Eighteen Years' Residence in Eastern Africa.* 2nd ed. London: Frank Cass, 1968.

Krapf, Johann Ludwig, and Johannes Rebmann. *A Nika-English Dictionary.* London: Society for Promoting Christian Knowledge, 1887.

Kresse, Kai. "Debating Maulidi: Ambiguities and Transformations of Muslim Identity on the Swahili Coast." In *The Global Worlds of the Swahili: Interfaces of Islam, Identity, and Space in 19th- and 20th-Century East Africa,* edited by Roman Loimeier and Rudiger Seesemann, 209–28. Berlin: LIT Verlag, 2006.

———. *Philosophizing in Mombasa: Knowledge, Islam, and Intellectual Practice on the Swahili Coast.* Edinburgh: Edinburgh University Press, 2007.

———. "The Uses of History: Rhetorics of Muslim Unity and Difference on the Kenyan Swahili Coast." In *Struggling with History: Islam and Cosmopolitanism in the Western Indian Ocean,* edited by Edward Simpson and Kai Kresse, 223–60. New York: Columbia University Press, 2008.

Kurzman, Charles, ed. *Modernist Islam, 1840–1940: A Sourcebook.* New York: Oxford University Press, 2002.

Kusimba, Chapurukha M. "Social Context of Iron Forging on the Kenya Coast." *Africa* 63 (1996): 194–210.

Kusimba, Sibel. "What Is a Hunter-Gatherer? Variation in the Archaeological Record of Eastern and Southern Africa." *Journal of Archaeological Research* 13, no. 4 (2005): 337–66.

Kyle, Keith. *The Politics of the Independence of Kenya.* Basingstoke, UK: Palgrave Macmillan, 1999.

Laband, John. *Bringers of War: The Portuguese in Africa during the Age of Gunpowder and Sail from Fifteenth to Eighteenth Century.* London: Frontline Books, 2013.

Larson, Pier M. *History and Memory in the Age of Enslavement: Becoming Merina in Highland Madagascar, 1770–1822.* Portsmouth, NH: Heinemann, 2000.

———. *Ocean of Letters: Language and Creolization in an Indian Ocean Diaspora.* Cambridge: Cambridge University Press, 2009.

LaViolette, Adria. "Craft and Industry." In *The Swahili World,* edited by Stephanie Wynne-Jones and Adria Jean LaViolette, 319–34. New York: Routledge, 2017.

LaViolette, Adria, and Jeffrey Fleisher. "The Urban History of a Rural Place: Swahili Archaeology on Pemba Island, Tanzania, 700–1500 AD." *IJAHS* 42, no. 3 (October 2009): 433–55.

LaViolette, Adria, and Stephanie Wynne-Jones. "The Swahili World." In *The Swahili World*, edited by Stephanie Wynne-Jones and Adria Jean LaViolette, 1–14. New York: Routledge, 2017.

Lewis, Bernard. *Islam: From the Prophet Muhammad to the Capture of Constantinople*. Vol. 2, *Religion and Society*. New York: Harper and Row, 1974.

Lodhi, Abdulaziz Y. "African Settlements in India." *Nordic Journal of African Studies* 1, no. 1 (1992): 83–86.

Loimeier, Roman. "Traditions of Reform, Reformers of Tradition: Case Studies from Senegal and Zanzibar/Tanzania." In *Diversity and Pluralism in Islam Historical and Contemporary Discourses amongst Muslims*, edited by Zulfikar Hirji, 135–62. London: IB Tauris, 2010.

Lonsdale, John. "The Moral Economy of Mau Mau: Wealth, Poverty, and Civic Virtue in Kikuyu Political Thought." In *Unhappy Valley: Conflict in Kenya and Africa*, edited by Bruce Berman and John Lonsdale. Vol. 2. London: James Currey, 1992.

———. "When Did the Gusii (or Any Other Group) Become a Tribe?" *Kenya Historical Review* 5, no. 1 (1977): 123–33.

———. "Writing Competitive Patriotisms in Eastern Africa." In *Recasting the Past: History Writing and Political Work in Modern Africa*, edited by Derek R. Peterson and Giacomo Macola, 251–68. Athens: Ohio University Press, 2009.

Lowe, Christopher. "Talking about 'Tribe': Moving from Stereotype to Analysis." Africa Policy Information Center, November 1997. http://www.africafocus.org/docs08/ethno801.php.

Lynch, Gabrielle. *I Say to You: Ethnic Politics and the Kalenjin in Kenya*. Chicago: University of Chicago Press, 2011.

MacArthur, Julie. *Cartography and the Political Imagination: Mapping Community in Colonial Kenya*. Athens: Ohio University Press, 2016.

Macgaffey, Wyatt. "Changing Representations in Central African History." *Journal of African History* 46, no. 2 (2005): 189–207.

Machado, Pedro. *Ocean of Trade: South Asian Merchants, Africa and the Indian Ocean, c. 1750–1850*. Cambridge: Cambridge University Press, 2014.

Maho, Jouni. "A Classification of the Bantu Languages: An Update of Guthrie's Referential System." In *The Bantu Languages*, edited by Derek Nurse and Gérard Philippson, 639–51. London: Routledge, 2003.

Manger, Leif O. *The Hadrami Diaspora: Community-Building on the Indian Ocean Rim*. New York: Berghan Books, 2010.

Marck, Jeff, and Koen Bostoen. "Proto Oceanic Society (Austronesian) and Proto East Bantu Society (Niger-Congo), Residence, Descent and Kin Terms ca. 1000 BC." In *Kinship, Language, and Prehistory: Per Hage and the Renaissance in Kinship Studies*, edited by Doug Jones and Bojka Milicic, 83–94. Salt Lake City: University of Utah Press, 2011.

Martin, Bradford G. "Arab Migrations to East Africa in Medieval Times." *IJAHS* 7, no. 3 (1974): 367–90.

Mathews, Nathaniel. "Imagining Arab Communities: Colonialism, Islamic Reform, and Arab Identity in Mombasa, Kenya, 1897–1933." *Islamic Africa* 4, no. 2 (2013): 135–63.

Mazrui, al-Amin bin Ali al-. *Guidance (Uwongozi) by Sheikh al-Amin Mazrui: Selections from the First Swahili Islamic Newspaper; A Swahili-English Edition*. Edited by Kai Kresse and Hassan Mwakimako. Boston: Brill, 2016.

———. *The History of the Mazruʻi Dynasty of Mombasa*. Translated by J. McL. Ritchie. Oxford: Oxford University Press, 1995.

Mazrui, Alamin M. *Kayas of Deprivation, Kayas of Blood: Violence, Ethnicity and the State in Coastal Kenya*. Nairobi: Kenya Human Rights Commission, 1998.

Mazrui, Ali A., presenter and writer. "The Nature of a Continent." In *The Africans: A Triple Heritage*. 1986, aired on BBC TV. 1 hr.

McDow, Thomas Franklin. *Buying Time: Debt and Mobility in the Western Indian Ocean*. Athens: Ohio University Press, 2018.

McIntosh, Janet. *The Edge of Islam: Power, Personhood, and Ethnoreligious Boundaries on the Kenya Coast*. Durham, NC: Duke University Press, 2009.

———. "Elders and 'Frauds': Commodified Expertise and Politicized Authenticity among Mijikenda." *Africa* 79, no. 1 (2009): 35–52.

McIntosh, Roderick J. *Ancient Middle Niger: Urbanism and the Self-Organizing Landscape*. New York: Cambridge University Press, 2005.

McIntosh, Susan Keech. *Beyond Chiefdoms: Pathways to Complexity in Africa*. Cambridge: Cambridge University Press, 2005.

McMahon, Elisabeth. "'A Solitary Tree Builds Not': Heshima, Community, and Shifting Identity in Post-emancipation Pemba Island." *IJAHS* 39, no. 2 (June 2006): 197–219.

McPherson, Kenneth. *The Indian Ocean: A History of People and the Sea*. New Delhi: Oxford University Press, 1998.

Meier, Prita. *Swahili Port Cities: The Architecture of Elsewhere*. Bloomington: Indiana University Press, 2016.

Metcalf, Thomas R. *Ideologies of the Raj*. Cambridge: Cambridge University Press, 1997.

———. *Imperial Connections: India in the Indian Ocean Arena, 1860–1920*. Berkeley: University of California Press, 2008.

Meyer, Andrie, and Chris Cloete. "Architectural Traditions of Mapungubwe and Bambandyanalo (K2)." *Journal for Transdisciplinary Research in Southern Africa* 6, no. 1 (April 4, 2010): 241–70.

Middleton, John. *The World of the Swahili: An African Mercantile Civilization*. New Haven, CT: Yale University Press, 1992.

Miller, Joseph Calder. "Introduction: Listening for the African Past." In *The African Past Speaks: Essays on Oral Tradition and History*, edited by Joseph Calder Miller, 1–59. Hamden, CT: Archon, 1980.

Mirza, Sarah, and Margaret Strobel. *Three Swahili Women: Life Histories from Mombasa, Kenya*. Bloomington: Indiana University Press, 1989.

Mohlig, W. J. G., and Bernd Heine. *Historical Phonological Atlas of the Bantu Languages of Kenya*. Language and Dialect Atlas of Kenya 6. Berlin: Dietrich Reimer, 1980.

Morton, R. F. *Children of Ham: Freed Slaves and Fugitive Slaves on the Kenya Coast, 1873 to 1907*. Boulder, CO: Westview, 1990.

———. "The Shungwaya Myth of Mijikenda Origins: A Problem of Late Nineteenth-Century Kenya Coastal History." *IJAHS* 5, no. 3 (1972): 397–423.

Muriuki, Godfrey. *A History of the Kikuyu: 1500–1900*. Oxford: Oxford University Press, 1974.

Mutoro, Henry. *A Nearest Neighbour Analysis of the Mijikenda Makaya on the Kenya Coastal Hinterland*. Nairobi: Department of History, University of Nairobi, 1985.

Mwakimako, Hassan. "The Historical Development of Muslim Courts: The Kadhi, Mudir and Liwali Courts and the Civil Procedure Code and Criminal Procedure Ordinance, c. 1963." *Journal of Eastern African Studies* 5, no. 2 (May 1, 2011): 329–43.

New, Charles. *Life, Wanderings, and Labours in Eastern Africa*. 3rd ed. London: Cass, 1971.

Ngala, Ronald G. *Nchi Na Desturi Za Wagiriama* [The country and customs of the Giriama]. Nairobi: Eagle, 1949.

Ng'weno, Bettina. "Inheriting Disputes: The Digo Negotiation of Meaning and Power through Land." *African Economic History*, no. 25 (1997): 59–77.

Nimitz, August. *Islam and Politics in East Africa: The Sufi Order in Tanzania*. Minneapolis: University of Minnesota Press, 1980.

Nugent, Paul. "Putting the History Back into Ethnicity: Enslavement, Religion, and Cultural Brokerage in the Construction of Mandinka/Jola and Ewe/Agotime Identities in West Africa, c. 1650–1930."

Comparative Studies in Society and History 50, no. 4 (October 1, 2008): 920–48.

Nurse, Derek. "Historical Texts from the Swahili Coast Part I." *Afrikanistische Arbeitspapiere* 37 (1994): 47–85.

———. "Historical Texts from the Swahili Coast Part II." *Afrikanistische Arbeitspapiere* 42 (1995): 41–72.

———. "Segeju and Daisū: A Case Study of Evidence from Oral Tradition and Comparative Linguistics." *History in Africa* 9 (1982): 175–208.

———. "South Meets North: Ilwana = Bantu + Cushitic on Kenya's Tana River." In *Mixed Languages,* edited by Peter Bakker and Maarten Mous, 213–22. Amsterdam: IFOTF, 1994.

Nurse, Derek, and Thomas Hinnebusch. *Swahili and Sabaki: A Linguistic History.* Berkeley: University of California Press, 1993.

Nurse, Derek, and Gérard Philippson. *The Bantu Languages.* London: Routledge, 2003.

Nurse, Derek, and Thomas T. Spear. *The Swahili: Reconstructing the History and Language of an African Society, 800–1500.* Philadelphia: University of Pennsylvania Press, 1984.

Ochieng', William Robert. *A Pre-colonial History of the Gusii of Western Kenya from c. A.D. 1500 to 1914.* Kampala: East African Literature Bureau, 1974.

Ominde, Simeon H. *Land and Population Movements in Kenya.* London: Heinemann, 1968.

Orchardson-Mazrui, Elizabeth. "Expressing Power and Status through Aesthetics in Mijikenda Society." *Journal of African Cultural Studies* 11, no. 1 (June 1998): 85–102.

Osborne, Myles. *Ethnicity and Empire in Kenya: Loyalty and Martial Race among the Kamba, c. 1800 to the Present.* New York: Cambridge University Press, 2014.

Overton, John. "The Origins of the Kikuyu Land Problem: Land Alienation and Land Use in Kiambu, Kenya, 1895–1920." *African Studies Review* 31, no. 2 (September 1988): 109–26.

Owen, W. F. W. *Narrative of Voyages to Explore the Shores of Africa, Arabia and Madagascar.* London: R. Bentley, 1833.

Parkin, David. *Sacred Void: Spatial Images of Work and Ritual among the Giriama of Kenya.* Cambridge: Cambridge University Press, 1991.

———. "Swahili Mijikenda: Facing Both Ways in Kenya." *Africa* 59, no. 2 (1989): 161–75.

Parsons, Kate. "The Aesthetic and Spiritual Contexts of Giriama Vigango in Kenya and Their Relationship to Contemporary Sculptural Form." *Azania* 35 (2000): 226–30.

Pawełczak, Marek. *The State and the Stateless: The Sultanate of Zanzibar and the East African Mainland; Politics, Economy and Society, 1837–1888*. Warsaw: SOWA, 2010.

Pearson, Michael N. *The Indian Ocean*. London: Routledge, 2003.

———. "Littoral Society: The Case for the Coast." *Great Circle* 7, no. 1 (1985): 1–8.

———. *Port Cities and Intruders: The Swahili Coast, India, and Portugal in the Early Modern Era*. Baltimore: Johns Hopkins University Press, 1998.

———. *The Portuguese in India*. Cambridge: Cambridge University Press, 2006.

Peterson, Derek R. "Colonial Rule and the Rise of African Politics (1930–1964)." In *The Oxford Handbook of Kenyan Politics*, edited by Nic Cheeseman, Karuti Kanyinga, and Gabrielle Lynch, 29–42. New York: Oxford University Press, 2020.

———. *Ethnic Patriotism and the East African Revival: A History of Dissent, c. 1935–1972*. Cambridge: Cambridge University Press, 2013.

Peterson, Derek R., and Giacomo Macola. "Introduction: Homespun Historiography and the Academic Profession." In *Recasting the Past: History Writing and Political Work in Modern Africa*, 1–30, edited by Derek R. Peterson and Giacomo Macola. Athens: Ohio University Press, 2009.

Pouwels, Randall L. "The Battle of Shela: The Climax of an Era and a Point of Departure in the Modern History of the Kenya Coast." *Cahiers d'Études Africaines* 31, no. 123 (1991): 363–89.

———. *Horn and Crescent: Cultural Change and Traditional Islam on the East African Coast, 800–1900*. Cambridge: Cambridge University Press, 1987.

———. "Oral Historiography and the Problem of the Shirazi of the East African Coast." *History in Africa* 11 (1984): 237–67.

Prange, Sebastian R. *Monsoon Islam: Trade and Faith on the Medieval Malabar Coast*. Cambridge: Cambridge University Press, 2018.

Prestholdt, Jeremy. *Domesticating the World: African Consumerism and the Genealogies of Globalization*. Berkeley: University of California Press, 2008.

———. "Politics of the Soil: Separatism, Autochthony, and Decolonization at the Kenyan Coast." *Journal of African History* 55, no. 2 (July 2014): 249–70.

———. "Portuguese Conceptual Categories and the 'Other' Encounter on the Swahili Coast." *Journal of Asian & African Studies* 36, no. 4 (November 2001): 383–406.

Prins, A. H. J. *The Coastal Tribes of the North-Eastern Bantu (Pokomo, Nyika, Teita)*. London: International African Institute, 1952.

———. *East African Age Class Systems*. Groningen, Netherlands: J. B. Wolters, 1953.

———. *The Swahili-Speaking Peoples of Zanzibar and the East African Coast: Arabs, Shirazi and Swahili*. London: International African Institute, 1967.

Raj, Kapil. "Circulation and the Emergence of Modern Mapping: Great Britain and Early Colonial India, 1764–1820." In *Society and Circulation: Mobile People and Itinerant Cultures in South Asia, 1750–1950*, edited by Claude Markovits, Jacques Pouchepadass, and Sanjay Subrahmanyam, 23–54. Delhi: Permanent Black, 2003.

Ranger, Terence O. "The Invention of Tradition Revisited: The Case of Africa." In *Legitimacy and the State in Twentieth Century Africa*, edited by Terence Ranger and Olufemi Vaughan, 62–111. London: Palgrave Macmillan, 1993.

Ray, Daren E. "From Constituting Communities to Dividing Districts: The Formalization of a Cultural Border between Mombasa and Its Hinterland." In *Borderlands in World History*, edited by Paul Readman, Cynthia Radding, and Chad Bryant, 101–20. London: Palgrave Macmillan, 2014.

———. "Recycling Interdisciplinary Evidence: Abandoned Hypotheses and African Historiologies in the Settlement History of Littoral East Africa." *History in Africa* 49 (December 23, 2022): 97–130.

Ray, Himanshu Prabha. *The Archaeology of Knowledge Traditions of the Indian Ocean World*. Abingdon, UK: Routledge, 2020.

Ray, Himanshu Prabha, and Edward A. Alpers, eds. *Cross Currents and Community Networks: The History of the Indian Ocean World*. Oxford: Oxford University Press, 2007.

Rinn, Ulrich. "Mwaka Koga: The Development of Syncretistic Rituals in a Globalising World." In *Unpacking the New: Critical Perspectives on Cultural Syncretization in Africa and Beyond*, edited by Afe Adogame, Magnus Echtler, and Ulf Vierke, 349–67. Berlin: LIT Verlag, 2008.

Risso, Patricia. *Oman and Muscat: An Early Modern History*. New York: St. Martin's Press, 1986.

Robinson, David. *Paths of Accommodation: Muslim Societies and French Colonial Authorities in Senegal and Mauritania, 1880–1920*. Athens: Ohio University Press, 2000.

Ruel, Malcolm. "The Structural Articulation of Generations in Africa (L'articulation Structurelle Des Générations En Afrique)." *Cahiers d'Études Africaines* 42, no. 165 (January 1, 2002): 51–81.

Russell, Thembi, Fabio Silva, and James Steele. "Modelling the Spread of Farming in the Bantu-Speaking Regions of Africa: An Archaeology-Based Phylogeography." *PLOS ONE* 9, no. 1 (January 31, 2014): e87854.

Sahlins, Marshall. *What Kinship Is—and Is Not*. Chicago: University of Chicago Press, 2014.

Salim, Ahmed Idha. "The Movement for 'Mwambao' or Coast Autonomy in Kenya, 1956–63." In *Hadith*, edited by Bethwell A. Ogot, 2:212–28. Nairobi: East African Publishing House, 1970.

———. *The Swahili-Speaking Peoples of Kenya's Coast, 1895–1965*. Nairobi: East African Publishing House, 1973.

Sassoon, Hamo. "Excavations at the Site of Early Mombasa." *Azania* 15, no. 1 (January 1, 1980): 1–42.

Schoenbrun, David L. *A Green Place, a Good Place: Agrarian Change, Gender, and Social Identity in the Great Lakes Region to the 15th Century*. Portsmouth, NH: Heinemann, 1998.

———. *The Historical Reconstruction of Great Lakes Bantu Cultural Vocabulary: Etymologies and Distributions*. Sprache und Geschichte in Afrika, Supplement 9. Cologne, Germany: Rüdiger Köppe Verlag, 1997.

Sheriff, Abdul. *Dhow Cultures of the Indian Ocean: Cosmopolitanism, Commerce, and Islam*. New York: Columbia University Press, 2010.

———. *Slaves, Spices, and Ivory in Zanzibar: Integration of an East African Commercial Empire into the World Economy, 1770–1873*. London: James Currey, 1987.

Sheriff, Abdul, and Engseng Ho. *The Indian Ocean: Oceanic Connections and the Creation of New Societies*. London: Hurst, 2014.

Shetler, Jan Bender. *Imagining Serengeti: A History of Landscape Memory in Tanzania from Earliest Times to the Present*. Athens: Ohio University Press, 2007.

Shipton, C., R. Helm, N. Boivin, A. Crowther, P. Austin, and D. Q. Fuller. "Intersections, Networks and the Genesis of Social Complexity on the Nyali Coast of East Africa." *African Archaeological Review* 30, no. 4 (December 1, 2013): 427–53.

Simpson, Edward, and Kai Kresse. *Struggling with History: Islam and Cosmopolitanism in the Western Indian Ocean*. New York: Columbia University Press, 2008.

Soper, Robert C. "Kwale: An Early Iron Age Site in Southeastern Kenya." *Azania* 2 (1967): 1–17.

Spear, Thomas T. *The Kaya Complex: A History of the Mijikenda Peoples of the Kenya Coast to 1900*. Nairobi: Kenya Literature Bureau, 1978.

―――. "Neo-traditionalism and the Limits of Invention in British Colonial Africa." *Journal of African History* 44, no. 1 (January 1, 2003): 3–27.

―――. "Swahili History and Society to 1900: A Classified Bibliography." *History in Africa* 27 (2000): 339–73.

―――. "Traditional Myths and Historian's Myths: Variations on the Singwaya Theme of Mijikenda Origins." *History in Africa* 1 (1974): 67–84.

―――. *Traditions of Origin and Their Interpretation: The Mijikenda of Kenya*. Athens: Ohio University Center for International Studies, 1981.

Spear, Thomas T., and Richard Waller, eds. *Being Maasai: Ethnicity and Identity in East Africa*. Athens: Ohio University Press, 1993.

Srinivas, Smriti, Bettina Ng'weno, and Neelima Jeychandran. "Introduction: Many Worlds, Many Oceans." In *Reimagining Indian Ocean Worlds*, edited by Smriti Srinivas, Bettina Ng'weno, and Neelima Jeychandran, 1–22. New York: Routledge, 2020.

Stephens, Rhiannon. *A History of African Motherhood: The Case of Uganda, 700–1900*. New York: Cambridge University Press, 2015.

Strandes, J. *The Portuguese Period in East Africa*. Edited by James Kirkman. Translated by J. F. Wallwork. Nairobi: East African Literature Bureau, 1961. Originally published as *Die Portugiesenzeit von Deutsch—und Englisch-Ostafrika*. Berlin: Reimer, 1899.

Swartz, Marc J. *The Way the World Is: Cultural Processes and Social Relations among the Mombasa Swahili*. Berkeley: University of California Press, 1991.

Taasisi ya Uchunguzi wa Kiswahili [Institute of Kiswahili Research]. *Kamusi ya Kiswahili-Kiingereza*. Dar es Salaam: Institute of Kiswahili Research, 2001.

Tapper, Richard. "Anthropologists, Historians, and Tribespeople on Tribe and State Formation in the Middle East." In *Tribes and State Formation in the Middle East*, edited by Philip S. Khoury and Joseph Kostiner, 48–73. Berkeley: University of California Press, 1990.

Theal, George McCall. *Records of South Eastern Africa*. 7 vols. London: William Clowes and Sons, 1899.

Tolmacheva, Marina, trans. *The Pate Chronicle*. East Lansing: Michigan State University Press, 1993.

Tonkin, Elizabeth. "Processes of Identity, Ethnicising and Morality." In *Ethnicity in Africa: Roots, Meanings, and Implications*, edited by Louisa de la Gorgendiere, Kenneth King, and Sarah Vaughan, 237–59. Edinburgh: Center of African Studies, University of Edinburgh, 1996.

Townsend, Norman. "Age, Descent and Elders among Pokomo." *Africa* 47, no. 4 (December 1977): 386–97.
Vail, Leroy. "Introduction: Ethnicity in Southern African History." In *The Creation of Tribalism in Southern Africa*, edited by Leroy Vail, 1–20. Berkeley: University of California Press, 1991.
Vansina, Jan. *How Societies Are Born: Governance in West Central Africa before 1600*. Charlottesville: University of Virginia Press, 2004.
———. *Paths in the Rainforests: Toward a History of Political Tradition in Equatorial Africa*. Madison: University of Wisconsin Press, 1990.
Vernet, Thomas. "East African Travelers and Traders in the Indian Ocean: Swahili Ships, Swahili Mobilities, 1500–1800." In *Trade, Circulation, and Flow in the Indian Ocean World*, edited by Michael Pearson, 167–203. New York: Palgrave Macmillan, 2015.
———. "Re-considering the Swahili City-States in the Early Modern Era: New Evidences and Renewed Paradigms." Paper presented at the Zanzibar Indian Ocean Research Institute Inaugural Conference, Zanzibar City, Tanzania, August 16, 2008.
Walker, Iain. *Becoming the Other, Being Oneself: Constructing Identities in a Connected World*. Newcastle upon Tyne, UK: Cambridge Scholars Publishers, 2010.
Waller, Richard. "Age and Ethnography." *Azania* 34, no. 1 (January 1, 1999): 135–44.
Walsh, Martin T. "Mijikenda Origins: A Review of the Evidence." *Transafrican Journal of History* 21 (1992): 1–18.
———. "The Segeju Complex? Linguistic Evidence for the Precolonial Making of the Mijikenda." In *Contesting Identities: The Mijikenda and Their Neighbors in Kenyan Coastal Society*, edited by Rebecca Gearhart and Linda Giles, 25–51. Trenton, NJ: Africa World Press, 2013.
Walshaw, Sarah C. "Converting to Rice: Urbanization, Islamization and Crops on Pemba Island, Tanzania, AD 700–1500." *World Archaeology* 42, no. 1 (March 2010): 137–54.
Wamwere, Koigi wa. *Towards Genocide in Kenya: The Curse of Negative Ethnicity*. Nairobi: MvuleAfrica Publishers, 2008.
Watkins, O. F. "The Report of the Kenya Land Commission, September, 1933." *Journal of the Royal African Society* 33, no. 132 (July 1934): 207–16.
Wehr, Hans. *A Dictionary of Modern Written Arabic*. Edited by J. Milton Cowan. 3rd ed. London: MacDonald & Evans, 1980.
Weitzberg, Keren. *We Do Not Have Borders: Greater Somalia and the Predicaments of Belonging in Kenya*. Athens: Ohio University Press, 2017.

Werner, Alice. *The Bantu Coast Tribes of the East Africa Protectorate.* London: Royal Anthropological Institute of Great Britain and Ireland, 1915.

———. "Swahili History of Pate." *Journal of the African Society* 14 (1914): 148–61, 278–97, 392–413.

Wilkinson, John C. *The Arabs and the Scramble for Africa.* Bristol, CT: Equinox Publishing, 2014.

Willis, Justin. "The Makings of a Tribe: Bondei Identities and Histories." *Journal of African History* 33, no. 2 (1992): 191–208.

———. *Mombasa, the Swahili, and the Making of the Mijikenda.* New York: Oxford University Press, 1993.

Willis, Justin, and George Gona. "Tradition, Tribe, and State in Kenya: The Mijikenda Union, 1945–1980." *Comparative Studies in Society and History* 55, no. 2 (March 2013): 448–73.

Wilson, Thomas H. "Spatial Analysis and Settlement Patterns on the East African Coast." *Paideuma: Mitteilungen Zur Kulturekunde* 28 (1982): 201–19.

———. "Swahili Funerary Architecture of the North Kenya Coast." In *Swahili Houses and Tombs of the Coast of Kenya,* edited by James de Vere Allen and Thomas H. Wilson, 33–46. London: Art and Archaeology Research Papers, 1979.

Wright, David K. "New Perspectives on Early Regional Interaction Networks of East African Trade: A View from Tsavo National Park, Kenya." *African Archaeological Review* 22, no. 3 (2005): 111–40.

Wright, Henry T. "The Comoros and Their Early History." In *The Swahili World,* edited by Stephanie Wynne-Jones and Adria Jean LaViolette, 266–76. New York: Routledge, 2017.

Wynne-Jones, Stephanie. *A Material Culture: Consumption and Materiality on the Coast of Precolonial East Africa.* Oxford: Oxford University Press, 2016.

Young, M. Crawford. "Nationalism, Ethnicity, and Class in Africa: A Retrospective." *Cahiers d'Études Africaines* 26, no. 103 (January 1, 1986): 421–95.

Zein, Abdul Hamid el-. *The Sacred Meadows: A Structural Analysis of Religious Symbolism in an East African Town.* Evanston, IL: Northwestern University Press, 1974.

Index

Page numbers in italics refer to figures and maps.

adzomba, 49, 154, 157, 159
Africa: ancestry, 5, 24, 29, 30, 31–32, 35, 39, 43, 50; customs, 89, 146; history, 10, 18, 56, 77; identity, 3–4, 7–8, 32, 80–81, 209; nationalism, 221, 245; politics, 5, 25, 32, 113, 220, 228; regions, 2, 4, 12, 14, 18, 29, 47, 63
Afro-Arab Youth League (AAYL), 223–24
Afro-Asian Association (AAA), 196–97, 202–5, 209–10, 213
age-sets, 101–4, 107–8, 120, 128–30. *See also* patrician status; title societies; wealth inequality
Almeida, Captain Francisco de, 97
al-Shabaab, 236
Anderson, Benedict, 7–8
Arab: community, 171–72, 202, 209–10; culture, 18, 25, 58, 114, 143, 147, 228; identity, 178, 186–88, 208–9, 214; immigrants, 16, 76–77, 90–91, 124, 149–50, 163–65, 200, 222; language, 18, 124–25, 143, 193, 206–8; nationalism, 223; people, 168–69, 195–96, 204; politics, 220–23, 230, 234; religion, 150; travelers, 115, 136, 155
Arab administration, 173, 177, 182, 184, 194, 213. *See also liwali* (pl. *maliwali*)
Armitage, David, 13
Atlantic Ocean, 134
autoethnography, 210–12. *See also* Frank, William; Ngala, Ronald

Bagamoyo, 86
Bajun, 48, 118, 132, 173, 226, 232. *See also* Swahili
Bang, Anna, 142–43
Bantu: dialects, 99, 101, 219–20; heritage, 32, 49–50, 71; language, 4, 14, 32–33, 33, 37–41, 44–48, 241–42; loanwords, 104; people, 16, 18, 20, 22, 55–56, 233; society, 31, 40, 45–47, 62, 65, 77–78, 97–100; speakers, 53, 59, 67, 95, 98; traditions, 111–12. *See also* littoral; Proto-Bantu; Sabaki
bao, 111–12, 135
Baratum line, 172, 181, 183–86, 188
Barghash bin Sa'id. *See* Busaidi, Sultan Barghash bin Sa'id al-
Barth, Fredrik, 6–7. *See also* basic anthropological model *under* ethnicity
Batawi, 90–91. *See also* Pate
Battuta, Ibn, 89, 115, 143
Bauri, Ahmed al-, 118–20
Bauri, Hasan al-, 120
Bauri, Munganaja al-, 120
Bauri, Yusuf bin Hasan al-, 120–22, 126
Beech, Merwyn, 187
Belfield, Governor, 180, 184
Benyegundo Hill, 15–17, 88, 129. *See also* Rabai
Binns, Edward K., 199
Bocarro, 103–4. *See also* writers *under* Portugal
Bostoen, Koen, 38, 40
Brantley, Cynthia, 179–80

319

Bresnahan, David, 175
British Empire: colonization, 167–71, 178, 192–93, 212–14; decolonization, 219–20; East Africa Protectorate, 188–90, 195–99, 214; imperialism, 139–41, 145, 148, 160–63, 165, 178; politics, 180–82, 223, 227–29, 236. *See also* England; Great Britain
Buganda Kingdom, 54
Bure, 184
Busaidi, Seyyid Saʻid bin Sultan al-, 135, 139–43, 146, 148, 160, 229
Busaidi, Sultan Barghash bin Saʻid al-, 148–49, 161
Busaidi, Sultan Khalifa al-, 144

caffres. See *kafiri*
Cape of Good Hope, 82
Caruso, Joseph, 221
Casale, Giancarlo, 116
Central Kenya Bantu, 23, 41, 51, 97–101, 104, 112, 220, 259n56. *See also* Daisu *under* ethnic groups (Tanzania); Kamba; Kikuyu; Mosseguejos; Segeju
Central Sudanian, 40, 41, 44
chakacha, 2
Chakravarti, Ananya, 6
Champion, Arthur M., 35–36, 179–80
Changamwe, 118, 177. *See also* Miji Tatu
Chaudhuri, K. N., 19
Chʻeng-shih, Tuan, 58
Chimijikenda speakers: community, 66–67, 70, 113, 117, 146, 151–53, 156, 159, 169; customs, 81, 91, 94, 101–6, 194, 196, 211; dialects, 88, 98–100, 99, 107–8, 151; identity, 204–5; people, 14–15, 17, 23, 30–31, 173–74, 182, 185–89, 197–98, 201–3; politics, 120, 123, 127–28, 140–43, 152–55, 177–78, 210, 214, 221, 237; religion, 139, 147, 150, 160–65, 213; speech, 33, 46, 51, 63–64, 66, 84–86, 145, 168. *See also* Mijikenda
China, 115
Chonyi, 87, 129, 151, 173, 188. *See also* Mijikenda

Christianity, 114–15, 120–22, 135, 156, 161–63, 194–95, 200, 213. *See also* Islam
Chwaka, 87, 88
cis-oceanic history, 13, 18, 19, 24, 51, 77, 79, 97, 107, 135, 143, 164, 194, 236, 242, 244
clan confederations, 82–83, 85–86, 91–92, 94–96, 102–8, 113, 122–23, 129–31, 135, 169–70
clans, 52–55, 68, 71, 73, 78, 99–101, 105, 188, 214
Coast African Association, 224–26
coastal strip, 161, 169–73, 178, 183, 185, 189, 221–30, 234
Coast Arab Association (CAA), 195–98, 203, 205
Coast People's Party, 229–32
Cohen, Ronald, 10–11
colonialism, 3, 5, 8–9, 17, 108
Comorian, 4, 14, 92, 145, 263n45. *See also* languages *under* Sabaki; Shicomorian
Comoros Islands, 4, 14, 55, 66, 77, 86, 92, 147
conurbation, 86, 87, 88, 136
coral architecture, 73–74, 77, 82, 86, 89–90, 96–97, 105, 107, 135
Cunha, Captain Nuño da, 116. *See also* Portugal
Cushitic agropastoralists, 56–58, 61–62, 67, 71, 73. *See also* Eastern Cushitic; Southern Cushitic

da Gama, Vasco, 81, 114. *See also* Portugal
Daḥlān, Aḥmad Zaynī, 148
Dar al-Islam, 112, 114, 123, 243–45. *See also* Islam
Dar es Salaam, 163
decolonization, 25, 217–19, 227, 244. *See also* Foster-Sutton's Regional Boundaries Commission; Robertson Commission
Denge, Joseph, 48
Digo, 48, 188, 236; confederations, 67, 151, 157, 172–73, 180, 198–99; conversion, 156–59, 165, 201, 205, 209, 214; Kenya Land Commission, 203–4; politics, 163–64, 220, 233–36, 235, 244; region,

320 Index

129; road, 137, 164. *See also* Mijikenda
Digo Association, 201
Digo National Union, 219, 233–34, 235
Digo Welfare Association, 201
dini ya kienyeji (traditional religion), 139, 157, 165, 200. *See also* Christianity; Islam
Duruma, 36, 129, 151, 153, 163–64, 172–73, 175, 188, 203–4, 233–34. *See also* Mijikenda
Dzoka, Gona, 52–53

Early Tana Tradition (ETT) ware, 62–63, 96. *See also* pottery
East African Association, 195
East African Estates, 172
Eastern Cushitic, 112. *See also* Oromo
Egypt, 208
Ehret, Christopher, 33, 40, 44. *See also* linguistics
Elwana, 4, 77, 99. *See also* languages *under* Sabaki
England, 131. *See also* Great Britain
Enkenseni, Ruth, 240
Eriksen, Thomas, 7
escarpment, Kenya's coastal, 14–18, 55, 59–63, 65, 67, 77, 81, 83–84, 86, 91, 98, 100, 105–7, 123, 127, 139, 152–53, 155, 157, 163
Essorami, Sulaiman bin Said bin Ahmed, 144–45
Ethiopia, 18
ethnic groups (Kenya): Gusii, 3; Kalenjin, 3, 8; Luhya, 3, 8; Luo, 3; Maasai, 3, 101; Waata, 1. *See also* Elwana; Kamba; Kikuyu; Mijikenda; Pokomo; Swahili; Taita
ethnic groups (Tanzania): Chagga, 145, 245; Daisu, 98, 99; Nyamwezi, 145, 153; Shambara, 188
ethnicity: basic anthropological model, 6–7, 9–11; boundaries, 6–7, 9, 217; groups, 4–5, 8, 193–96; ideology, 2–3, 5, 24–25, 48, 244–45; patriots, 192–95, 205, 213–14, 221; research, 6–7, 19. *See also* Africa; kinship; Swahili

Faza, 87, 118, 122, 128, 173, 231. *See also* Miji Tisa

Fleisher, Jeffrey, 86–88, 96
foraging, 61–62, 67. *See also* Cushitic agropastoralists; Laa
Fort Jesus, 120–23, 126–27, 135, 158, 164
Foster-Sutton's Regional Boundaries Commission, 229–30, 233
France, 131, 148
Frank, William, 191, 210–11, 213–14
Friday Mosque, 157

Galla threat, 104–7. *See also* Oromo
Gazi, 148, 158, 160–61
Gedi, 90
Gellner, Ernest, 7–8
Germany, 148, 161–63, 170–71, 188
Ghassany, Muyaka bin Haji al-. *See* Muyaka
Gibson, Arthur, 181–82
Giriama: clan confederation, 59, 93–94, 103–4, 123, 210; customs, 210–11, 239–40; discrimination, 139, 151–57, 164, 172–73, 178–89, 209; politics, 197, 206, 221–22; region, 129, 210. *See also* Giriama Uprising *under* rebellion; Mijikenda
Glassman, Jonathan, 19
Govi, Thomas, 53, 68
Great Britain, 4, 23, 25, 173–75, 244. *See also* England
Great Lakes, 32, 37, 40, 41, 42, 43, 45, 51, 54, 245
Guillain, Charles, 125, 128
Gujerat, 11
Gunya. *See* Bajun

Habib Swaleh. *See* Layl, Habib Swaleh Jamal al-
Hadhramy, Liwali Salih bin Muhammed al-, 126–27
Hardinge, Arthur, 162–63, 173
Hassan, Issack, 192–94
He, Zheng, 115
healing, 52–54, 62, 72, 94
Hedabu Hill, 135. *See also* Lamu
Helm, Richard, 59, 61, 77, 84
Hemed, Mbaruk bin, 140–41
Hemsted, Charles, 181
heterarchy, 68, 82, 84, 88, 92, 107, 115, 153
Hindu, 6, 13, 18

Index   321

Hinnebusch, Thomas, 59–61, 63–64, 66, 68
Ho, Enseng, 11
Hobley, Charles, 171, 174–76, 179–82
Hobsbawm, Eric, 7–8
Horowitz, David, 7
Horton, Mark, 69–71, 74, 86

Ibadi, 142, 148–49, 160–61
Iberia, 114
Idrisi, Abu Abdullah al-, 72
Iliffe, John, 112
Imperial British East Africa Company, 161–62
imperialism, 13, 23–25, 111, 138–39, 170, 226, 237, 242; European, 8, 149, 161, 167, 173–75, 212, 213, 236; of Mombasa, 128, 131–32, 135; Omani, 142, 164, 175; Portuguese, 114–16, 135; rivalries and, 8, 113, 118, 127; upcountry, 225
India: immigration, 167; politics, 116, 119–22, 136, 143, 163, 195; region, 2, 13
Indian Ocean: colonialism, 168, 188; commerce, 96, 112–13, 116, 125, 142, 243; region, 1–4, 12–13, 17, 25, 32, 112; scholars, 6, 11, 18–19, 24, 244; settlement, 45, 51; traders, 58, 73, 75–76, 78–79, 85, 89–90. *See also* littoral
Inland Niger Delta, Mali, 68
Interim Independent Boundaries Review Commission (IIBRC), 191–92
Iraq, 208
Irvine, Janice, 43
Isaacman, Allen, 3, 8
Isaacman, Barbara, 3, 8
Islah, al- (Mombasa), 207–12
Islam: commerce, 73, 165; commitment, 91, 121, 144–45, 156–64, 182, 186, 205, 209, 214; law, 176–77; mosques, 69–71, 74, 82, 86, 171, 196; nationalism, 124, 223; orthodoxy, 139, 142, 145, 147–49, 159, 209, 212–13; practices, 78, 142, 229; religion, 4, 15, 71–72, 74, 76, 147–48, 242; traditions, 46–47, 49, 72–73, 75, 77, 138–39, 207; zones, 170–73, 175, 189. *See also* Christianity; *dini ya kienyeji* (traditional religion); Muslims; Sufism

Japan, 116
Jefa, Abdulla, 186
Jenkins, Richard, 6
Jenne-jeno, Mali, 68
Jibana, *129*, 151, 172–73, 187–88. *See also* Mijikenda
Johnson, Frederick, 88–89
Jomvu, 118, *129*, 172, 176–78, 189. *See also* Miji Tisa; Nine Tribes; Tissia Taifa
Jones, John, 185

kafiri, 91, 93, 106, 123, 150–52, 155, 163, 165
Kaloleni, 63
Kamba, 1, 3, 18, 98, 151–54, 172–74, 188, 205, 210, 219–20, 232–33, 242–44. *See also* ethnic groups (Kenya)
Kambe, 93, *129*, 151, 173, 187, 188, 210. *See also* Mijikenda
Kaskazi areal group, 33, 41, 42–44, 47. *See also* language *under* Bantu
Katwa, 118. *See also* Miji Tisa
Kau, 86, 87
Kauma, *129*, 151, 156–58, 173, 183, 185, 188. *See also* Mijikenda
kaya (pl. *makaya*): confederation, 198, 202; cultural heritage, 77, 175; fortified town, 15, 70, 77, 84, 91, 105; ritual centers, 150, 153, 154–59, 165, 174–75, 189, 242. *See also* Chimijikenda speakers; *kaya* complex; Mijikenda
kaya complex, 15, 17, 84–85, 104, 107
Kaya Fungo, 179–81
Kenya: coastal, 13–14, 18, 20–21, 38, 51, 59, 83–84, 104, 168; commerce, 107; communities, 82, 98, 111, 160, 192–93; country, 1, 4, 17, 24, 37, 136, 160–61, 241, 245; culture, 1–2, 8, 31; ecology, 55, 65, 68, 78–79, 85; historians, 8, 11, 54; National Museums of, 1; north, 61; politics, 23, 217–19, 227–30, 235, 244; Supreme Court, 217–18. *See*

also littoral
Kenya African Democratic Union (KADU), 218–19, 225, 227, 229, 233, 235
Kenya African National Union (KANU), 218–19, 226–27, 229, 233
Kenya African Union (KAU), 219–20
Kenya Land Commission, 201–4, 213, 219, 234
Kenya Protectorate, 173, 223–24
Kenyatta, Jomo, 219
Kenyatta, Uhuru, 217–18
Kielwana, 14, 33, 63–65, 98. *See also* Elwana; languages *under* Sabaki
Kikuyu, 3, 8, 195, 201–2, 206, 219, 225–26, 232–33. *See also* ethnic groups (Kenya)
Kilifi, 86, 87, 118, 127–30, 157, 161, 198–99, 222, 231, 232
Kilifi African Peoples Union, 221–22
Kilindini, 118, 126–27, 131, 136, 196. *See also* Miji Tatu; Thalatha Taifa; Three Tribes
Kilindini (town), 118, 123, 127
Kilwa, 86, 89–90, 115, 161
Kilwa Chronicle, 49–50
Kimvita, 46, 88–89. *See also* Miji Tisa; Mvita
Kindy, Hyder al-, 196, 213, 226–28
kinship, 29–32, 34–36, 38–40, 43–44, 47–50, 241–42
Kinyika, 151. *See also* languages *under* Sabaki; Wanyika
Kipokomo, 14, 33, 46, 63–65, 101, 105, 147. *See also* Pokomo
Kiswahili: community, 61, 71–72, 76–77, 86, 90–91, 113, 116–18, 124; customs, 194; dialects, 88, 98–101, 105, 132, 144, 166, 206; hierarchy, 91–93; identity, 168, 202, 204; language, 33, 38, 46, 51, 63–66, 145, 190, 193; literature, 49; military, 122–24; people, 2, 14, 17–19, 23, 195, 208, 237; politics, 115, 119–20, 136, 140–43, 149, 152–55, 189, 200–203, 209, 221; religion, 139, 147–49, 159, 163–64, 209, 213, 239; towns, 114; traditions, 97, 104, 111–12. *See also* Sabaki; Swahili

Kiti, Toya wa, 62
Kodesh, Neil, 54
Kongowea, 88–89, 97, 111. *See also* Mombasa; Mvita
Krapf, John Ludwig, 46, 81, 93, 96–97, 105–6, 151–53, 156, 232
Kresse, Kai, 207
Kuri, Canon Samuel, 200
Kusi areal group, 33, 41
Kwale District, 198–99, 220, 222, 231, 232–33, 236
Kwale ware, 56–63. *See also* pottery

Laa, 62. *See also* foraging; Langulo
Lacy, William de, 182, 185
Lakes Bantu, 41, 42, 45, 47, 259n49
Lake Victoria, 45
Lamu, 86, 87, 92, 99, 130–35, 139–40, 143, 147, 161, 173, 184, 192, 233
Lamu Archipelago, 15, 69–70, 80, 86, 88, 231
Land and Freedom Army, 219–21. *See also* Mau Mau Emergency
Langulo, 59, 62
Larson, Pier, 3, 8–9
Layl, Habib Swaleh Jamal al-, 146–47
Legislative Council, 195, 222–24, 229
Lenga, Swalehe, 156–57. *See also* Mtanganyiko
lexis, 32, 34, 66
lìàngò, 42–47, 49, 51, 76
linguistics: dialects, 87–88; implications, 63, 88, 123; reconstructions, 32–34, 33, 37–40, 41, 53, 57, 61; societal change, 64–65, 95. *See also* Bantu; lexis; morphology; phonology; Sabaki; syntax
littoral: geography, 5, 12, 53; identity, 2–4, 20–21; society, 12–13, 16–17, 24, 32, 51. *See also* Indian Ocean; Pearson, Michael; SEALINKS project
liwali (pl. *maliwali*), 124–28, 130, 133–34, 139, 140–41, 160, 177, 185, 211
Local Native Councils (LNCs), 194–99, 213
Lonsdale, John, 8
lukólò, 44–47, 53, 55, 67
Luna, Kathryn de, 38

Index 323

Lynch, Gabrielle, 8

Ma'amiri, Muhammad bin Sa'id al-, 126
MacArthur, Julie, 8, 230
Macedo, Marcal de, 121
MacGaffey, Wyatt, 35
Machado, Pedro, 13
Mackawi, Mafudh, 222–24
Madagascar, 8, 11, 18
Mafia (island), 86
Magarini Syndicate, 184–85
mahaji, 155–58, 162–64, 182, 186
majimboism, 225, 233
makaya. See *kaya*
Malabar, 11, 13
Malindi, 1, 86–90, 98–100, 104, 115–21, 126–27, 146, 161, 172–78, 181–89, 198, 210, 231, 240
maliwali. See *liwali*
Manar, al- (journal), 207
Mappila, 18
Marck, Jeff, 38, 40
Maria Theresa dollars, 94
Mas'udi, Abū al-Ḥasan al-, 72, 92
matrilineage, 29, 35–37, 44, 49, 92, 158
Matthews, Nathaniel, 209
maulidi celebrations, 147, 153, 208
Maulidi ya Nabi festival, *81*, 81, 137–39, *138*, 164
Mau Mau Emergency, 219–20, 232, 244
Mauritius, 2, 6, 146
Mazrui, Ali, 135
Mazrui, Ali bin Salim al-, 200–201, 207
Mazrui, Liwali Ahmed bin Muhammad al-, 131–33
Mazrui, Liwali Rashid bin Salim al-, 141
Mazrui, Mbaruk bin Hemed al-, 140–41
Mazrui, Mbaruk bin Rashid al-, 160–65
Mazrui, Mohammed bin Uthman al-, 126–28
Mazrui, Nasir bin Abdalla al-, 125–26
Mazrui, Sheikh al-Amin bin Ali al-, 23, 205–14, 236
Mazrui, Sheikh Ali bin Abdullah al-, 148–50, 164
Mbodzi-Matsezi Union, 198–99
Mboya, Paul, 210
Mboya, Tom, 222
McIntosh, Roderick, 68
McIntosh, Sarah Keech, 68
Mecca, 148–50
Mekatilili wa Mwenza, 179–81, 240
Meyr, Hans, 89, 100
Mgande, Lucas, 104
mganga, 52, 62, 72, 206
Mgombani, 59
Middleton, John, 86
Mijikenda: community, 25, 32, 48–49, 53, 61, 154, 164, 240–42; customs, 31, 35–36, 51, 53, 55, 62, 104, 240; identity, 9, 11, 72, 108, 193, 197, 212, 245; language, 66; modern, 98; people, 1, 3–4, 15–19, 21, 195, 213, 236–37, 241; politics, 92–93, 222, 227–32, 233, 235; traditions, 82–83, 102, 134; tribes, 168, 202. See also Chimijikenda speakers; Chonyi; Digo; Duruma; ethnicity; Giriama; Jibana; Kambe; Kauma; *kaya* (pl. *makaya*); *kaya* complex; Rabai; Ribe
Mijikenda Union, 23, 198–201, 207, 210, 214, 222, 229, 232
Miji Tatu, 22, 118–19, 126–27, 141, 158. See also Thalatha Taifa; Three Tribes
Miji Tisa, 23, 118–19, 126–30, 141, 161. See also Nine Tribes; Tissia Taifa
Ming dynasty, 115. See also He, Zheng
Mir Ali Bey, 116–17
Mngumi, Zahidi bin, 132–33
Mogadishu, 89
moieties, 113–14, 123, 127, 130–32, 136. See also politics *under* Africa
Mombare, Dahlu wa, 93
Mombasa: architecture, 90; clans, 104, 168; communities, 220, 232, 236, 238–39; conquest, 97, 115–21, 123, 128; dialects, 101, 193, 206; identity, 170; labor demands, 179; lands, 186–87; Makadara Grounds, 137–38; people, 175–76, 197; politics, 125–26, 130–32, 134, 139–41,

143, 146–55, 160–64, 195, 223, 227, 234; region, 9, 14–15, 17, 22, 25, 29, 86, *87, 129,* 171–72, 208; religion, 149, 158, 162, 209; trade, *87,* 87; traditions, 46, 61, 94, 125, 211; travel, 178–79; urban contexts, 169
Mombasa Republican Council (MRC), 218, 236
Mombasa Times, 196, 208
Monclaro, Father, 100
Montgomery, Harold, 184
morphology, 32, 34
Mosseguejos, 97–101, *99, 104. See also* Segeju
Mount Kenya, 45
Mozambique, 13, 18, 55, 81, 116–17, 122, 134, 145
Mozungullos, 100, 104, 106. *See also* Wanyika
Mtanganyiko, 156–58, 162
Mtongwe, 158, 175, 204
Mtwapa, 86, *87,* 118, *129,* 161
Muhammad (the Prophet), 81, 137, 146. *See also* Islam
muji (pl. *miji*), 21–24, 68–69, 206, 208, 209, 211, 241
Mundu, Chibo wa, 95
mung'aro, 102–3
Muramba, Johnstone, 80, 85
Muslims, 54, 69, 71, 72, 93, 114, 145, 182; community, 124, 138, 143, 151, 157–58, 170–71, 176, 204, 205–9; converts, 139, 147, 149–50, 154–56, 159–60, 165, 186, 189; customs, 158–59; identity, 69, 121, 209–10, 242; immigrants, 15, 90, 91, 138, 142, 144, 186; merchants, 73, 89, 152; officials, 173; organizations, 137, 146, 150; politics, 93, 114, 123, 135–36, 144, 154–56, 161, 173, 178, 189, 200, 214, 223, 227, 229, 236; reformers, 75, 138, 147–49. *See also* Digo; Islam; *mahaji;* Swahili
Mutwafy, Hamis bin Kombo al-, 161, 163
Muyaka, 111, 137, 141–42
Mvita, 97, 117, 118, 123, 126, 127, 131, 136. *See also* Miji Tisa; Shehe Mvita

Mwakimako, Hassan, 207
Mwambao, 224–27, 229–31, *231, 235,* 237, 244–45
Mwambao United Front, 218, 227, 229
Mwamure, Mitsanze, 95
Mwana Mkisi, 92, 97. *See also* Mombasa
Mwangea, Mount, 14, *57,* 61, 179–81
Mwapodzo, Kivoyero, 158–59
Mwarandu, Joseph, 239–40
Mwavuo, Ngoyo wa, 180

Nabahani, 90–91, 125, 130–31, 136. *See also* Oman
Nahda, 148–49. *See also* Oman
Nairobi, 195, 212, 236
Naji, Abdullah Said, 1–2
Nassir, Abdilahi, 217, 229, 237
Nassir, Gamal Abdel, 223–27
Ndendeuli, 10. *See also* Tanzania
Ndoro, Kaura wa, 183
Ndzovu, Bukardi, 29, 48, 52, 59
New, Charles, 94, 101, 154
Ngala, Ronald, 210–11, 214, 221–25, 229
Nguli Kibanda, 128–30
Nilo-Saharan languages, 40–43, *41, 45, 47*
Nine Tribes, 195–96, 200. *See also* Miji Tisa; Tissia Taifa
Northeast Coast (NEC) Bantu, *57, 58–59,* 78, *99. See also* Proto–Northeast Coast (NEC) Bantu
Nugent, Paul, 9
Nurse, Derek, 59–61, 63–64, 66, 68
nyika, 100, 106, 136, 150. *See also* Wanyika
Nyika Native Reserve, 171, 174, 178, 181, 183–84, 189
*nyùmbá, 46–49, 67, 76

Odinga, Raila, 217–18
Official Gazette (Kenya), 167, 175, 190, 210
Oman: language, 141, 143; politics, 90, 104, 112, 122–28, 131–36, 139–50, 170, 190; region, 4, 11, 15, 23–24, 173, 179, 244; religion, 160–63; rule, 178. *See also* Omani *under* imperialism

Index   325

Omar, Fathil bin, 185
Omwe, 86, 87
oral traditions, 15–17, 19–21, 31, 49, 53–54, 62, 82–84, 93, 118
Oromo, 82–83, 101, 104–6, 112, 128, 146, 153, 236, 242. *See also* Galla threat
Ottoman Empire, 112, 115–17, 122–23, 131
Ozi River, 161

Pangani River, 87, 141
Pare, 33, 37, 55, 57, 59, 122
Pastoral Neolithic, 56, 57, 59–60, 63. *See also* pottery
Pate, 86, 87, 90–91, 99, 105, 118, 122–32, 134–36, 139, 143, 173, 201
patrician status, 92–94, 97, 100–102, 106–7, 126, 134, 146, 156. *See also* wealth inequality
patrilineage, 29, 35–38, 44, 46, 49, 91–92, 115, 119, 197
Paziani borderlands, *183*, 183–86
Pearson, J. M., 176–77
Pearson, Michael, 12–13, 119, 166. *See also* littoral
Pemba Island, 86–88, *87*, 99, 124, 128, 131, 136, 139, 149, 153, 244
Periplus of the Erythraean Sea (anonymous), 56–58, 115
Persia: immigrants, 16, 76–77, 97, 144, 149–50, 168–69, 202; language, 18
Persian Gulf, 70, 125
Philip II (king), 120–21. *See also* monarchy *under* Portugal
Philippines, 2, 111
phonology, 32, 34, 66
plantation economy, 146–47
Pokomo, 2, 4, 17–18, 43, 50, 92, 220, 226–28, 232
Pongwe, 172
Portugal: commerce, 112–13, 119; culture, 123; empire, 4, 11, 88–89, 97, 114–21, 124, 135–36, 170, 203–4, 233–34, 244; language, 15, 84; Lisbon, 120; monarchy, 119; nation, 18, 25, 131; people, 114–15; tribute, 140–41; visitors, 91, 97, 100, 106, 111, 122; writers, 86, 98, 103–4, 114. *See also* Portuguese *under* imperialism
pottery, 56, 57, 59–62, 67, 74–75, 77–78. *See also* Early Tana Tradition (ETT) ware; Kwale ware; Pastoral Neolithic
Pouwels, Randall, 133
Prange, Sebastian, 13
precolonial era, 2–5, 7–9, 19–21, 24
Prestholdt, Jeremy, 114
Prins, A. H. J., 37
protectorates: British East Africa, 162–63, 165–69, 171, 174, 176, 178–79, 181–82, 186, 188–90, 191–92, 195, 214, 218–19, 221, 223–27, 232, 236; German East Africa, 148, 163; Mombasa, 140–41
Proto-Bantu, 33, 37, 38, 42, 44, 47, 101, 241. *See also* Bantu
Proto–Central Kenya Bantu. *See* Central Kenya Bantu
Proto-Chimijikenda, 66, 263n47. *See also* Chimijikenda speakers
Proto-Kilimanjaro-Taita Bantu, 33, *41*, 57
Proto-Kiswahili, 63, 65, 71, 72, 263n40. *See also* Kiswahili
Proto–Lakes Bantu. *See* Lakes Bantu
protolanguages, 32, 38–42, *41*, 243
Proto–Mashariki Bantu, 32–33, *33*, 37–42, 47, 95, 101, 243, 257nn23–24
Proto–Northeast Coast (NEC) Bantu, 14, 33, *33*, 37, *41*, 42, 45, 47, 55–56, 58, 60, 65, 67, 101, 245. *See also* Northeast Coast (NEC) Bantu
Proto-Pare. *See* Pare
Proto-Ruvu. *See* Ruvu
Proto–Sabaki Bantu, 14, 17, 33, 37, 45–47, 53–55, 60, 64–66, 243. *See also* Sabaki
Proto–Savanna Bantu, 33
Proto-Seuta. *See* Seuta
Proto-Shicomorian. *See* Comorian
Proto–Southern Cushitic, 61. *See also* Southern Cushitic
Proto–Upland Bantu, 45, 259n56. *See also* Central Kenya Bantu; Proto-Kilimanjaro-Taita Bantu
Pumwani, 184

Qur'an, 72–73, 137, 157–58, 239. *See also* Islam

Rabai: clan confederation, 14–17, *16*, 29–30, 36, 167, 177, 179, 241; politics, 120, 128, 151–53, 156, 188; region, 52, 87, 88, 94, 100, 129, 166, 172, 173, 175; tribe, 210. *See also* Mijikenda; Mombasa

Ramadan, 162

Ranger, Terence, 8

rebellion: Giriama Uprising, 178–82, 184, 189, 240, 286n55; Mazrui Revolt, 160–64; Oman, 127; Portugal, 120–21; Sheikh Rumba, 126. *See also* Mazrui, Mbaruk bin Rashid al-; Mekatilili wa Mwenza

Rebmann, Thomas, 156

religion, traditional. See *dini ya kienyeji*

Reunion (island), 146

Ribe, 48, 93, 103, 123, 128–30, 151, 155, 156, 163–64, 173, 210–11. *See also* Mijikenda

ritual: analysis of, 21, 48, 51, 241, 245; ceremonies, 39, 43, 45, 100, 102–3, 153; identity, 20–21, 199, 200, 241–42; knowledge, 72; practices, 20, 25, 31, 35; specialists, 62, 75, 92, 107, 143, 165. See also *kaya* (pl. *makaya*); *uganga*

Riyadha Mosque, 80, 147. *See also* mosques *under* Islam

Riyamy, Nasor Said, 238

Robertson Commission, 227–30

Rumba, Sheikh, 126

Ruvu, *33, 37, 55, 57,* 59. *See also* Proto–Northeast Coast (NEC) Bantu

Sabaki: identity, 169, 193, 198, 245; languages, 4, *33,* 38, 44–48, 50–51, 62, 64, 69, 84–85, 93, 95–96, 112–13, 188–90, 241–43; loanwords, 104, 124–25; politics, 120, 123, 127, 136, 142, 167, 236; religion, 139, 159; research, 49; settlements, 62–63, 104–5, 112–15; society, 77–78, 91, 244; speakers, 20–22, 24–25, 31–32, 78, 83, 86, 169–70, 176, 194, 212–13; speech communities, 35, 54, 61, 64, 67–68, 71, 77–78, 98, 106, 152, 212, 219, 232; trade, 81–82. *See also* speech community

Sabaki River, *57,* 60, 128, 136, 171, 179–80, 183–84, 187–89, 210

Sahifa (newspaper), 205–9, 212

Salafi reformers, 138

Salim, A. I., 168

Salim, Ali bin, 207. *See also* Mijikenda Union

Salim, Liwali Ali bin, 184–85, 195–96

Salim, Mfaki bin, 176–78

Saudi Arabia, 138

schema: colonial, 25, 170–71, 173, 209; concept of, 19–21, 54, 67, 77, 135, 165, 212–14, 236, 243–44; kinship, 31–32, 35–37, 42, 44, 47–51, 76, 200; littoral, 82, 100, 104, 113, 119, 123, 130, 243; Omani, 145, 152; oral traditions, 105; political, 92, 113, 119, 128, 141–42, 192, 213, 225; religious, 72, 155–59, 165; spatial, 68–69, 76

Schoenbrun, David, 39–42. *See also* linguistics

SEALINKS project, 12. *See also* littoral

Segeju, 17, 98, *99,* 172, 236. *See also* ethnicity; Mosseguejos

Seuta, *33, 37, 55, 57,* 145. *See also* Proto–Northeast Coast (NEC) Bantu

Seyyidie Province, 172–73

Seyyid Sa'id. *See* Busaidi, Seyyid Sa'id bin Sultan al-

Shafii, 148, 158

Shahriyar, Buzurg ibn, 72

Shaka, 118. *See also* Miji Tisa

Shanga, Lamu Archipelago, 69–77, 90–91, 244. *See also* mosques *under* Islam; town building

Shatry, Shariff Muhammad, 222–24

Shehe, Omar bin Athman bin, 185

Shehe Mvita, 97, 144, 239. *See also* Mvita

Sheriff, Abdul, 11, 18

Shia, 149

Shicomorian, 14, *33,* 63–66, 77, 92–93, 113. *See also* Comorian

Shimba Hills, 14, 63, 129, 172, 220, 233

Index   327

Shirazi, 144, 177. *See also* Persia
Shungwaya, 16–17, 60–61, 83–85, 98, 104–5, 107, 198, 202, 210–11
Siku ya Kibunzi, 238–39
Sind, 11
Sīrāfī, Abū Zayd al-, 72
Siyu, 173
Skene, Ralph, 184–86
slavery, 132–34, 146, 153–54, 180, 184, 205–6, 228–29
Somalia, 14, 17, 55, 61, 131, 230, 236
Southern Cushitic, 44, 45, 56, 57, 58–61, 63, 66–67, 71, 73, 78; Tale, 44–45. *See also* Proto–Southern Cushitic
Southern Nyanza areal group, 41, 45
Spear, Thomas, 9–10, 17, 48–49, 53, 59, 62, 83–85, 93, 95
speech community: concept, 21, 33; reconstruction, 64, 64–65. *See also* Sabaki
Sperling, David, 155–56, 158–59
Sri Lanka, 2
Sufism, 142, 146–50, 159, 164, 194, 205, 213
Sultan Barghash. *See* Busaidi, Sultan Barghash bin Saʿid al-
Sunni, 142–43, 148–50, 160–61
Suudi faction, 130–32, 134, 136
Swahili: civilization, 82, 144; community, 25, 32, 49–50, 74, 81, 171–72, 175, 186, 232, 236–37, 242; customs, 35–36; identity, 168, 170, 193, 212; language, 4; modern, 98; New Year, 25; people, 1–2, 9, 11, 15–18, 21, 188, 196, 213, 228, 240; politics, 92, 200–204, 230, 233; racialization of, 196–97, 214; society, 68, 77, 195, 202. *See also* Kiswahili
Swahilini, 228–29, 244
syntax, 32, 34

taifa ~ ṭāʾifa, 23, 141, 193, 206–8, 211. *See also* Thalatha Taifa; Tissia Taifa
Taita, 3, 48, 205, 232–33; language, 33, 259n56. *See also* ethnic groups (Kenya)
Taita District, 231, 232
Taita Hills, 45, 59, 172

Takaungu, 148, 153–54, 157, 160–62, 178
Tana River, 60, 64–66, 77, 86, 98, 99, 220, 226, 235
Tangana, 118, 158. *See also* Miji Tatu
Tanganyika, 229, 233
Tanzania, 10, 40, 45, 59, 86, 98, 128, 131, 148, 151, 161
Taylor, W. E., 128
ten-mile strip. *See* coastal strip
Thalatha Taifa, 141, 143, 158, 160, 172, 173, 177, 292. *See also* Miji Tatu; Three Tribes
Three Tribes, 195–96, 204, 219, 228, 234. *See also* Miji Tatu; Thalatha Taifa
Tissia Taifa, 141, 143, 160–61, 172–73, 176–78, 195. *See also* Miji Tisa; Nine Tribes
title societies, 101–2, 104, 107, 152. *See also* patrician status; wealth inequality
Tonkin, Elizabeth, 3
town building, 67–70, 73–78, 82, 85–86, 91. *See also* Shanga, Lamu Archipelago
tradition, 29–30. *See also* ancestry *under* Africa
tribalism: African, 3, 5–8, 10, 23, 55; ideology, 191–94, 200–208, 212–14; politics, 219–20, 229–30, 232–33, 237
Tsaka, William, 50, 166–67
Tsori, Ali Abdallah, 155, 157
Twelve Tribes, 197–98, 200–205, 208–10, 213, 222–27. *See also* Miji Tatu; Miji Tisa

Uganda, 40, 210, 229
uganga, 52–53, 55, 62, 68–69, 77–78, 94, 212; relationship to Islam, 69, 71–75, 143, 147, 159. *See also* healing; Islam
Umba River, 61, 86, 87
Unguja (island). *See* Zanzibar
United States, 131, 142, 153
ustaarabu, 144, 150, 206, 236
uungwana, 144, 206

Vail, Leroy, 8
Vanga, 86, 87, 162, 231

328 Index

vaya, 94–95, 180. *See also* patrician status; title societies
violence: ceremonial, 80, 82–83, 95, 101–3; commercial, 80–81, 83, 97, 133–36; conquest, 114, 116–18, 122–23, 130; interpersonal, 105–6; raiding, 82–83, 90, 97, 104–8, 115–18, 123, 125, 128–30. *See also* rebellion
Vumba, 86, 87, 88, 96

Wadigo, 175, 233–34. *See also* Digo
waganga. See *mganga*
Wahhabis, 149
Waller, Richard, 108
Walsh, Martin, 98
Wamiji Association, 23, 238–39
Wanje, 180–81
Wanyika, 100, 106, 126, 140, 150–52, 159–60, 162, 164–65, 170–71, 173–77, 181–88, 197, 200–201, 210. See also *nyika;* Young Nyika Association
Wanyumba, David, 232
Wapwani, 206–8, 238, 244
Wassin, 86, 87, 140–41, 202
Waswahili, 145, 147, 150, 211. *See also* Swahili

watan, 206–8
watoro, 153–54, 160, 164, 182–85
waungwana, 148–50, 239. See also *uungwana*
wealth inequality, 82–83, 91, 93–96, 106–7, 133
Wilkinson, John, 148
Willis, Justin, 9, 17, 168–69, 198
Witu, 170, 231
Witu Sultanate, 161, 170
World War I, 181, 195, 213
World War II, 219
Wynne-Jones, Stephanie, 96

Yarubi, Sultan bin Seif al-, 122
Yemen, 115–16, 142, 146–47, 208
Young Duruma Association, 201
Young Nyika Association, 197–98
Yunus, Sheikh Ali Muhamad bin, 228

Zanzibar: community, 122, 127, 139, 212–13; politics, 141–46, 149–52, 159–65, 167, 170–73, 202–3; region, 19, 86, 99, 116, 204–5; sultanate, 223–30, 234, 245
Zena faction, 130–36
Zimba cannibals, 117–18, 123